Standards of Decision in Law

Standards of Decision in Law

Psychological and Logical Bases for the Standard of Proof, Here and Abroad

"ONCE you hear the details/ VICTORY, IT IS HARD to distinguish IT FROM defeat." — Jean-Paul SARTRE —

Kevin M. Clermont

ZIFF PROFESSOR OF LAW, CORNELL UNIVERSITY

CAROLINA ACADEMIC PRESS

Durham, North Carolina

Library of Congress Cataloging-in-Publication Data

Clermont, Kevin M.
  Standards of decision in law : psychological and logical bases for the standard
of proof, here and abroad / Kevin M. Clermont.
    pages cm
  Includes bibliographical references and index.
  ISBN 978-1-61163-373-3 (alk. paper)
  1. Burden of proof. 2. Burden of proof--Psychological aspects. I. Title.

  K2263.C54 2013
  347'.06019--dc23

                          2013007280

                CAROLINA ACADEMIC PRESS
                      700 Kent Street
              Durham, North Carolina 27701
                Telephone (919) 489-7486
                    Fax (919) 493-5668
                    www.cap-press.com

For Jian,
my beloved little daughter about to enter her age of decisions

And for Adrienne,
my mirific adult daughter who has made great decisions

Contents

Table of Methodological Notes

Standards of Decision in Law

Chapter I

Role of Standards of Decision in Law

The principal task of the law's actors is decisionmaking.[1] Decisionmaking necessarily takes place in a world of uncertainty.[2] A legal decisionmaker accordingly needs to know not only what the issue is, but also how certain he or she must be to decide it in a particular way.

Procedure aims to improve that decisionmaking.[3] In fact, much of procedure aims at facilitating optimal decisionmaking in the face of uncertainty. A central and critical task of procedure, then, is to specify the degree of sureness required to support a particular decision: the standard of decision.

---

1. "So thoroughly immersed is law in the business of decision that one might easily be tempted to say that decision is its sole activity." Thomas A. Cowan, Decision Theory in Law, Science and Technology, 17 Rutgers L. Rev. 499, 507 (1963).

2. "Most legal decision making, like that in many other areas of complex activity, is done under conditions of uncertainty." Michael J. Saks & Robert F. Kidd, Human Information Processing and Adjudication: Trial by Heuristics, 15 Law & Soc'y Rev. 123, 126 (1981). One can play with the notion of uncertainty, of course. For example, "to be certain of uncertainty ... is to be certain of at least one thing." Milton Dawes, Multiordinality: A Point of View, ETC, Summer 1986, at 128, 131; cf., e.g., Neal Gabler, The Elusive Big Idea, N.Y. Times, Aug. 14, 2011 (Sunday Review), at 1 (announcing as the big idea that we are in a post-idea era). Philosophers can do more than play with the notion. See, e.g., Daniel Greco, Probability and Prodigality, 4 Oxford Stud. Epistemology (forthcoming 2012), available at http://web.mit.edu/dlgreco/www/ProbAndProd.pdf (objecting to the view that what we know has a probability of one); Gary Lawson, Proving the Law, 86 Nw. U. L. Rev. 859, 871–74 (1992) (discussing possible Cartesian arguments regarding uncertainty). For some propositions in closed systems, uncertainty will seem rather thin, except in the metaphysical sense that nothing is absolutely certain. But in almost all circumstances calling for the application of law, out in the real world, uncertainty will be a palpable concern. See William Twining, Rethinking Evidence 104 (2d ed. 2006) (rebutting "the myth of certainty").

3. "Legal procedure is the methodology of the law, and it is by understanding and improving this methodology that we can best hope to make our justice system more reliable and fair." E. Allan Lind, The Psychology of Courtroom Procedure, in The Psychology of the Courtroom 13, 14 (Norbert L. Kerr & Robert M. Bray eds., 1982).

People use the term "standard of decision" loosely to refer to any legal standard, including substantive criteria. Thus, the reasonable-person standard of care in negligence law is often called a standard of decision. But herein I propose to speak of standard of decision in a narrower sense. It will mean the law's designation of the required likelihood for rendering decision.

Indeed, I propose to discuss in detail only those standards of decision employed in connection with ordinary legal decisions of a binary nature. For example, either the defendant will be found negligent or not, that is, whether the defendant violated the reasonable-person standard of care. Although the decision may be binary, the level of sureness is not. So, the standard of decision specifies how sure the factfinder must be to decide the defendant was negligent under the applicable substantive criterion. It governs the separate step that the factfinder must take to determine, say, whether it was more likely than not that the defendant failed to exercise the required level of care.

Mine still remains a big subject. My kind of standard of decision comprises the standards of original decision, the standards of review of that decision, and the standards for reviewing the reviewer. It includes the most conspicuous standard of decision, which is called the standard of proof: this particular measure of persuasion, or degree of belief, specifies the sureness required of a factfinder to decide that a contested fact exists. Moreover, this matter of a standard of decision arises in connection with every single legal decision ever to be made, whether of law or fact. Testing the degree of certainty must precede every decision by a legal actor. The teacher and scholar consequently must immerse himself or herself in these standards to understand almost any legal subject, from pleading hurdles to appellate review on the procedural side of the fence, and from the law of arrest to equal protection as one moves toward the substantive side.

Despite its range, my subject may seem arcane. But my experience introducing the law to undergraduates suggests that a true/false dichotomy as to legal questions tends to seduce the laity and so makes any standard of decision a special source of confusion to outsiders. In teaching an introductory course, one thus must spend an inordinate amount of time on the subject of standards of decision. The effort is enough to convince at least the teacher that the subject is an extraordinarily important key to understanding and resolving many different legal problems. My much longer experience in teaching law students has repeatedly confirmed that insight. Stepping outside the classroom, I contend that the subject is far from arcane but is instead intensely practical. It really matters to the legal outcome, whether or not lay people are aware of its role.

Thus, the so-called standard of decision in law is a broad and important subject. It has long intrigued me. It has led me over the years to think hard, read widely, and write periodically on the subject, yielding a series of articles.[4]

Formulating a Standard of Decision in Law

How does the law fix the standard of decision? Let us consider at this introductory stage the standard of proof as an example.

Because procedure is a means to the end, embodying process values as well as outcome values,[5] the procedural law should set the standard of proof at a level that serves the legal system's multiple aims. That is, the law should instrumentally set the required likelihood at a level that optimizes society's goals. In a given circumstance, the law may aim to minimize overall expected error costs, to decrease dangers of deception or bias or to disfavor certain claims, or to avoid a special kind of error such as convicting the innocent.

In so doing, the law has settled on three standards of proof that apply in different circumstances: (1) The standard of *preponderance of the evidence* translates into more-likely-than-not. It is the usual standard in civil litigation, but it appears throughout law. (2) Next comes the intermediate standard or standards, often grouped under the banner of *clear and convincing evidence* and roughly translated as much-more-likely-than-not. These variously phrased but essentially similar standards apply to certain issues in special situations, such as when terminating parental rights.[6] (3) The standard of *proof beyond a rea-*

4. The principal articles were Kevin M. Clermont, Procedure's Magical Number Three: Psychological Bases for Standards of Decision, 72 Cornell L. Rev. 1115 (1987); Kevin M. Clermont & Emily Sherwin, A Comparative View of Standards of Proof, 50 Am. J. Comp. L. 243 (2002), translated in 47 China L.J. 117 (2002), reprinted in Kuo-Chang Huang, New Perspective of Civil Procedure Theory ch. 2 (2005); Kevin M. Clermont & Emily Sherwin, A Comparative Puzzle: Standards of Proof, in Law and Justice in a Multistate World 629 (James A.R. Nafziger & Symeon C. Symeonides eds., 2002); Kevin M. Clermont, Standards of Proof in Japan and the United States, 37 Cornell Int'l L.J. 263 (2004), translated in 33 J. Japanese Inst. Int'l Bus. L. 611, 779 (2005), reprinted in Theories of American Civil Procedure 139 (Masahiko Omura & Koichi Miki eds. & trans., 2006); Kevin M. Clermont, Standards of Proof Revisited, 33 Vt. L. Rev. 469 (2009); Kevin M. Clermont, Conjunction of Evidence and Fuzzy Logic, http://ssrn.com/abstract=2115200 (Dec. 12, 2012); Kevin M. Clermont, Aggregation of Probabilities and Illogic, 47 Ga. L. Rev. 165 (2012); Kevin M. Clermont, Death of Paradox: The Killer Logic Beneath the Standards of Proof, 88 Notre Dame L. Rev. 1061 (2013).

5. See Robert S. Summers, Evaluating and Improving Legal Processes—A Plea for "Process Values," 60 Cornell L. Rev. 1 (1974).

6. See Santosky v. Kramer, 455 U.S. 745 (1982).

sonable doubt translates to mean proof to a virtual-certainty. It very rarely prevails outside criminal law.

Most significantly, the law today seems to limit the choice to no more than these three standards selected from among the infinite range of probabilities stretching from more-likely-than-not to virtual-certainty. The law did not always recognize this limitation, but with time the law acknowledged that the feasible spectrum of standards had coalesced irresistibly into three. Why? Well, the cognitive psychology literature suggests that these threefold standards accord with how humans naturally process information.

Much more on this later on. And much more on what these standards of proof really mean. But for now I note that all other standards of decisionmaking, such as appellate review of judicial decisions, do and should follow the same pattern. Thus, the many conceivable standards of review distill into simple disagreement, clear error, and the almost-certain error of an irrationality test.

Formulating a Standard of Decision Outside Law

As I have suggested, lay people do not warm to the idea of a standard of decision. Yet, decisionmaking under uncertainty constitutes a fact of life outside the law too. One can speak of decisions of whether to go out to the movies tonight. Or whether to marry this particular person. There will be substantive criteria for decision, but also a standard of decision. A mistake on going to the movies might not be serious, but a false positive, or negative, in marriage can be extraordinarily costly.

Take sports as a prime example. Sport is defined as an activity not only physical and competitive, but also governed by rules. So it is apt to have the same concerns as law. Indeed, in organized sports, there are makers of written rules and also rule-enforcing officials. The official when enforcing the rules must apply a standard of decision.

Appeal, if any, will operate by a standard of review (and possibly a standard for the commissioner to review the reviewer). Of late, some sports, such as football, have introduced video review of the call on the field for certain kinds of calls. What standard of review should these sports employ, given that they have already decided to adopt video replay?

The National Football League directs the reviewing referee to overturn on-field calls only when he sees "indisputable visual evidence," something like the criminal standard of beyond a reasonable doubt. That is, the call on the field is insulated from review, so that it should ordinarily stand even if probably wrong.

Professor Mitchell Berman of the University of Texas, however, disagrees with the propriety of that standard. "The near-consensus in favor of highly deferential standards of review for instant replay in sports is puzzling, however, for there is obvious reason to prefer a more neutral standard."[7] His argument is that the standard of review in this setting should aim at minimizing errors. It should pursue that aim up to the point that the marginal cost of review comes to exceed its marginal benefit. Assuming unbiased on-field calls, the standard of indisputable visual evidence will produce too many false negatives, even though it reduces false positives. Instead, a nondeferential standard would best achieve error minimization, he argues.

He then meets the counterarguments. First, he argues that there is no reason to suspect the on-field official has epistemic advantages that make his call more likely correct than the reviewer's call. Multiple camera angles capture views, played in slow motion, that give the reviewer the edge. If the on-field official had a favorable vantage for a particular call, the reviewer could take that into account. The reviewer should reverse only if convinced, all things considered, that the on-field official was more likely than not incorrect. Second, Berman maintains that there is little reason to weigh erroneous reversals of on-field calls as more costly than erroneous affirmances. He disbelieves that reversals will diminish the respect for the on-field officials, given that the visual evidence of on-field mistakes is already available widely. Also, he notes that reversing under the lower standard of probable mistake is less of a rebuke than reversing under the higher standard of truly egregious blunder. He goes on to discount the counterargument that reversal causes more anguish to one set of fans, because of the endowment effect based on loss aversion, than pleasure to another set. He not only doubts this endowment effect, but also questions whether the league's rule should be concerned with such matters of entertainment satisfaction. Third, although he concedes that a lower standard of review would increase the number of challenges, he observes that the league already limits the number of challenges allowed and could further control that number. Avoiding delay thus is not a sufficient argument to justify a high standard of review.

On balance, although he admits there is room for some empirical and evaluative argument, he thinks under the current state of knowledge of the game that nondeferential review is preferable to the standard of indisputable visual evidence. His arguments are fascinating, not only for their content but also for their similarity to all the common arguments on the law's standards of decision.

---

7. Mitchell N. Berman, Replay, 99 Calif. L. Rev. 1683, 1742 (2011).

Of course, his analysis may reflect only how a law professor thinks about sports. But I think it actually reflects how people think about the world. Instead of sports, one could look to the world of art. Questionable artwork that a court declares to be authentic often will not sell in the market as an authentic work, a market driven by art buyers' decisions. "Judges now recognize that while their word is law in the courtroom, in the art world their verdicts can be overturned by a higher authority: the market."[8] An expert explained, "In civil litigation the standard of proof is 'more likely than not.' Now picture yourself walking into a gallery and seeing a Picasso. You ask, 'Did Picasso paint that?,' and the dealer says, 'Yes, more likely than not.' You wouldn't buy that."[9]

My point here is that my subject is far from parochial. Although I set the discussion in the realm of law, my concerns are universal. I shall take the legal subject well beyond the borders of the United States. And I shall take the subject well beyond the traditional borders of the law, by going heavily into psychology and logic because my ultimate concern is with how people do and should think.

Formulating an Aim for This Book

An ultimate concern with how people think seems a bit presumptuous for a professor of law. But this book does not aim at originally discovering truths about cognition or pioneering new realms for logic. Instead, this book aims at specifying how American law should answer the ubiquitous question of what it should tell its decisionmakers about the required level of sureness in making their decisions. To pursue that aim, the book utilizes psychological and philosophical learning developed by the experts.

Thus I build out from my expertise in law. Ultimately, my conclusions as to the law will have significance beyond law's realm. As already suggested, the notion of standard of decisions is not at all limited to the law, but instead it pervades all varieties of decisionmaking. In that sense, I am using law as an exemplar.

To get at the answer to the question of what are proper standards of decision in law, with this introduction behind me (Chapter I), I shall begin by looking at the answers that American lawmakers have already given (Chapter II). Next I shall look for lessons in the light cast by empiricists (Chapter III) and by experts on how people think (Chapter IV). That pursuit will lead to

---

8. Patricia Cohen, Ruling on Artistic Authenticity: The Market vs. the Law, N.Y. Times, Aug. 5, 2012, at C1, C5.

9. Id. at C5 (quoting art-law specialist Ronald D. Spencer).

my fundamental conceptualization of standards of proof (Chapter V). Only then shall I be prepared to turn to what other countries have had to say on standards of proof, in the past and currently (Chapter VI). The book's concern in closing becomes how American law should adjust standards of decision in order to accommodate the empirical, psychological, theoretical, logical, historical, and comparative dimensions (Chapter VII).

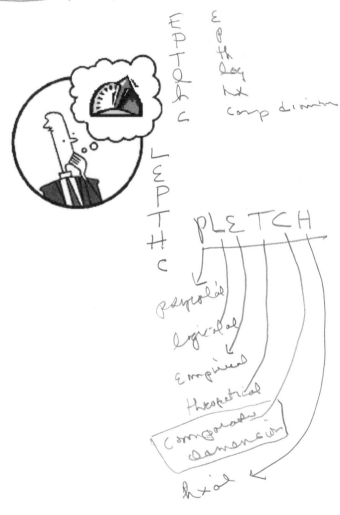

Chapter II

Varieties of Standards of Decision

This chapter will explore the law's variety of decisional standards to uncover a pattern (Part A). It will then turn to cognitive psychology to explain the existence of that pattern (Part B). Finally it will apply the lessons from that explanation to illuminate a sampling of doctrinal corners of the law (Part C).

A. Patterned Taxonomy

To begin, I divide the subject of standards of binary decision into the standards of original decision, the standards of review, and the standards for reviewing the reviewer. To illustrate these standards generously, I shall mine civil and criminal and administrative procedure for doctrines, and indeed go beyond the realm of procedure. As I shall be sketching these examples at best pithily, I am sure that experts in those fields and doctrines could quibble with some of my formulations, but I hope that they would accept my basic descriptions.

1. Standards of Original Decision

Examples of standards of original decision form the most diverse group, because of the wide range of initial decisions made by legal actors. I here develop three such examples, but I shall later suggest the range of other examples.

a. Standard of Proof

As a first example, reconsider in more detail the kind of standard of decision called the standard of proof, measure of persuasion, or degree of belief.[10]

---

10. See generally Richard H. Field, Benjamin Kaplan & Kevin M. Clermont, Materials for a Basic Course in Civil Procedure 1344–50 (10th ed. 2010); 2 McCormick on Evidence

It is the most conspicuous, expressive, and understandable example, and so I use it throughout the book as my prime example.

This example comprises the various standards of sureness required of a factfinder to decide that a contested fact exists. I refer to factfinding in its broad sense, as covering anything that a court or like institution subjects to the proof process in order to establish what the system will treat as truth. The subject includes many applications of law to fact, and also odd kinds of facts such as a prediction of an event,[11] but for simplicity I shall usually refer to the whole as "facts." The various standards differ in how likely the particular fact must be.

Magisterially, but opaquely, the law tells its decisionmaker, once done with receiving and considering the evidence by whatever psychological path the de-

---

§§ 339–341 (Kenneth S. Broun gen. ed., 6th ed. 2006); 9 John H. Wigmore, Evidence §§ 2497–2498 (James H. Chadbourn rev. 1981).

11. For an example, a court has to gauge the sureness of a future imprecise event when determining, for pretrial detention of juveniles, whether a serious risk of future criminal conduct exists. See Schall v. Martin, 467 U.S. 253, 278 (1984). Also, the Supreme Court contemplated the likelihood of a conjectural event—uncovering tainted evidence in another way—when it ruled that in order to avoid the exclusionary rule, the prosecution had to establish by a preponderance the evidence's "inevitable discovery," rejecting both a lower and a higher "quantum of proof." Nix v. Williams, 467 U.S. 431, 444 & n.5 (1984). The oddity in these examples springs from what some call an iterated epistemological operator. See Susan Haack, The Embedded Epistemologist: Dispatches from the Legal Front, 25 Ratio Juris 206, 212 (2012) (giving as an example that "the Texas death-penalty statute requires prosecutors … to prove *beyond a reasonable doubt* that *there is a probability* that the defendant will be dangerous in future ('definitely maybe,' as my students say)" (footnote omitted)); infra note 492 and accompanying text. *On the one hand,* when trying to determine how likely an event is likely, the solution lies in collapsing the iterations into a single measure. See Hagerty v. L & L Marine Servs., Inc., 788 F.2d 315, 319 ("we conclude that a plaintiff can recover only where he can show that the toxic exposure more probably than not will lead to cancer" (emphasis omitted)), modified on other grounds, 797 F.2d 256 (5th Cir. 1986). *On the other hand,* sometimes the questions do not collapse and so the standard of proof applies in ordinary fashion to a probabilistic proposition, as when a judge has to decide how sure it was that reasonable minds could differ. See Wampler v. Indianapolis Colts, No. 1:11-CV-0606-TWP-TAB, 2012 WL 3309009, at *8 (S.D. Ind. Aug. 13, 2012) ("Whether it was actually a lie depends on your conception of nudity. If a person uses latex body paint to cover his or her private parts, does that constitute nudity? Perhaps reasonable minds could disagree on this issue. (And the answer may turn on the quality and opaqueness of the paint at issue.) The relevant point is that the Club reasonably construed Ms. Wampler's statement as a lie." (emphasis omitted)). The *distinction* lies in whether the two probabilities contribute to determining one fact's existence or whether the factfinder is trying to determine two facts' coexistence.

cisionmaker chooses, to apply the standard of proof. That is, the law tells the decisionmaker to determine sureness and measure it against the legally established standard of proof. The law, most theorists, and I/all proceed on the assumption that the decisionmaker—after having somehow processed the evidence concerning a factual contention—dutifully tries in this subsequent step, within human limits, to apply the given standard of proof in testing the burdened party's contention.

The law will have already chosen the standard, specifying the required degree of persuasion. There was a choice of available standards from an array of candidates. A task of the law was making the choice appropriate to the situation: the law may have aimed (1) to minimize overall expected error costs, (2) to decrease dangers of deception or bias or to disfavor certain claims, or (3) to avoid a special kind of error such as convicting the innocent.[12] My current interest is merely to describe the range of choices. Beyond observing the desirability of the law's being able to choose among at least three standards, I shall not spend much time in criticizing the law's reasons for choosing a particular standard of proof for a specific issue.

At one end of the usual array is the preponderance standard, which most people read as meaning that the fact is probable. At the other end, proof beyond a reasonable doubt means to most people a very high degree of probability. In the United States, that array also includes clear and convincing proof in the middle. These different standards apply in different circumstances:

- The standard of preponderance of the evidence translates to more likely than not. It occupies the bottom end of the usual scale of likelihood that extends above equipoise.[13] This standard will act to minimize the expected cost of error if an error against the plaintiff is just as costly as an error against the defendant. It is the usual standard in civil litigation, but it appears throughout law. Considerable debate still revolves around its

12. See 2 McCormick on Evidence, supra note 10, §§ 340–341; V.C. Ball, The Moment of Truth: Probability Theory and Standards of Proof, 14 Vand. L. Rev. 807, 815–17 (1961); David Kaye, The Limits of the Preponderance of the Evidence Standard: Justifiably Naked Statistical Evidence and Multiple Causation, 1982 Am. B. Found. Res. J. 487.

13. In statistical terminology, "likelihood" (the chance that the data would be observed, given a hypothesis as true) is not wholly equivalent to "probability" (the chance that a hypothesis is true, given the observed data). See, e.g., Richard M. Royall, Statistical Evidence: A Likelihood Paradigm 5–6, 28 (1997). But for most people, likelihood means probability. I use likelihood here in that way, with perhaps the connotation of an intuitive measure of probability and with the incidental benefit of conforming to the law's common and probabilistic usage of "more likely than not."

precise practical meaning, but nearly everyone in common-law countries now accepts the propriety of this standard.[14]

- Next comes the intermediate standard or standards, often grouped under the banner of clear and convincing evidence and roughly translated into much more likely than not. Judicial formulations include "clear, cogent, and convincing," "clear, satisfactory, and convincing," "clear, precise, and indubitable," "clear and irresistible," and "convincing beyond reasonable controversy."[15] These apply to special cases and issues, when interests more important than money or property are at stake.[16] Continuing debate here focuses on the practical meaning of clear and convincing evidence, while debate of late has markedly decreased on potential but unrealized differences among the distinctive formulations of this intermediate standard.[17]

- The standard of proof beyond a reasonable doubt translates as proof almost to a certainty. This standard stands at the top end of the likelihood scale that is feasible in our unavoidably uncertain world. The standard supposedly must be set this high in criminal cases, because the error of convicting the innocent is especially costly. This high standard rarely prevails outside criminal law.[18] Again, arguments persist about the practical meaning of this standard of proof too, but here arguments also persist over its propriety.[19]

---

14. See 2 McCormick on Evidence, supra note 10, §339; J.P. McBaine, Burden of Proof: Degrees of Belief, 32 Calif. L. Rev. 242, 247–51 (1944).

15. McBaine, supra note 14, at 253 ("Much of the trouble in this class of cases … is caused by the use of phrases which describe the quality of the evidence rather than the [required] state of mind of the judge or the jury ...."); see id. at 254 & n.24 (describing decisions as "confused and confusing").

16. On certain issues in civil cases, some courts have imposed a stricter standard than preponderance of the evidence. See, e.g., Johnson v. Johnson, 90 S.E. 516 (N.C. 1916) (involving fraud and undue influence). In certain kinds of civil cases, this stricter standard applies generally to all the elements. See, e.g., Santosky v. Kramer, 455 U.S. 745 (1982) (involving termination of parental rights). For other issues and cases as to which this stricter standard may apply, see 9 Wigmore, supra note 10, §2498. Compare Microsoft Corp. v. i4i Ltd. P'ship, 131 S. Ct. 2238 (2011) (applying this standard to assertions of patent invalidity), with Grogan v. Garner, 498 U.S. 279, 286 (1991) (refusing to apply this standard to dischargeability in bankruptcy).

17. See 2 McCormick on Evidence, supra note 10, §340.

18. There are holdings that whenever in a civil case a criminal act is alleged, proof of the act must be beyond a reasonable doubt. An example would be proof of forgery in a proceeding to set aside an allegedly forged deed. But this view has not been widely adopted in common-law countries. See id. §341.

19. See id.; McBaine, supra note 14, at 255–58.

Note that the application of the standard of proof is left to the first-instance factfinder. The standard of review for factfinding is deferential. Whether the trial judge is reviewing the jury or whether the appellate court is reviewing the trial judge, the reviewer must be restrained in substituting its view of the facts. In brief, the standard of proof is really only a guide to the first-instance factfinder, rather than an enforced standard of decision.

Important Methodological Note:
Standards As a Step Function

Throughout, the law is seeking to minimize the expected cost of error, with broad recognition of the variety of costs. But it typically chooses among only three choices in degrees of sureness. The law did not always recognize this limitation:

> Even the most direct evidence can produce nothing more than such a high degree of probability as amounts to moral certainty. From the highest degree, it may decline by an infinite number of gradations, until it produce in the mind nothing more than a mere preponderance of assent in favour of the particular fact.[20]

With time the law acknowledged that the conceivable spectrum of standards had coalesced irresistibly into three.[21] Thus, Professor J.P. McBaine could eventually write:

> The only sound and defensible hypotheses are that the trier, or triers, of facts can find what (a) *probably* has happened, or (b) what *highly probably* has happened, or (c) what *almost certainly* has happened. No other hypotheses are defensible or can be justified by experience and knowledge.[22]

Of course, a continuum is conceivable, and it might even in some ways be theoretically desirable, even if very dangerous practically. That is to say,

---

20. Thomas Starkie, A Practical Treatise on the Law of Evidence 449 (Boston, Wells & Lilly 1826) (discussing "degrees of evidence").

21. See Addington v. Texas, 441 U.S. 418, 423 (1979) ("the evolution of this area of the law has produced across a continuum three standards or levels of proof for different types of cases"); Edmund M. Morgan, Instructing the Jury upon Presumptions and Burden of Proof, 47 Harv. L. Rev. 59, 60 (1933) (discussing three standards of proof).

22. McBaine, supra note 14, at 246–47 (footnote omitted).

it might be that if we knew more about the base rates for the type of case or about the realities of the particular case itself, we would adjust the standard of proof. For example, a variable standard of proof, set on a case-by-case basis by the ideal judge, could serve accuracy by offsetting the unavailability or inadmissibility of evidence in the particular case.[23] More generally, in an idealized system, one could argue that the standard of proof should slightly vary case-by-case and indeed issue-by-issue in response to the expected utility of each outcome.[24]

However, we do not live in an ideal world, and so the path of the law has not led toward variable standards of proof. Instead, the law has evolved toward standards applicable for broad categories of cases and issues—while making only gross adjustments by rule as to whole categories of cases or issues when substantive considerations, such as the high social cost of criminally convicting the innocent, counsel adjustment. Thus, only three discrete standards exist in usual practice.

A separate question is what the factfinder does with any of the three discrete standards. Some observers steadfastly believe that triers of fact will appropriately adjust an established standard up or down according to the circumstances.[25] Variability in application of standards is surely an empirical fact.[26] But one point of this book will be that reliance on such adjustment is neither realistic nor desirable.

Preponderance of the Evidence

Debate over the meaning of preponderance persists. The range of the debate is wide, in that authorities take one of three broad positions: (1) some argue that preponderance of the evidence actually involves balancing the items of evidence on each side, despite the obscurity of this approach and its divorce

---

23. See Dominique Demougin & Claude Fluet, Deterrence Versus Judicial Error: A Comparative View of Standards of Proof, 161 J. Institutional & Theoretical Econ. 193 (2005) (arguing by sophisticated analysis for a variable standard of proof).

24. See Richard A. Posner, An Economic Approach to Legal Procedure and Judicial Administration, 2 J. Legal Stud. 399, 414–16 (1973) (using economic analysis); cf. Richard D. Friedman, Standards of Persuasion and the Distinction Between Fact and Law, 86 Nw. U. L. Rev. 916, 926 (1992) (extending the arguments to law-determining).

25. See, e.g., Richard Eggleston, Evidence, Proof and Probability 117–18, 131, 140 (2d ed. 1983).

26. See infra Chapter III.

from any discernible purpose; (2) many hold that preponderance has some probabilistic meaning in terms of more likely than not; or (3) others argue that preponderance demands the factfinder's belief in the fact, as opposed to a belief in its likelihood.[27] The modern view converges on the middle option.

The key idea when elaborating that middle option is that the law adopts the preponderance standard for civil cases, rather than some higher standard, in order to minimize overall expected error costs. In setting the standard at more likely than not, the law has overcome the appealing but unsound lay intuition that the standard should not allow recovery to turn on a slight shift away from evenly balanced evidence.[28]

The argument for the preponderance standard is strong, because it seems demonstrably optimal given two conditions that are plausible. The first condition is that an error in favor of the plaintiff is neither more undesirable nor less undesirable than an error in favor of the defendant, or that a dollar mistakenly paid by the defendant (a false positive) is just as costly to society as a dollar mistakenly uncompensated to the plaintiff (a false negative).[29] The second condition is that the goal is to minimize the sum of expected costs from

---

27. See John Leubsdorf, Preponderance of the Evidence: Some History 3–7 (unpublished manuscript 2012).

28. A separable question is whether the law should deliver partial relief following partial proof. See Timothy A.O. Endicott, Vagueness in Law 72–74 (2000); Michael Abramowicz, A Compromise Approach to Compromise Verdicts, 89 Calif. L. Rev. 231 (2001). The answer is not obviously affirmative. See Kaye, supra note 12 (showing the current law's economic superiority to an expected-value approach that would award damages proportional to probabilistic certainty). After cataloging the prevalence of fuzzy concepts in law, Professor Katz concludes that law is correct to draw lines in the fuzz and so separate all-or-nothing remedies; he argues that law must establish discontinuities in order to retain its rational coherence. See Leo Katz, Why the Law Is So Perverse 157–81 (2011). Most significantly, I add that partial relief would have to contend with the difficulty that the system does not, and logically could not as I shall eventually develop, charge the factfinder to find upon imperfect evidence the degree to which the plaintiff is right.

29. "[I]n civil actions, unlike criminal actions, there is no particular reason to disadvantage one party substantially. We are interested in finality and dispatch, but, given whatever sacrifices are necessary to achieve that, we want to find facts correctly as often as possible. And that means that there is no particular reason to disadvantage either plaintiffs or defendants in the placing of the risk of nonpersuasion. We cannot say, as we do in criminal cases, that saving one innocent defendant is worth absolving x number of guilty ones." Ralph K. Winter, Jr., The Jury and the Risk of Nonpersuasion, 5 Law & Soc'y Rev. 335, 337 (1971) (footnote omitted); see Richard A. Posner, Economic Analysis of Law §21.2 (8th ed. 2011); Kaye, supra note 12, at 496 n.39; Frank I. Michelman, The Supreme Court and Litigation Access Fees: The Right to Protect One's Rights (pt. 1), 1973 Duke L.J. 1153, 1177–97.

these two types of error, that is, the system wants to keep the amounts suffered mistakenly to a minimum.[30]

Accepting that these conditions generally prevail outside the criminal law— and discounting more intangible possibilities, such as there being differential marginal utilities of wealth that are worthy of consideration in this context— the preponderance standard should perform better than any other nonvariable standard of proof. The reason is that by so deciding in accordance with apparent probabilities, the legal system in the long run will make fewer errors than, for example, the many false negatives that a virtual-certainty standard would impose.

Formal proofs indeed show that the preponderance standard minimizes not only the expected number of erroneous decisions but also the expected sum of wrongful amounts of damages. For an idea of a proof, let p be the apparent probability that the defendant is liable (for D dollars). If $p > \frac{1}{2}$, call it p_1; and if $p \leq \frac{1}{2}$, call it p_2. On the one hand, under the preponderance standard, the expected sum of false positives and false negatives over the run of cases is $\sum[(1 - p_1)D + p_2 D]$. On the other hand, under a very high standard that eliminates false positives, the analogous sum is $\sum[p_1 D + p_2 D]$. Because $(1 - p_1)$ is less than p_1, the preponderance standard lowers the system's expected error costs.[31]

Important Methodological Note:
Equipoise As a Range

Equipoise lies just below the preponderance standard. I want to make three points in connection with the concept of equipoise.

First, it embodies a range of cases, not merely a point of precise 50-50 balance.[32] A range of evidential states may strike the factfinder as evenly

---

30. See Posner, supra note 24, at 400–02; infra text accompanying note 52.

31. See D.H. Kaye, The Error of Equal Error Rates, 1 Law Probability & Risk 3, 7 (2002) (arguing that the $p > \frac{1}{2}$ rule is appealing because "it minimizes expected losses"); David Hamer, Probabilistic Standards of Proof, Their Complements and the Errors That Are Expected to Flow from Them, 1 U. New Eng. L.J. 71 (2004); cf. Neil Orloff & Jery Stedinger, A Framework for Evaluating the Preponderance-of-the-Evidence Standard, 131 U. Pa. L. Rev. 1159 (1983) (considering bias in the distribution of errors).

32. See Neil B. Cohen, Conceptualizing Proof and Calculating Probabilities: A Response to Professor Kaye, 73 Cornell L. Rev. 78, 90–91 (1987); Neil B. Cohen, Confidence in Probability: Burdens of Persuasion in a World of Imperfect Knowledge, 60 N.Y.U. L. Rev. 385, 418–19 (1985).

balanced. The psychological truth is that equipoise is a zone broader and fuzzier that a point probability would suggest. For reasons that will become increasingly clear in this discussion, a useful way to envisage the whole scale of likelihood is as a set of categories, or intervals, of likelihood. Each category, such as more likely than not, embodies some range of approximate likelihood, rather than a point. Equipoise is no different from the other categories. Equipoise being a zone means that the burden of persuasion will affect many more cases than those few in which the conflicting evidence results precisely in a dead heat.

   Second, the law handles a finding of equipoise by means of the burden of persuasion.[33] If the evidence ends up in the zone of the evenly matched, the burden-bearer loses. That observation usually generates the reaction that the burden of persuasion does not matter much. After all, in theory, it works only as a tiebreaker. But, in practice, lawyers and judges fight and suffer over it. Why? Well, ties constitute a zone, as just explained. Moreover, given the selection effect, close cases are common.[34] But still other reasons for caring lie in psychology. How the law frames a question— whether the plaintiff or the defendant bears the risk of nonpersuasion of a fact, that is, whether the plaintiff or the defendant appears to start from "zero"—matters.[35] An anchoring heuristic lowers the willingness of the factfinder to determine that the burdened party has prevailed, because people fail to adjust fully from a given starting point, even if the starting point was arbitrarily set.[36]

   Good courts recognize all this. For example, in a habeas corpus case, at issue was what effect the burden of persuasion has on the decision of fitness to stand trial.[37] The state court, the Illinois Supreme Court, had said, "the burden of proof becomes significant in a given case only when the evidence is so nicely balanced that neither fitness nor unfitness is established by a preponderance of the evidence," and stated such cases would be "rare." The federal court, the United States Court of Appeals for the Seventh Circuit,

---

33. See Field et al., supra note 10, at 1328–32; Ball, supra note 12, at 817–18; Posner, supra note 24, at 408–09.

34. See George L. Priest & Benjamin Klein, The Selection of Disputes for Litigation, 13 J. Legal Stud. 1 (1984).

35. See Eyal Zamir & Ilana Ritov, Loss Aversion, Omission Bias, and the Burden of Proof in Civil Litigation, 41 J. Legal Stud. 165, 197 n.23 (2012).

36. See infra text accompanying note 211.

37. United States *ex rel.* Bilyew v. Franzen, 686 F.2d 1238, 1245, 1247–48 (7th Cir. 1982).

disagreed, attacking the simplistic model of probability that underlay the state court's view:

> The model supposes that the evidence at a fitness hearing can be toted on a scale of probabilities from zero to one, with zero representing certain unfitness and one representing certain fitness.... Since the number one half is infinitely rare among the numbers between zero and one, the occasions when the burden of proof makes a difference must be rare also.
>
> There are at least three objections to such a theory of the burden of proof. First, factfinders do not discern a continuous spectrum of evidentiary weights. While there is an unaccountably infinite supply of numbers between zero and one, a judge or a jury can experience only a small, finite number of degrees of certainty that a defendant is fit to stand trial. A defendant may be absolutely fit, most likely fit, hard-to-tell-but-probably fit, etc., but before long any additional gradations of fitness are imperceptible. Thus cases when the evidence of fitness and unfitness seem in balance are not unique among some infinite variety of evidentiary balances, but instead are among a much smaller number of possibilities that may be perceived by the factfinder.
>
> Second, the statement that cases where the evidence is equipoised are "rare" assumes without justification that the weights of evidence are distributed in a fashion that makes equipoise rare. The contrary assumption, that there are relatively many close cases, similarly lacks justification. Perhaps the Illinois Supreme Court intended to state an empirical judgment about the relative frequency of hard cases in which the burden of proof is determinative, but instead the Court appears simply to have swallowed the unjustified logic that when probabilities are evenly distributed equipoise occurs infrequently.
>
> Finally, the allocation of the burden of proof probably is important throughout the hearing, not just at the end when all the evidence has been received and is being weighed by the factfinder. The party with the burden of proof must put on its evidence first, and goes first with closing argument. While these procedural differences do not by themselves violate due process, they suggest a weakness in a model of burdens of proof that requires the evidence be evaluated all at once at the close of the proceedings. More likely is

ML is

➤ that the factfinder (to the extent it is familiar with and knows who has the burden of proof) makes use of the burden throughout its reception of the evidence, viewing the burdened party's evidence more skeptically as it comes in.

Third, the law does not worry overly about allocating the burden of persuasion. The plaintiff must prove affirmatively the elements of the claim. True, the defendant will bear the burden on affirmative defenses. Also, presumptions and other special rules can shift the original burden from one side to the other. Speaking generally, the law will shift the burden from the plaintiff if one or more of four factors is big enough to shift noticeably the balance of costs and benefits: (1) the plaintiff's relative expense of presenting evidence to support his position on the issue, (2) the plaintiff's likelihood of being correct on the issue, (3) the relative amount at stake for the plaintiff, and (4) the relative social cost of an erroneous decision against the plaintiff.[38] But the default rule is to burden the plaintiff, and so on most issues and most of the time the plaintiff is the burden-bearer.[39]

Shift the rln

Given that the factfinder will rely on the burden of persuasion much more often than most people would guess and thus that the burden decides a lot of cases—because of both the zone of frequent evidential ties and the framing effect—why does the law so blithely allocate the burden routinely to the plaintiff?

The law's purpose therein might reflect a general hostility toward plaintiffs, who usually seem intent on disrupting the status quo,[40] or might reflect a specific substantive policy, such as avoiding the costs of enforcement that would be incurred in what is admittedly a close case.[41] This approach to the burden of persuasion disadvantages plaintiffs by influencing the outcome of litigation.

An arguably better reason is that loss aversion and omission bias support burdening the plaintiff.[42] The idea is that the disutility generated by a loss of something exceeds the utility reaped from an equal gain. A similar

---

38. See Bruce L. Hay, Allocating the Burden of Proof, 72 Ind. L.J. 651, 677 (1997); Fleming James, Jr., Burden of Proof, 47 Va. L. Rev. 51, 60–61 (1961).

39. See Field et al., supra note 10, at 1332–44.

40. See Albert Kiralfy, The Burden of Proof 1 (1987) ("In addition, all legal systems see litigation as troublesome, time-consuming and expensive, and place the person who instigates it under some disadvantages.").

41. See Posner, supra note 29, §22.4.

42. See Zamir & Ritov, supra note 35, at 187–97.

idea is that harmful commissions inflict more cost psychologically than do harmful omissions. Accordingly, people perceive the loss to the defendant by a judgment of recovery as larger than the gain to the plaintiff, while such a judgment requires the system to elevate action over inaction and so risk incurring regret costs. Another way to make this point is that a mistake against a defendant is more costly than a mistake against a plaintiff and therefore, just as the system is wary of convicting the innocent, the system should be somewhat wary of finding for the plaintiff in a civil case. Or in still other words, the law should be more reluctant to decide for the plaintiff than for the defendant. Putting the burden of persuasion on the plaintiff accommodates this reluctance, without raising the standard of proof.

This argument that the system should recognize the perceived psychological effects is not wholly satisfying. On the one hand, there is the question of whether law should accommodate psychological costs at all. Perhaps the law should just ignore the two facts that people perceive a $100 judgment against the defendant as more costly than the plaintiff's failure on the $100 claim and that decisionmakers tend to prefer not to stick their necks out by taking action.[43] On the other hand, because psychological studies indicate that people incline against imposing losses on others despite offsetting gains and they incline, even more effectively, toward inaction on decisions affecting others, we can assume that the factfinder will have impulses against the plaintiff already.[44] Imposing the burden of persuasion on the plaintiff might overly augment this natural inclination. Perhaps the burden should instead be imposed on the defendant to counteract the inclination.

Even accepting one or more of these arguments for burdening the plaintiff, it appears that imposing the burden of persuasion on the plaintiff is an adequate cure. These are not good arguments for taking the additional step of raising the plaintiff's standard of proof.

In any event, the preceding ideas—that standards of decision invoke a range of likelihoods rather than a point, and that we need to recognize the burden of persuasion really matters—are powerful. For example, the range of each of the natural categories of complex probabilities and the impreci-

---

43. Cf. Winter, supra note 29, at 343 n.1 (commenting that "[t]here may well be some predisposition to disfavor plaintiffs because they are 'accusers,'" but adding that "[s]uch a view seems to me ... more emotional than rational and wholly inappropriate in a highly commercialized and insured society").

44. See Zamir & Ritov, supra note 35, at 171–86 (describing experiments that tend to show that factfinders do in fact incline against plaintiffs).

sion of boundaries between them, combined with a proper judicial reluctance to force precise cutoffs on the jury, may help to explain some of the judicial reluctance to overturn decisions by the jury.

Clear and Convincing Evidence

The key idea here is coalescence over time of possibly multiple intermediate standards into a single one.[45] Thus a court in a suit for contract reformation could utter the following description of the single standard with a straight face:

> A safeguard, however, has been enunciated which requires a higher degree of proof than mere preponderance of the evidence. The standard has been described in the case in various ways—clear and conclusive, Davidson v. Greer, 35 Tenn. (3 Sneed) 384 (1855); clear, certain and satisfactory, Bailey v. Bailey, 27 Tenn. (8 Humph) 230 (1847); clear, convincing and satisfactory, Jones v. Jones, 150 Tenn. 554, 266 S.W. 110 (1925); clear, cogent and convincing, Whitaker v. Moore, 14 Tenn. App. 204 (1938); full, clear and unequivocal, Perry v. Pearson, 20 Tenn. (1 Humph) 431 (1839); clear, exact and satisfactory, Rogers v. Smith, 48 S.W. 700 (Tenn. Ch. App.1898).[46]

The court then said, "This brings us to the more difficult question to be resolved, viz., does the proof meet the more stringent test?" It concluded that the plaintiff did meet the standard.

But what does that unitary standard really mean? The evolving view is that all the various formulations mean "highly probable." This formulation did constitute a big step forward. At least, the law became simpler. "Adopting this defi-

---

45. See Am-Pro Protective Agency, Inc. v. United States, 281 F.3d 1234, 1239–40 (Fed. Cir. 2002) (equating the "well-nigh irrefragable proof" standard to clear and convincing). Compare Molyneux v. Twin Falls Canal Co., 35 P.2d 651, 655–56 (Idaho 1934) (saying that "clear, positive, and unequivocal" imposes an impermissibly heavier burden than "clear and convincing"), and Howard Newcomb Morse, Evidentiary Lexicology, 59 Dick. L. Rev. 86, 86 (1954) (saying that the intermediate category contains many separate standards), with Paul C. Giannelli, Understanding Evidence §4.03[B] (3d ed. 2009) (implying that only one intermediate standard exists), Geoffrey C. Hazard, Jr, John Leubsdorf & Debra Lyn Bassett, Civil Procedure §11.14 (6th ed. 2011) (same), and Roger C. Park, David P. Leonard, Aviva A. Orenstein & Steven H. Goldberg, Evidence Law §4.04 (3d ed. 2011) (same).

46. Rentenbach Eng'g Co., Constr. Div. v. Gen. Realty Ltd., 707 S.W.2d 524, 527 (Tenn. Ct. App. 1985).

nition of clear and convincing evidence—that the factfinder believes that the truth of the facts asserted is highly probable—will also begin to provide, through its simplicity, some much-needed clarity to an evidentiary area that has plagued Kansas, and other jurisdictions, for years.... All contrary holdings of this court are disapproved, and the Kansas pattern jury instruction(s) on this issue will require modification."[47]

For an example of this modern view, the trial court had charged the jury in a criminal case: "The defendant has the burden of proving that he is not responsible for criminal conduct by reason of insanity by clear and convincing evidence. To be clear and convincing, evidence should be clear in the sense that it is certain, plain to the understanding, unambiguous, and convincing in the sense that it is so reasonable and persuasive as to cause you to believe it." The state supreme court reversed, on the ground that the charge set the standard too high: "We hold that the trial court erred in giving the instructions it did in the case at bench. In this context, the better instruction would inform a jury that clear and convincing evidence is evidence that makes the existence of the issue propounded 'highly probable.'"[48] Yet it quoted with approval a lower court: "The use of the term 'certain' is so likely to mislead in defining clear and convincing evidence that, rather than attempting to parse degrees of certainty on a scale from reasonable to moral to absolute, we would avoid its usage altogether."[49]

Thus, the standard's position as intermediate between preponderance and reasonable doubt might be more instructive than its expression in terms of probability. An example comes from a recent fraud case on the civil side:

> Under Hawai'i law, "clear and convincing" evidence is "defined as an intermediate standard of proof greater than a preponderance of the evidence, but less than proof beyond a reasonable doubt required in criminal cases." This standard requires "that degree of proof which will produce in the mind of the trier of fact a firm belief or conviction as to the allegations sought to be established, and requires the existence of a fact be highly probable."
>
> The "clear and convincing" standard "has been applied to a wide variety of civil cases where for policy reasons the courts require a higher than ordinary degree of certitude before making factual findings." This standard "is typically used in civil cases involving allegations of fraud or some other quasi-criminal wrongdoing by the

---

47. *In re* B.D.-Y., 187 P.3d 594, 602 (Kan. 2008).
48. State v. King, 763 P.2d 239, 241–44 (Ariz. 1988).
49. State v. Renforth, 746 P.2d 1315, 1318 (Ariz. Ct. App. 1987).

defendant." In such cases, "the interests at stake … are deemed to be more substantial than mere loss of money and some jurisdictions accordingly reduce the risk to the defendant of having his reputation tarnished erroneously by increasing the plaintiff's burden of proof."[50]

Important Methodological Note:
Standard As a Policy Judgment

As I have said, in setting a standard of proof for a category of cases or issues, the law apparently seeks to minimize the expected cost of error. This focus might seem short-sighted, however, as it ignores to some degree the possibilities of optimizing incentives for primary conduct. A broader focus would suggest that the law should look not only at the disutilities of erroneous judgments, but also at the utilities of correct findings of liability and nonliability.[51] That is, it could well be that the law, in civil as well as criminal cases, should aim beyond minimizing the sum of expected costs from the two types of erroneous decisions, measured from an ex post perspective. Going forward from decision, correct decisions matter too, in that they increase the deterrent effect and reduce the chilling effect of the law's applications. From a social welfare point of view, the law should set the standard of proof only after taking these effects into account.[52]

---

50. Tauese v. State, Dep't of Labor & Indus. Relations, 147 P.3d 785, 819–20 (Haw. 2006) (citations omitted) (quoting Masaki v. Gen. Motors Corp., 780 P.2d 566, 574–75 (Haw. 1989) (observing also, "The law has evolved three standards of levels of proof for different types of cases.")).

51. See Larry Laudan & Harry D. Saunders, Re-thinking the Criminal Standard of Proof: Seeking Consensus About the Utilities of Trial Outcomes, 7 Int'l Comment. on Evidence iss. 2, art. 1 (2009), available at http://ssrn.com/abstract=1369996, at 3–4, 9–16; cf. Larry Laudan, Is It Finally Time to Put "Proof Beyond a Reasonable Doubt" Out to Pasture?, in The Routledge Companion to Philosophy of Law 317 (Andrei Marmor ed., 2012), available at http://ssrn.com/abstract=1815321, at 11–14 (observing that the usual approach assumes that the procedural rules and the adjudicators are not biased in producing results, because otherwise the standard would have to be adjusted to offset the bias).

52. See Louis Kaplow, Burden of Proof, 121 Yale L.J. 738 (2012); see also Fredrick E. Vars, Toward a General Theory of Standards of Proof, 60 Cath. U. L. Rev. 1 (2010) (using a sophisticated utility analysis to set the standard for the issue of mental incapacity in will contests).

Moreover, in any such analysis, the law must recognize a broad variety of costs. Including some costs, though, is debatable: I have already questioned including the possible biases of adjudicators; the psychological effects of loss aversion and omission bias; the substantive hostility to plaintiffs; the economic consideration of the parties' differing marginal utilities of wealth; and the availability and admissibility of evidence particular to the case. Yet even if the law were to ignore these ephemeral costs, and instead look more basically at the expected cost of each outcome, questions would remain as to how particularized the analysis should be with regard to the specific type of case and issue in dispute.

The principal concern of this book is not this societal choice in setting the standard optimally, but lies instead in understanding and applying whatever standard is chosen. Still, my prior conclusions—that the available standards constitute not a spectrum but rather a starkly limited set, and that the law tends to fix standards applicable across broad categories of cases and issues—do make the task of choosing the standard a good deal less difficult to perform. In brief, society can address the policy task grossly.

Beyond a Reasonable Doubt

In criminal cases, at least for the elements of the crime, the degree of persuasion must be beyond a reasonable doubt. Acceptance of some such high standard has been wide, since ancient times and both here and abroad.[53] The

---

53. See Barbara J. Shapiro, "Beyond Reasonable Doubt" and "Probable Cause": Historical Perspectives on the Anglo-American Law of Evidence (1991); Loretta B. DeLoggio, "Beyond a Reasonable Doubt"—A Historic Analysis, N.Y. St. B. J., Apr. 1986, at 19; Federico Picinali, Is "Proof Beyond a Reasonable Doubt" a Self-Evident Concept? Considering the U.S. and the Italian Legal Cultures Towards the Understanding of the Standard of Persuasion in Criminal Cases, 9 Global Jurist iss. 4, art. 5, at 3–9 (2009), available at http://www.bepress.com/gj/vol9/iss4/art5/; Steve Sheppard, The Metamorphoses of Reasonable Doubt: How Changes in the Burden of Proof Have Weakened the Presumption of Innocence, 78 Notre Dame L. Rev. 1165 (2003); see also Barbara J. Shapiro, "To a Moral Certainty": Theories of Knowledge and Anglo-American Juries 1600–1850, 38 Hastings L.J. 153 (1986) (tracing a somewhat equivalent phrase); Barbara Shapiro, Changing Language, Unchanging Standard: From "Satisfied Conscience" to "Moral Certainty" and "Beyond Reasonable Doubt," 17 Cardozo J. Int'l & Comp. L. 261 (2009); cf. Chris N. Heffer, The Language of Certainty and the Convictions of Certainty: Is "Sure" an Impossible Standard of Proof, 5 Int'l Comment. on Evidence iss. 1, art. 5 (2007), available at http://www.bepress.com/ice/vol5/iss1/art5/ (defending England's use of "sure" as the standard). But cf.

key idea to elaborate now is how a very established standard can remain so very confusing and even somewhat contested.[54]

One of the best-known formulations of reasonable doubt is that of Chief Justice Shaw, even though it leaves a lot up in the air, or even augments the amount in the air:

> It is not mere possible doubt; because every thing relating to human affairs, and depending on moral evidence, is open to some possible or imaginary doubt. It is that state of the case, which, after the entire comparison and consideration of all the evidence, leaves the minds of jurors in that condition that they cannot say they feel an abiding conviction, to a moral certainty, of the truth of the charge.[55]

The basic notion is not that all doubt must be gone, but that all doubt be gone that would make a reasonable person hesitate to act. The proof must be so convincing that a reasonable person would not hesitate to act upon it in the most important of the person's own affairs even when a falsely positive decision would be dreadful.

Nevertheless, it is safe to say that debates still rage about how to phrase the definition for the jury,[56] and that courts regularly get reversed for straying into supposed synonyms.[57] The debates have naturally led to proposals, adopted in some courts, that the judge should not try to define "beyond a reasonable doubt,"[58] given that delivering the unadorned phrase to the jury is constitutionally permissible.[59] The next step would be to propose that the phrase "beyond a reasonable doubt" not be uttered at all. The motive might be the belief

---

James Q. Whitman, The Origins of Reasonable Doubt: Theological Roots of the Criminal Trial 4 (2008) (arguing that the reasonable-doubt-type standard originated "to make conviction *easier*, by assuring jurors that their souls were safe if they voted to condemn the accused"); Randolph N. Jonakait, Finding the Original Meaning of American Criminal Procedure Rights: Lessons from Reasonable Doubt's Development, 10 U. N.H. L. Rev. 97 (2012); James Q. Whitman, Response to Shapiro, 2 Law & Human. 175 (2008).

54. See Dan Simon, In Doubt 195–97 (2012).

55. Commonwealth v. Webster, 59 Mass. (5 Cush.) 295, 320 (1850).

56. See, e.g., Picinali, supra note 53, at 23–28.

57. See, e.g., Cage v. Louisiana, 498 U.S. 39 (1990) (rejecting "grave uncertainty" and "actual substantial doubt").

58. See, e.g., Note, Reasonable Doubt: An Argument Against Definition, 108 Harv. L. Rev 1955 (1995). But cf. Jon O. Newman, Beyond "Reasonable Doubt," 68 N.Y.U. L. Rev. 979, 984 (1993) ("I find it rather unsettling that we are using a formulation that we believe will become less clear the more we explain it.").

59. See Victor v. Nebraska, 511 U.S. 1 (1994).

that the phrase makes the burden on the prosecution seem either too low[60] or too high.[61]

Even more significantly, dispute persists over whether the criminal standard should be anywhere close to the level of this elevated standard. But only radicals push for revision, because an elevated standard is settled law, even if we do not know exactly what it means. Indeed, a surprising aspect here is just how long the basic policy decision of a very high standard has gone unquestioned.

To understand the radicals, begin with this accepted statement of our law: "There is always in litigation a margin of error, representing error in factfinding, which both parties must take into account. Where one party has at stake an interest of transcending value—as a criminal defendant his liberty—this margin of error is reduced as to him by the process of placing on the other party the burden of producing a sufficiency of proof in the first instance, and of persuading the factfinder at the conclusion of the trial of his guilt beyond a reasonable doubt. Due process commands that no man shall lose his liberty unless the Government has borne the burden of producing the evidence and convincing the factfinder of his guilt."[62] For more on the fear of convicting the innocent, the case to cite is *In re Winship*:

> The reasonable-doubt standard plays a vital role in the American scheme of criminal procedure. It is a prime instrument for reducing the risk of convictions resting on factual error. The standard provides concrete substance for the presumption of innocence—that bedrock

---

60. See, e.g., Lawrence M. Solan, Refocusing the Burden of Proof in Criminal Cases: Some Doubt About Reasonable Doubt, 78 Tex. L. Rev 105, 118 (1999) (arguing that the current standard makes the jury think the defendant has the burden of persuasion, and endorsing as an alternative: "If, based on your consideration of the evidence, you are firmly convinced that the defendant is guilty of the crime charged, you must find him guilty. If, on the other hand, you are not firmly convinced of defendant's guilt, you must give defendant the benefit of the doubt and find him not guilty." (quoting State v. Medina, 685 A.2d 1242, 1251–52 (N.J. 1996))).

61. See, e.g., Larry Laudan, Truth, Error, and Criminal Law: An Essay in Legal Epistemology 82 (2006) (arguing that the current standard is too subjective, and suggesting as an alternative: "If there is credible, inculpatory evidence or testimony that would be very hard to explain if the defendant were innocent, and no credible, exculpatory evidence or testimony that would be very difficult to explain if the defendant were guilty, then convict. Otherwise, acquit."); Larry Laudan, Is Reasonable Doubt Reasonable?, 9 Legal Theory 295 (2003) (arguing that the current standard is virtually indistinguishable from a standard that any doubt, even an inarticulable one, can justify acquittal).

62. Speiser v. Randall, 357 U.S. 513, 525–26 (1958).

"axiomatic and elementary" principle whose "enforcement lies at the foundation of the administration of our criminal law."

The requirement of proof beyond a reasonable doubt has this vital role in our criminal procedure for cogent reasons. The accused during a criminal prosecution has at stake interest of immense importance, both because of the possibility that he may lose his liberty upon conviction and because of the certainty that he would be stigmatized by the conviction. Accordingly, a society that values the good name and freedom of every individual should not condemn a man for commission of a crime when there is reasonable doubt about his guilt.

Moreover, use of the reasonable-doubt standard is indispensable to command the respect and confidence of the community in applications of the criminal law. It is critical that the moral force of the criminal law not be diluted by a standard of proof that leaves people in doubt whether innocent men are being condemned. It is also important in our free society that every individual going about his ordinary affairs have confidence that his government cannot adjudge him guilty of a criminal offense without convincing a proper factfinder of his guilt with utmost certainty.[63]

In that case, Justice Harlan's concurrence even more clearly laid out the underlying reasoning:

The standard of proof influences the relative frequency of these two types of erroneous outcomes. If, for example, the standard of proof for a criminal trial were a preponderance of the evidence rather than proof beyond a reasonable doubt, there would be a smaller risk of factual errors that result in freeing guilty persons, but a far greater risk of factual errors that result in convicting the innocent. Because the standard of proof affects the comparative frequency of these two types of erroneous outcomes, the choice of the standard to be applied in a particular kind of litigation should, in a rational world, reflect an assessment of the comparative social disutility of each.

. . . .

In this context, I view the requirement of proof beyond a reasonable doubt in a criminal case as bottomed on a fundamental value de-

---

63. *In re* Winship, 397 U.S. 358, 363–64 (1970) (Brennan, J.) (quoting Coffin v. United States, 156 U.S. 432, 453 (1895)).

termination of our society that it is far worse to convict an innocent man than to let a guilty man go free.[64]

There is the nub, traceable to Blackstone's famous maxim—"it is better that ten guilty persons escape, than that one innocent suffer"[65]—and thence back through the ages to the Bible.

True, a few have questioned the Blackstonian ratio in the past, but their opposition perhaps worked more to support Blackstone. Otto von Bismarck supposedly felt that "it is better that ten innocent men suffer than one guilty man escape."[66] And Felix Dzerzhinsky, founder of the Bolshevik secret police, went further: "Better to execute ten innocent men than to leave one guilty man alive."[67]

Recently, however, some more thoughtful people have raised challenges that only appear to come from a like angle.[68] Their launch point is the sound observation that Blackstone, and the Supreme Court, made a basic mistake in looking at the utilities only of erroneous judgments, thus ignoring the utilities of correct convictions and acquittals. Additionally, Blackstone should not have been looking at errors rather than utilities, nor should he have been expressing his result in the unavoidably arbitrary form of a ratio. Instead, proper decision theory would ask for the social utility of all four possible outcomes, which then neatly generate the optimal standard of proof, p^*, by this formula:

$$p^* = \frac{1}{1 + \frac{U_{TC} - U_{FA}}{U_{TA} - U_{FC}}}$$

where U represents the utility of a true conviction, false acquittal, true acquittal, or false conviction. The standard p^* can vary anywhere from 0 to 1, depending on the utilities assigned.

The radical conclusion would be that on any reasonable estimation of utilities, the current criminal standard of proof is much higher than optimal. The law seems to have focused heavily on the risk of false conviction, while ignor-

---

64. Id. at 371–72 (Harlan, J., concurring).
65. 4 William Blackstone, Commentaries *352 (1769).
66. See John W. Wade, Uniform Comparative Fault Act, 14 Forum 379, 385 (1979).
67. See Alexander Volokh, *n Guilty Men*, 146 U. Pa. L. Rev. 173, 195–96 (1997).
68. See Laudan & Saunders, supra note 51, at 3, 14–16; cf. Erik Lillquist, Recasting Reasonable Doubt: Decision Theory and the Virtues of Variability, 36 U.C. Davis L. Rev. 85 (2002) (arguing for a variable standard). As already suggested, good reason exists for not trying to squeeze the four utilities into consideration of only the two erroneous decisions. See supra text accompanying note 51.

ing altogether the utility of true conviction.[69] The effect of this narrow focus is obvious: it will make the phrase $(U_{TC} - U_{FA})$ small and $(U_{TA} - U_{FC})$ large, and thus make the entire denominator just slightly larger than 1, giving p^* a value around .90. If instead the law included in its focus the utility of true conviction, which is considerable in that it provides just deserts and serves many other values such as deterrence and incapacitation, then $(U_{TC} - U_{FA})$ would jump in size and p^* would plummet.

For example, setting $U_{TC} = 5$ utils, $U_{FC} = -10$, $U_{FA} = -1$, and $U_{TA} = 1$, would mean that although this Blackstone-influenced society still is valuing a false conviction as ten times worse than a false acquittal, nevertheless this society's p^* equals .65. The radicals' point, however, is not that their illustrative utilities are accurate. Their point is instead that society has not made the needed determination of utilities to justify its high standard of proof for criminal cases. The law, through the legislature, has never tried to make or estimate the calculation, but instead jumped to the conclusion of a very high standard of proof. Therefore, the radicals find stunning the law's unthinking persistence over the centuries in maintaining an elevated standard of proof.

My reaction, however, is that if the lawmakers were to reconsider the very high standard of proof, they should discover it to be a good deal more complicated than a mere probability threshold. I shall explain the complications in Chapter V. For now suffice it to say, the criminal standard of proof has a component that would still require the factfinder to eliminate all reasonable possibility of innocence before conviction of any person, even if the lawmakers were to adopt the radical proposal to lower the required showing of guilt.

In general, arguing that a standard of proof reduces to a simple threshold, to say nothing of a precisely quantified threshold, is a misguided endeavor. This reductionism helps in this introductory chapter to convey the range of standards, but a much more sophisticated conceptualization is mandatory before one pushes reform.

b. Harmless Error

My second example is the harmless-error doctrine, which shifts the concern from likelihood of fact to likelihood of effect or noneffect. Trial courts can face the issue of harmlessness, as on some new-trial motions: not every error duly objected to during the course of trial—even if inadequately cured and properly renewed—requires a new trial; instead, after unearthing error,

---

69. See Ronald J. Allen & Larry Laudan, Deadly Dilemmas, 41 Tex. Tech. L. Rev. 65, 68 (2008).

the trial court normally must decide whether the error failed to change the outcome.[70]

Appellate courts most often act as original decisionmakers with respect to harmlessness too.[71] Thus, in exploring the range of original decisions pertinent to this chapter, both appellate and trial courts deserve consideration. Indeed, the legal decisionmaker need not be a court at all, as the upcoming example of police actions will drive home. Nonetheless, for simplicity I shall discuss harmless error in the terms of an appellate doctrine, just as many authorities do.

After an appellate court unearths error, it normally must decide whether the error failed to change the outcome.[72] Approaches differ on the standard of decision, that is, how likely this noneffect must be for the court to deem the error harmless.[73] The conflict among approaches has lasted for centuries.[74] Moreover, courts often mask their standard in idiosyncratic terminology, a practice that by now has helped to produce "verbal chaos"[75] or vague tests like "substantial rights."[76] Although the confusion leads some observers to despair of precision,[77] an appellate court must apply *some* standard of decision:

> Easier was the [harmless error] command to make than it has been always to observe. This, in part because it is general; but in part also because the discrimination it requires is one of judgment transcending confinement by formula or precise rule. That faculty cannot ever be wholly imprisoned in words, much less upon such a criterion as

---

70. See Fed. R. Civ. P. 61; Fed. R. Crim. P. 52(a); Fed. R. Evid. 103(a). See generally 3B Charles Alan Wright, Nancy J. King & Susan R. Klein, Federal Practice and Procedure §§ 851–855 (3d ed. 2004); 11 Charles Alan Wright, Arthur R. Miller & Mary Kay Kane, Federal Practice and Procedure §§ 2881–2888 (2d ed. 1995).

71. See 28 U.S.C. § 2111; Daniel J. Kornstein, A Bayesian Model of Harmless Error, 5 J. Legal Stud. 121, 140–42 (1976). See generally McDonough Power Equip., Inc. v. Greenwood, 464 U.S. 548, 553–54 (1984). But cf. infra note 170 (discussing appellate review of the trial judge's harmless-error determination).

72. But cf. Kornstein, supra note 71, at 129, 131–33 ("Under existing law, certain constitutional errors—coerced confessions, denial of the right to counsel, and a biased judge, for example—call for automatic reversal, without a determination whether such errors affected the judgment." (footnotes omitted)).

73. See id. at 143–44.

74. See Field et al., supra note 10, at 1430–32.

75. Kornstein, supra note 71, at 122.

76. Fed. R. Civ. P. 61; cf. Kotteakos v. United States, 328 U.S. 750, 765 (1946) ("fair assurance" of harmlessness).

77. E.g., Hazard et al., supra note 45, § 15.9; 11 Wright, Miller & Kane, supra note 70, § 2883; see Kornstein, supra note 71, at 121 & n.5.

what are only technical, what substantial rights; and what really affects the latter hurtfully....

....

All this hardly needs to be said again. But it must be comprehended and administered every day. The task is not simple, although the admonition is. Neither is it impossible. By its very nature no standard of perfection can be attained. But one of fair approximation can be achieved. Essentially the matter is one for experience to work out. For, as with all lines which must be drawn between positive and negative fields of law, the precise border may be indistinct, but case by case determination of particular points adds up in time to discernible direction.[78]

With respect to an error on a constitutional matter, the court might require the appellee to show harmlessness "beyond a reasonable doubt."[79] On a nonconstitutional matter, the court might require the appellee's showing of noneffect to be "highly probable."[80] This latter standard—requiring the nonaggrieved party to show the noneffect of error on outcome to be highly probable—has commonly applied in civil cases,[81] while the higher standard most often applies in criminal cases.[82] Nonetheless, other courts sometimes choose to follow a different approach, almost taking an independent view of the case by re-

---

78. Kotteakos v. United States, 328 U.S. 750, 761–62 (1946) (citation omitted).

79. Yates v. Evatt, 500 U.S. 391, 403 (1991); Rose v. Clark, 478 U.S. 570, 582 (1986); Delaware v. Van Arsdall, 475 U.S. 673, 684 (1986); Chapman v. California, 386 U.S. 18, 24 (1967). The more recent cases have in a sense watered down the so-called Chapman standard by increasing the categories of error subject to harmless-error analysis instead of automatic reversal, but wherever applicable the quoted Chapman standard remains unchanged. See United States *ex rel.* Miller v. Greer, 789 F.2d 438, 442–45 (7th Cir. 1986) (en banc), rev'd on other grounds sub nom. Greer v. Miller, 483 U.S. 756 (1987).

80. McQueeney v. Wilmington Trust Co., 779 F.2d 916, 928 (3d Cir. 1985).

81. See Roger J. Traynor, The Riddle of Harmless Error 35, 50 (1970) ("Any test less stringent entails too great a risk of affirming a judgment that was influenced by an error. Moreover, a less stringent test may fail to deter an appellate judge from focusing his inquiry on the correctness of the result and then holding an error harmless whenever he equated the result with his own predilections.... Like all too easy affirmance, all too ready reversal is also inimical to the judicial process. Again, nothing is gained from such an extreme, and much is lost. Reversal for error, regardless of its effect on the judgment, encourages litigants to abuse the judicial process and bestirs the public to ridicule it.").

82. See Stephen A. Saltzburg, The Harm of Harmless Error, 59 Va. L. Rev. 988, 993 n.14 (1973) (arguing for the higher harmless-error standard, by analogy to the criminal law's beyond-a-reasonable-doubt standard of proof).

quiring the appellee merely to show "more probably than not" that the error did not change the outcome.[83]

Thus, Chief Justice Roger J. Traynor managed to perceive a pattern of three defensible standards: "What degree of probability should [the appellate court] require that the judgment is contaminated? Should it affirm if it believes that it is more probable than not that the error did not affect the judgment? Highly probable that it did not? Almost certain that it did not?"[84] And if the standards take those quantum steps within this range, then those are the only three feasible standards for an appellee to escape reversal for a found error. Neither standards less demanding nor standards more demanding than those three would make much sense.[85]

Courts, however, have complicated the pattern by sometimes speaking in terms of the appellant's burden. Although this kind of shift in burden does not substantially simplify or aid the court's decisionmaking, it does substantially affect imagery.[86] The shift necessitates creating three analogous standards: the appellant might show a "slightest possibility,"[87] "reasonable possibility,"[88] or "substantial possibility"[89] that the error changed the outcome and thus was prejudicial.[90]

---

83. E.g., United States v. Stiger, 413 F.3d 1185, 1190 (10th Cir. 2005) ("The government bears the burden to show that a nonconstitutional error is harmless by a preponderance of the evidence."); Haddad v. Lockheed Cal. Corp., 720 F.2d 1454, 1459 (9th Cir. 1983).

84. Traynor, supra note 81, at 34.

85. See Haddad v. Lockheed Cal. Corp., 720 F.2d 1454, 1458 n.7 (9th Cir. 1983) ("Where an error could have been and was the subject of an objection at trial, then appellate courts have three possible standards of review: harmless beyond a reasonable doubt; high probability of harmlessness; and more probably than not harmless.").

86. See Traynor, supra note 81, at 25–26; 11 Wright, Miller & Kane, supra note 70, § 2883, at 448; cf. John T. McNaughton, Burden of Production of Evidence: A Function of a Burden of Persuasion, 68 Harv. L. Rev. 1382, 1382–83 (1955) (discussing and distinguishing burdens of production and persuasion in general).

87. E.g., United States v. Adams, 385 F.2d 548, 550–51 (2d Cir. 1967).

88. E.g., Fahy v. Connecticut, 375 U.S. 85, 86 (1963).

89. E.g., Turlington v. Phillips Petroleum Co., 795 F.2d 434, 444 (5th Cir. 1986).

90. The flip can occur with respect to standards of proof too. A rare example occurs when the law requires a defendant to show merely a specific possibility of disparate racial impact to justify its behavior. See Herman N. (Rusty) Johnson, Jr., The Evolving Strong-Basis-in-Evidence Standard, 32 Berkeley J. Emp. & Lab. L. 347, 375–79 (2011).

Yet, again, terminology applied to the low end of the scale of possibilities is far from uniform.[91] Perhaps it will improve now that the Supreme Court has broadly indicated in a civil case that it is the appellant's burden to show effect[92]—which would rephrase the former civil standard of highly probable noneffect into a requirement that the appellant show a substantial possibility of the error's effect on outcome. Meanwhile, the Supreme Court in its verbalizations in criminal cases has occasionally oscillated between the usual standard of noneffect beyond a reasonable doubt and a flipped standard requiring the appellant to show a reasonable possibility of the error's effect on outcome.[93]

Once the courts get into this lower scale of possibilities by imposing the burden on the appellant, it becomes more conceivable for a court to reduce reversals by tightening up the standard. A court might even abandon the realm of the "possible" for that of the "probable," requiring the appellant to show "affirmatively" that the error more probably than not changed the outcome.[94]

This elaboration of the harmless-error standards positions me to assert now as a matter of theory that there are not just three available standards of decision, but three more standards that invoke mirror-image categories beyond

---

91. See, e.g., Press-Enter. Co. v. Superior Court, 478 U.S. 1, 14 (1986) (distinguishing, without definition, "substantial probability" from "reasonable likelihood" of prejudice in context of denying public access to criminal proceedings); cf. United States v. Bagley, 473 U.S. 667, 682–84 (1985) (using "reasonable probability" test to assess effect of prosecution's failure to disclose evidence favorable to accused); People v. Watson, 299 P.2d 243, 254–55 (Cal. 1956) (converting a "miscarriage of justice" standard into a test for a "reasonably probable" effect).

92. Shinseki v. Sanders, 556 U.S. 396, 409–11 (2009).

93. E.g., Chapman v. California, 386 U.S. 18, 24 (1967); cf. Strickland v. Washington, 466 U.S. 668, 693–94 (1984) (saying that the appellant must show a "reasonable probability" that ineffective assistance of defense counsel affected the outcome, meaning "a probability sufficient to undermine confidence in the outcome" but a showing less than "more likely than not").

94. E.g., Moise v. Fairfax Mkts., Inc., 236 P.2d 216, 218–19 (Cal. Ct. App. 1951), noted in 25 S. Cal. L. Rev. 348 (1952); cf. Palmer v. Hoffman, 318 U.S. 109, 116 (1943) (ruling that the appellant "carries the burden of showing that prejudice resulted"); Vincent v. Young, 324 F.2d 266, 269 (10th Cir. 1963) (implying preponderance standard).

equipoise. The array of standards reflect seven nonnumerical and approximate categories of likelihood: (1) slightest possibility, (2) reasonable possibility, (3) substantial possibility, (4) equipoise, (5) probability, (6) high probability, and (7) near certainty.

Appellee's Burden to Show Noneffect

0 ————————————————————————————————————> 1

Slightest Possibility	Reasonable Possibility	Substantial Possibility	Equipoise	Probability (or Preponderance)	High Probability (or Clear and Convincing)	Near Certainty (or Beyond a Reasonable Doubt)
Near Certainty	High Probability	Probability	Equipoise	Substantial Possibility	Reasonable Possibility	Slightest Possibility (or Scintilla Test)

1 <———————————————————————————————————— 0

Appellant's Burden to Show Effect

Important Methodological Note:
Effect of the Burden Allocation

As just suggested, a useful way to envisage the scale of probabilities is as a set of categories, or intervals, of likelihood. They extend in nonnumerical form from a probability of zero, up to a probability of one. But each of the seven categories embodies some range of probabilities, rather than a point.

As earlier suggested, the law not only sets the standard of proof but also allocates the burden of proof, and the allocation of the burden of persuasion has a considerable effect on the outcome of close cases. Here I want to discuss the effect of that allocation on the phrasing of the standard of decision.

Shifting the burden from the appellee to show harmless error onto the appellant to show prejudicial error, which involves traveling the likelihood scale in the opposite direction, exposes the equivalences among the categories of likelihood.

First, taking as an example a particular category such as beyond a reasonable doubt, a shift in the burden from appellee to appellant changes the terminology from highest probability to lowest possibility.

Second, the affirmance/reversal result for the category in question changes, too. On the scale of probabilities the slightest-possibility-of-effect standard for the appellant represents the same category of likelihood as the noneffect-beyond-a-reasonable-doubt standard for the appellee. The former rule provides that a case falling in the slightest-possibility-of-effect category contains prejudicial error, while the latter rule provides that an appellee reaching the equivalent category establishes harmless error. But the former rule would produce many more reversals. The reason is that the party with the burden gets its desired result if it reaches the specified category. The minimally strong case for reaching the category changes upon shifting of the burden, because the direction of entering the category flips as the burden shifts. Although the appellee must work all the way up to the highest probability, the appellant need only dip his or her toe into the lowest possibility. Thus, a court would almost automatically reverse if it required the appellant to show merely the slightest possibility of effect, because any error on a relevant matter could meet this test.

Third, the analog in terms of a standard of decision, then, does not lie opposite a given category of likelihood, but on the diagonal down to the left. The substantial equivalent of the noneffect-beyond-a-reasonable-doubt standard for the appellee is the reasonable-possibility-of-effect standard for the appellant. The Supreme Court has recognized this equivalence for the harmless error doctrine in paraphrasing "beyond a reasonable doubt" as "whether there is a reasonable possibility that the evidence complained of might have contributed to the conviction."[95] Likewise, the standard that is equivalent to highly probable noneffect, as used in civil cases, is the substantial possibility of an effect.[96]

---

95. Chapman v. California, 386 U.S. 18, 24 (1967) (quoting Fahy v. Connecticut, 375 U.S. 85, 86–87 (1963)).

96. See McQueeney v. Wilmington Trust Co., 779 F.2d 916, 927 n.19 (3d Cir. 1985) (describing unnamed standard higher than reasonable possibility).

I do not mean to suggest that the extreme slightest-possibility standard does not exist. But to require the proponent to raise only some possibility, whether or not reasonable, is a very lenient standard of decision, sometimes called the scintilla test.[97]

An incidental insight here is that there can be a standard of proof higher than beyond a reasonable doubt. The aforementioned slightest-possibility standard of an error's effect is really the analog of requiring from the appellee absolute certainty that the error did not change the outcome. More generally, a decisionmaker can in practical terms demand absolute certainty from the proponent of a fact by deciding against him or her if the opponent could raise the slightest doubt. Occasional tests for frivolity invoke this standard.[98] In the very old days, courts more often spoke of a burden to banish all doubts, and still today courts slip into talk of certainty sometimes.[99] But this ultra-demanding standard is today more common outside the law than within it. After all, anything is possible in almost all the circumstances that call for the application of law.

Note that the existence of this new standard of proof does not imply the existence of an additional category of likelihood. The new standard simply involves entering the highest category of likelihood from the opposite direction.

c. Police Actions

The third example involves the street actions of police officers, which shifts the focus more squarely onto criminal procedure and more explicitly onto the lower end of the probability scale. My concern is with the standards of decision that the police themselves must use, although later their decisions may very well be subject to objective judicial review.[100]

---

97. See Jerome A. Hoffman, Alabama's Scintilla Rule, 28 Ala. L. Rev. 592 (1977).

98. See infra text accompanying note 276; cf. Eggleston, supra note 25, at 139–40 (describing extremely high standard of proof used in some parentage cases in Australia, wherein decision for plaintiff "should not be given if there was even the slightest room for doubt").

99. See Twining, supra note 2, at 104.

100. See 2 Wayne R. LaFave, Jerold H. Israel, Nancy J. King & Orin S. Kerr, Criminal Procedure § 3.3(a), at 107–08 (3d ed. 2007).

Police need not justify with any suspicion their street activity that does not entail detention or search.[101] When facing a decision to detain or search, however, police on the street cannot act on their slightest suspicion, which means an "inchoate and unparticularized suspicion or 'hunch'" or, arguably, the *slightest possibility*.[102] But they can stop and frisk based on "reasonable suspicion," which means reasonable grounds to suspect criminal conduct or, arguably, a *reasonable possibility*.[103] And they can arrest or search based on "probable cause," which is a vague standard meaning a substantial reason to suspect, say, that the arrestee committed the crime in question and which in turn might mean a *substantial possibility*[104] or might, as academics often contend, mean something more demanding such as more likely than not.[105]

---

101. See Michigan v. Chesternut, 486 U.S. 567, 576 (1988).

102. Terry v. Ohio, 392 U.S. 1, 27 (1968). For a thorough search performed at the nation's borders, officers need no more than a "mere suspicion" of illegal activity. Rodriguez-Gonzalez v. United States, 378 F.2d 256, 258 (9th Cir. 1967); cf. United States v. Ramsey, 431 U.S. 606, 616–19 (1977) (saying that a routine border search requires no suspicion).

103. See 2 LaFave et al., supra note 100, §3.8(d) (treating these so-called Terry stops). For a prolonged detention at a border to await a suspect's bowel movement, officers need a "reasonable suspicion" of alimentary-canal smuggling, United States v. Montoya de Hernandez, 473 U.S. 531, 541 (1985), a standard that "lies somewhere in the nebulous region between mere suspicion and probable cause." Gregory L. Waples, Note, From Bags to Body Cavities: The Law of Border Search, 74 Colum. L. Rev. 53, 75 (1974).

104. See 2 LaFave et al., supra note 100, §3.3(b), at 114–15; C.M.A. McCauliff, Burdens of Proof: Degrees of Belief, Quanta of Evidence, or Constitutional Guarantees?, 35 Vand. L. Rev. 1293, 1303–07 (1982). For a border search involving examination of body cavities, officers need a "plain suggestion" of body-cavity smuggling, which arguably is equivalent to this version of probable cause. Henderson v. United States, 390 F.2d 805, 808 (9th Cir. 1967); see Almeida-Sanchez v. United States, 413 U.S. 266, 269 (1973) (requiring probable cause for a roving highway patrol to stop and search vehicles for illegal aliens away from the border). In the related setting of issuing an arrest or search *warrant*, which involves the same probable-cause standard of original decision (although perhaps a more deferential standard of review), see 2 LaFave et al., supra note 100, §3.3(a), at 107, the Court has defined probable cause as a "fair probability" or "substantial chance of criminal activity." New York v. P.J. Video, Inc., 475 U.S. 868, 876–78 (1986) (quoting Illinois v. Gates, 462 U.S. 213, 238, 244 n.13 (1983)); cf. Safford Unified Sch. Dist. No. 1 v. Redding, 557 U.S. 364, 371 (2009) ("Perhaps the best that can be said generally about the required knowledge component of probable cause for a law enforcement officer's evidence search is that it raise a 'fair probability' or a 'substantial chance' of discovering evidence of criminal activity. The lesser standard for school searches could as readily be described as a moderate chance of finding evidence of wrongdoing." (quoting Illinois v. Gates, 462 U.S. 213, 238, 244 n.13 (1983))).

105. Even if the law does not ratchet up the meaning of "probable cause" generally, its test might be the more-likely-than-not standard when the arrest-or-search issue is, say,

At any rate, all these standards stand in stark contrast to the standard for conviction—proof beyond a reasonable doubt. They lie at the low end of the scale of likelihood. As we have just seen, the law could shift the burden and speak instead in terms of standards at the high end. But it is wise not to do so. Speaking in terms of slightest suspicion, reasonable suspicion, and substantial suspicion facilitates direct application of the standard of decision—rather than imposing a burden on the suspect. The police can look directly at the suspicion to measure it—rather than comparing some fact to its negation, which is a mental process of greater complication, as I shall eventually show.

Moreover, all these standards for police actions stand as discrete standards, constituting "a step profile of the criminal justice system."[106] Some courts[107] and observers[108] have argued for a sliding scale of suspicion, whereby the required degree of suspicion would move up with greater invasion of privacy and down with greater need for action. But the Supreme Court has rejected such an approach as too subtle and manipulable, saying that "the protections intended by the Framers could all too easily disappear in the consideration and balancing of the multifarious circumstances presented by different cases, especially when that balancing may be done in the first instance by police officers engaged in the 'often competitive enterprise of ferreting out crime.'"[109]

---

whether a crime has occurred. See 2 LaFave et al., supra note 100, § 3.3(b), at 115. The "probable cause" test might be still more stringent for certain kinds of searches, such as one involving intrusion into the human body. See id. at 111 & n.40. The "probable cause" test could also change as the criminal setting alters from police actions. See 4 id. §§ 13.1(b) (prosecutorial decision to charge), 14.3(a) (preliminary hearing), 15.2(f) (grand jury). And of course, the meaning of "probable cause" has changed over time. See Wesley MacNeil Oliver, The Modern History of Probable Cause, 78 Tenn. L. Rev. 377 (2011). I contend, however, that any such changes occur by quantum leap from one customary category of likelihood to another, thus illustrating a major point of this book.

106. 1 Wayne R. LaFave, Substantive Criminal Law § 1.4(a), at 27 (2d ed. 2003).

107. E.g., United States v. Chaidez, 919 F.2d 1193, 1197 (7th Cir. 1990) (2–1 decision) (adopting, in order to validate a detention, a sliding scale for police stops, "a continuum in which the necessary degree of confidence increases with the degree of intrusion").

108. E.g., Edward L. Barrett, Jr., Personal Rights, Property Rights, and the Fourth Amendment, 1960 Sup. Ct. Rev. 46, 63–65. But when discussing conceivable standards of decision, one must be careful to distinguish proposals that would change the underlying issue to be decided. E.g., Craig M. Bradley, Two Models of the Fourth Amendment, 83 Mich. L. Rev. 1468, 1481–91 (1985) (arguing for overt shift of focus from degree of suspicion to overall reasonableness).

109. Dunaway v. New York, 442 U.S. 200, 213 (1979) (quoting Johnson v. United States, 333 U.S. 10, 14 (1948)); see also Anthony G. Amsterdam, Perspectives on the Fourth Amendment, 58 Minn. L. Rev. 349, 393 (1974) (saying that a sliding scale "converts the fourth amendment into one immense Rorschach blot"); cf. United States v. Montoya de Hernan-

Important Methodological Note:
Magical Numbers Three and Seven

The number three seemed to acquire a bit of magic in connection with the standards of proof. But it loses much of the magic when one realizes that the police example's triad of slightest suspicion, reasonable suspicion, and probable cause do not necessarily all fall on the same side of equipoise, and when one further realizes that the potentially multiple meanings of probable cause, as well as the stringent standard for conviction, mean that more than three standards are at play in this sample drawn from criminal law. Indeed, it is easy to get to seven standards by fleshing out the criminal process's use—during its various steps and for special issues such as searches involving bodily intrusions—of the levels of likelihood between probable cause and beyond a reasonable doubt.

More generally, a discussion of decisionmaking in some corner of the law might involve only one or two standards, or occasionally four or more. True, the number three still predominates in the broad range of examples. One explanation for the prominence of three is that many examples involve a court's expressly picking one standard from three arguable choices. In that situation, the court's and the parties' natural and observable tendency is to think in terms of high-low-and-middle candidates, once they perceive the task as choosing a standard from a scale.

Another explanation for three's prominence is that many examples involve a choice among the three standards that all lie on one side of equipoise. If the task is to gradate how bad a bad act is, the scale will be bad, worse, and worst. Or black things are classifiable as black, blacker, and blackest. Once the court's judgment has surpassed equipoise, the three categories nicely conform to language's structure of adjective, comparative, and superlative. And so, likely acts are classifiable as more likely than not, much more likely than not, and almost certain.

The more solid lesson, however, is that choosing a standard from a scale involves resort to a likelihood scale that comprises seven intervals. These seven consist of two sets of three, appearing as mirror-image categories around equipoise: (1) slightest possibility, (2) reasonable possibility, (3) substantial possibility, (4) equipoise, (5) probability, (6) high probability, and (7) near certainty. Thus, the multiplicity of standards applied in crim-

dez, 473 U.S. 531, 541 (1985) (rejecting any standard between "reasonable suspicion" and "probable cause").

inal law presents no difficulty for the model I am building. By contrast, opting for a sliding scale would clash with my model and, more importantly, with the overwhelmingly dominant approach of the law to likelihood determinations.

2. Standards of Review

Standards of review are analogous to standards of original decision, but a standard of review specifies how certain the reviewer must be of error by the original decisionmaker in order to overturn the original decision. Also, somewhat in contrast to the diverse standards of original decision, standards of review in different legal settings display a high degree of structural similarity. Here I sketch three examples of tripartite standards of review. I begin by shifting the main focus back to the civil side, and chiefly in the federal courts.

a. Review of Trial Judges by Appellate Courts

My first example arises from an appellate court's reviewing the trial judge for error. When considering a reviewable issue,[110] the appellate court must apply a standard of review.[111] Such a standard specifies how certain the appellate court must be of error by the trial judge in order to overturn the original decision.

Scholars and practitioners expend a lot of attention on the standard of review,[112] because it is so practically important.[113] "There are few aspects more crucial to a successful appeal than understanding the appropriate standard of

---

110. Appellate courts simply will not review certain issues; for example, a federal plaintiff gets no review of a remittitur that he has accepted. See Donovan v. Penn Shipping Co., 429 U.S. 648 (1977). Unreviewability is not a standard of decision, but rather an allocation of decisionmaking authority.

111. But cf. Mary M. Schroeder, Address, Appellate Justice Today: Fairness or Formulas, 1994 Wis. L. Rev. 9, 10–11, 27 (1994) (arguing that appellate courts overly rely on standards of review to duck actual decisionmaking, but really attacking only overuse of deferential standards).

112. E.g., Steven Alan Childress & Martha S. Davis, Federal Standards of Review (4th ed. 2010); Harry T. Edwards & Linda A. Elliott, Federal Courts Standards of Review (2007); J. Eric Smithburn, Appellate Review of Trial Court Decisions (2009).

113. See Joshua B. Fischman & Max M. Schanzenbach, Do Standards of Review Matter? The Case of Federal Criminal Sentencing, 40 J. Legal Stud. 405 (2011).

appellate review."[114] The degree of appellate scrutiny is indeed such an important part of the reviewability doctrines that the parties in their briefs must specifically state the applicable standard of review for each issue on appeal.[115]

For any particular reviewable issue, the appellate courts' selection of a standard of review will rest on a complex balancing of the needs for appellate review of the issue (such as controlling possible abuses of power by the trial judge and maintaining uniformity of the law) against the policies that favor limited review (such as conserving judicial resources and enhancing the appellate court's effective functioning, as well as augmenting the trial court's sense of responsibility and image of legitimacy). For an example, the reviewer must be reluctant to substitute its view of the facts. The basis for deference is that review is more concerned with getting the law right for the sake of society than correcting the facts for the sake of a party; that the factfinder is more apt to be right, having actually heard the evidence; and that intrusive review has many costs, including the long-run detrimental effect on the factfinder's sense of responsibility and image of legitimacy and on the reviewer's effective functioning as its workload increases.

Many are the formulations of the standard of review, but they appear to congregate around three basic standards:[116]

- First, on so-called issues of law, the appellate court normally engages in plenary or nondeferential review, employing a virtually de novo approach. It will reverse if it disagrees with the trial judge's resolution and so thinks error in ascertainment of the correct law to be more likely than not.[117]

---

114. Gregory A. Castanias & Robert H. Klonoff, Federal Appellate Practice and Procedure in a Nutshell 176 (2008). But see Scott Rempell, Judging the Judges: Appellate Review of Immigration Decisions, 53 S. Tex. L. Rev. 477, 481–82 (2012) ("Seldom discussed, however, are the evaluative processes appellate courts employ that increase their oversight over the immigration agency's factual determinations."); John Stick, Can Nihilism Be Practical?, 100 Harv. L. Rev. 332, 362 n.130 (1986) (suggesting that standards of review are open to judicial manipulation).

115. See Fed. R. App. P. 28(a)(9)(B), (b)(5).

116. See Richard H.W. Maloy, "Standards of Review"—Just a Tip of the Icicle, 77 U. Det. Mercy L. Rev. 603, 610–11 (2000); cf. United States v. Boyd, 55 F.3d 239, 242 (7th Cir. 1995) ("We are not fetishistic about standards of appellate review. We acknowledge that there are more verbal formulas for the scope of appellate review (plenary or de novo, clearly erroneous, abuse of discretion, substantial evidence, arbitrary and capricious, some evidence, reasonable basis, presumed correct, and maybe others) than there are distinctions actually capable of being drawn in the practice of appellate review.").

117. See Jack H. Friedenthal, Mary Kay Kane & Arthur R. Miller, Civil Procedure § 13.4 (4th ed. 2005); 9C Charles Alan Wright & Arthur R. Miller, Federal Practice and Procedure

- Second, on issues of judge-found fact, the appellate court normally defers to the trial court's view, for the reasons just explained. It will reverse only if the trial judge's view is clearly erroneous and thus generates "the definite and firm conviction that a mistake has been committed."[118]
- Third, in performing certain functions, the appellate court will intrude only in the most extreme circumstances. An instance is granting mandamus for abuse of discretion. An appellate court will grant a petition for mandamus only upon a clear and indisputable showing that the trial judge has committed reversible error.[119] If the trial error alleged is abuse of discretion, then this threshold test of clear and indisputable error means at least "clear abuse of discretion."[120] That standard of review seems equivalent to almost-certain error.

---

§ 2588 (3d ed. 2008); Patrick W. Brennan, Standards of Appellate Review, 33 Def. L.J. 377, 406–07 (1984).

118. United States v. U.S. Gypsum Co., 333 U.S. 364, 395 (1948); see Fed. R. Civ. P. 52(a)(6); Field et al., supra note 10, at 1459–62; Federal Civil Appellate Jurisdiction: An Interlocutory Restatement, Law & Contemp. Probs., Spring 1984, at 13, 55–58. In a different context, applying the rule that a court can escape the law-of-the-case doctrine if the prior decision was clearly erroneous, the Seventh Circuit explained, perhaps too colorfully and strongly: "In any event, under the clearly-erroneous standard, we cannot meddle with a prior decision of this or a lower court simply because we have doubts about its wisdom or think we would have reached a different result. To be clearly erroneous, a decision must strike us as more than just maybe or probably wrong; it must, as one member of this court recently stated during oral argument, strike us as wrong with the force of a five-week-old, unrefrigerated dead fish. To be clearly erroneous, then, the [earlier] panel's decision must be dead wrong, and we do not believe it is." Parts & Elec. Motors, Inc. v. Sterling Elec., Inc., 866 F.2d 228, 233 (7th Cir. 1988). In reality, reversals for clear error of fact do occur. See Robert Anderson IV, Law, Fact, and Discretion in the Federal Courts: An Empirical Study, 2012 Utah L. Rev. 1, 38, 49–50.

119. See 28 U.S.C. § 1651(a) (authorizing issuance of writ); 16 Charles Alan Wright, Arthur R. Miller & Edward H. Cooper, Federal Practice and Procedure §§ 3932–3936 (2d ed. 1996). There are other necessary conditions for granting mandamus: (a) the case must be one that could ultimately be within the appellate court's jurisdiction but the petitioner has no other means to get adequate relief and (b) a cost-benefit analysis must favor interlocutory review. See id. But under current doctrine, these conditions entail decisional steps separate from the threshold determination of probability of error, which is the only step involving a standard of review.

120. See Will v. Calvert Fire Ins. Co., 437 U.S. 655, 665 n.7 (1978) (plurality opinion); id. at 676 (Brennan, J., dissenting); In re Drexel Burnham Lambert Inc., 861 F.2d 1307 (2nd Cir. 1988) (asking "whether the district judge's decision is a rational one finding support in the record"); Field et al., supra note 10, at 1578; Friedenthal et al., supra note 117, § 13.3; George V. Burke, Annotation, Mandamus as Appropriate Remedy to Control Action of Federal Court in Civil Case—Supreme Court Cases, 57 L. Ed. 2d 1203, 1212–13 (1979).

The need to fit issues into one of these three boxes will, of course, present some difficult characterization problems.[121] A prime example is the mixed questions of fact and law.[122]

Abuse of Discretion

This mention of abuse of discretion reveals that appellate courts do verbalize other formulations. Courts refer to an abuse-of-discretion standard of review for certain applications of law to fact.[123] To illustrate, the core decision on a motion for a new trial on the ground of misconduct of counsel lies within the trial judge's discretion, and the appellate court will reverse only if there was an abuse of that discretion.[124]

How such a standard correlates with the tripartite scale just described is not immediately apparent. "Abuse of discretion is thus a nebulous concept which remains essentially undefined."[125] Nonetheless, in practice, review of discretionary decisions seems to replicate in parallel the traditional triple standards of appellate review. In the usual situation, such as review of a decided motion

---

121. When the Supreme Court clarified that the clear-error standard applies even to factfindings based on documentary evidence, Anderson v. City of Bessemer City, N.C., 470 U.S. 564, 574–75 (1985), it went on to say, quite questionably: "When findings are based on determinations regarding the credibility of witnesses, Rule 52(a) demands even greater deference to the trial court's findings …." Id. at 575; see Amadeo v. Zant, 486 U.S. 214, 227 (1988). The Court's explanation of this statement hinted at raising the standard of review in such circumstances to a test of almost certain error, which would constitute a very surprising alteration of the applicable standard. If instead the Court merely meant to nudge the standard slightly higher, then I argue, as for other such minor adjustments, this alteration would be neither realistic nor desirable. Cf. Charles Alan Wright & Mary Kay Kane, The Law of Federal Courts § 96, at 689 (7th ed. 2011) (arguing for "a single standard of review" of factfindings).

122. See 9C Wright & Miller, supra note 117, § 2589; Randall H. Warner, All Mixed Up About Mixed Questions, 7 J. App. Prac. & Process 101 (2005); cf. Martin B. Louis, Allocating Adjudicative Decision Making Authority Between the Trial and Appellate Levels: A Unified View of the Scope of Review, the Judge/Jury Question, and Procedural Discretion, 64 N.C. L. Rev. 993 (1986) (comparing the fact/law boundary regarding the jury right).

123. See generally Sarah M.R. Cravens, Judging Discretion: Contexts for Understanding the Role of Judgment, 64 U. Miami L. Rev. 947 (2010).

124. See City of Cleveland v. Peter Kiewit Sons' Co., 624 F.2d 749, 756 (6th Cir. 1980) (applying deferential standard in reversing denial of new trial based on misconduct of counsel); Pettingill v. Fuller, 107 F.2d 933, 936 (2d Cir. 1939) (reversing grant for abuse of discretion).

125. Federal Civil Appellate Jurisdiction: An Interlocutory Restatement, supra note 118, at 62; cf. Lawson Prods., Inc. v. Avnet, Inc., 782 F.2d 1429, 1438–39 (7th Cir. 1986) (justifying the lack of clarity).

for a new trial on the ground of misconduct of counsel, most observers would say "that only if an appellate court is convinced that the court below was clearly wrong will it reverse."[126] In other situations, however, the appellate court might be more willing[127] or more reluctant[128] to intercede, given stronger or weaker reasons for review rather than deference. This variety of meanings justifies a generalization: "Discretionary decisions fall into three categories, with corresponding limitations on appellate review."[129]

---

126. Friedenthal et al., supra note 117, § 13.4, at 643; see Anderson v. Air W., Inc., 542 F.2d 522, 524 (9th Cir. 1976); Hazard et al., supra note 45, § 15.9; cf. Cooter & Gell v. Hartmarx Corp., 496 U.S. 384, 401 (1990) ("When an appellate court reviews a district court's factual findings, the abuse-of-discretion and clearly erroneous standards are indistinguishable ....").

127. See, e.g., Pearson v. Dennison, 353 F.2d 24, 28 n.6 (9th Cir. 1965) ("What we mean, when we say that a court abused its discretion, is merely that we think that it made a mistake."); cf. Cooter & Gell v. Hartmarx Corp., 496 U.S. 384, 405 (1990) ("A district court would necessarily abuse its discretion if it based its ruling on an erroneous view of the law ...."); Schenck v. City of Hudson, 114 F.3d 590, 593 (6th Cir. 1997) ("A district court abuses its discretion when it applies the incorrect legal standard, misapplies the correct legal standard, or relies upon clearly erroneous findings of fact.").

128. See, e.g., Delno v. Mkt. St. Ry. Co., 124 F.2d 965, 967 (9th Cir. 1942) (dictum) ("Discretion ... is abused only where no reasonable man would take the view adopted by the trial court."); cf. supra note 120 (discussing "clear abuse of discretion").

129. Federal Civil Appellate Jurisdiction: An Interlocutory Restatement, supra note 118, at 62. Although one of the three categories discussed therein seems to be unreviewable discretion, theoretically there should also exist a highly deferential standard of review. "Unfortunately [abuse of discretion] covers a family of review standards rather than a single standard, and a family whose members differ greatly in the actual stringency of review." Am. Hosp. Supply Corp. v. Hosp. Prods. Ltd., 780 F.2d 589, 594 (7th Cir. 1986) (Posner, J.) (describing three standards: simple disagreement, strong conviction of error, and virtually complete deference); cf. Maurice Rosenberg, Judicial Discretion of the Trial Court, Viewed from Above, 22 Syracuse L. Rev. 635, 650–53 (1971) (describing a similar set of three "gradations of discretion," in addition to unreviewable discretion; noting also that the "slight abuse of discretion" standard is equivalent to review on questions of law, making "discretion" somewhat of a misnomer). But cf. Henry J. Friendly, Indiscretion About Discretion, 31 Emory L.J. 747 (1982) (observing many different verbal formulas in practice and arguing for a sliding scale in theory).

Important Methodological Note:
De Novo Review

In addition to the three standards of review that we have seen in play, courts could conceivably conduct review on a truly de novo basis. Truly de novo review would entail making a fresh decision, whether reached by ignoring completely the prior determination or by using the prior decisionmaker's record or even by weighing the prior decision as evidence.

However, truly de novo review is quite rare in U.S. law. Admittedly, courts use the term all the time, but they simply mean that the review is nondeferential.[130] The appellate court will look for likely error, but will not start over:

> And "de novo," while reflecting the usual Latin obscurantism of the law, does not really mean the judge will decide as on a clean slate without considering the decision of the administrator (or on appeal the decision also of the trial court). Even the most egocentric federal judge applying de novo review will give some weight to what the presumably more expert or experienced plan administrator actually did, even if that weight is applied sub rosa or subconsciously.[131]

It can sometimes be unclear whether nondeferential review or truly de novo review is appropriate.[132]

---

130. See Bose Corp. v. Consumers Union of U.S., Inc., 466 U.S. 485, 514 n.31 (1984) ("The independent review function is not equivalent to a 'de novo' review of the ultimate judgment itself, in which a reviewing court makes an original appraisal of all the evidence to decide whether or not it believes that judgment should be entered for plaintiff."); see also Salve Regina Coll. v. Russell, 499 U.S. 225, 232 (1991) ("Independent appellate review necessarily entails a careful consideration of the district court's legal analysis, and an efficient and sensitive appellate court at least will naturally consider this analysis in undertaking its review."). Compare Alan D. Hornstein, Appellate Advocacy in a Nutshell 37 (2d ed. 1998) ("Even with respect to the purely legal decision, however, there is an inertial force that the party seeking reversal of a trial judge's ruling must overcome."), with Robert L. Stern, Review of Findings of Administrators, Judges and Juries: A Comparative Analysis, 58 Harv. L. Rev. 70, 72 n.7 (1944) ("although appellate courts purport to respect the legal conclusions they are reviewing, in practice this probably amounts to little more than following the judgment below if the appellate court thinks the considerations are so evenly balanced that there is no reason for reversal").

131. Mood v. Prudential Ins. Co. of Am., 379 F. Supp. 2d 267, 271 (E.D.N.Y. 2005).

132. See Amadasu v. Ngati, No. 05-CV-2585 (RRM) (LB), 2012 WL 3930386 (E.D.N.Y. Sept. 9, 2012) (discussing the split over whether the district court can or must consider new arguments and evidence when reviewing "de novo" a magistrate judge under 28 U.S.C. §636(b)(1)).

> Where it exists, truly de novo review is not really review at all, but an original decision, a retrial. The relevant concept then is the standard of original decision, such as the standard of proof. Thus, de novo review does not merit more discussion in this section on standards of review.

Plain Error

Another specialized formulation is the vaguely defined plain-error doctrine, which allows an appellate court to reach an issue not raised by the parties.[133] The power to reverse for plain error is an exception to the adversary principle of party-presentation, which typically sticks a party with a formulation or application of law to which it failed to object. Of course, any such exercise of this plain-error power could reflect appellate whim and so could be difficult to restrain. But the cases do suggest that this exceptional power is very sparingly exercised and normally will be invoked only to correct an obvious error that caused a miscarriage of justice. That is, the plain-error doctrine requires a clear and convincing showing of reversible error, as well as of the error's net harm if left uncorrected.

As the first of its decisional steps, the appellate court requires a showing of "obvious" error. Obviousness takes into account the standard of appellate review that will apply. Thus, in measuring obviousness, the appellate court apparently should apply a standard that is one notch more deferential than the usual standard of review.[134]

Next, the appellate court requires a showing of prejudicial effect, with a likelihood greater than that required under the harmless-error doctrine and

---

133. See Fed. R. Civ. P. 51(d)(2); Fed. R. Crim. P. 52(b); Fed. R. Evid. 103(e). The plain-error doctrine is invoked most often in connection with faulty jury instructions, see, e.g., Ratay v. Lincoln Nat'l Life Ins. Co., 378 F.2d 209 (3d Cir.1967) (involving faulty instructions as to the standard of proof), but sometimes for other errors. Compare City of Newport v. Fact Concerts, Inc., 453 U.S. 247 (1981) (finding plain error as to the law applied on punitive damages), with Nimrod v. Sylvester, 369 F.2d 870 (1st Cir. 1966) (finding no plain error as to instructions).

134. See Rojas v. Richardson, 703 F.2d 186, 190, vacated on other grounds, 713 F.2d 116 (5th Cir. 1983); P.P. Mast & Co. v. Superior Drill Co., 154 F. 45, 51 (6th Cir. 1907); 1 Michael H. Graham, Handbook of Federal Evidence § 103:9 (6th ed. 2006); Hornstein, supra note 130, at 42.

perhaps dependent on the circumstances of the case. Here appellate courts act in the general interest of justice, looking more to the public's interest than to the party's forfeited interest. On the one hand, even though in applying the doctrine a court will often verbally stress the harm to the appellant, the court in effect does so only to measure the indirect harm to the system. On the other hand, the appellate court will apply the doctrine only to relieve the appellant's earlier "forfeiture" by omitting timely assertion of a right, rather than a "waiver" by voluntary and intentional relinquishment of a known right.[135]

b. Review of Juries by Trial Judges

As a second example, consider that a trial judge, upon motion to review the jury's factfinding,[136] selects the standard of review from a tripartite scale:

- The judge conceivably might inquire whether he or she thinks that the jury erred and the movant should have prevailed. This is similar to the standard used on a motion for judgment on partial findings, when a jury is not sitting.[137] Under federal jury practice, however, the judge cannot so substitute his or her own view for the jury's.[138]
- The judge should grant a motion for a new trial on the ground that the verdict was "against the weight of the evidence" if, looking at all the evidence, he or she is clearly convinced that the jury was in error.[139] Courts

---

135. See United States v. Olano, 507 U.S. 725, 733 (1993); United States v. Young, 470 U.S. 1, 15–20 (1985); 19 James Wm. Moore et al., Moore's Federal Practice § 206.06[2] (3d ed. 2011); 1 Christopher B. Mueller & Laird C. Kirkpatrick, Federal Evidence §§ 1:21–:22 (3d ed. 2007).

136. I am speaking here only of judicial review of the jury. A new-trial motion can raise other kinds of error for original decision. For example, the trial judge must employ a standard of original decision, not a standard of review, on a motion for a new trial on the ground of newly discovered evidence. The standard of decision on the criminal side for such a motion is whether the new evidence would more likely than not alter the outcome. See INS v. Abudu, 485 U.S. 94, 107 n.12 (1988); 3 Charles Alan Wright & Sarah N. Welling, Federal Practice and Procedure § 584 (4th ed. 2011). However, the standard might effectively be higher on the civil side, see Field et al., supra note 10, at 1437, and be lower in administrative proceedings, see Booz v. Sec'y of Health & Human Servs., 734 F.2d 1378, 1381 (9th Cir. 1984).

137. See Fed. R. Civ. P. 52(c); 9C Wright & Miller, supra note 117, § 2573.1.

138. Nonetheless, inclusion of this version of a "thirteenth juror" approach as an available standard of review is not fanciful, because some states seem to employ it on new-trial motions. See Hazard et al., supra note 45, § 11.28.

139. See Fed. R. Civ. P. 59(a)(1)(A); 11 Wright, Miller & Kane, supra note 70, § 2806; see also id. § 2807 (discussing review of the size of the verdict for excessiveness or inadequacy).

employ various verbal formulas to express this standard. It is apparent, however, that this standard lies between the low standard for judgment on partial findings and the high standard for judgment n.o.v.[140]

· The judge can grant a motion for judgment n.o.v. if, looking at the evidence in the light reasonably most favorable to the nonmovant, the judge thinks that a reasonable jury could not find for the nonmovant.[141] This is a demanding standard. Although courts employ many different verbal formulas, these again "are largely battles of words."[142] In essence, the

---

Some courts, including the Supreme Court in Gasperini v. Center for Humanities, Inc., 518 U.S. 415, 423–25 (1996), rephrase the federal test for review of the size of the verdict as whether the award "shocks the conscience." This phrasing might lead in effect to the more hands-off test of irrationality, as suggested by the trial judge's saying in Coward v. Ruckert, 113 A.2d 287, 290 (Pa. 1955): "When the jury's verdict, at the time of its rendition, causes the trial judge to lose his breath, temporarily, and causes him to almost fall from the bench, then it is truly 'shocking to the judicial conscience'. That is the effect the jury's verdict had on the trial judge in the present case, and we can truly say it was the first such shock so experienced in almost ten years of trial experience on the bench." But, in actual practice, federal judges have not been shy about stepping in to control large awards. See Eric Schnapper, Judges Against Judges—Appellate Review of Federal Civil Jury Verdicts, 1989 Wis. L. Rev. 237, 313–36.

140. Regarding this middle standard, "clearly convinced of error" seems equivalent to "convinced of clear error." They require the same degree of likelihood of error. In other contexts, however, one must beware that similarly subtle verbal shifts do not reflect a change in the standard of decision or the underlying issue.

141. See Fed. R. Civ. P. 50(b); 9B Wright & Miller, supra note 117, §§ 2524–2529. As reflected in the new name for a motion for judgment n.o.v.— "renewed motion for judgment as a matter of law"—the same legal standard for granting the motion applies in the pre-verdict setting on a motion for judgment as a matter of law, which used to be called a motion for a directed verdict. See id. § 2524. Likewise the same standard prevails on summary judgment. See Anderson v. Liberty Lobby, Inc., 477 U.S. 242, 250–52 (1986). In practice, the movant may find it harder to succeed on these earlier motions because the judge often prefers to await verdict in order to lessen intrusion upon the jury and to facilitate appellate review and because the earlier motions usually rest upon a less complete and effective airing of the evidence. In other words, by *denial* the judge can avoid decision on the earlier motions, but before *grant* of either a summary judgment or a directed verdict the movant must meet the n.o.v. standard. See Louis Kaplow, Multistage Adjudication, 126 Harv. L. Rev. (forthcoming 2013), available at http://ssrn.com/abstract=2154683 (developing the difference between standards for granting and denying). Cutting the other way, however, is the factor that granting an earlier motion avoids having to overturn a jury verdict and saves time and money, while the early timing of the motion may hide the difficulty of factual issues that a full airing would reveal. In other words, even the standards for denying these motions may be the same. See Field et al., supra note 10, at 187–88, 1360–62.

142. Hazard et al., supra note 45, § 11.21, at 490.

granting judge must think not merely that the jury was wrong or even that it was clearly wrong, but that it acted irrationally.[143]

Imagine a single disputed issue of typical fact, for which the likelihood of error in a verdict for the proponent is one at W and zero at Z. Imagine further that either the proponent or the opponent on the issue moves after an unfavorable verdict. Then, the judge's belief that the jury erred can range in seven categories or degrees of likelihood, from almost certainty down to slightest possibility, as shown in the figure.[144]

To illustrate, if in the judge's view the likelihood of jury error lies between X and X′, but the jury has nevertheless found for the proponent, then the judge

---

143. Although wholly different standards are feasible, they would not necessarily require the judge to make a finer gradation of probability of error. For instance, a state court might deny the n.o.v. motion whenever there is the slightest possibility of the jury's being correct, more or less as under the generally rejected scintilla test. See 9B Wright & Miller, supra note 117, § 2524. This extreme standard exists on the usual scale of seven intervals of likelihood, involving only a shift in the burden of persuasion. See supra text accompanying note 97.

144. This figure is a remote adaptation of the representation of burden of production in 9 Wigmore, supra note 10, § 2487, at 298. The alterations in part reflect the diagrammatic concerns expressed in McNaughton, supra note 86, at 1384–85. See also William Powers, Jr. & Jack Ratliff, Another Look at "No Evidence" and "Insufficient Evidence," 69 Tex. L. Rev. 515, 520 (1991) (treating Texan standards of review).

should correct the jury's clear error by granting the opponent's motion for a new trial. Note, in particular, that this diagram represents the likelihood of jury error, not the judge's view of the evidential probability that the disputed fact exists.

Important Methodological Note:
Multi-Step Decisionmaking

The typical formulation of the judgment n.o.v. test—if, looking at the evidence in the light reasonably most favorable to the nonmovant, the judge thinks that a reasonable jury could not find for the nonmovant—sounds like a two-step decisional process, different in kind from the process for new-trial motions. But the n.o.v. process does not truly involve two separate decisions.

The federal judge asks only whether he or she is so sure that the jury erred that he or she can say that a jury could not rationally so decide. This involves envisaging the thought process of rationally functioning jurors as, first, they filter the evidence in the rational manner most favorable to the nonmovant, believing what the rational jury could believe of the favorable evidence and disbelieving what it could disbelieve of the unfavorable evidence; and as, second, they view the resultant inferences in the rational manner most favorable to the nonmovant. These are merely logical subdivisions of the jurors' thought process, not separate decisional steps for the judge. The judge inquires whether the jury was wrong to the point of irrationality. Recreating the thought process of most-favorable but still-rational jurors is simply a way of testing whether the verdict falls beyond the irrationality line. Looking at the case in the way reasonably most favorable to the nonmovant—thus looking at all but incredible evidence favorable to the nonmovant and the unquestionable evidence favorable to the movant, and then asking whether a reasonable jury could not find for the nonmovant—merely constitutes the natural way a judge would determine whether the jury almost certainly erred.

Although federal n.o.v. practice is therefore not a two-step process, this is not to say that multi-step processes do not exist. Plain error is the example last raised above: obviousness of error and likelihood of effect are two separate issues. Back to discussing trial motions, a state court might adopt a true two-step process for n.o.v. decisions, as by mechanically looking only at the evidence favorable to the nonmovant and then applying the irrationality test.[145] And a federal court in fact employs a multi-step decisional process for n.o.v. insofar as it applies separate preliminary requirements under the guise of initial burden of production—such as a rule that the burdened side must initially produce some evidence of certain kinds to avoid adverse decision[146]—but the federal approach is to apply the one-step irrationality standard of review once that side meets the preliminary requirements.

c. Review of Administrators by Judges

The third example comes from administrative law and entails judicial review of administrative factfinding.[147] It exhibits greater use of highly deferential review. One view puts it thus:

> Three subsections of [the Administrative Procedure Act, 5 U.S.C. § 706(2),] deal with review of facts, and each prescribes a different level of judicial deference to agency fact-finding. Subsection (A)'s "arbitrary and capricious" test, which applies generally to informal rulemaking and informal adjudication, is in theory the most deferential standard; it is often interpreted to mean only that the administrator's decision have some rational basis. The "substantial evidence" test prescribed by subsection (E) invites somewhat closer judicial scrutiny: there must be enough evidence in the record as a whole that a reasonable person could have reached the conclusion that the agency did. The substan-

---

145. See J.P. McBaine, Recent Decision, Trial Practice: Directed Verdicts; Federal Rule, 31 Calif. L. Rev. 454, 460–61 (1943).

146. See Field et al., supra note 10, at 1356–60.

147. Again, the precise subject here is standards of review. Administrative law could also provide rich examples of standards of original decision. For example, a recent study discusses the "substantially unlikely" standard in immigration law, under which a mandatorily detained noncitizen may get a bond hearing only if he can show that the government is substantially unlikely to prevail on the merits later. Julie Dona, Note, Making Sense of "Substantially Unlikely": An Empirical Analysis of the Joseph Standard in Mandatory Detention Custody Hearings, 26 Geo. Immigr. L.J. (forthcoming 2012), available at http://ssrn.com/abstract=1856758. The study's data suggest that the immigration judges in fact require the noncitizen's position to be beyond a reasonable doubt.

tial evidence test is most often applied to proceedings where there has
been a formal trial-type hearing. Finally, subsection (F) indicates that
in some instances, the court can find the facts de novo.[148]

Other scholars, however, argue that the arbitrary-and-capricious and substantial-
evidence standards should be and are equivalent,[149] both being significantly
more deferential than the clearly erroneous test applied to judicial factfinding
and thus being basically the same as the irrationality test applied to jury factfinding.[150] Whatever the merits of this debate, it seems to take place on the familiar scale of likelihood degrees. A more fundamental debate occurs between
such views and the familiar pleas for the establishment or recognition of a sliding scale of review standards.[151]

Administrative law provides other examples, as similar debates concern judicial deference to agency decisionmaking on mixed questions[152] or even questions of law.[153] Yet my three examples of standards of review—review of judges,
jurors, and administrators—more than suffice because of their basic similar-

---

148. Ernest Gellhorn & Barry B. Boyer, Administrative Law and Process in a Nutshell
59 (2d ed. 1981); see Ernest Gellhorn & Ronald M. Levin, Administrative Law and Process
in a Nutshell 98–102, 111–15 (5th ed. 2006).

149. See, e.g., 2 Richard J. Pierce, Jr., Administrative Law Treatise § 11.4 (5th ed. 2010);
Matthew J. McGrath, Note, Convergence of the Substantial Evidence and Arbitrary and
Capricious Standards of Review During Informal Rulemaking, 54 Geo. Wash. L. Rev. 541
(1986).

150. See, e.g., Richard J. Pierce, Jr., Sidney A. Shapiro & Paul R. Verkuil, Administrative Law and Process § 7.3.3 (5th ed. 2009); Bernard Schwartz, Administrative Law §§ 10.11,
.39 (3d ed. 1991); Stern, supra note 130, at 89.

151. Compare, e.g., Kenneth Culp Davis, Administrative Law Text 525, 529–30, 535–38
(3d ed. 1972), and Roy A. Schotland, Remarks, Scope of Review of Administrative Action,
34 Fed. B.J. 54, 59 (1975), with, e.g., Sch. Dist. of Wis. Dells v. Z.S. ex rel. Littlegeorge, 295
F.3d 671, 674 (7th Cir. 2002) (saying "that 'it is possible, though not always easy,' to distinguish among the canonical standards of review, such as substantial evidence and clear error,
noting that 'this court has expressed skepticism in the past about the ability of judges to
apply more than a few standards of review,'" and conceding that "in any event the cognitive limitations that judges share with other mortals may constitute an insuperable obsta-
cle to making distinctions any finer than that of plenary versus deferential review" (quoting
Aegerter v. City of Delafield, Wis., 174 F.3d 886, 889 (7th Cir. 1999))).

152. See Gellhorn & Levin, supra note 148, at 102–07 (discussing various standards of
review for mixed questions); Charles H. Koch, Jr., Judicial Review of Administrative Discretion, 54 Geo. Wash. L. Rev. 469, 491–94 (1986).

153. See Chevron, U.S.A., Inc. v. Natural Res. Def. Council, Inc., 467 U.S. 837 (1984);
Gellhorn & Levin, supra note 148, at 79–97 (discussing various standards of review for
legal questions); Pierce et al., supra note 150, § 7.4 (discussing degrees of deference ac-
corded to agency conclusions of law).

ity. Together they reveal the prominence, and suggest the propriety, of a tripartite scale of probability of error. So I proceed to the next grouping of standards.

3. Standards for Renewed Review

Standards for reviewing the reviewer are very similar to standards of review, but such a standard of renewed review specifies how certain the backup reviewer must be of error by the preceding reviewer in order to overturn its decision. To focus the concern, three related notions need distinguishing. First, certain issues may be unreviewable on renewed review, which would render the concept of standard of decision irrelevant. Second, renewed review could be a truly fresh review, which would make the standard of initial review the relevant concept. Third, the higher reviewer may have to review an original decision by the reviewer below (for example, the highest court's review of the intermediate court's original decision on harmless error), so that here too the standard of initial review would become the relevant concept.

In a true situation of reviewing the reviewer, the applicable standard of renewed review on a matter of law might remain nondeferential. If the review entailed considering factual matters, a deferential standard of renewed review would become appropriate. If the initial reviewer's review itself was deferential, the standard of renewed review might occasionally edge up a notch toward greater deference, especially where the motivation for additional review is merely correctness review rather than institutional review.[154] In other words, the standards of renewed review fall into place on the tripartite scale of probability of error, as the following three examples confirm.[155]

a. Review by Supreme Courts

The obvious first example arises from the existence of a higher level of appellate courts. Consider the Supreme Court's review of a federal court of ap-

---

154. See Paul D. Carrington, Daniel J. Meador & Maurice Rosenberg, Justice on Appeal 2–4 (1976).

155. These examples come from federal civil court proceedings, although similar examples exist in state law, see, e.g., Hornstein, supra note 130, at 59–65 (second level of appellate review), criminal law, see, e.g., Carrington et al., supra note 154, at 103–18 (state and federal review of state convictions), and administrative law, see, e.g., Schwartz, supra note 150, § 10.10 (renewed review of agency findings). In short, examples could come from any part of the legal system with two or more levels of review.

peals' review. For most issues fully reviewed on the merits, the Court asks whether it disagrees with the court of appeals' resolution. But for certain issues of fact, the Court has shaped the two-court rule, under which the Court will not correct findings concurred in by two courts below "in the absence of a very obvious and exceptional showing of error";[156] although vague, this seems to mean that the court of appeals must have committed clear error in its own deferential review.[157] Finally, the standard of almost certain error theoretically goes unused, at least in full review on the merits.

b. Review of Magistrate Judges

The second example derives from the growing use of federal magistrate judges.[158] Among other functions, magistrate judges can determine nondispositive pretrial matters in civil cases.[159] In such cases, reconsideration by the district judge can occur.[160] Thereafter, appeal may occasionally go to the court of appeals.[161] The court of appeals thus plays a third-tier role similar to the Supreme Court's usual role, presumably applying the Supreme Court's standards of renewed review.[162]

---

156. Graver Tank & Mfg. Co. v. Linde Air Prods. Co., 336 U.S. 271, 275 (1949); see Eugene Gressman, Kenneth S. Geller, Stephen M. Shapiro, Timothy S. Bishop & Edward A. Hartnett, Supreme Court Practice 270–73 (9th ed. 2007); Reynolds Robertson & Francis R. Kirkham, Jurisdiction of the Supreme Court of the United States §333, at 659–61 (Richard F. Wolfson & Philip B. Kurland eds., 2d ed. 1951); Wright & Kane, supra note 121, §108; cf. Stern, supra note 130, at 89–93, 121–22 (disapproving largely of the rule).

157. See Rogers v. Lodge, 458 U.S. 613, 623 (1982); cf. Anderson v. Liberty Lobby, Inc., 477 U.S. 242, 252–56 (1986) (holding that a first-line reviewer looks only for error in the original decisionmaker's application of its own standard of decision). Elevated standards may also apply in granting certiorari on the basis of likelihood of error, see Gressman et al., supra note 156, at 272, 276–80, or in the Court's deciding to dispose of a case summarily, see id. at 342–56.

158. See Tim A. Baker, The Expanding Role of Magistrate Judges in the Federal Courts, 39 Val. U. L. Rev. 661 (2005); Judith Resnik, Tiers, 57 S. Cal. L. Rev. 837, 867–69, 984 (1984). As to the review of a *master*'s findings and conclusions, see 9C Wright & Miller, supra note 117, §§2584, 2613–2615.

159. See 28 U.S.C. §636(b)(1)(A).

160. See Fed. R. Civ. P. 72(a) ("set aside any part of the order that is clearly erroneous or is contrary to law"); 12 Charles Alan Wright, Arthur R. Miller & Richard L. Marcus, Federal Practice and Procedure §3069 (2d ed.1997); cf. Resnik, supra note 158, at 985–90, 1027–28 (questioning the role of the district judge's de novo determinations on dispositive pretrial matters).

161. See 15A Charles Alan Wright, Arthur R. Miller & Edward H. Cooper, Federal Practice and Procedure §3901.1 (2d ed. 1992).

162. Cf. Wolff v. Wolff, 768 F.2d 642, 647, 649 (5th Cir. 1985) (suggesting a rule analogous to the Supreme Court's two-court rule).

c. Review of Trial Motions

The third and most interesting example entails the federal court of appeals' reviewing the trial court's review of the *civil jury's factfinding*. The preceding examples help to put in a revealing light this prime example, exposing that here too a tripartite scale of probabilities appears to reign:

- The court of appeals reviews a grant or denial of an n.o.v. motion as a matter of law, asking whether it disagrees with the trial judge's decision.[163]
- In reviewing a *grant* of a motion for a new trial on the ground that the verdict was against the weight of the evidence, the court of appeals reviews the discretionary element with deference.[164]
- When reviewing a *denial* of such a new-trial motion, whereby the trial judge and the sacrosanct jury concurred, the court of appeals exhibits the highest deference.[165] This highly deferential standard will result in extremely few reversals, because only the combination of a very faulty judge and jury and an extraordinarily lopsided case would prompt the appellate court to be almost certain that the trial judge erred in failing to find the jury in clear error.[166]

---

163. See 9B Wright & Miller, supra note 117, §§ 2524, 2540; William P. McLauchlan, An Empirical Study of Civil Procedure: Directed Verdicts and Judgments Notwithstanding Verdict, 2 J. Legal Stud. 459, 464–68 (1973) (suggesting, albeit in a flawed empirical study, that appellate courts exhibit little diffidence). The same nondeferential standard applies to review of directed verdicts. See 9B Wright & Miller, supra note 117, § 2536. And the same standard applies to review of challenges to so-called impossible verdicts: an appellate court will normally treat the decisions as matters of law, because they entailed the irrationality test. See Fairmount Glass Works v. Cub Fork Coal Co., 287 U.S. 474, 483–84 (1933); 11 Wright, Miller & Kane, supra note 70, §§ 2807, 2820. But the Supreme Court has recently suggested that a layer of deference should apply when a federal habeas court reviews the state appellate court's affirmation of a denial of an n.o.v. motion. See Coleman v. Johnson, 132 S. Ct. 2060 (2012).

164. See Conway v. Chem. Leaman Tank Lines, Inc., 610 F.2d 360, 362, 367 n.9 (5th Cir. 1980) (reversing for "abuse of discretion," which means "that the court has clearly erred"); 11 Wright, Miller & Kane, supra note 70, § 2819; see also id. § 2820 (discussing appellate review of the size of the verdict for excessiveness or inadequacy).

165. See Ga.-Pac. Corp. v. United States, 264 F.2d 161, 166 (5th Cir. 1959) (reversing for "clear abuse of discretion"); Sears v. Pauly, 261 F.2d 304, 309 (1st Cir. 1958) (affirming, while observing that an appellate court can find abuse "only in a very unusual case").

166. Indeed, older views suggested that the appellate court should even treat the facts as unreviewable. See 12 Moore et al., supra note 135, § 59.54[4][a]. But cf. Paul D. Carrington, The Power of District Judges and the Responsibility of Courts of Appeals, 3 Ga. L. Rev. 507, 525 (1969) ("For me, the power of the trial judge to set aside a verdict that he does not like is made more tolerable if he is subject to a measure of review in the exercise of that power.").

Appellate Review of New-Trial Motions, Generalized

If the focus were to broaden to appellate review of the full variety of new-trial motions, however, I would find it harder to rebut the argument that an explicit or implicit sliding scale governs in lieu of three discrete standards. For the federal courts of appeals' review of new-trial decisions in civil cases, no accepted set of standards of review or renewed review currently exists. Instead, the applicable standard seems to depend on three factors. These factors reflect reasons for or against deference to the trial judge, and the weight of these factors in the particular case's circumstances determine the standard that the appellate court will apply.

First, the most significant factor is the degree to which proper decision depends on the decisionmaker's presence at the trial. On the one hand, an appellate court will not defer on so-called issues of law when reviewing a new-trial decision; for example, after the trial judge decides a new-trial motion on the ground of judicial mistake of law in conducting the trial, as in instructing the jury, the appellate court may reverse if it merely disagrees with the trial judge's view of the law.[167] On the other hand, an appellate court will defer considerably on issues of fact[168] and on like issues for which presence at trial is important; for an example already mentioned, the appellate court will not freely substitute its view for the trial judge's with respect to a new-trial motion based on misconduct of counsel.[169]

Because of the broad and varied nature of the new-trial device and because of the complexities of the new-trial decisional process, numerous similar examples exist where the appellate court will show deference.[170] It is difficult to know exactly how much deference these nonlegal decisions enjoy, because appellate courts use varying and vague language to describe the standard of review. Presumably, however, deference theoretically should steadily increase with the importance of being present at trial.[171] The reasons for such defer-

---

167. See Allstate Ins. Co. v. Springer, 269 F.2d 805, 808 (6th Cir. 1959). Similarly, the appellate court freely reverses for errors in handling the procedural law associated with new-trial motions. See Marsh v. Ill. Cent. R.R. Co., 175 F.2d 498, 500 (5th Cir. 1949); Louis, supra note 122, at 1038–46 (exploring law/discretion boundary in appellate review of procedural issues).

168. Any findings of fact by the trial judge are subject to the deference of the clearly erroneous standard. See La Fever, Inc. v. All-Star Ins. Corp., 571 F.2d 1367, 1368 (5th Cir. 1978).

169. See supra note 124 and accompanying text.

170. See 11 Wright, Miller & Kane, supra note 70, §2818, at 195–96 (mentioning misconduct by jury, unfair surprise, and falsified testimony). Indeed, whenever the new-trial review extends to a trial judge's harmless-error determination, the appellate court will show some deference, thus encouraging broad statements to the effect that all new-trial motions are within the trial court's discretion. E.g., id. §2803, at 46–48.

171. See Ehret Co. v. Eaton, Yale & Towne, Inc., 523 F.2d 280, 285 (7th Cir. 1975) ("the trial judge's opportunity to view the 'living courtroom' must be given great weight, especially when assessing the intent of the parties").

ence are familiar: society's interest in getting the right answer by reexamination is usually greater on general legal issues than on specific nonlegal issues, because any review is more concerned with getting the law consistently right for the sake of society than correcting the facts for the sake of a party; anyway, having actually heard the evidence, the trial judge is more apt to be right on nonlegal issues than the appellate court; and even when possibly more adept on nonlegal issues, the appellate court by intruding will probably not generate sufficient benefits to offset the many costs, including the long-range detrimental effects on the trial judges' sense of responsibility and image of legitimacy and on the appellate courts' effective functioning as appeals consequently multiply.[172] Conceivably, these reasons could act as independently variable factors that would help determine the appropriate level of deference.

Second, another factor at play is the specific ground for the new-trial motion. On the one hand, a motion based on the judge's own misbehavior arguably calls for less deferential review, because of the desire to control judicial abuse.[173] On the other hand, there is at least verbal allegiance to higher than usual deference for a decision of any motion made on the ground that the verdict was against the weight of the evidence, because of the jury's sacrosanctity.[174] Also, for somewhat unclear reasons, there may be higher than usual deference for motions on the ground of newly discovered evidence.[175]

Third, yet another factor is the grant/denial distinction. It nicely reveals the doctrinal confusion. On the one hand, arguable reasons exist to treat a grant of any new-trial motion with more deference than a denial. The appeal of a grant usually comes after a second trial that has survived any new-trial motion, and

---

172. See generally Charles Alan Wright, The Doubtful Omniscience of Appellate Courts, 41 Minn. L. Rev. 751, 779–82 (1957).

173. See Hazard et al., supra note 45, § 11.25. In fact, however, the appellate courts seem slow to fault fellow judges. See 11 Wright, Miller & Kane, supra note 70, § 2809.

174. See, e.g., Harris v. Quinones, 507 F.2d 533, 535–36 (10th Cir. 1974) (affirming grant of new trial on ground that verdict was against weight of evidence under a "gross abuse of discretion" standard); cf. Lind v. Schenley Indus. Inc., 278 F.2d 79, 90 (3d Cir. 1960) (saying that "close[r] scrutiny is required in order to protect the litigants' right to jury trial," but the court was reviewing a conditional new-trial grant on ground that verdict was against weight of evidence). In fact, however, the appellate courts seem quite willing to reverse grants of jury-based new motions. See, e.g., Taylor v. Washington Terminal Co., 409 F.2d 145, 149 (D.C. Cir. 1969) (reversing grant, while still observing that an appellate court must give "considerable deference" to trial judge's application of his or her own deferential standard).

175. See Pettingill v. Fuller, 107 F.2d 933, 936 (2d Cir. 1939) (dictum) (discussing deference to denial of such motion); 12 Moore et al., supra note 135, § 59.54[4][c]. But cf. Thomas v. Nuss, 353 F.2d 257, 259–60 (6th Cir. 1965) (affirming denial under the usual abuse-of-discretion standard).

consequently the appellate court will be reluctant to upset the fair second trial to reinstate the contrary first result.[176] Also, wrongly reversing a grant ensures injustice, but wrongly reversing a denial leads only to a new trial where justice may still be done.[177] On the other hand, the opposite tendency to reverse grants and affirm denials would reduce the number of retrials. Also, when a new-trial motion entails factual reconsideration of the jury's factfinding (as on review of a decision on a new-trial motion based on the ground that the verdict was against the weight of the evidence), much more persuasive reasons exist to treat a denial with more deference than a grant (a denial means that the trial judge and the sacrosanct jury concurred, so that the appellate court should be extremely reluctant to intercede).[178]

The result of all these factors is considerable confusion, inadvertently encapsulated by one court in this circuit: "The scope of appellate review of the trial court's [new-trial] decision is narrow as the trial judge's discretion is broad, and reversal warranted only when he has abused it."[179] We cannot expect appellate courts to conform strictly to the currently confused law, and in fact they are left fairly free to exercise whatever review they wish. Perhaps an explicit sliding scale of standards of review would at least clean up the theory.

Nevertheless, even if theoretical clarification were to result, such an approach would be unilluminating and undesirable. Instead, I submit that a definite improvement would flow from recognizing only three review standards for decisions on new-trial motions. At one extreme, all issues currently classified as matters of law should still undergo review as such, with the appellate court asking whether it simply disagrees with the trial judge's decision and thus reversing if it thinks error to be more likely than not. At the other extreme, on factual reconsideration the appellate court should reverse a denial of a motion on the ground that the verdict was against the weight of the evidence (or that the verdict was excessive or inadequate) only if it is almost certain that the trial judge erred. All other reviewable new-trial issues should receive customary middle-level scrutiny, by which the appellate court looks for clear (or highly probable) error, in recognition of the importance of the decisionmaker's having been actually present at trial.

---

176. See Friedenthal et al., supra note 117, at 597–98.

177. See Recent Decision, Appellate Review in the Federal Courts of Orders Granting New Trial, 13 Stan. L. Rev. 383, 388–89 (1961).

178. See Friedenthal et al., supra note 117, at 598–99. But see Cassandra Burke Robertson, Judging Jury Verdicts, 83 Tul. L. Rev. 157, 213–15 (2008).

179. Sulmeyer v. Coca Cola Co., 515 F.2d 835, 852 (5th Cir. 1975).

This formulation of three standards roughly conforms to the present state of the doctrine, and likely even more closely to what most courts do as opposed to what they say. It covers the same range as the current standards, but reduces potentially infinite gradations to the three discrete standards of probable, highly probable, and almost certain error. This easy formulation would improve comprehension and application by the courts. It would also better control them. Moreover, quantum leaps adequately serve the policies behind variable deference on review. Indeed, because the limited choice of standards illuminates the policy question, courts may be able more soundly to effectuate those policies by choosing the appropriate standard, once three and only three discrete standards of new-trial review come to be recognized.

B. Cognitive Explanation

In this part, I shall argue that human limitations on cognition explain the observed pattern among legal standards of decision. My point will not be that people cannot analyze precise probabilities. My point will be that people cannot do more than coarsely place stimuli on a scale, including when they try to gradate perceived probabilities. Thus, however useful the probability calculus is in certain endeavors, like gambling or manipulating statistical evidence, precise or complex probabilities have no role to play in handling legal standards of decision.[180]

1. Cognitive Limitations

Cognitive psychology is a fascinating latter-day branch of the relatively young science of psychology.[181] In the 1950s, as behaviorism fell from favor, and with impetus from breakthroughs in computer science and linguistics and developmental psychology, the discipline of cognitive psychology arose. It comprises the study of how we detect, transform, store, retrieve, and use information from our environment.

---

180. On the integration of statistical evidence with the standard of proof, see infra note 576 and accompanying text.

181. See generally Robert L. Solso, Cognitive Psychology 1–21 (1979). To set the subject in the broadest context, see Howard Gardner, The Mind's New Science (1985).

To look ahead, the cognitive psychology literature suggests that limited, step-like standards of decision accord with how humans naturally process information. Studies of humans' absolute judgment, short-term memory, and use of biased heuristics all support the "bounded rationality" of humankind.[182] In particular, our cognitive limitations leave us able only weakly to judge probabilities. Such judgments usually find expression in terms of a very limited set of broad and fuzzy categories such as more likely than not, high probability, and almost certainty. Perhaps the law, by an intuitive but wise reconciliation with humans' cognitive limitations, has optimized by conforming to the coarsely gradated scale of likelihood already in people's customary use. If so, this development carries some lessons.

One lesson already drawn is that all standards of probabilistic decision-making, such as new-trial review of jury decisions and appellate review of judicial decisions, follow the same pattern. Thus, the many conceivable standards of review distill into simple disagreement, clear error, and the almost certain error of an irrationality test.

Another lesson, which I shall more fully draw in the next section, is that lawmakers in specifying a standard of decision should express their choice in familiar nonnumerical language and should steadfastly choose from the customary standards already in use. The available standards will adequately cover the range of underlying policies, and a range of choices limited to quantum leaps will indeed illuminate the policy question.[183] Familiar language will improve comprehension by the decisionmakers. In application, those decisionmakers should abide by the familiar standards. Learning and accepting this lesson would make for a sounder procedure that better fits humans. As Niels Bohr warned, "I try not to speak more clearly than I think."[184]

a. Absolute Judgment

Today, cognitive psychologists generally agree on an information-processing model, which postulates that information proceeds through a series of identifiable stages including a sensory system, a memory system with short-term and long-term components, and a response system. A pioneering article by

---

182. Herbert A. Simon, Models of Man 199 (1957).

183. Cf. K.C. Cole, Sympathetic Vibrations: Reflections on Physics as a Way of Life 117 (1985) (analogizing discrete states of mind to quantum mechanics).

184. See Richard Rhodes, The Making of the Atomic Bomb 77 (1986).

Harvard and later Princeton Professor George Armitage Miller,[185] which stressed the limits that exist at various stages of our processing of information, proved influential.[186] Among the limits he discussed were those on absolute judgment and on short-term memory. After describing his pertinent findings on those two subjects, I shall mention a few other relevant limitations on cognitive powers, closing this section with thoughts on the theoretical and practical significance of my rudimentary social-science survey.

Professor Miller used the techniques of information theory to analyze the data of other researchers who had tested absolute judgment, that is, how accurately people can identify various magnitudes of any one stimulus.[187] As the typical experiment increased in a single dimension the number of different values of the stimulus presented repetitively to the subject, the subject at some fixed limit began to make significant errors by confusing the different values. This upper limit, or channel capacity, differed for different kinds of stimuli, but the mean for the different kinds was about seven distinct values and the deviation was remarkably small. Thus, there is a clear and definite limit on the amount of information that an observer can transmit through absolute judgments. Even this simplified explanation probably sounds obscure, but some examples should help.

First, consider an experiment in absolute judgment of tone. The experimenter asked listeners to identify different pitches by assigning arbitrary numerals to them; he presented the different pitches repetitively, but in random order; and after each response, he corrected any misidentification. If there were only a few different pitches, the listener could, after a preliminary training period, distinguish them with no confusion. If there were many different pitches, confusions were frequent. The average channel capacity seemed to be about six pitches.

> The result means that we cannot pick more than six different pitches
> that the listener will never confuse. Or, stated slightly differently, no
> matter how many alternative tones we ask him to judge, the best we

---

185. George A. Miller, The Magical Number Seven, Plus or Minus Two: Some Limits on Our Capacity for Processing Information, 63 Psychol. Rev. 81 (1956).

186. See Gardner, supra note 181, at 89–91; Solso, supra note 181, at 445.

187. See Miller, supra note 185, at 81–89. Although not entirely distinct, relative judgment concerns the considerable capacity of people to distinguish between two or more different stimuli that they can compare directly. Absolute judgment instead involves reference to a remembered scale. See William N. Dember & Joel S. Warm, Psychology of Perception 113, 116–17 (2d ed. 1979).

can expect him to do is to assign them to about six different classes without error.[188]

The result held across a broad range of frequencies, prompting an interesting aside:

> For example, if you can discriminate five high-pitched tones in one se-
> ries and five low-pitched tones in another series, it is reasonable to
> expect that you could combine all ten into a single series and still tell
> them all apart without error. When you try it, however, it does not work.
> The channel capacity for pitch seems to be about six and that is the best
> you can do.[189]

Moreover, another experiment with different loudnesses yielded similar results.

Second, experimenters asked observers to interpolate visually between two
scale markers. In each trial the experimenters presented a pointer position
from a set of five, ten, twenty, or fifty pointer positions to the subjects, who
either (1) used any integer from zero to one hundred to locate the position or
(2) knew which pointer positions could occur in the set being presented and
chose one of them as a response. The two versions of the experiments yielded
virtually identical results: "[T]here are between 10 and 15 distinct positions
along a linear interval. This is the largest channel capacity that has been measured for any unidimensional variable."[190] Other experiments involved visually
judging the size of squares, the curvature and length and direction of lines,
and the hue and brightness of colors. These yielded analogous results, although
with significantly smaller channel capacities.[191]

---

188. Miller, supra note 185, at 84.

189. Id. On the oddity of absolute pitch, see W. Dixon Ward, Absolute Pitch, in The Psychology of Music 265 (Diana Deutsch ed., 2d ed. 1999).

190. Miller, supra note 185, at 86; see Dember & Warm, supra note 187, at 113–19.

191. The observed differences in channel capacities from 4 to 15 for different kinds of stimuli have more to do with differences in the types of experiments than differences in cognitive
capabilities. For example, defining end-points or "anchors," as in the linear interpolation experiment, should and does by itself increase channel capacity to 9 or 10. See Wendell R. Garner, Uncertainty and Structure as Psychological Concepts 72–74 (1962); Earl A. Alluisi, Conditions
Affecting the Amount of Information in Absolute Judgments, 64 Psychol. Rev. 97, 101–02
(1957) (treating differences among individuals and among experimental conditions); cf. A.W.
MacRae, Channel Capacity in Absolute Judgment Tasks: An Artifact of Information Bias?, 73
Psychol. Bull. 112, 116, 119–20 (1970) (arguing that channel capacity eventually decreases as
the number of different values of stimulus presented to the subject increases, as well as de-
creasing if the number of response categories does not equal the number of stimulus values).
But upon purifying the experimental structure, the channel capacity actually drops below seven.
See Nelson Cowan, The Magical Number 4 in Short-Term Memory: A Reconsideration of

Third, the senses of taste and touch also came under scrutiny. Experimenters tested absolute judgments of the concentration of salt solutions. Another tested the skin's discrimination by using vibrators and by varying intensity, duration, and location. These experiments suggested channel capacities from four to seven.

In sum, we have built-in cognitive limitations. As Professor Miller concluded, "[W]e possess a finite and rather small capacity for making such unidimensional judgments and ... this capacity does not vary a great deal from one simple sensory attribute to another."[192] At least for most of us, this limited capacity means around seven or fewer distinguishable categories.

This conclusion may seem counterintuitive or unrealistic. After all, in the real world we can distinguish, say, many hundreds of faces. However, faces differ in many independently variable attributes, allowing us to make multidimensional and hence finer distinctions. Experimenters have in fact tested absolute judgment of stimuli varying in two or more dimensions; for example, subjects had to judge both the pitch and the loudness of tones, the position of a dot in a square, or both the saltiness and the sweetness of solutions. These experiments indicate that additional dimensions increase channel capacity, although the effect is not fully cumulative. "The point seems to be that, as we add more variables to the display, we increase the total capacity, but we decrease the accuracy for any particular variable. In other words, we can make relatively crude judgments of several things simultaneously."[193]

The basic idea of limited capacity for absolute judgment extends beyond sensory stimuli.[194] Probability is not unlike those studied sensory stimuli.[195]

Mental Storage Capacity, 24 Behav. & Brain Sci. 87 (2001).

192. Miller, supra note 185, at 86. More elaborate and technical work supporting Miller's basic conclusions appears in later reports, such as Garner, supra note 191; 2 Handbook of Perception: Psychophysical Judgment and Measurement (Edward C. Carterette & Morton P. Friedman eds., 1974); Richard M. Shiffrin & Robert M. Nosofsky, Seven Plus or Minus Two: A Commentary on Capacity Limitations, 101 Psychol. Rev. 357 (1994) (updating the literature); see James Bieri, Alvin L. Atkins, Scott Briar, Robin Lobeck Leaman, Henry Miller & Tony Tripodi, Clinical and Social Judgment 79–82, 97–99, 102–04 (1966) (including similar results of odor experiments).

193. Miller, supra note 185, at 88; see Bieri et al., supra note 192, at 63–75, 97–104, 231–32; infra note 233.

194. Most significantly, an important book extends these conclusions concerning absolute judgment from the domain of sensory stimuli to the fields of clinical and social judgment. Bieri et al., supra note 192, at 62, 95–96, 106–08, 230–32; cf. John Volkmann, Scales of Judgment and Their Implications for Social Psychology, in Social Psychology at the Crossroads 273, 286 (John H. Rohrer & Muzafer Sherif eds., 1951) (suggesting a general psychology of discrimination "whose statements are independent of the particular aspect that is being discriminated").

195. "The subjective assessment of probability resembles the subjective assessment of phys-

Indeed, the research on absolute judgment carries over to all rating tasks, because absolute judgment and any rating task both involve some scale that is memory-based.[196] Professor Miller himself made an observation concerning scaling that has implications for many kinds of rating tasks: "It is interesting to consider that psychologists have been using seven-point rating scales for a long time, on the intuitive basis that trying to rate into finer categories does not really add much to the usefulness of the ratings."[197]

b. Short-Term Memory

According to the predominant cognitive model, between the sensory system, which gathers and selects among thousands of environmental stimuli, and the long-term memory (LTM), which stores vast quantities of knowledge, lies the short-term memory (STM).[198] In a sense, we "live" in STM, which constitutes our "now" as well as the locus of reasoning. There we work with arriving information, as by transforming it, transferring it to permanent storage, or using it to produce responses. An important operation there is rehearsal, a sort of repetition or elaboration of the information that serves to maintain the

---

ical quantities such as distance or size." Amos Tversky & Daniel Kahneman, Judgment Under Uncertainty: Heuristics and Biases, 185 Science (n.s.) 1124, 1124 (1974); see Dirk Wendt, On S.S. Stevens' Psychophysics and the Measurement of Subjective Probability and Utility, in Social Attitudes and Psychophysical Measurement 303, 307–08 (Bernd Wegener ed., 1982).

196. See Alexander A. Petrov & John R. Anderson, The Dynamics of Scaling: A Memory-Based Anchor Model of Category Rating and Absolute Identification, 112 Psychol. Rev. 383 (2005) (observing individuals' variability and the sensitivity of scales).

197. Miller, supra note 185, at 84; see Yanlong Sun, Hongbin Wang, Jiajie Zhang & Jack W. Smith, Probabilistic Judgment on a Coarser Scale, 9 Cognitive Sys. Res. 161, 163 (2008) ("The general conclusion of this literature is that a five to nine point rating scale will capture almost all the information, but finer scales will rarely result in a loss of information."); cf. Garner, supra note 191, at 74–75, 87–90 (slight but appreciable increase in information transmission as number of response categories increases toward number of stimulus values). Compare Percival M. Symonds, On the Loss of Reliability in Ratings Due to Coarseness of the Scale, 7 J. Experimental Psychol. 456, 460 (1924) (arguing for seven categories in rating scales), with J.P. Guilford, Psychometric Methods 289–91 (2d ed. 1954) (arguing that more categories can be useful).

198. See generally David H. Dodd & Raymond M. White, Cognition 62–85 (1980); Roberta L. Klatzky, Human Memory 87–176 (2d ed. 1980); Solso, supra note 181, at 147–202; George A. Miller, Information and Memory, Sci. Am., Aug. 1956, at 42.

item in STM or to transfer it to LTM. Without rehearsal, information will leave STM as forgotten in less than a half-minute, either by temporal decay or by interference from other information.

Professor Miller's classic article emphasized the limited capacity of STM.[199] Extensive data indicate that the typical individual can handle only about seven items in STM.[200] Subjects can hold and recall about seven unconnected digits, letters, or words. Additional items result in displacement from STM, which means forgetting unless the subject has managed to transfer the information to LTM. Thus, there is a clear and definite limit on the number of items that a person can retain in STM.

We have ways of circumventing this cognitive limitation. We can organize or "recode" information into larger units or "chunks," each of which uses up only one of the available slots in STM. For example, we can retain seven unconnected words, although each contains several morphemes, phonemes, and letters; we can also group words into larger chunks by means of semantic and syntactic structure, effectively increasing our memory span. For another example, after referring to a telephone book, we can by chunking digits retain in STM a full telephone number, including area code, until we complete the call. "The point is that recoding is an extremely powerful weapon for increasing the amount of information that we can deal with. In one form or another we use recoding constantly in our daily behavior."[201]

Perhaps a causal relation exists between the limited capacity of STM and the limit on absolute judgment. To the experts any such causal relation long remained obscure.[202] But recently, neuroscience research has suggested a connection.[203] The idea is that a cluster of neurons must fire to recall sequentially each chunk of information, but its effective firing necessitates the momentary

---

199. See Miller, supra note 185, at 91–95.

200. There are relatively small differences among individuals' STM capacities. See Klatzky, supra note 198, at 98–100; cf. Michael S. Humphreys, Mary Jean Lynch, William Revelle & James W. Hall, Individual Differences in Short-Term Memory, in 1 Individual Differences in Cognition 35 (Ronna F. Dillon & Ronald R. Schmeck eds., 1983) (giving more general treatment of theory and method).

201. Miller, supra note 185, at 95.

202. See id. at 91, 96; Arthur J. Sandusky, Memory Processes and Judgment, in 2 Handbook of Perception, supra note 192, at 61, 62–64, 79–81.

203. See Christian Bick & Mikhail I. Rabinovich, Dynamical Origin of the Effective Storage Capacity in the Brain's Working Memory, 103 Physical Rev. Letters no. 218101 (2009) (describing theory); Mikhail I. Rabinovich & Pablo Varona, Robust Transient Dynamics and Brain Functions, 5 Frontiers in Computational Neuroscience art. 24, at 6–7 (2011), http://www.frontiersin.org/computational_neuroscience/10.3389/fncom.2011.00024/

suppression of other clusters. The greater the number of competing clusters, the exponentially more difficult it becomes to suppress all the other clusters. About seven clusters is the maximum number that can effectively suppress competitors and hence perform STM functions, such as creating a scale for absolute judgment.

c. More General Limitations

Other significant cognitive limitations exist, whether by design of our nervous system or by adaptation to our environment. Consider the process of judgment or, roughly speaking, categorization. Here cognitive limitations operate on both the input and the output levels to skew judgment.

Where the input is coming from humans, limits on their perception, memory, and communication make the incoming information suspect. As an example, I need only refer to the fairly startling work on the unreliability of eyewitness testimony.[204] Moreover, the humans generating the input can intentionally manipulate it by capitalizing on the cognitive limitations of others. I again need only mention the studies showing the power of lawyers to influence witnesses and factfinders by careful choice of language.[205]

As to the output side, limits on reception, processing, and response all affect human ability to convert information into a judgment. On the one hand,

---

full (citing initial experimental support); Sun et al., supra note 197, at 163 (citing brain-imaging results).

204. See, e.g., Elizabeth F. Loftus, James M. Doyle & Jennifer E. Dysart, Eyewitness Testimony (4th ed. 2007); Robert Buckhout, Eyewitness Testimony, in Memory Observed 116 (Ulric Neisser ed., 1982); Gary L. Wells, The Eyewitness, in The Psychology of Evidence and Trial Procedure 43 (Saul M. Kassin & Lawrence S. Wrightsman eds., 1985); cf. Sheri Lynn Johnson, Cross-Racial Identification Errors in Criminal Cases, 69 Cornell L. Rev. 934 (1984) (providing specific illustration); Eyal Zamir, Ilana Ritov & Doron Teichman, Seeing Is Believing: The Anti-Inference Bias, http://ssrn.com/abstract=1989561 (June 24, 2012) (discussing people's general preference for direct evidence).

205. See, e.g., Lori B. Andrews, Exhibit A: Language, Psychol. Today, Feb. 1984, at 28, 30 (recounting, for example, an experiment showing a short film of an auto accident and later questioning subjects, with this result: "When a definite article was used in the question ('Did you see the broken headlight?' rather than 'Did you see a broken headlight?'), witnesses responded with more certainty—but also were twice as likely to 'remember' a broken headlight ... when there was none."); John M. Conley, William M. O'Barr & E. Allan Lind, The Power of Language: Presentational Style in the Courtroom, 1978 Duke L.J. 1375. Compare Victor Gold, Covert Advocacy: Reflections on the Use of Psychological Persuasion Techniques in the Courtroom, 65 N.C. L. Rev. 481 (1987) (raising concerns), with J. Alexander Tanford & Sarah Tanford, Better Trials Through Science: A Defense of Psychologist-Lawyer Collaboration, 66 N.C. L. Rev. 741 (1988) (calming concerns).

individual traits and states, attitude, ego-involvement, and social influence may skew judgment. Study of "hot" cognition of this sort intrudes on the fields of personality and social psychology.[206] For example, one study confirmed that in judging probability of an outcome—an activity "central to the application of the law"—subjects tended to depart from rational estimates when the outcome was costly or beneficial to the subject, although the direction and degree of departure depended on the individual.[207] On the other hand, humans demonstrate systematic skewing even in handling emotionally and motivationally neutral information. This latter proposition merits a more expansive illustration squarely back in the field of cognitive psychology. For that illustration, consider the specific task of judging probabilities.[208]

Experiments have shown that as intuitive statisticians, we do not naturally use precise tools like multiple regression or Bayes' theorem, but instead we cope by using a limited number of rules of thumb called heuristics.[209] One such approach in common use is the "availability heuristic": when asked to estimate the probability of an event we try to recall or imagine examples, and the ease of so doing determines the estimated probability. Another is the "anchoring heuristic": when asked to make a judgment, we adjust up or down from some initial value, which may be a given starting point or may constitute a natural anchor or may come from a partial calculation. The last of the three major heuristics is the "representativeness heuristic": when asked to categorize something, we do so according to the degree its salient features resemble a particular category's characteristic features. Often these heuristics prove quite

206. See, e.g., Orville G. Brim, Jr., David C. Glass, David E. Lavin & Norman Goodman, Personality and Decision Processes (1962); Muzafer Sherif & Carl I. Hovland, Social Judgment (1961).

207. A.T. Carr, People, Probabilities and the Law, in Law and Psychology 157, 157, 162 (Sally Lloyd-Bostock ed., 1981).

208. See generally Dodd & White, supra note 198, at 349–59; Heuristics and Biases (Thomas Gilovich, Dale Griffin & Daniel Kahneman eds., 2002); Robin M. Hogarth, Judgement and Choice (2d ed.1987); Judgment Under Uncertainty (Daniel Kahneman, Paul Slovic & Amos Tversky eds., 1982); Richard Nisbett & Lee Ross, Human Inference (1980); Ward Edwards & Detlof von Winterfeldt, Cognitive Illusions and Their Implications for the Law, 59 S. Cal. L. Rev. 225, 227–51 (1986); Paul Slovic, Toward Understanding and Improving Decisions, in 2 Human Performance and Productivity: Information Processing and Decision Making 157 (William C. Howell & Edwin A. Fleishman eds., 1982).

209. However, it is possible that humans are employing a different system of probability, namely, quantum probability, which yields patterns that psychologists have been calling heuristics. See Emmanuel M. Pothos & Jerome R. Busemeyer, Can Quantum Probability Provide a New Direction for Cognitive Modeling?, 35 Behav. & Brain Sci. (forthcoming 2012).

useful. However, because such approaches neglect relevant information, systematic judgmental biases often result.

For specific instances, reconsider the three heuristics sequentially. In a study of the availability heuristic, the participants judged homicides to be more than five times as frequent as suicides in the United States, although suicides were actually thirty percent more frequent; people tend to overestimate the frequency of dramatic or sensational events, examples of which come readily to mind.[210] In a study of the anchoring heuristic, the experimenters—who gave subjects random starting percentages, told them those percentages were random, and asked them to adjust those percentages to their best estimate of the percentage of African countries in the United Nations—found that those with higher starting points ended up with higher estimates; people tend to adjust the anchor inadequately in light of additional information.[211] In a study of the representativeness heuristic, the subjects gave virtually the same probability that a stereotypically described man was a lawyer, regardless of whether they were told that the personality sketch came at random from sketches of thirty lawyers and seventy engineers or from sketches of seventy lawyers and thirty engineers; people tend to categorize on the basis of similarity to prototype, ignoring base-rate data.[212]

The three heuristics appear in many variants, and together they dominate the unaided judging of probabilities by almost all of us, including skilled statisticians, without our awareness.[213] Another reason that humans do not naturally use perfectly "rational" techniques, but instead use less accurate "intuitive"

---

210. See Sarah Lichtenstein, Paul Slovic, Baruch Fischhoff, Mark Layman & Barbara Combs, Judged Frequency of Lethal Events, 4 J. Experimental Psychol.: Hum. Learning & Memory 551, 553–59 (1978).

211. See Tversky & Kahneman, supra note 195, at 1128. Another example of the anchoring heuristic comes from a study involving subjects asked to estimate quickly, without paper and pencil, the product of 8x7x6x5x4x3x2x1, while another group faced 1x2x3x4x5x6x7x8; the first group's median estimate was 2250, while the other's was 512; the correct answer is 40,320. Id.

212. See Daniel Kahneman & Amos Tversky, On the Psychology of Prediction, 80 Psychol. Rev. 237, 241–43 (1973). The gambler's fallacy (for example, the belief that the chance of heads is high after a string of tails, based on the view that heads will yield a more representatively random sequence) stems from the same representativeness heuristic. See Tversky & Kahneman, supra note 195, at 1125.

213. See Tversky & Kahneman, supra note 195, at 1130; cf. Amos Tversky & Daniel Kahneman, Extensional Versus Intuitive Reasoning: The Conjunction Fallacy in Probability Judgment, in Heuristics and Biases, supra note 208, at 19 (treating biases in combining probabilities).

techniques, is that they often utilize the automatic level rather than the systematic level of their metaphorically dual cognitive processes.[214]

Training of and increased effort by the person judging probabilities offer only a limited hope of debiasing and thus improving judgment.[215] Incidentally, the foregoing and other studies show that people are overconfident in their judgments and that they persevere in incorrect judgments in the face of inconsistent new information.[216]

In sum, for these and other reasons people perform many probabilistic tasks quite weakly—in the laboratory, in everyday life, and in the courtroom.[217] Thus, it is safe to assume that legal decisionmakers frequently assess and reassess probabilities not too scientifically and not too well: they tend to take a largely intuitive, and often inaccurate, stab at judgment.[218]

---

214. See generally Daniel Kahneman, Thinking, Fast and Slow (2011); Anna Ronkainen, Dual-Process Cognition and Legal Reasoning, in Argumentation 2011: International Conference on Alternative Methods of Argumentation in Law 1, 1 (Michal Araszkiewicz et al. eds., 2011), available at http://ssrn.com/abstract=2004336 ("The dual-process framework is a set of theories on human cognition in which cognition is seen as consisting of (at least) two substantially different yet interdependent systems: the older, faster, partly unconscious and automatic System 1 and the newer, slower, fully conscious and considered System 2."); Mark Spottswood, Reassessing Bayesian and Story-Comparison Models of Proof in Light of Dual-Process Cognition, http://ssrn.com/abstract=2083280 (Aug. 17, 2012).

215. See Judgment Under Uncertainty, supra note 208, chs. 28–32; Edwards & von Winterfeldt, supra note 208, at 238–46, 269; Slovic, supra note 208, at 175, 179. See generally Thomas S. Wallsten, The Theoretical Status of Judgmental Heuristics, in Decision Making Under Uncertainty 21 (Roland W. Scholz ed., 1983).

216. See Heuristics and Biases, supra note 208, chs. 13–16; Judgment Under Uncertainty, supra note 208, chs. 20–23; Asher Koriat, Sarah Lichtenstein & Baruch Fischhoff, Reasons for Confidence, 6 J. Experimental Psychol.: Hum. Learning & Memory 107, 108 (1980).

217. See generally Saks & Kidd, supra note 2 (describing literature on behavioral decision theory, explaining heuristic biases in legal setting, showing how lawyers can exploit those biases, and arguing that legal system should counteract those biases by steps such as expert testimony on mathematical aids to decisionmaking). The authors richly support my statement as to weak performance, as well as their statement "that in many contexts decision makers' intuitive, common-sense judgments depart markedly ... from the actual probabilities." Id. at 127.

218. See David Kaye, The Laws of Probability and the Law of the Land, 47 U. Chi. L. Rev. 34, 52–53 (1979); Saks & Kidd, supra note 2, at 145–49; David A. Schum & Anne W. Martin, Formal and Empirical Research on Cascaded Inference in Jurisprudence, 17 Law & Soc'y Rev. 105, 143–44 (1982); Tanford & Tanford, supra note 205, at 748–59; Tversky & Kahneman, supra note 195, at 1130; Matthew L. Spitzer, Book Review, 9 Hofstra L. Rev. 1621, 1625–36 (1981); cf. Albert J. Moore, Trial by Schema: Cognitive Filters in the Courtroom, 37 UCLA L. Rev. 273, 278–303 (1989) (emphasizing schema theory).

The more general theoretical point here, which this survey merely suggests but the literature more amply supports, is that significant cognitive limitations leave humans to contend with their bounded rationality.[219] Shakespeare gauged us as "noble in reason! how infinite in faculties!"[220] Professor Miller would seem to have reduced that assessment to seven, plus or minus two. The truth, as usual, lies in between.[221] Study of the human mind does induce marvel, but also a realization of its limitations. Knowledge of those limitations can only improve the mind's product.

Practical applications abound. The recent past, especially since the 1970s, has revealed many applications of psychology in general to law.[222] I have already suggested some examples of applying specifically the knowledge of cognitive limitations to law, such as becoming wary of eyewitness testimony. I believe there could be many such applications directly to procedural mechanics. An obvious example of where awareness of, say, limits on memory could help to shape procedure involves the body of rules governing jury practice: the possibility of jurors' taking notes, asking questions, and receiving written or taped instructions; the timing of those instructions; and the use of special verdicts and split trials.[223]

---

219. See Gardner, supra note 181, at 360–80; Slovic, supra note 208, at 158–59, 170; see also Robert L. Sinsheimer, The Brain of Pooh: An Essay on the Limits of Mind, 59 Am. Scientist 20 (1971).

220. William Shakespeare, Hamlet act II, sc. 2, line 317.

221. Some disagreement exists in the scientific world, of course, over the details and implications of the body of research on cognitive limitations. In particular, reactive scholarship increasingly maintains that the prevailing view ignores our capabilities and overstates our limitations. See, e.g., Simple Heuristics That Make Us Smart (Gerd Gigerenzer et al. eds., 1999); Wallace D. Loh, Social Research in the Judicial Process 574–81 (1984) (treating eyewitness testimony); Alex Stein, Are People Probabilistically Challenged?, 111 Mich. L. Rev. 855 (2013) (reviewing Kahneman, supra note 214). See generally Helmut Jungermann, The Two Camps on Rationality, in Decision Making Under Uncertainty, supra note 215, at 63; Elizabeth F. Loftus & Lee Roy Beach, Book Review, 34 Stan. L. Rev. 939, 950–56 (1982). One must "recognize that the glass is both half full and half empty." Id. at 956.

222. See, e.g., Handbook of Psychology and Law (D.K. Kagehiro & W.S. Laufer eds., 1992). But see David N. Robinson, Psychology and Law (1980) (questioning wisdom of psychosocial invasion of law). From these applications of psychology within law, one should distinguish efforts that utilize the psychologist's "outside" perspective to study law as a social system. Compare Lawrence M. Friedman, The Law and Society Movement, 38 Stan. L. Rev. 763, 777–78 (1986) (taking outside perspective), with John Monahan & Laurens Walker, Teaching Social Science in Law: An Alternative to "Law and Society," 35 J. Legal Educ. 478, 478–79 (1985) (taking inside perspective).

223. See Field et al., supra note 10, at 1401–03, 1416–18, 1425–27; Andrews, supra note 205, at 32–33; Shari Seidman Diamond, Mary R. Rose, Beth Murphy & Sven Smith,

My immediate interest, however, lies in a more indirect contribution that cognitive psychology could make to procedural doctrine. It would come from understanding the role that cognitive limitations have played in the evolution of doctrine concerning decisionmaking, as well as the role that awareness of cognitive limitations should play in reshaping this doctrine. At that interest I aimed this selective social-science survey, and so to standards of decision I now return.

2. Psychology's Illumination of Standards

In the realm of standards of decision, we have now seen that a natural set of seven categories of likelihood prevails in legal usage: (1) slightest possibility, (2) reasonable possibility, (3) substantial possibility, (4) equipoise, (5) probability, (6) high probability, and (7) almost certainty. Next, a survey of cognitive limitations revealed that humans are boundedly rational, with the number seven curiously playing a prominent role in the variety of mental limitations. As a matter of absolute judgment, and possibly owing to limits on short-term memory, we can identify only about seven magnitudes of any one sensory stimulus. This limitation leads directly to "resolution errors." The survey also showed that in additional ways, we perform rather weakly in judging probabilities. These "genuine biases" lead to other sorts of judgment errors.[224]

My conjecture in 1987 was that all these ideas were connected, so that limitations on human capabilities might underlie the systematic structure of standards of decision.[225] That is, all these ideas perhaps combine, albeit after some subtle but sizable leaps of reasoning peculiarly subject to misunderstanding, to imply that humans can effectively place on a scale only a limited number of

---

Juror Questions During Trial: A Window into Juror Thinking, 59 Vand. L. Rev. 1925 (2006); Joel D. Lieberman, The Psychology of the Jury Instruction Process, in Jury Psychology 129 (Joel D. Lieberman & Daniel A. Krauss eds., 2009); Leonard B. Sand & Steven Alan Reiss, A Report on Seven Experiments Conducted by District Court Judges in the Second Circuit, 60 N.Y.U. L. Rev. 423 (1985); cf. Paul Bergman, The War Between the States (of Mind): Oral Versus Textual Reasoning, 40 Ark. L. Rev. 505 (1987) (arguing that orality induces intuitive thinking, while writing induces analytical thinking). See generally Victor J. Gold, Jury Wobble: Judicial Tolerance of Jury Inferential Error, 59 S. Cal. L. Rev. 391 (1986) (calling for application of knowledge of cognitive limitations to reform of trial procedure and evidence law); Lind, supra note 3, at 14 ("It is important to keep in mind, though, that the psychological investigation of procedure has just begun. Like much of the law, the law of procedure is based to a large extent on untested assumptions about how people behave.").

224. Sun et al., supra note 197, at 162–63.

225. Kevin M. Clermont, Procedure's Magical Number Three: Psychological Bases for Standards of Decision, 72 Cornell L. Rev. 1115 (1987).

categories of probabilities. The law's approach in following a gradated scale of likelihood might rest on an intuitive recognition of this particular cognitive limitation.

Since 1987, a few others have come aboard. Here is a very recent example: "Psychologists are uncertain just how nuanced human [probability] judgments actually are. No doubt the human [probability] scale is not calibrated in hundredths: outside of games of chance and similar contexts in which we internalize frequentist probabilities, it would be bizarre to claim to be, say, .58 confident that p. Beyond that, however, about all that psychologists are agreed upon is that, between the poles of being 'certain' that some proposition is true and being precisely in 'equipoise,' humans can reliably distinguish only among limited categories of subjective confidence, frequently grouping their judgments in such broad clusters as more likely than not, very likely, and almost certain."[226]

More importantly, recent experimental research provides direct support for the conjecture. An important study from 2007 supports the notion that humans utilize a coarse internal scale for probabilities, producing a resolution error in judgment separate from the effect of heuristics and other biases.[227] The researchers conducted two experiments that involved estimation of the winning probability for various poker hands covering the whole range from zero to one. In the first experiment, the subjects estimated the probability freely as a percentage from 0 to 100. But each subject's responses tended to cluster in a small number of groups, averaging about five groups, although the number and location of the groups differed for the individual subjects. Because the subjects might be using a coarse scale simply for ease, the second experiment made the subjects respond in a terms of a coarse scale and a finer scale. The finer scale produced lower accuracy and also lower consistency between repeated trials, while it imposed a heavier mental load and caused a longer response time. In other words, the finer detail in response was random, apparently being generated by an internally coarse scale actually in use by the subjects.

Moving back into the legal domain, an experiment reported in 2013 showed that jury instructions that try to nudge the jurors down from a clear-and-convincing standard tend to push the standard all the way down to a preponderance standard.[228] Mock jurors, recruited and replying online, considered

---

226. Berman, supra note 7, at 1711 n.66.
227. Sun et al., supra note 197.
228. David L. Schwartz & Christopher B. Seaman, Standards of Proof in Civil Litigation: An Experiment from Patent Law, 26 Harv. J.L. & Tech. (forthcoming 2013), available at http://ssrn.com/abstract=2110342.

the invalidity of a patent for obviousness after receiving a usual kind of clear-and-convincing instruction (defined as "highly probable," and higher than preponderance but lower than beyond a reasonable doubt), a usual preponderance instruction ("more probable than not," and lower than clear-and-convincing and reasonable-doubt standards), or the instruction recently mandated by the Supreme Court[229] (a clear-and-convincing instruction with an additional sentence saying that the "burden of proving obviousness is more easily satisfied when, as in this case, the prior art on which the claim of obviousness is based was not considered by the Examiner"). The clear-and-convincing instruction led 27% of that group of subjects to find the patent invalid, while the preponderance instruction led 38% to find the patent invalid, but the subjects receiving the Supreme Court's modification performed in a manner not statistically significantly different from the preponderance-instruction subjects.

a. Using Nonprecise Standards

One could theorize that, in dealing with a probabilistic environment, each of us constantly evaluates probabilities. After a lifetime of evaluating situations that cover the whole range of probability, but given a limited channel capacity, each of us has internalized a stable scale of likelihood with a small number of categories that fall between the ideal end-points of absolute certainty. When we receive as input the depiction of a new amorphous set of circumstances, we process its likelihood in part by referring to our coarsely graded scale of likelihood, with our optimal output often being a response in the form of one of its coarse categories.

We could, of course, go to the trouble of giving a verbal or even a numerical response that appears more precise. It is true that sometimes such attempts at precision would pay off. First, mathematical tools can aid in producing finer probabilistic distinctions for certain tasks, as when working with statistical frequency data.[230] Second, restructured tasks can help because more complicated decisionmaking processes can sometimes offset the crudeness of intuitive probabilistic determinations,[231] as in processes involving a sequence of separate de-

---

229. See Microsoft Corp. v. i4i Ltd. P'ship, 131 S. Ct. 2238 (2011).

230. See L. Jonathan Cohen, The Probable and the Provable 256–58 (1977); Laurence H. Tribe, Trial by Mathematics: Precision and Ritual in the Legal Process, 84 Harv. L. Rev. 1329, 1346–47 (1971).

231. See Slovic, supra note 208, at 179; cf. Miller, supra note 185, at 90 ("We are not completely at the mercy of this limited span [of absolute judgment], however, because we have a variety of techniques for getting around it and increasing the accuracy of our judgments. The three most important of these devices are (a) to make relative rather than ab-

cisional steps,[232] a multidimensional inquiry,[233] or a relative judgment;[234] one especially effective restructuring is to seek hypothesized frequency information rather than asking for the probability of a unique event.[235] Third, decisionmakers can somewhat improve their performance on some tasks, as by means of training and increased effort, although the limited feasibility of such improvement obviously differs for administrators, judges, and jurors.[236] So, in some settings—for example, where we are averaging estimated probabilities—we should try to express all the available accuracy by a finely gradated response.

In the ordinary task of unaided categorization of amorphous likelihood, however, we can at best make little more than a stab at judgment. Usually there is no reason to expect a more precise response to be much more accurate or to transmit much more information. Not only do we encounter limitations on absolute judgment and short-term memory, but in dealing accurately with

---

solute judgments; or, if that is not possible, (b) to increase the number of dimensions along which the stimuli can differ; or (c) to arrange the task in such a way that we make a sequence of several absolute judgments in a row.").

232. Separate decisional steps, some of which are overtly probabilistic, are common in law. See supra text accompanying note 145. Note, however, that any separate step involving a standard of decision would proceed in the usual fashion.

233. See supra text accompanying note 193. A truly multidimensional test is unwieldy in law and consequently rare. It would entail simultaneous measurement in terms of clearly separable dimensions, as opposed to (1) a sequential process of initial inquiry into factors that might affect the choice of standard of decision, followed by application of the chosen standard, (2) a decision on a complex issue such as reasonableness, on which many factors bear but to which an ordinary standard of decision applies, or (3) a multifactored placement along what the decisionmaker sees as a single dimension, such as in measuring need for a remedy or perhaps even probability of an event. A possible example of a multidimensional inquiry in civil procedure is the power test of personal jurisdiction: the court may decide on the basis of both the level of the defendant's state-directed activity and the degree of unrelatedness between the plaintiff's claim and that activity, see Kevin M. Clermont, Principles of Civil Procedure 256–65 (3d ed. 2012), although categorization along the latter dimension becomes very coarse, see William M. Richman, Review Essay, 72 Calif. L. Rev. 1328, 1337–40 (1984).

234. See supra note 187 and accompanying text. Some such decisional processes are loosely called balancing. See T. Alexander Aleinikoff, Constitutional Law in the Age of Balancing, 96 Yale L.J. 943, 945 (1987).

235. See Leda Cosmides & John Tooby, Are Humans Good Intuitive Statisticians After All? Rethinking Some Conclusions from the Literature on Judgment Under Uncertainty, 58 Cognition 1 (1996); Steven Strogatz, Chances Are, http://opinionator.blogs.nytimes.com/2010/04/25/chances-are/ (Apr. 25, 2010); Sun et al., supra note 197, at 162.

236. See supra note 215 and accompanying text.

probabilities we also must overcome special shortcomings such as heuristics and other biases. Accordingly, most tasks do not warrant a response finer than selecting one from a few categories of likelihood. Indeed, regardless of any small differences among experts and nonexperts as to competence in evaluating likelihood, the considerable costs and insignificant benefits of utilizing precise standards of decision support avoiding them for all legal decisionmakers.

Yet one could accept that the coarseness of human judgment justifies utilizing a particular set of a few discrete standards for decisional output, and still one could argue for much more precision in articulating those standards to decisionmakers.[237] Indeed, lawmakers could begin to state the standards in numerical terms.[238] Quantification, however, would not be wise, at least in the prevailing legal system. First, quantification by itself imposes some costs in terms of accuracy and other values—arguably by such effects as inaccurate meshing with soft or unquantifiable variables and the dehumanization of the legal process[239]—even though theorists often overstate those costs.[240] Second, expressly translating a level of probability into something like a point estimate could be illusory, because probability in connection with standards of decision is a complex concept.[241] Third, there is no convincing reason to expect that quantification would effectively invoke our nonprecise internal scale of judgment, or otherwise accord with the ingrained way of human thinking just described;[242] although expressly requiring an elevated numerical probability could effectively signal the need to apply a higher standard of decision,[243] it is doubtful that the number would convey a sound sense of what the standard

---

237. See, e.g., John Kaplan, Decision Theory and the Factfinding Process, 20 Stan. L. Rev. 1065, 1073 (1968) (1968); Kornstein, supra note 71, at 121–22.

238. See, e.g., Peter Tillers & Jonathan Gottfried, Case Comment—United States v. Copeland, 369 F. Supp. 2d 275 (E.D.N.Y. 2005): A Collateral Attack on the Legal Maxim That Proof Beyond a Reasonable Doubt Is Unquantifiable?, 5 Law Probability & Risk 135 (2006).

239. See Tribe, supra note 230, at 1389–93.

240. See Patricia G. Milanich, Decision Theory and Standards of Proof, 5 Law & Hum. Behav. 87, 90, 94–96 (1981); Saks & Kidd, supra note 2, at 124–25, 148–54.

241. See infra Chapter V.

242. See Alf C. Zimmer, Verbal vs. Numerical Processing of Subjective Probabilities, in Decision Making Under Uncertainty, supra note 215, at 159, 180.

243. See Dorothy K. Kagehiro, Defining the Standard of Proof in Jury Instructions, 1 Psychol. Sci. 194 (1990) (reviewing research on juror comprehension that found a stricter standard of proof decreased the proportion of plaintiffs' victories significantly only if it was stated in terms of a quantified probability, that is, "you must be at least [51%/71%/91%] certain of the truth of the plaintiffs' case").

means.[244] Therefore, lawmakers should, and wisely do, speak in nonnumerical terms.

b. Using Customary Standards

As to why the law should speak not only in nonprecise terms but specifically in terms of the customary seven categories of likelihood, the basic reason is that referring to this scale is routinely straightforward and hence easy. Shared experience in the same culture has led most of us into some degree of agreement on a scale with which the seven categories in legal usage are compatible.[245] The coarsely gradated, customary scale of likelihood is ready for use in the minds of lawmakers and also of decisionmakers, whether for repeated use by officials like judges or on a one-shot basis by people like jurors.

I am not suggesting communicating and comprehending standards of decision will ever be easily effective.[246] What I am saying is that if a standard of decision were to invoke one of the customary seven categories, the lawmaker's tasks of articulation and communication and the decisionmaker's tasks of comprehension and application would become easier and more effective. The legal system could thereby act with surer footing.

Indeed, the argument for employing only the relatively clear customary standards of decision grows stronger as the psychological and legal realities come more fully into joint consideration. First, the empirical evidence laid out in the next chapter shows that lawmakers have trouble communicating any

244. Cf. id. at 198 (hypothesizing optimistically that "our mock jurors may have abstracted the relevant certainty level from the quantified definitions and converted it into subjective categories representing 'moderate certainty,' 'higher certainty,' and 'highest certainty,'" and thereby acknowledging that the categories did the real decisional work).

245. Experiments on people's formation of scales for judging sensory stimuli support the plausibility of such convergence. See Bieri et al., supra note 192, at 29 ("somewhat analogous to an equal-interval scale"); Guilford, supra note 197, at 312–17; Sherif & Hovland, supra note 206, at 34–36, 68–69, 179–83; Allen Parducci, Category Ratings: Still More Contextual Effects!, in Social Attitudes and Psychophysical Measurement, supra note 195, at 89, 89, 101–02; Volkmann, supra note 194, at 288–90. Some support for such convergence in connection with judging probabilities appears in the important work of one researcher, although he used a distinguishable experimental design. Zimmer, supra note 242, at 180.

246. Recent research suggests, however, that it might be feasible to construct and employ an ordinally ranked vocabulary of likelihood that would improve effective interpersonal communication. See Mandeep K. Dhami & Thomas S. Wallsten, Interpersonal Comparison of Subjective Probabilities: Toward Translating Linguistic Probabilities, 33 Memory & Cognition 1057 (2005); Frederick Mosteller & Cleo Youtz, Quantifying Probabilistic Assessments, 5 Stat. Sci. 2 (1990).

standard whatsoever. Unusual standards would only increase the confusion. Second, to the extent that decisionmakers exhibit disuniformity in handling any standard, abandoning the customary standards would only accentuate their problem. To the extent the law sticks to customary standards, disuniform handling should be lessened.

Lawmakers' Use

The lawmaker ordinarily will require the decisionmaker to consider a situation's probability in determining whether it reaches the level of probability required by the standard of decision. Theoretically, as explained above, the decisionmaker's psychologically optimal output is in terms of the customary seven categories of likelihood. From that point, I argue that lawmakers should cast any standard of decision in terms that fit this optimal output, at least in the absence of a strong legal reason to the contrary.

Further, and critically, I argue that such a contrary reason is lacking, because lawmakers can adequately serve the often imprecise policies underlying the standard of decision by choosing from the set of seven categories, thus moving up or down by fairly small quantum leaps rather than by unrealistically finer degrees. My argument, however, is not as extreme as it might sound. I am merely saying that, as specifying a standard of decision necessarily entails drawing a dividing line on the spectrum of likelihood, lawmakers can defer to psychological limitations and still serve legal policies by drawing the line at the most appropriate of the customary categories rather than inventing an unusual cutoff.

Consequently, lawmakers should, and wisely do, speak of slightest possibility, reasonable possibility, substantial possibility, equipoise, probability, high probability, and almost certainty—or they speak in apparent synonyms such as preponderance of the evidence, clear and convincing evidence, and proof beyond a reasonable doubt. I am not claiming that use of these phrases will solve communication problems, because such words do mean different things to different people. I am theorizing that we generally share a customary scale and arguing that lawmakers should strive to utilize it. In fact, the very imprecision of such a vocabulary reinforces the argument in favor of employing only a limited set of customary standards of decision. A fortiori, an explicit or implicit sliding scale of standards is neither realistic nor desirable.

Once articulated, the standard must be passed to the decisionmakers for comprehension and application. To maximize the chances of their invoking the desired standard, especially in settings like jury trial,[247] the decisionmak-

---

247. See Guilford, supra note 197, at 293 (treating construction of cues); Amiram El-

ers need careful explanations. Admittedly, the decisionmaker may not be able or inclined to handle the standard in strict accordance with the law. But the chances of the decisionmaker's doing so are maximal if the desired standard gets expressed in customary terms.

Decisionmakers' Use

Because of the decisionmaker's difficulty in dealing with likelihood and the potency of the customary seven categories, any hope that the decision-maker would reliably adjust the standard up or down instinctively by fine de-grees appropriate to the circumstances seems quite unrealistic. Instead, the hope and duty should be that the decisionmaker will stick with the articu-lated standard.

An important but heretofore nonobvious point is that although cognitive limitations have generated the customarily coarse scale of likelihood, applica-tion of a standard of decision does not require the decisionmaker to maintain in mind the full scale. Using the whole scale of gradations from zero to one would be a considerable mental task that would exhaust short-term memory. Instead the standard specifies an "action threshold," which says that the likeli-hood must equal or exceed a certain level. The lawmaker needs only to spec-ify one of the customary gradations as the action threshold, and the decisionmaker needs only to understand that threshold. The mental task of absolute judgment thus becomes the much more feasible task of categorizing the likelihood into one of two categories: strong enough to pass the standard or not.

My argument ultimately is that all such action thresholds for decisionmak-ers should be one of the seven customary gradations of likelihood. Striving to utilize noncustomary standards of decision does not seem a feasible or worth-while goal.

c. Reflecting Back on Psychology

In sum, on the basis of this theorizing, I argue that lawmakers should for-mulate and decisionmakers should use standards of decision in terms of the cus-tomary seven nonnumerical categories. I am not saying that people would find handling a novel standard impossible. I am saying that any such standard would be difficult to articulate and communicate and comprehend and apply,

---

work & Bruce D. Sales, Jury Instructions, in The Psychology of Evidence and Trial Proce-dure, supra note 204, at 280 (reviewing literature on making instructions understandable).

would risk confusion and possibly abuse by the decisionmaker, and would in-evitably drift toward one of the customary standards—and that these costs more than offset any benefit of utilizing an unusual standard.

Note that mine is not a defeatist attitude. I am not suggesting that we sur-render to our cognitive limitations. Knowledge of limitations enables us to de-vise techniques, nonlegal and legal, to function better. The end is to make sound procedure better fit humans, and not the impracticable reverse.[248] In the context of the Fourth Amendment, Professor Amsterdam phrased this en-gineering challenge thus:

> The motto, I suppose, is that any number of categories, however shaped, is too few to encompass life and too many to organize it man-ageably. The question remains at what level of generality and in what shape rules should be designed in order to encompass all that can be encompassed without throwing organization to the wolves. The ques-tion must be answered with a due regard for the practical workings of the institutions that administer, and are governed by, any particular set of rules.[249]

In mapping the cognitive limitations, I have referenced psychological the-ories. But finally I want to argue that my position does not depend on the va-lidity of those psychological theories.

I do think that the law's reaction to an ingrained scale for categorizing like-lihood explains the observed systematic structure of standards of decision. But I admit that in several important ways my explanation involves speculation. First, the psychological evidence is difficult to interpret, incomplete in cover-age, and not free from doubt.[250] Second, experimental or other proof of the ex-

---

248. My allusion is to human factors engineering, which involves tailoring things to fit human limitations. See, e.g., Alphonse Chapanis, "Words, Words, Words," 7 Hum. Factors 1 (1965).

249. Amsterdam, supra note 109, at 377. A more general formulation appeared in Fred-erick Pollock, A First Book of Jurisprudence 45 (5th ed. 1923) ("The law cannot be more finely graduated than the means of ascertaining facts .... Hence the development of law is largely bound up with the development of procedure. As improved procedure enables the law to grapple with complex facts, the aspirations of lawyers and citizens are enlarged .... But even in the most advanced polity we shall find now and then that the subtilty of foren-sic and judicial thought outruns the possibilities of effectual inquiry and administration.").

250. See Robert R. Scott, Error and Rationality in Individual Decisionmaking: An Essay on the Relationship Between Cognitive Illusions and the Management of Choices, 59 S. Cal. L. Rev. 329, 330–37 (1986).

planation in the legal setting is lacking and seems infeasible.[251] Third, and as a parting shot at human cognition, any such specific explanation is suspect because people are notoriously bad at causal analysis.[252] I am therefore willing to concede that the psychological theorizing beneath my explanation—a somewhat persuasive and ultimately reassuring explanation as it contends anew that the law's experience represents wisdom—constitutes merely a plausible reason for observed phenomena.

Nevertheless, a merely plausible explanation suffices for my purposes. My position rests more on sensible inferences from observing the law's systematic standards than on definitive science. Given the empirical tendency of legal doctrine to converge on the customary seven nonnumerical categories of likelihood, given the general theoretical point of bounded rationality, and given at least one plausible explanation, I am prepared to believe that there is *some* significant reason for the systematic structure of standards of decision. Magic is not at work, and the real reason likely lies in the law's reaction to some limitations that would serve as an equivalent theoretical basis for my position.

This thesis of some kind of actual causation, when combined with the considerable consequential costs and insignificant policy benefits of utilizing unusual standards of decision, supports restricting legal standards of decision to the customary seven nonnumerical categories of likelihood.

C. Doctrinal Application

The first part of this chapter uncovered a pattern among standards of decision. The second part developed both a thesis of cognitive causation and also several largely independent lessons. This third part will provide additional examples that demonstrate how helpful those lessons are in the practical task of stating doctrine.

The very variety of the first part's examples suggested that those examples do not exhaust the list. The ultimate list is long because numerous legal decisionmakers must decide countless kinds of issues, and each of those issues requires a standard of decision. The differences among the underlying issues account for the increasing variety in the longer list and for the occasional

---

251. See infra Chapter III.

252. See Nisbett & Ross, supra note 208, at 113–38 (outlining major sources of error in causal analysis, including overreliance on representativeness and availability heuristics).

nonobviousness of the connection between examples. What links the examples, however, is that their standards of decision all involve an apparently gradated scale of likelihood. This makes the second part's conclusions relevant to all the examples.[253]

Indeed, I maintain that the conclusions are relevant to any decisionmaking that involves placement on a scale. A ready example that goes well beyond the kind of examples already offered comes from modern equal-protection analysis. It entails the two accepted tests of rational basis and strict scrutiny, and also the contested intermediate standard that requires substantial relation to an important governmental interest for gender and illegitimacy classifications.[254] There could indeed be more than three tests, though, because the two accepted tests use both sides of the probability scale.[255] Any such test is essentially inquiring whether sufficient need exists for the government's classifying of persons.[256] As the initial step in deciding how to evaluate that need, however, there was a choice between (1) selecting among the extremely lenient rational-basis test that requires only a possible need, zero or one or more intermediate standards, and the extremely stringent strict-scrutiny test that requires very probable need and (2) selecting from a sliding scale of standards. This basic choice relates to the concerns of this book.[257]

In my studies, practice, teaching, and research, I have long struggled with standards of decision occurring over many areas of law. Here are three more examples of original decision drawn from civil procedure, all employing the lower end of the scale of likelihood.

---

253. See, e.g., Christopher M. Pietruszkiewicz, Conflating Standards of Review in the Tax Court: A Lesson in Ambiguity, 44 Hous. L. Rev. 1337, 1362–75 (2008).

254. See 3 Ronald D. Rotunda & John E. Nowak, Treatise on Constitutional Law § 18.3 (4th ed. 2008).

255. See James A. Kushner, Substantive Equal Protection: The Rehnquist Court and the Fourth Tier of Judicial Review, 53 Mo. L. Rev. 423 (1988) (arguing that a fourth tier—"rational basis with teeth"—exists).

256. See Moshe Cohen-Eliya & Gila Stopler, Probability Thresholds as Deontological Constraints in Global Constitutionalism, 49 Colum. J. Transnat'l L. 75, 77 (2010) ("a judicial inquiry into the probability of harm to state interests should be a prime determinant in constitutional rights adjudication").

257. See Pietruszkiewicz, supra note 253, at 1365–66 ("In the review of legislative activity, there are only three traditional standards of legislative review—strict scrutiny, intermediate scrutiny, and rational basis. In each of these cases, nontraditional notions of review are limited, and the standards of review are necessarily limited to the traditional standards." (footnotes omitted)). But see San Antonio Indep. Sch. Dist. v. Rodriguez, 411 U.S. 1, 98 (1973) (Marshall, J., dissenting) (arguing against a few discrete standards and for "a spectrum of standards").

1. Pleading

Bell Atlantic Corp. v. Twombly[258] and *Ashcroft v. Iqbal*[259] are the two recent cases in which the U.S. Supreme Court revolutionized the law on pleading.[260] The Court unearthed, in Federal Rule of Civil Procedure 8(a)(2)'s required "showing," a requirement above and beyond claimants' having to give notice. The requirement involves asking, given the facts nonconclusorily pled by the plaintiff, whether inferring the moving defendant's liability on a cause of action is "plausible" in light of the judge's judicial experience and common sense.[261]

Plausibility

To satisfy this new factual-sufficiency test, the plaintiff must plead facts and perhaps some evidence. The plaintiff should give a particularized mention of the factual circumstances of each element of the cause of action. The degree of particularization should be sufficient to make reasonably possible an inference of liability, with the judge testing that plausibility not of each fact but only of the moving defendant's ultimate liability on the particular cause. The judge performs the decisional task (1) by ignoring any conclusory allegation, such as a bald assertion that an element exists, and (2) by accepting the remaining allegations as true and then weighing the plausibility of the liability

---

258. 550 U.S. 544 (2007) (dismissing an antitrust complaint that alleged an agreement in conclusory terms based upon information and belief, with the lack of detail owing to the fact that the plaintiffs had no proof in hand without discovery).

259. 556 U.S. 662 (2009) (dismissing a civil rights complaint, while clarifying the intricate workings and broad applicability of Twombly).

260. See generally Kevin M. Clermont & Stephen C. Yeazell, Inventing Tests, Destabilizing Systems, 95 Iowa L. Rev. 821 (2010) (criticizing the new regime); Kevin M. Clermont, Three Myths About Twombly-Iqbal, 45 Wake Forest L. Rev. 1337 (2010) (exploring the new regime).

261. See Pamela Atkins, Twombly, Iqbal Introduce More Subjectivity to Rulings on Dismissal Motions, Judge Says, 78 U.S.L.W. 2667, 2667 (2010) ("J. Douglas Richards, ... who represented the plaintiff in Twombly, called the kind of reasoning judges have to do under the new standard for assessing pleadings 'ugly' and agreed with [District Judge Sidney H.] Stein, that the standard is based on a judge's personal perspective and experience of 'how the world works.' Richards called this result the 'antithesis of justice,' 'deeply troubling,' and 'moving in the direction of yahoo justice' because it encourages bias."). However, the shock of this admitted subjectivity is lessened by the realization that ordinarily a reasonable factfinder, including a jury, can bring life experience and common sense to bear on the particular case. See J. Alexander Tanford, An Introduction to Trial Law, 51 Mo. L. Rev. 623, 700 (1986).

inference in light of his or her judicial experience and common sense as applied in the case's particular context. This new approach will most seriously impact the plaintiff who needs discovery to learn the required factual particulars.

The first step for the judge is to trim out conclusory allegations. The plaintiff now must state facts in nonconclusory form, subject to Rule 11.[262] As always, the pleader need not offer proof.[263] Nor need the pleader even try to show that proof is possibly obtainable, although the judge's expectation of discovery yielding proof will affect the plausibility test. No inconsistency necessarily exists between nonconclusoriness and plausibility testing. Instead, the court must take the nonconclusory allegations to be true facts.

The second step—testing the plausibility of liability—is unavoidably probabilistic in nature.[264] It asks whether liability is a "reasonable inference," given those accepted facts.[265] It thus asks whether the assertion of liability is reasonably possible:[266]

> "Plausibility" in this context does not imply that the district court should decide whose version to believe, or which version is more likely than not. Indeed, the Court expressly distanced itself from the latter approach in *Iqbal*, "the plausibility standard is not akin to a probability requirement." As we understand it, the Court is saying instead that the plaintiff must give enough details about the subject-matter of the case to present a story that holds together. In other words, the court will ask itself *could* these things have happened, not *did* they happen.[267]

---

262. See Clermont & Yeazell, supra note 260, at 849 (explaining the interaction of Rule 8 and Rule 11).

263. See 61B Am. Jur. 2d Pleading §919 (1999).

264. See Bell Atl. Corp. v. Twombly, 550 U.S. 544, 556 (2007) ("Asking for plausible grounds to infer an agreement does not impose a probability requirement at the pleading stage; it simply calls for enough fact to raise a reasonable expectation that discovery will reveal evidence of illegal agreement."); see also Ashcroft v. Iqbal, 556 U.S. 662, 678 (2009) ("The plausibility standard is not akin to a 'probability requirement,' but it asks for more than a sheer possibility that a defendant has acted unlawfully." (quoting Twombly, 550 U.S. at 556)). These statements reject only a standard as high as more-likely-than-not. They do not disavow any and all probabilistic standards.

265. Iqbal, 556 U.S. at 678; see also Nicholas Tymoczko, Note, Between the Possible and the Probable: Defining the Plausibility Standard After Bell Atlantic Corp. v. Twombly and Ashcroft v. Iqbal, 94 Minn. L. Rev. 505, 515 (2009).

266. See Iqbal, 556 U.S. at 681.

267. Swanson v. Citibank, N.A., 614 F.3d 400, 404 (7th Cir. 2010) (quoting Iqbal, 556 U.S. at 678).

The precise question for decision, it seems, is whether a factfinder, if it were to accept as true the pleaded nonconclusory facts, could reasonably find the moving defendant to be liable on the merits of the cause of action.

This plausibility step is an artificial and unprecedented sort of decisional task. Although the standard of reasonable possibility prevails on summary judgment,[268] this new pleading test proceeds without the evidential development and procedural protections applicable upon summary judgment. It authorizes decision of the factual dispute as to liability without suitable procedures, even if applies only a low standard of likelihood.[269]

Frivolity

Even before *Twombly* and *Iqbal*, dismissing a complaint composed of frivolous allegations would not have been controversial.[270] A complaint that the judge perceives as frivolous will not survive a pleading challenge. The way this works is that the court will disregard an allegation in a pleading that contradicts a proposition judicially noticed. The court reads the attacked pleading as if such untenable allegations were omitted, so that a demurrer or motion to dismiss does not admit any allegation in the attacked pleading running counter to the court's judicial knowledge. The classic illustrative case at common law was *Cole v. Maunder*,[271] where an allegation that stones were thrown "*molliter et molli manu*" ("gently and with a gentle hand") was held not to be admitted by demurrer, "for the judges say that one cannot throw stones molliter." In *Southern Ry. Co. v. Covenia*,[272] the court took judicial notice that a child under two years of age was unable to have any earning capacity and held on demurrer that an allegation that such a child performed valuable services did not stand as admitted.

---

268. See Clermont, supra note 260, at 1357–59; Clermont & Yeazell, supra note 260, at 833–34; supra note 141.

269. See Allan R. Stein, Confining Iqbal, 45 Tulsa L. Rev. 277, 284 (2009) ("To allow a judge to make those determinations based on his own sense of history and human behavior without the benefit of an adversarial presentation of the facts is the precise definition of prejudice: he is pre-judging, without regard to the evidence.").

270. Cf. Clinton v. Jones, 520 U.S. 681, 708 (1997) ("Most frivolous and vexatious litigation is terminated at the pleading stage or on summary judgment, with little if any personal involvement by the defendant. See Fed. Rules Civ. Proc. 12, 56."). Also, appellate courts may give summary disposition to frivolous appeals. See Aaron S. Bayer, "I Know a Frivolous Appeal When I See One," Nat'l L.J., Mar. 12, 2012, at 32.

271. (1635) 2 Rolle's Abr. 548 (K.B.), in James Barr Ames, A Selection of Cases on Pleading at Common Law 2, 2 (Cambridge, Mass., John Wilson & Son 1875) (translating the case from Law French to English).

272. 29 S.E. 219, 220 (Ga. 1896).

This frivolity test is similar to *Twombly-Iqbal*, in that they both involve the reasonable-possibility test. But obviously, *Twombly-Iqbal* has a broader application than judicial notice. The broader application flows from *Twombly-Iqbal*'s call for greater judicial activism in invoking the test, and perhaps also from *Twombly-Iqbal*'s shifting the burden from the opponent's having to show that no reasonable possibility exists to the proponent's having to show that a reasonable possibility exists.[273]

"Frivolous" is a slippery word, however.[274] In other contexts, it may invoke a different standard of decision. A particularly instructive context is the frivolity test under 28 U.S.C. § 1915 for proceeding in forma pauperis, a test that comes early and with no procedural protections, and can even come sua sponte before answer. In *Denton v. Hernandez*,[275] the Supreme Court explained:

> As we stated in *Neitzke* [*v. Williams*, 490 U.S. 319 (1989)], a court may dismiss a claim as factually frivolous only if the facts alleged are "clearly baseless," 490 U.S., at 327, a category encompassing allegations that are "fanciful," id., at 325, "fantastic," id., at 328, and "delusional," ibid. As those words suggest, a finding of factual frivolousness is appropriate when the facts alleged rise to the level of the irrational or the wholly incredible ....

Thus, the § 1915 standard is demanding on the defendant, who has to show no-slightest-possibility.[276]

---

273. Other contexts exist where "frivolous" refers to the proponent's inability to generate a reasonable possibility. See, e.g., Bell v. Hood, 327 U.S. 678, 684–85 (1946) (authorizing dismissal for lack of subject-matter jurisdiction if the proponent cannot establish the federal-question claim's factual and legal viability to a reasonable possibility), discussed in Kevin M. Clermont, Jurisdictional Fact, 91 Cornell L. Rev. 973, 1011–13 (2006) (also including discussion of removal's fraudulent joinder doctrine).

274. On the variety of other frivolity tests, see Suja A. Thomas, Frivolous Cases, 59 DePaul L. Rev. 633 (2010).

275. 504 U.S. 25, 32–33 (1992) (authorizing dismissal of proceedings in forma pauperis that are delusional or wholly incredible, such that the opponent can show that the proponent would be unable to generate the slightest possibility).

276. See generally Milton Roberts, Annotation, Standards for Determining Whether Proceedings In Forma Pauperis Are Frivolous and Thus Subject to Dismissal Under 28 U.S.C.A. § 1915(d), 52 A.L.R. Fed. 679 (1981) (collecting cases in its supplement to §§ 5–6, 8–9). Thus, § 1915 operates much like the old so-called scintilla test for judgment as a matter of law, which in effect required the opponent to banish the slightest possibility, whether or not reasonable. See supra text accompanying note 97; Eastway Constr. Corp. v. City of New York, 637 F. Supp. 558, 565 (E.D.N.Y. 1986) ("'Frivolous' is of the same order of magnitude as 'less than a scintilla.'"), modified on other grounds, 821 F.2d 121 (2d Cir. 1987).

So the accepted frivolity tests shed light on the new pleading test. *Twombly-Iqbal* gives scant procedural protections similar to those of *Denton*, but requires the *plaintiff* to make the tangibly stronger showing of *plausibility*. Thus the new cases on pleading have stepped up from the older frivolity tests, no matter how those are understood. The plaintiff now must show, at the very outset, a reasonable possibility of the defendant's liability.

"Plausibility with Teeth"

An even more demanding pleading test is conceivable. For example, the Court has interpreted "strong inference" in the Private Securities Litigation Reform Act of 1995[277] to mean that the plaintiff's allegations must make the inference of scienter cogent and at least as compelling as any opposing inference of nonfraudulent intent, and hence more than merely plausible or reasonable.[278]

Analogously, some courts and observers have interpreted the much more generally applicable *Twombly-Iqbal* to demand more than a showing of reasonable possibility, with some even seeing the new cases as requiring a showing on the pleadings of more likely than not.[279] This book's framework argues against such view.

It is unlikely that the Court meant to adopt a standard that would require the plaintiff to show by pleadings alone more than a reasonable possibility. The latter standard prevails on summary judgment. Any articulation and application of the new *Twombly-Iqbal* test that require a stronger likelihood show-

---

277. 15 U.S.C. §78u-4(b)(2).

278. Tellabs, Inc. v. Makor Issues & Rights, Ltd., 551 U.S. 308, 324 (2007); cf. Geoffrey P. Miller, Pleading After Tellabs, 2009 Wis. L. Rev. 507, 532 (arguing that the statute has converted the motion to dismiss in securities cases into a hybrid falling somewhere between Rule 12(b)(6) and Rule 56).

279. See, e.g., Rory Bahadur, The Scientific Impossibility of Plausibility, 90 Neb. L. Rev. 435, 467 (2011) ("plausibility is virtually indistinguishable from a more likely than not analysis"); Jesse Jenike-Godshalk, Comment, "Plausible Cause"?: How Criminal Procedure Can Illuminate the U.S. Supreme Court's New General Pleading Standard in Civil Suits, 79 U. Cin. L. Rev. 791, 793 (2010) ("As this Comment shows, in Twombly and Iqbal the Supreme Court adopted a standard of pleading that shares many similarities with probable cause. In particular, the new civil pleading standard is a form of 'comparative plausibility' that appears to be, in practice, tantamount to a standard of more-likely-than-not probability—the same quantum of proof required by probable cause."); cf. *In re* Text Messaging Antitrust Litig., 630 F.3d 622, 629 (7th Cir. 2010) (Posner, J.) ("The fact that the allegations undergirding a claim could be true is no longer enough to save a complaint from being dismissed; the complaint must establish a nonnegligible probability that the claim is valid; but the probability need not be as great as such terms as 'preponderance of the evidence' connote.").

ing on the pleadings than does summary judgment on the evidence after discovery would be hard to justify.[280]

Instead, it would make policy sense to require a weaker claim at the pleading stage, but we can be pretty confident the Court was not adopting a low standard either. There is a limited number of choices among decisional standards, and so any standard less demanding than summary judgment's reasonable-possibility test would equate to the slightest-possibility or scintilla standard. Nothing in *Twombly* or *Iqbal* suggests that the Court meant such a low standard. The Court rejected a test that would knock out only "allegations that are sufficiently fantastic to defy reality as we know it: claims about little green men, or the plaintiff's recent trip to Pluto, or experiences in time travel."[281] More convincingly, *Twombly* and *Iqbal* were not adopting a scintilla test because it would not serve the Justices' gatekeeping purpose.

In sum, the gradated scale of likelihood illuminates the policy and interpretation problem. It is doubtful that the Court meant anything as radical as requiring the plaintiff to show by the complaint that liability is substantially possible. But it surely meant to require the plaintiff to show more than the slightest possibility. The narrowed choice thus reveals that *Twombly-Iqbal* must have imposed a reasonable-possibility standard. One can argue about whether the Court should have invented a testing of complaints for factual sufficiency, but not about what standard of decision governs under its scheme.

2. Jurisdictional Fact

What kind of factual showing must the plaintiff make in order to establish, say, personal jurisdiction in a civil case? Well, proof of such jurisdictional facts would appear to be an ordinary task, subject to the ordinary standard of proof. The ordinary standard of proof—our default rule—is preponderance of the evidence, because it serves the neutral policy of error-cost minimization. In theory, then, to prove an issue of jurisdictional fact the plaintiff must present a preponderance of the evidence.[282]

---

280. Admittedly, it is possible that the Court was relaxing the traditional summary-judgment standard by its decision in Scott v. Harris, 550 U.S. 372 (2007). It is, however, unlikely that the Court would bump the established standard from reasonably possible to substantially possible without any explanation.

281. Iqbal, 556 at 696 (Souter, J., dissenting).

282. See, e.g., Landoil Res. Corp. v. Alexander & Alexander Servs., Inc., 918 F.2d 1039, 1043 (2d Cir. 1990); Travelers Indem. Co. v. Calvert Fire Ins. Co., 798 F.2d 826, 831–32 (5th Cir. 1986), on rehearing, 836 F.2d 850 (5th Cir. 1988); Farmer Boys' Catfish Kitchens

Real difficulties in regard to this simple picture arise, however, whenever there is a similarity of the facts entailed in the jurisdictional determination and those on the merits. Then the generally accepted standard drops to some sort of reasonable likelihood, or a prima facie showing, of jurisdiction.[283] This is a purposely malleable standard that varies primarily with the nature of the issue: in establishing jurisdiction, this standard requires, for example, a relatively strong showing on identity of the tortfeasor, but only a weak one on results of the tortious act. Indeed, this standard of decision risks becoming a sliding scale on the lower end of the scale of likelihood.

Assume that a woman brings a paternity suit at home in Illinois against an absent man on allegations of in-state impregnation, and that the defendant from Ohio denies the factual allegations. More particularly, Shirley of Illinois has brought a paternity action against Jim of Ohio in an Illinois state court. She claims, in essence, that he sired her child out of wedlock and has failed in his duty to provide support. She alleges that "during the time biologically certain to have been the instant of conception, your Plaintiff had sexual intercourse with your Defendant in Cook County, Illinois, and with no other person." She mentions no other connection of Jim to Illinois. He has received in-hand service of process in Ohio pursuant to the Illinois long-arm statute. Further imagine that the defendant denies that he was "the author of acts or omissions within the state." The defendant says that he attended a big and wild traveling party that began in Gary, Indiana, but in his foggy recollection he does not think that he ever met the plaintiff or had sex with anyone. He has now, by his attorney, submitted a motion to dismiss for lack of personal jurisdiction, and his papers in support spell out his denial of the complaint's allegations. The defendant's challenge is not to the state's constitutional or statutory reach, but rather to the plaintiff's factual allegations.

Surely, Jim's denial cannot suffice to defeat personal jurisdiction, because that result would effectively repeal the long-arm statute. Just as surely, Shirley must do more than *allege* that the defendant is the author of in-state acts or omissions, because that standard would obviously have all sorts of illogical consequences.[284] After all, we would probably want to allow a defaulting defendant

---

Int'l, Inc. v. Golden W. Wholesale Meats, Inc., 18 F. Supp. 2d 656, 659 (E.D. Tex. 1998); New Eng. Welding Contractors, Inc. v. Hydra-Mach. Sales, Inc., 704 F. Supp. 315, 315 (D. Mass. 1989); 2 Robert C. Casad & William B. Richman, Jurisdiction in Civil Actions § 6-1[3][b], at 11 & n.21 (3d ed. 1998).

283. See, e.g., 2 Casad & Richman, supra note 282, § 6-1[3][c], at 14–15.

284. Even so, there is some case support for this position that allegations suffice. E.g., Schermerhorn v. Hoiland, 337 N.W.2d 692, 693–94 (Minn. 1983) ("In other words, at this juncture, we take as true that defendant Raymond Johnson was a co-owner of the plane with defendant Loren Nogosek, who at relevant times was a Minnesota resident, and that

to raise, say, mistaken identity as a jurisdictional defense when seeking relief from judgment. If not, we would have created a worldwide service provision, requiring only the plaintiff's say-so to force the defendant to appear.

It is thus clear that the court must actually determine whether jurisdiction exists. What showing, then, must the plaintiff make to establish challenged jurisdiction? She should not have to *prove* her cause of action in order to establish jurisdiction, because that standard would likewise have all sorts of obviously illogical consequences.[285] A preliminary hearing on jurisdiction would entail a full-dress trial on the merits as to all issues of liability, with troublesome judge/jury problems and difficult res judicata or law of the case implications.[286] If the defendant won that hearing, he would get not a conclusive judgment on the merits but only a dismissal for lack of jurisdiction; and meanwhile he would have relinquished his right not to have to litigate the merits in that forum. If he instead defaulted, he could force a trial on all the issues of li-

---

the negotiations for the sale of the airplane to Minnesota plaintiffs were initiated by defendant Johnson's co-owner in Minnesota.... Here the plaintiffs have alleged facts that, if true, show that defendant Johnson purposely availed himself, through his co-owner, of the privilege of conducting activities within Minnesota."). Indeed, in this confused area, one can find case support for just about any position.

285. Even so, there is some case support for this position. E.g., H.V. Allen Co. v. Quip-Matic, Inc., 266 S.E.2d 768, 769 (N.C. Ct. App.) (2–1 decision) (finding no jurisdiction on both parties' appeals, so dismissing defendant's victory on the merits, while observing: "The only possible subsection which might apply in the instant case is subsection (1) ['any cause of action arising ... [o]ut of any contract made in this State or to be performed in this State']. Yet the record fails to show that a contract was ever made in North Carolina between plaintiff and defendant. Plaintiff certainly alleged that a binding contract was entered into, but defendant vigorously denied any contract. It cannot be conclusively stated that a contract was made at all, and therefore this subsection is inapplicable."), appeal dismissed, 273 S.E.2d 298 (N.C. 1980).

286. See N. Am. Video Corp. v. Leon, 480 F. Supp. 213, 216 (D. Mass. 1979) ("If the [preponderance] course were undertaken, the court might be deciding key fact issues that, if the doctrine of estoppel were not applied, would be resubmitted for jury determination at trial, thus making wasteful use of scarce judicial resources and also creating a possibility of inconsistent findings by the court on motion and the jury at trial. If estoppel were applied on the basis of the court's resolution of the issues, thereby precluding waste and inconsistency, then either the court must impanel a jury just to try those issues for disposition of the motion—a dubious procedure at best—or else the parties would effectively be denied jury trial on those issues because the court's findings on them when determining the motion would preclude their resubmission at jury trial."); cf. Kevin M. Clermont, Sequencing the Issues for Judicial Decisionmaking: Limitations from Jurisdictional Primacy and Intrasuit Preclusion, 63 Fla. L. Rev. 301, 338 (2011) (arguing against intrasuit preclusion).

ability in his home state because these would be jurisdictional facts subject to collateral attack; and thus the statutory objective of forcing the defendant, when appropriate, to defend his conduct in the state where it took place would be nullified.[287]

The answer, therefore, must lie in requiring the plaintiff to show the court something between mere allegation and full proof: a prima facie showing. The temptation could arise for legislators or courts to take advantage of the malleability of the prima facie term by attempting to adjust the standard with infinite fineness in response to the contested fact's importance. But the boundedly rational human mind cannot reliably make such fine adjustments, and so the law should not call upon it to do so. Just as the traditional standards of proof above equipoise have coalesced around (1) preponderance of the evidence, (2) clear and convincing evidence, and (3) beyond a reasonable doubt, the standards of decision below equipoise should follow a quantum-step approach that recognizes only the gradations of (1) slightest possibility, (2) reasonable possibility, and (3) substantial possibility.

The task for the law, then, is to assign an appropriate standard of decision to each contested jurisdictional element, one that reflects the direct costs of applying the standard and the element's importance in terms of the expected cost of resultant errors, giving due weight to the differential between the policy against failing to provide a forum to the plaintiff (type II error) and the policy against failing to limit the burden on the defendant (type I error).[288] The aim is to minimize the sum of the costs, but the trick is to specify properly the sources and magnitudes of all the various costs. Above, it was the costs of applying a preponderance standard to overlapping jurisdictional issues—direct costs such as holding a full-dress hearing, and also the consequences as to jury right, preclusive effect, and subsequent attack—that drove the standard down to prima facie proof. Here, it is primarily the varying differential between type I and type II error costs that causes further adjustment in the meaning of prima facie for different jurisdictional elements, so that courts will demand a stronger jurisdictional showing on the defendant's identity than on the act's location. This task of assigning the appropriate standard of decision to each element is a typical and traditional one for the law, made easier by the

---

287. Again, these dread consequences are not fanciful, as confused courts sometimes do allow lowly merits to be litigated under the guise of a collateral attack for lack of personal jurisdiction. E.g., Pardo v. Wilson Line, Inc., 414 F.2d 1145 (D.C. Cir. 1969) (allowing defendants who had defaulted to prove there had been no fraudulent transfer within the long-arm statute).

288. See Richard A. Posner, Frontiers of Legal Theory 366–67 (2001).

realization that the choice is among only the quantum steps on the lower half of the probability scale.

On the one hand, think of mistaken identity for a defendant who defaulted because he had no connection whatsoever with a totally misled plaintiff. Upon enforcement of the default judgment at the defendant's home, the system would intuitively let him maintain that the in-state actor had not been him, even if the plaintiff could make a plausible showing of same name and likeness. Fore-closing collateral attack would be unfair. Indeed, that result would create a worldwide service provision. No defendant could risk defaulting, because too much would be at stake under conditions too uncertain.

On the other hand, the system would incline to treat location of the juris-dictional act differently. It would lean toward not allowing the defendant to litigate fully that locational fact on collateral attack. If the plaintiff could show a prima facie likelihood that the act took place on the right side of the Illinois border, the defendant should have appeared in the first forum to litigate. If the defendant chooses to default, the collaterally attacking defendant can main-tain as to location only that the plaintiff cannot make a plausible showing. This resistance to relief explains why, when courts or commentators want to justify the existence of collateral attack, they never talk of location but instead always use examples closer to the identity end of the spectrum.[289]

Thus, in any specific case, there appears to be a spectrum, or rather a hier-archy, of facts. In the hypothesized paternity case, there is:

- identity (nexus to defendant);[290]
- intercourse (act);[291]

---

289. E.g., Bd. of Trs., Sheet Metal Workers' Nat'l Pension Fund v. Elite Erectors, Inc., 64 F. Supp. 2d 839, 845–47 (S.D. Ind. 1999) (using example of defendant who can show he was never partner of person who signed contract), rev'd on other grounds, 212 F.3d 1031 (7th Cir. 2000).

290. See Jackson v. FIE Corp., 302 F.3d 515, 524 (5th Cir. 2002) (allowing collateral at-tack, while observing: "To prove that the judgment was void for lack of personal jurisdic-tion, Fratelli Tanfoglio raises an assertedly meritorious defense (identity of the pistol's manufacturer) that the district court's default judgment on the merits had flatly rejected. Because the identity of the pistol's manufacturer has ramifications for both jurisdiction and the merits, the 'foundational principle' embodied in Rule 60(b)(4) collides head-on with a well-established rule of claim preclusion.").

291. See Morris v. SSE, Inc., 843 F.2d 489, 492 (11th Cir. 1988) (reversing pretrial dis-missal for lack of jurisdiction, where the issue was the defendant's in-state acts, and ob-serving: "In the context of a motion to dismiss for lack of personal jurisdiction in which no evidentiary hearing is held, the plaintiff bears the burden of establishing a prima facie case of jurisdiction over the movant, non-resident defendant.... A prima facie case is established

- location (nexus to sovereign);[292]
- impregnation (result);[293] and
- failure to support (legal liability).[294]

The legal system would apply a high standard of decision to identity for jurisdictional purposes, requiring the plaintiff to get at least to equipoise on that issue. Meanwhile, it would require the plaintiff merely to allege failure to support, and not to prove it at all for jurisdictional purposes, leaving the parties to litigate legal liability only on the merits. It would then apply the prima facie standard of decision to the facts in-between, but prima facie would imply a different rigor for the different facts: the system might require the "slightest possibility" for the result of impregnation, meaning little more than good-faith allegation; "reasonable possibility" for the location of the act, implying that reasonable fact finders could differ; and the higher showing of a "substantial possibility" for the fact of intercourse.

From a morass of confused cases on a procedural point of significance, there emerges a startlingly clear rule that covers jurisdictional issues. On any factual element or legal question of personal jurisdiction whenever properly challenged, the proponent of jurisdiction must make the usual showing of more likely than not, subject to this exception: if that element or question overlaps the merits of the claim, the proponent need provide only prima facie proof to establish the forum's authority. Depending on the particular threshold issue's importance, "prima facie" might mean any of the standards below the more-

---

if the plaintiff presents sufficient evidence to defeat a motion for a directed verdict." (citations omitted)).

292. See Wyatt v. Kaplan, 686 F.2d 276, 280 (5th Cir. 1982) ("he must also make a prima facie showing that the tort occurred within the state"), reh'g denied with opinion, 712 F.2d 1002 (5th Cir. 1983); Dustin v. Cruise Craft, Inc., 487 F. Supp. 67, 69 (D.N.H. 1980) (upholding jurisdiction when "one might justifiably conclude that the boat as likely capsized in New Hampshire territorial waters as in Maine territorial waters").

293. See Mountain States Sports, Inc. v. Sharman, 353 F. Supp. 613, 617 (D. Utah 1972) ("However, the court interprets the Utah law to require only a good faith allegation of injury in order to vest the court with power to proceed to trial.").

294. See Prod. Promotions, Inc. v. Cousteau, 495 F.2d 483, 491 (5th Cir. 1974) (considering a pretrial dismissal for lack of jurisdiction and observing that "the task required only a prima facie showing of the facts on which jurisdiction was predicated, not a prima facie demonstration of the existence of a cause of action.... In order to make a prima facie showing of the facts on which jurisdiction was predicated under the contract portion of the statute, appellant did not have to show prima facie evidence of a breach of contract. Rather, appellant had to present prima facie evidence that (1) a contract to be performed in whole or in part within Texas existed between itself and appellees and (2) the present suit arose out of that contractual arrangement.").

likely-than-not standard, namely, slightest possibility, reasonable possibility, sub-stantial possibility, or equipoise. That lower standard will allow the judge to decide efficiently but definitively whether the forum has authority to decide the merits—doing so without entailing or foreclosing any decision on the mer-its, a decision to which a higher standard would apply.

This prima facie standard applies to the jurisdictional issue regardless of the procedural setting in which it arises. The same standard for jurisdiction applies before, during, and after trial. Only the burden of production shifts in collateral attacks.

This prima facie standard applies to all the various types of jurisdiction. Admittedly, most of the cases and discussions involve personal jurisdiction, because modern long-arm statutes have made overlapping jurisdictional is-sues commonplace. Nonetheless, the same considerations apply to nonper-sonal jurisdiction of either the in rem or the quasi in rem variety; if the jurisdiction and the merits overlap as to an issue, then a lower standard should apply to that jurisdictional issue.[295] The prima facie standard applies to subject-matter jurisdiction too. Indeed, the prima facie standard applies to all the other threshold issues that go to the forum's authority.[296]

Important Methodological Note:
Standards of Decision for Issues of Law

Was it correct to say above that the prima facie standard applies to all jurisdictional issues, whether they are questions of law or fact (or are mixed questions)? Consideration of this point is all too obviously necessitated by long-arm statutes that refer to acts such as "commission of a tortious act

---

295. See Fla., Dep't of State v. Treasure Salvors, Inc., 621 F.2d 1340, 1345–46 (5th Cir. 1980) (applying a lower standard to ownership in the unusual situation where deciding who owns the thing determines whether in rem jurisdiction exists), rev'd on other grounds, 458 U.S. 670 (1982).

296. I develop this argument much more fully, and extend it to all of the forum-authority defenses, from subject-matter jurisdiction to venue, in Clermont, supra note 273 (includ-ing discussion of federal question's substantiality rule and removal's fraudulent joinder doc-trine); Brief of Amicus Curiae Professor Kevin M. Clermont in Support of Respondent, Lozman v. City of Riviera Beach, Fla., 133 S. Ct. 735 (2013) (No. 11-626), available at 2012 WL 3027162 (applying the theory to a specific case involving the meaning of "vessel" for ad-miralty jurisdiction and the merits).

within this State." So, what is the required showing on the legal question of whether the alleged facts constitute a tort?

This seemingly straightforward inquiry raises the profound question of how the notion of standard of decision applies to issues of law. The apparent difficulty of this question could counsel its avoidance when possible. Thus, the wise course may be for jurisdictional statutes to avoid the use of terms, like "tortious," that connote a legal outcome.[297] Similarly, when left free to shape doctrine, courts might try to eliminate any legal overlap between the jurisdiction and the merits, or read the jurisdictional statute to require the plaintiff merely to allege something like "the facts *might* constitute a cause of action."[298] If, however, the court finds such avoidance to be statutorily foreclosed, the court has to face the profound but neglected question of the standard of decision for law.

Happily, that question turns out to have a relatively straightforward answer. Simply put, at least for the purposes of the required jurisdictional showing of prima facie proof, no momentous distinction lies between fact and law, they being epistemological equivalents.[299] "If one makes any propositional claims about what the law *is*, regardless of what one has in mind by 'law,' one is making claims of fact."[300]

---

297. See Prod. Promotions, Inc. v. Cousteau, 495 F.2d 483, 491 (5th Cir. 1974) (distinguishing long-arm statute for contract actions, which usually does not read as if it requires proof of the cause of action); 1 Casad & Richman, supra note 282, §4-2[2][a][iii]; cf. Adolf Homburger, The Reach of New York's Long-Arm Statute: Today and Tomorrow, 15 Buff. L. Rev. 61, 86–87 (1965) (noting that this whole prima facie problem can generally be avoided by ensuring that jurisdictional facts do not overlap the merits).

298. See Baldwin v. Household Int'l, Inc., 36 S.W.3d 273, 277 (Tex. App. 2001) ("When reaching a decision to exercise or decline jurisdiction based on the defendant's alleged commission of a tort, the trial court should rely only upon the necessary jurisdictional facts and should not reach the merits of the case. In other words, ultimate liability in tort is not a jurisdictional fact, and the merits of the cause are not at issue. When the plaintiff alleges an action in tort that arose out of an act committed in Texas, the necessary proof is only that the purposeful act was committed in this State.... The act or omission within the state is a sufficient basis for the exercise of jurisdiction to determine whether or not the act or omission gives rise to liability in tort." (citations omitted)).

299. See Ronald J. Allen & Michael S. Pardo, The Myth of the Law-Fact Distinction, 97 Nw. U. L. Rev. 1769, 1770 (2003) ("Thus, the quest to find 'the' essential difference between the two that can control subsequent classifications of questions as legal or factual is doomed from the start, as there is no essential difference.").

300. Gary Lawson, Proving the Law, 86 Nw. U. L. Rev. 859, 865 (1992); see id. ("a proposition by definition is the sort of statement that can be either true or false"); id. at

At trial, however, the treatment of law does differ from that of fact. The reason, which I shall eventually develop, is that we expect the trial factfinder to account for the imperfections of trial evidence by ignoring indeterminate, or uncommitted, belief and then comparing belief in a fact's truth to belief in its falsity. The "proof" of law (like pretrial prima facie proof of fact) does not require these extra steps and so involves only a direct estimation of likelihood, such as reasonably possible.

Perhaps because of that difference upon trial, or perhaps because the process of determining law comprises a usually internal and fairly intuitive or automatized chain of cognition, we tend not to speak of standards of decision for law. "By and large, the law says nothing to initial decision-makers who wonder what standard of proof they should apply to propositions of law. Fact finders are always given a standard; law finders are generally on their own."[301] They just have to find the law (or make conclusions of law)—doing so by a process that goes largely unexamined.

Nevertheless, even if unexamined, standards of decision for law are in play.[302] To establish any proposition, whether of fact or law and in any context, we look to evidence. That look must entail three steps: we will apply rules of admissibility of evidence, we will employ analytic methods for measuring and adding the significance or weight of that evidence, and we will require the combined evidence's weight to meet some standard before declaring the proposition established.[303] The concern here is the last of the necessary steps, which is applying the standard of decision. "The need for standards of proof and the effect of standards of proof on interpretative outcomes are independent of the admissibility and significance rules of one's theory of interpretation."[304] One simply cannot talk about accepting a proposition without, at least implicitly, invoking a standard of decision. The necessity of a standard of decision is therefore just as real for law as for fact.

---

863 ("Whatever one's metaphysical theory of law may be, any positive propositions derived from that theory are, from an epistemological standpoint, claims of fact.").

    301. Id. at 888.

    302. Burdens of proof for law are consequently in play too, even if we tend not to speak of them either. See id. at 868, 895. Often, it is obvious which party is pushing an issue of law and so bears the burden of persuasion. Yet burdens on law can shift under the influence of canons of interpretation. See id. at 877. The judge thereby will come from one direction while going toward a particular view of any interpretative problem, and so should put the risk of nonpersuasion on the party urging that view.

    303. See id. at 861–77.

    304. Id. at 875.

The standard of decision for law normally is more likely than not.[305] Sometimes the standard of decision differs from this neutral one, in order to avoid the special costs of error in one particular direction. The most prominent example is where a clear-statement rule, such as the rule of lenity in criminal law, raises the bar for finding a change in the law.[306] When a clear-statement rule prevails, the evidence must unmistakably compel the interpretation being urged. For one specific example, finding a statutory exception to full faith and credit requires an "affirmative showing" of a "clear and manifest" congressional purpose.[307]

Getting back to the subject of jurisdictional issues of law that overlap the merits, the standard of decision should lower in order to minimize costs. It is true that a full-proof approach for jurisdictional issues of law does not pose judge/jury problems, and that jurisdictional issues of law raise res judicata and other problems in less intense form than do jurisdictional facts. Consequently, some cases do seem weakly to suggest that all jurisdictional issues of law must be determined in the normally full fashion.[308] Nonetheless, this simply cannot be. For jurisdictional issues of law that overlap the merits, the full-proof approach would open default judgments to subsequent attack for failure to state a claim, which would be unacceptable as a normal matter. In short, the court should avoid treating an attack on jurisdiction as the equivalent of a demurrer.[309]

---

305. The focus here is initial decisionmaking, not appellate review. See id. at 883–88. Moreover, the focus is law determining, not lawmaking. See Friedman, supra note 24, at 935–38.

306. See Lawson, supra note 300, at 888–90. Presumptions used in legal interpretation, such as the presumption of territoriality used within the realm of legislative jurisdiction, can play a similar role. See EEOC v. Arabian Am. Oil Co., 499 U.S. 244 (1991).

307. Kremer v. Chem. Constr. Corp., 456 U.S. 461, 485 (1982).

308. E.g., Stevens v. Redwing, 146 F.3d 538 (8th Cir. 1998) (ruling that because an inmate failed to present prima facie evidence showing that his claims were within the scope of the Missouri long-arm statute, there was no personal jurisdiction over defendants, but also determining that his causes of action were not legally sound).

309. See Petters v. Petters, 560 So. 2d 722, 724 (Miss. 1990) ("It is easy to see that Rule 12(b)(2) (personal jurisdiction) and Rule 12(b)(6) (failure to state a claim) inquiries are separate and distinct. A non-resident's amenability to suit here in no way turns on the viability of the claim the plaintiff asserts. Conversely, that the plaintiff's claim is without merit is never sufficient to establish lack of personal jurisdiction. The non-resident does not prevail on his Rule 12(b)(2) motion by convincing the court that the plaintiff's suit is groundless." (citations omitted)).

> In the legal analysis of jurisdictional issues that overlap the merits, the plaintiff should survive by making some sort of plausible showing, which might not measure up to more likely than not. That is, the plaintiff should have to make only a prima facie showing of a favorable outcome on a particular legal issue that overlaps the merits.[310] This threshold legal decision will not fix the law applicable on the merits in the instant case or any future case; instead, the decision will determine only whether jurisdiction exists.[311]

3. Jurisdictional Amount

The realm of subject-matter jurisdiction provides the third example. It lies in the prominent requirement of a specified amount in controversy, which just below its surface entails a standard of decision.

On inquiry into jurisdictional amount the preponderance standard applies, usually without discussion, in the absence of other considerations.[312] A key

---

310. See Zeunert v. Quail Ridge P'ship, 430 N.E.2d 184, 187 (Ill. App. Ct. 1981) ("When a defendant challenges jurisdiction, a court will make a preliminary inquiry as to whether the complaint states a legitimate cause of action 'to insure that acts or omissions which form the basis of a cause of action that is patently without merit will not serve to confer jurisdiction.'" (quoting Wiedemann v. Cunard Line Ltd., 380 N.E.2d 932, 938 (Ill. App. Ct. 1978))).

311. See Longines-Wittnauer Watch Co. v. Barnes & Reinecke, Inc., 209 N.E.2d 68, 83 (N.Y. 1965) (concurring opinion) ("I think that, without prejudice to the determination of questions of liability at the trial, enough has been shown to indicate the existence of a substantial controversy which if resolved in plaintiff's favor on the facts and the law, would warrant the assumption of jurisdiction under [the long-arm statute].... Since products or some related form of liability (if established) would mean that the infant plaintiff's injuries arose out of the particular business transaction engaged in by the nonresident manufacturer in the purposeful circulation of this hammer in the stream of commerce in New York State, enough has been shown prima facie to warrant upholding jurisdiction to try this issue.").

312. See McNutt v. Gen. Motors Acceptance Corp., 298 U.S. 178, 189 (1936) (holding in an injunction suit that amount in controversy was the loss that would result from enforcement of challenged regulation, and observing: "The authority which the statute vests in the court to enforce the limitations of its jurisdiction precludes the idea that jurisdiction may be maintained by mere averment or that the party asserting jurisdiction may be relieved of his burden by any formal procedure. If his allegations of jurisdictional facts are challenged by his adversary in any appropriate manner, he must support them by competent proof. And where they are not so challenged the court may still insist that the jurisdictional facts be es-

consideration, however, is that the court in deciding jurisdiction must avoid trying the merits. Indeed, overlap with the merits is a very common occurrence here, because most often the jurisdictional amount inquiry involves weighing the claim's worth. The standard then must lower.[313]

Although seldom recognized as such, the standard of decision must become one of prima facie proof. That prima facie standard is the well-known legal-certainty test.[314] To satisfy the jurisdictional amount requirement in a diversity case where the plaintiff has pleaded a claim for more than $75,000 against the defendant, the plaintiff needs to show only some possibility that the judgment could exceed $75,000 under the applicable *law*. This test is very easily passed, especially in unliquidated tort cases, because jurisdiction will exist even though a recovery over $75,000 is highly unlikely on the *facts*. That is, because here the jurisdictional amount and the merits overlap, courts ask for no more than a very modest showing to establish jurisdiction. The plaintiff need rebut contrary legal certainty by establishing a legal possibility of adequate recovery or, in other words, by establishing that a reasonable factfinder could award more than the jurisdictional amount consistently with the law. In sum, the legal-certainty test, as applied to the damages that might be recovered, is in essence a required showing of a reasonable possibility of exceeding the floor amount.[315]

Some courts will at an early stage dismiss occasional cases in which requested damages are very flagrantly exaggerated, but all tests routinely more rigorous than the reasonably possible standard have proved impractical.[316] This ongoing debate is so much more comprehensible if framed in terms of the stan-

---

tablished or the case be dismissed, and for that purpose the court may demand that the party alleging jurisdiction justify his allegations by a preponderance of evidence.").

313. See Smithers v. Smith, 204 U.S. 632, 645 (1907) ("lest, under the guise of determining jurisdiction, the merits of the controversy between the parties be summarily decided without the ordinary incidents of a trial"); Barry v. Edmunds, 116 U.S. 550, 565 (1886).

314. See Saint Paul Mercury Indem. Co. v. Red Cab Co., 303 U.S. 283 (1938); 14AA Charles Alan Wright, Arthur R. Miller & Edward H. Cooper, Federal Practice and Procedure §3702 (4th ed. 2011); cf. id. §3702.1 (discussing the differing standards of decision in the removal setting); 14C Charles Alan Wright, Arthur R. Miller, Edward H. Cooper & Joan E. Steinman, Federal Practice and Procedure §3725 (4th ed. 2009) (same).

315. See Fireman's Fund Ins. Co. v. Ry. Express Agency, Inc., 253 F.2d 780, 784 (6th Cir. 1958) ("Where the jurisdictional issue as to amount in controversy can not be decided without the ruling constituting at the same time a ruling on the merit of the case, the case should be heard and determined on its merits through regular trial procedure."); Stefania A. Di Trolio, Comment, Undermining and Unintwining: The Right to a Jury Trial and Rule 12(b)(1), 33 Seton Hall L. Rev. 1247, 1264 n.132, 1280 n.234 (2003).

316. See 14AA Wright, Miller & Cooper, supra note 314, §3707.

dard of decision. For example, a few courts, through some vague verbal formula, try to raise the bar, in effect by nudging the standard of decision up to a substantial possibility.[317] However, while courts are fairly adept at applying the reasonably possible standard, as on motion for summary judgment, courts would find curtailing the opponent's procedural opportunities for factual development, as by denying without full discovery and evidentiary hearing, to be more questionable as the standard for the proponent to meet elevates to substantial possibility or above. Moreover, an elevated standard would more often necessitate jurisdictional dismissals during or after trial, when the facts get better developed. These difficulties are unacceptable, and therefore the workable but lenient legal-certainty test still prevails.

Moving beyond issues of fact regarding damages in applying the legal-certainty test, courts should also require only a prima facie showing on related issues of law that overlap the merits. It is clear that the plaintiff need not survive the usual demurrer test for the legal sufficiency of the claim in order to establish that liability exists sufficiently for the possible judgment to meet the jurisdictional amount requirement.[318] Consistently, the plaintiff need not establish by a more-likely-than-not standard the measure of damages under the applicable law; for example, even if the availability of punitive damages remains unclear, a big enough claim for them will support jurisdiction.[319] Finally, the plaintiff should not have to establish the absence of valid defenses.[320] Here, however, courts begin to show more confusion

On the one hand, as courts move toward considering exclusive-remedy or limitation-of-liability provisions in the course of applying the legal-certainty test, they require a stronger showing.[321] For example, one court, in granting

---

317. E.g., Nelson v. Keefer, 451 F.2d 289 (3d Cir. 1971) (seeming to require, by its analogies to the new-trial test that equates the jury's clear error to its having decided in the absence of a substantial possibility, a showing of a substantial possibility of exceeding $75,000).

318. See Bell v. Hood, 327 U.S. 678 (1946).

319. See Columbia Pictures Corp. v. Grengs, 257 F.2d 45, 47 (7th Cir. 1958); see also Calhoun v. Ky.-W. Va. Gas Co., 166 F.2d 530, 531 (6th Cir. 1948) (upholding jurisdiction despite "very real controversy in respect to the applicable law of Kentucky" on damages); Duhon v. Conoco, Inc., 937 F. Supp. 1216, 1222 (W.D. La. 1996) (saying that "where it is unclear as to whether state law precludes recovery jurisdiction exists").

320. See Saint Paul Mercury Indem. Co. v. Red Cab Co., 303 U.S. 283, 289 (1938) (dictum).

321. E.g., Stuart v. Colo. Interstate Gas Co., 271 F.3d 1221 (10th Cir. 2001) (allowing, on jurisdictional attack, full legal testing of whether workers' compensation was the exclusive remedy); cf. Radil v. Sanborn W. Camps, Inc., 384 F.3d 1220 (10th Cir. 2004) (distinguishing factual testing on the same question).

a Rule 12(b)(1) motion based on lack of jurisdictional amount, got into a full-fledged consideration of the applicability and enforceability of a contractual ceiling on damages.[322] The court rejected the plaintiff's argument "that the liquidated damages provision does not apply because: (1) [the plaintiff] is seeking direct damages and this provision does not limit its recovery of direct damages; (2) it is unenforceable due to [the defendant's] willful and/or bad faith breach of the contract; and (3) it is unenforceable because it is contrary to the public policy embodied in the Kansas Salesperson Commission Statutes."[323] To do so, the court was perfectly willing to resolve "questions of law and disputed jurisdictional facts" on "a jurisdictional issue that was logically distinct from whether the defendant breached its contractual duties."[324]

On the other hand, other courts manage to avoid this result. They have recognized the undesirability of so getting into the merits on a jurisdictional motion. In particular, the Second Circuit in similar cases has refused to go that route, although it has rested its refusal on the shaky reason that the limitation-of-liability provision is an affirmative defense and therefore off-limits altogether on jurisdiction, even as to jurisdictional amount.[325]

The better approach—which incidentally is in the nature of a compromise between these two lines of precedent—would be to require, on overlapping fact or law arising in claim or defense, only a prima facie showing to establish jurisdictional amount, with the case then moving on to the merits.[326]

322. LDCircuit, LLC v. Sprint Commc'ns Co., 364 F. Supp. 2d 1246, 1263 (D. Kan. 2005) (refusing also to count damages for tortious interference claim that was "patently without merit").

323. Id. at 1251.

324. Id. at 1254.

325. E.g., Zacharia v. Harbor Island Spa, Inc., 684 F.2d 199 (2d Cir. 1982) (treating statutory cap); cf. Scherer v. Equitable Life Assurance Soc'y of U.S., 347 F.3d 394 (2d Cir. 2003) (disallowing use of res judicata, an affirmative defense, to whittle down the amount in controversy).

326. See Pratt Cent. Park Ltd. P'ship v. Dames & Moore, Inc., 60 F.3d 350, 362–63 (7th Cir. 1995) (Flaum, J., dissenting) ("But where the plaintiff has presented more than a colorable issue regarding the amount in controversy, courts should accept that presentation and move on. Otherwise, we are encouraging too much jurisdictional maneuvering at the outset of litigation.").

Chapter III

Empirical Data on How People Handle Different Standards of Proof

Throughout this book, I have tried to ground my empirical assertions in empirical research. But in this chapter I want to collect the studies that deal directly with legal standards of decision.

A. Range of Studies

1. Topics

The studies to date have mainly focused on standards of proof, rather than on the other standards of decision. Therefore, in this chapter, I shall focus on empirical work concerning the standards of proof.

There is, however, some more general work here and there.[327] Empirical results imply that differing standards of review actually do matter. For example, there is research showing higher reversal rates for nondeferential review (26%) than for deferential review under the clear-error standard (12%) in federal courts of appeal.[328] The study had gathered data from Lexis on about 10,000 published and unpublished 2008 opinions in civil and criminal cases issued by the First through Eleventh Circuits, including only cases that expressed a standard of re-

---

327. E.g., McCauliff, supra note 104, at 1324–33, 1335 (considering standards of decision more generally, and arguing that common confusion makes further proliferation of standards unwise).

328. Corey Rayburn Yung, Flexing Judicial Muscle: An Empirical Study of Judicial Activism in the Federal Courts, 105 Nw. U. L. Rev. 1, 20–21 (2011). Another study, using a different database, yielded analogous numbers of 31% and 22%. Anderson, supra note 118, at 24.

view. The result is reassuring, as it accords with expectations. One would expect, if all cases were appealed, a nondeferential standard to produce about a 25% reversal rate, given the tendency of expert decisionmakers to agree.[329] One would also expect a deferential standard to yield a lower reversal rate.[330]

As to the studies of the standard of proof, empiricists show their usual obsession with the criminal law. Thus, most studies focus on the beyond-a-reasonable-doubt standard.[331] This myopia has serious consequences. The criminal standard is so culturally loaded that subjects bring much information, misinformation, attitude, and emotion to the table. Results of the studies do not necessarily carry over to the lower and more arcane standards of proof.

2. Methodologies

Studying the ways that lawmakers and decisionmakers employ standards of proof is very difficult, obviously. One cannot rely on observation of outcome data.[332] One has to resort to indirect and artificial techniques, such as the self-reporting methodology that asks people what probability they associate with various standards of proof. A better approach would involve probing questionnaires for test subjects or even post-deliberation interviews with real jurors. Still better studies would construct simulations that use mock jurors who read or view case summaries, render verdicts, and answer questions. Simulations

---

329. In this part of his research project, Professor Yung did not control for much, although he did exclude immigration and habeas corpus cases for giving peculiarly deferential review. See Corey Rayburn Yung, Judged by the Company You Keep: An Empirical Study of the Ideologies of Judges on the United States Courts of Appeals, 51 B.C. L. Rev. 1133, 1155–61 (2010). In particular, he made no attempt to control for selection effect, although selection should dampen the effect of differing standards of review. See Yung, supra note 328, at 20 n.110. But in fact there is little selection effect on appeal. See Kevin M. Clermont, Litigation Realities Redux, 84 Notre Dame L. Rev. 1919, 1970–72 (2009).

330. See Clermont, supra note 329, at 1970–71. Yung's research also showed a reversal rate of 15% for the abuse-of-discretion standard. But that may reflect simply that this standard is an ambiguous one comprising deferential and nondeferential standards. See supra text accompanying note 125. Elsewhere, he found the substantial-evidence standard to yield a 15% reversal rate and the arbitrary-and-capricious standard to yield a 20% reversal rate. Corey Yung, Measuring Judicial Activism by Federal Appellate Judges, http://www.concurringopinions.com/archives/2009/05 (May 30, 2009) ("standards of review do affect reversal rates"). This spread may simply reflect confusion among judges as to how deferential these standards are supposed to be. See supra text accompanying note 149.

331. See Kagehiro, supra note 243, at 195.

332. See Schwartz & Seaman, supra note 228, at 23–27.

have the advantage of allowing the experimenter to manipulate the variables of interest while controlling the confounding variables.[333]

Striving for more direct and realistic experiments seems infeasible. One can grasp that point best by considering some past proposals for improving the experiments. One author suggested comparison of the results of real or mock trials with a statistician's probability calculations, using cases that permitted meaningful calculation of probabilities: "A comparison of the results might then enable us to decide what sort of probability figure is equivalent to proof 'beyond reasonable doubt.'"[334] Weighing such a suggestion reveals both how difficult staging such an experiment would be and how little it would likely reveal about standards of proof.

B. Findings of Studies

Nevertheless, the available empirical data do support the view that considerable confusion on standards of proof exists in practice—both with respect to articulation and communication of the standard by the lawgiver and also comprehension and application by the factfinder.

1. Articulation and Communication

The preceding chapter documented that lawmakers lack discipline in articulating the standards of proof. They speak loosely, and they proliferate the standards in use. When the law tries to communicate the chosen standard to the factfinder, the problems multiply. For example, there is agreement that judges have difficulty conveying to jurors the essence, to say nothing of the subtleties, of the standard of proof.[335]

Of course, steps that can be taken to improve communication, either by improving the language of the instructions or by revising the procedures for

---

333. See David DeMatteo & Natalie Anumba, The Validity of Jury Decision-Making Research, in 1 Psychology in the Courtroom 1, 8–9 (Joel D. Lieberman & Daniel A. Krauss eds., 2009).

334. H.J. Walls, What Is "Reasonable Doubt"? A Forensic Scientist Looks at the Law, 1971 Crim. L. Rev. 458, 469–70.

335. See Addington v. Texas, 441 U.S. 418, 424–25 (1979); Larson v. Jo Ann Cab Corp., 209 F.2d 929, 931–35 (2d Cir. 1954) (Frank, J.); Hazard et al., supra note 45, §11.14; 9 J. Wigmore, supra note 10, §2497, at 414–15; cf. Frederick Schauer, Slippery Slopes, 99 Harv. L. Rev. 361, 370–76 (1985) (discussing generally the problems of linguistic imprecision and limited comprehension in communicating legal principles).

delivering the instructions.[336] One desirable step, as already suggested, would be for lawgivers to deploy only a limited set of customary standards of proof.

2. Comprehension and Application

Likewise, there is agreement that juries have difficulty in comprehending the standards of proof.[337] Empirical research backs up that supposition.[338] Thus, we have long known that the usual judicial instructions do not communicate much to the jurors. In replies of 173 former jurors in the District of Columbia to a primitive questionnaire asking them to pick the most accurate definition of "preponderance of the evidence" from (1) one party's evidence is stronger than the other's, (2) a slow and careful pondering of the evidence, and (3) looking at the exhibits in the jury room, 76 of the jurors chose one of the latter two.[339] "Beyond a reasonable doubt" leads to legendary confusion too.[340]

The studies have inferred that this confusion leads to misapplication of the standards. The studies begin with the knowledge that most legal commentators interpret the preponderance standard as supposedly picking up anything above 50%, the intermediate standard as supposedly falling around 75%, and

---

336. See generally Amiram Elwork, Bruce D. Sales & James J. Alfini, Making Jury Instructions Understandable (1982); Field et al., supra note 10, at 1346–50 (discussing the route of improving pattern jury instructions on standards of proof); James R.P. Ogloff & V. Gordon Rose, The Comprehension of Judicial Instructions, in Psychology and Law 407 (Neil Brewer & Kipling D. Williams eds., 2005).

337. See United States v. Fatico, 458 F. Supp. 388, 409–10 (E.D.N.Y. 1978) (Weinstein, J.), aff'd, 603 F.2d 1053 (2d Cir. 1979); Eggleston, supra note 25, at 118–20.

338. See generally Kagehiro, supra note 243, at 194–95 (summarizing studies).

339. Kathleen F. O'Reilly, Why Some Juries Fail, D.C. B.J., Jan.–June 1974, at 69. In replies of 843 former jurors in Ohio to a questionnaire submitted by Judge Walter B. Wanamaker, 232 thought that the phrase "preponderance of the evidence" was the most difficult to understand. ("Proximate cause" was runner-up with 203 votes.) Trial by Jury, 11 U. Cin. L. Rev. 119, 192 (1937). In replies of 68 former jurors in Montana, 26 said that this phrase meant beyond a reasonable doubt. Bradley Saxton, How Well Do Jurors Understand Jury Instructions? A Field Test Using Real Juries and Real Trials in Wyoming, 33 Land & Water L. Rev. 59, 100 (1998).

340. See Picinali, supra note 53, at 11–14 (summarizing studies); David U. Strawn & Raymond W. Buchanan, Jury Confusion: A Threat to Justice, 59 Judicature 478, 481 (1976) (after giving potential jurors videotaped instructions, "only 50 per cent of the instructed jurors understood that the defendant did not have to present any evidence of his innocence, and that the state had to establish his guilt, with evidence, beyond any reasonable doubt").

the criminal standard as supposedly being in the 90%–95% range.[341] Now, we know that humans perform rather weakly in handling probabilities.[342] Small surprise, then, that the studies reveal that jurors and other lay people have difficulty in translating the standards of proof into numerical probabilities, not only doing so inaccurately compared to the expert commentators and but also responding inconsistently in that their outputs are all over the place.[343] Fear thus arises of juries' often demanding too much proof when applying the preponderance standard[344] and too little proof when applying the criminal standard,[345] if not simply utilizing highly variable criteria.

---

341. See Kagehiro, supra note 243, at 195; Joel D. Lieberman, The Psychology of the Jury Instruction Process, in 1 Psychology in the Courtroom, supra note 333, at 129, 133; Mc-Cauliff, supra note 104, at 1325, 1328, 1331 (surveying federal judges as to how they interpreted the three standards of proof, and getting mean responses of about 50%, 75%, and 90% but with some surprising spreads).

342. See supra text accompanying note 217.

343. See Christoph Engel, Preponderance of the Evidence Versus *Intime Conviction*: A Behavioral Perspective on a Conflict Between American and Continental European Law, 33 Vt. L. Rev. 435, 448–50 (2009) (summarizing studies showing that the beyond-a-reasonable-doubt standard translates into widely varying probabilities for jurors); Martin F. Kaplan, Cognitive Processes in the Individual Juror, in The Psychology of the Courtroom, supra note 3, at 197, 216–17 (summarizing studies showing variability in jurors' application of standards); Ogloff & Rose, supra note 336, at 418–19 (reporting that the mean instructed jury-eligible mock juror translated "beyond a reasonable doubt" as 95%, but the majority put it at 100% and almost a sixth put it at 80% or below).

344. Zamir & Ritov, supra note 35, at 187–97, used experimental results to argue that loss aversion and omission bias cause factfinders to require substantially stronger proof than 50%. But the apparently higher standard may reflect nothing more than the reality that equipoise is a range rather than the point of perfect balance. See supra text accompanying note 32. In any event, these online experiments asked one group of law students or lawyers to scale the persuasiveness of the plaintiff's position in a written scenario and asked another group to decide the case. While the first group set the persuasiveness around .6, slightly fewer than half of the second group found for the plaintiff.

345. See Berman, supra note 7, at 1717 ("high epistemic standards impose significant psychological demands on their addressees: they require people to act other than in accordance with what they strongly believe to be true"); Lillquist, supra note 68, at 111–16 (summarizing studies); Stuart Nagel, David Lamm & Marian Neef, Decision Theory and Juror Decision-Making, in The Trial Process 353, 368 (Bruce Dennis Sales ed., 1981) (using decision-theory methodology, which calculates an individual's standard from the individual's expressed utilities for the various outcomes, to peg "beyond a reasonable doubt" at about 55%). But see Anne W. Martin & David A. Schum, Quantifying Burdens of Proof: A Likelihood Ratio Approach, 27 Jurimetrics J. 383 (1987) (surveying a small sample of students for their self-reported odds of guilt required for conviction, and arriving at the equivalent of a 91% probability standard, except for murder's 99% standard).

Even if one questions the import of the self-reporting methodology,[346] one would have to admit that factfinders do have a difficult time with numbers.[347] This led me in Chapter II to recommend that the legal system restrict itself to nonquantified standards of decision.[348]

Two Classic Studies

A 1971 article by sociology Professors Simon and Mahan reported survey results from federal and state trial judges, persons diverted from the state jury pool, and introductory sociology students about the meaning they gave to the criminal and civil standards of proof.[349] For the beyond-a-reasonable-doubt standard, the judges' mean was 89%, the jurors' mean was 79%, and the students' mean was 89%. For preponderance, the judges' mean was 61%, the jurors' mean was 77%, and the students' mean was 76%. That is, judges, but not lay people, drew a sharp distinction between the criminal and civil standards of proof. Perhaps the civil standard remains arcane for the laity. However, the lay people had received judicial instructions of some sort on the criminal standard in the course of a mock criminal trial and were self-reporting by a questionnaire administered after deliberations, while the same people were simply asked in the body of that questionnaire for their translation of "preponderance of the evidence" into a probability.[350] This underplayed difference in method as to the two standards seems to constitute a substantial impediment to drawing a conclusion.

More interestingly, the article reported experiments involving that mock criminal trial.[351] The authors took 69 people from the jury pool, and played for

---

346. See Francis C. Dane, In Search of Reasonable Doubt: A Systematic Examination of Selected Quantification Approaches, 9 Law & Hum. Behav. 141, 143–44, 155 (1985) (criticizing the self-reporting methodology).

347. See Valerie P. Hans & Valerie F. Reyna, To Dollars from Sense: Qualitative to Quantitative Translation in Jury Damage Awards, 8 J. Empirical Legal Stud. 120, 131–46 (2011).

348. See supra text accompanying note 243. The discussion there covered Dorothy Kagehiro's work on quantification of standards.

349. Rita James Simon & Linda Mahan, Quantifying Burdens of Proof: A View from the Bench, the Jury, and the Classroom, 5 Law & Soc'y Rev. 319, 325–29 (1971).

350. See Rita James Simon, Judges' Translations of Burdens of Proof into Statements of Probability, 1969 Trial Law. Guide 103, 111 (elaborating somewhat the sketchily described methodology); Rita J. Simon & Linda Mahan, Probability Statements of Sufficiency of Proof in Criminal and Civil Trials, in A Handbook of Jury Research § 19 (Walter F. Abbott & John Batt eds., 1999) (same).

351. Simon & Mahan, supra note 349, at 322–25; see Rita James Simon, Murder, Juries, and the Press, Trans-action, May/June 1966, at 40, 41 (describing further the trial used).

them a 40-minute audiotape of a fictionalized version of the Sam Sheppard murder trial; the subjects next answered a questionnaire, then divided into groups of six for 30 minutes of deliberations to try to reach a unanimous verdict, and finally answered another questionnaire. For half the subjects, the initial questionnaire asked for a guilty/not-guilty decision, before asking for a probability estimate that the defendant committed the charged offense; for the other half, the initial questionnaire posed the two queries in reverse order. The subjects who first estimated a probability were much more apt to acquit: they had a 62% acquittal rate versus the other half of the subjects' 49%. Deliberations also moved the experimental subjects toward acquittal.[352] The post-deliberation questionnaire asked the subjects what probability of guilt they were requiring for conviction. Their mean was 79%, but their modal response was 100%: indeed, 25 of the 69 reported that they required 100%, while only 14 more fell in the 85%–95% range.[353]

To me, the authors' most interesting result was that asking jurors to quantify a probability assessment before rendering a verdict would affect the verdict.[354] This finding tends to support the view that quantification is not necessarily a step in applying the standard of proof.[355]

A 1996 article by psychology Professor Horowitz and law Professor Kirkpatrick reported an experiment to study the effect of the content of judicial instructions on the outcome of jury verdicts.[356] They took 80 six-person juries composed of jury-eligible adults, and played a one-hour audiotaped fictional murder trial performed by actors and shown with a synchronized

---

352. See Michael J. Saks, What Do Jury Experiments Tell Us about How Juries (Should) Make Decisions?, 6 S. Cal. Interdisc. L.J. 1, 38–39 (1997); infra text accompanying note 408.

353. The authors repeated the experiment with 88 students, who produced a similar pattern of results—except that the students were more inclined to acquit, with the 62%/49% split becoming 91%/80%. See Simon & Mahan, supra note 349, at 321. In a related study, Rita James Simon, "Beyond a Reasonable Doubt"—An Experimental Attempt at Quantification, 6 J. Applied Behav. Sci. 203 (1970), the author used rank-ordering methodology, which determines where a group of subjects' conviction threshold would fall on a presumably similar group's ranked probabilities that the defendant committed the act, to peg "beyond a reasonable doubt" for the students at 74%–80%.

354. See Simon & Mahan, supra note 349, at 322, 329. But see Dane, supra note 346, at 149–50 (failing to replicate this result).

355. See Koriat et al., supra note 216, at 108 (saying that quantification is a separate cognitive step following judgment as to certainty).

356. Irwin A. Horowitz & Laird C. Kirkpatrick, A Concept in Search of a Definition: The Effects of Reasonable Doubt Instructions on Certainty of Guilt Standards and Jury Verdicts, 20 Law & Hum. Behav. 655 (1996).

slideshow of the actors playing their roles.[357] The version of the trial was either one with evenly balanced evidence or one with strong but not overwhelming evidence of guilt. The trial judge's instructions included one of five definitions of reasonable doubt, ranging from the Federal Judicial Center's pattern instruction stressing the need to be firmly convinced of guilt[358] to an instruction that left the term undefined.[359] The subjects next answered a questionnaire, then deliberated until reaching a unanimous verdict, and finally answered another questionnaire. The results showed that the content of instructions has a big effect.[360]

The firmly convinced instruction was significantly the best at inducing verdicts of acquittal in the weak case and verdicts of conviction in the strong case. By contrast, the undefined instruction did not induce any significant reflec-

---

357. See Irwin A. Horowitz & David G. Seguin, The Effects of Bifurcation and Death Qualification on Assignment of Penalty in Capital Crimes, 16 J. Applied Soc. Psychol. 165, 173–74 (1986) (describing further the methodology).

358. This instruction read this way:

As I have said many times, the government has the burden of proving the defendant guilty beyond a reasonable doubt. Some of you may have served as jurors in civil cases, where you were told that it is only necessary to prove that a fact is more likely true than not true. In criminal cases, the government's proof must be more powerful than that, it must be beyond a reasonable doubt.

Proof beyond a reasonable doubt is proof that leaves you firmly convinced of the defendant's guilt. There are very few things in this world that we know with absolute certainty, and in criminal cases the law does not require proof that overcomes every possible doubt. If, based on your consideration of the evidence, you are firmly convinced that the defendant is guilty of the crime charged, you must find him guilty. If on the other hand, you think there is a real possibility that he is not guilty, you must give him the benefit of the doubt and find him "not guilty."

359. "The burden is on the prosecution to convince you beyond a reasonable doubt that the defendant committed the crime."

360. Accord Norbert L. Kerr, Robert S. Atkin, Garold Stasser, David Meek, Robert W. Holt & James H. Davis, Guilt Beyond a Reasonable Doubt: Effects of Concept Definition and Assigned Decision Rule on the Judgments of Mock Jurors, 34 J. Personality & Soc. Psychol. 282, 291–92 (1976) (describing the results of a study using mock jurors, and showing the effects of various reasonable-doubt instructions); Daniel B. Wright & Melanie Hall, How a "Reasonable Doubt" Instruction Affects Decisions of Guilt, 29 Basic & Applied Soc. Psychol. 91 (2007) (describing two experiments that investigated the effects of different reasonable-doubt instructions on mock jurors, and showing that the applied standard was lower when the reasonable-doubt instruction was given this elaboration: "You do not have to be certain of the defendant's guilt. You may be able to imagine a scenario in which the defendant is not guilty, but still believe the defendant is guilty 'beyond a reasonable doubt.'").

tion of the strength of evidence. Of the juries receiving that firmly convinced instruction, 0 of 8 convicted in the weak case and 6 of 8 convicted in the strong case. Of the juries receiving that undefined instruction, 4 of 8 convicted in the weak case and 5 of 8 convicted in the strong case. Content analysis of the deliberations showed that the jurors receiving the firmly convinced instruction spent more time discussing the evidence and the standard of proof, which they found accessible and understandable, than jurors receiving one of the other instructions.

Jurors self-reported the minimum probability of the defendant's committing the act that would justify voting for guilt. The thresholds reported before and after the deliberated verdict were overall quite low, at 63% and 64%, and did not differ significantly. The firmly convinced instruction did produce the highest numbers, 71% and 81%, which do significantly differ from each other. The undefined instruction produced 60% and 59%.

The Other Side of the Coin

Not all empirical reports are so gloomy. The existing research, even if imperfect, suggests that factfinders, instructed on finding a fact, can focus separately on the question of how probable it is that the fact is true. The just-described effect of differing instructions as to the criminal standard helps to demonstrate this point. Human decisionmaking on probability, moreover, can make coarse gradations, as recounted in Chapter II. Thus, with proper instruction, factfinding is not necessarily a mere on/off switch, but grossly can and usually does handle likelihood.

For example, a series of experiments in Germany showed "that different standards of proof are psychologically feasible."[361] Students applied a standard of either beyond a reasonable doubt or preponderance of the evidence to a body of evidence to decide a case and then reported their subjective probability. The subjects rendered conviction under a reasonable-doubt instruction only on a very high subjective probability, but under a preponderance standard the other subjects very neatly decided for the plaintiff if their subjective probability exceeded fifty

---

361. Engel, supra note 343, at 463; see id. at 460–61. His so-called Erfurt Experiments receive fuller description in Andreas Glöckner & Christoph Engel, Can We Trust Intuitive Jurors? An Experimental Analysis 9–11 (Max Planck Inst. for Research on Collective Goods, Preprint No. 2008/36, 2008), available at http://www.coll.mpg.de/pdf_dat/2008_36online. pdf. Interestingly, at the end of the questionnaire, the subjects translated their assigned standard into a probability. This step showed a much less pronounced distinction between criminal and civil standards across subjects, throwing the self-reporting methodology further into doubt. See id. at 15.

percent and for the defendant at or below fifty percent. The experiments thus yielded a statistically significant difference between the two standards of proof.

Thus, empirical research indicates that, despite the documented confusion, people can distinguish in application between the criminal standard and the preponderance standard upon proper instructions.[362] The ease of distinguishing between those standards may help to explain the fairly high frequency of agreement, say, between judge and jury as factfinder in both criminal and civil cases.[363] Indeed, an already-described recent study shows that the different standards of proof really matter to outcome, and might even hint that jurors can employ the clear-and-convincing standard of proof.[364] Although this study was typical in comparing subjects receiving different instructions, it implies that individual subjects would be at least as capable of distinguishing standards if they had multiple standards put before them.

Not only can factfinders, if told to do so, apply a simple standard of proof imposed by law, there is also good reason to think that those factfinders take the standard of proof seriously and try to follow instructions.[365] Therefore, it is possible that the different standards of proof work their intended effect.

---

362. See Saul M. Kassin & Lawrence S. Wrightsman, The American Jury on Trial: Psychological Perspectives 156 (1988) (reporting research that "suggests that, whether by instruction, intuition, or simply an appreciation for the differential consequences of criminal and civil decisions, juries are already sensitive to variations in the standard of proof"); Kaplan, supra note 343, at 216 ("It is also possible to observe the effects of differing judicial instructions on the [decisional] criteria."); Barbara D. Underwood, The Thumb on the Scales of Justice: Burdens of Persuasion in Criminal Cases, 86 Yale L.J. 1299, 1311 (1977) ("There is some evidence, then, that factfinders can distinguish among degrees of belief, and that rules about the burden of persuasion affect the outcome of cases.").

363. See Harry Kalven, Jr. & Hans Zeisel, The American Jury 55–65 (2d ed. 1971) (describing the impressive level of agreement between juries and judges); Kevin M. Clermont & Theodore Eisenberg, Litigation Realities, 88 Cornell L. Rev. 119, 144–46 (2002) (same).

364. Schwartz & Seaman, supra note 228, at 36. But see Elisabeth Stoffelmayr & Shari Seidman Diamond, The Conflict Between Precision and Flexibility in Explaining "Beyond a Reasonable Doubt," 6 Psychol. Pub. Pol'y & L. 769, 774–76 (2000) (summarizing studies in which mock jurors failed to distinguish a third standard of proof based on clear-and-convincing evidence).

365. See Terence Anderson, David Schum & William Twining, Analysis of Evidence 245 (2d ed. 2005).

3. Conclusions

a. Factfinders Have Difficulty in Comprehending Standards

These empirical studies conform to the lessons of psychological theory. Factfinders are going to have difficulty comprehending something as subtle as a standard of proof. Available empirical data tend to support the view that some confusion on standards of proof exists in practice, and that the confusion would grow as standards became more unusual. The results drive home the obvious need for better explanation to factfinders. Having to explain only the limited set of customary standards of decision would be a step in the right direction.

It could be, however, that trying to convey to the factfinder a required level of certainty will always remain a daunting endeavor. The standard of proof differs from more generally applicable standards of decision. Perhaps for factfinding a different approach is therefore in order: telling the factfinder not to measure absolutely the uncertainty, but asking it to compare relatively its belief in the disputed fact's truth to its belief in the fact's falsity. I shall use the modern theory of belief functions to elaborate such an approach in Chapter V.

b. Factfinders Have Difficulty in Handling Numbers

Factfinders cannot accurately and reliably convert their understanding of standards into a number representing probability. They cannot accurately and reliably convert their assessment of the evidence into a number. A decisional process that involved matching up those two numbers would not be notably dependable, even though it should do better than random.

Of course, this reality would matter only if factfinders actually employed that decisional process. As already noted, some of the research intimates that quantification is not necessarily a step in applying the standard of proof. My eventual conclusion will be that factfinders do not have to quantify their beliefs, nor do they even need to place those beliefs on a scale of likelihood.

An analogy helps here. Doctors notoriously overestimate the probability of disease after a positive test result. A positive mammogram entailed a 7.5% risk of breast cancer, but doctors overwhelmingly estimated the risk as lying between 70% and 80%. Theorists diagnosed the doctors' error as base-rate neglect.[366] But one could alternatively argue that in real life doctors are deciding only what to do next, whether to pursue further tests. The doctors' internal

---

366. See David M. Eddy, Probabilistic Reasoning in Clinical Medicine: Problems and Opportunities, in Judgment Under Uncertainty, supra note 208, at 249.

coarse scale, reflecting only an action threshold, does not project well onto an external risk scale that is continuous and precise. Asking them to estimate the risk is a task at which the doctors are not good, but it is also a job they are not ordinarily tasked with doing. In the experiment, the doctors gave high probability estimates, but perhaps merely as a way to express their considerable concern.[367]

More generally, one should not jump to any conclusion that the inability to handle numbers incapacitates decisionmakers for quantitative-like reasoning. Humans are capable not only of ordinal comparison between quantities without using numbers but also of cardinal measurement: "humans have a basic (and largely inborn, though improvable by training and experience) intuitive capacity for non-symbolic quantitative reasoning, a capacity that includes not only assessing and comparing magnitudes, but also performing on such magnitudes approximate mathematical operations: sums, subtractions, proportions, multiplications and divisions (and even approximate differentiation and integration)."[368]

c. Factfinders Nevertheless Can and Do Handle Likelihood

Despite considerable evidence that factfinders have difficulty in comprehending any standard of proof, and that they have difficulty in quantifying, there is some evidence that is more hopeful. Factfinders are not oblivious to the separate question of how probable it is that the fact is true. They can and do handle likelihood by making gross distinctions in probability.

d. Factfinders Can and Do Distinguish Between Standards

Thus, factfinders can and do distinguish in application between the preponderance standard and the criminal standard upon proper instructions. "In general, although some experiments have limitations that impact their external validity—such as the use of undergraduate psychology students rather than a more broadly representative population—and the evidence is not clear

---

367. See Sun et al., supra note 197, at 162–63, 169; cf. supra note 235 (suggesting that use of frequency information rather than probabilities would mitigate the doctors' mistake).

368. Giovanni Sartor, The Logic of Proportionality: Reasoning with Non-Numerical Magnitudes, 14 German L.J. (forthcoming 2013), available at http://ssrn.com/abstract= 2165545, at 13; see id. at 11 ("To express such nonnumerical cardinal evaluations we often refine our ordinal assessment with adverbs (we say, that this object is a little, fairly, a lot larger, or smaller, or quicker, etc., than that object).").

cut, they cumulatively suggest that jurors' decisions may be swayed by the standard of proof. In addition, they imply that the particular wording of jury instructions can play a significant role in jurors' decision making."[369]

Instructions that expressly differentiate the customary standards, defining the applicable standard by comparison to its competitors, should help the jurors. For example, the Federal Judicial Center's instruction on beyond a reasonable doubt expressly distinguishes the criminal from the civil standard,[370] just as a current federal pattern jury instruction for preponderance of the evidence tries to do.[371] Especially effective would be the Hawaiian approach to describing clear and convincing evidence by contrast to the other standards.[372]

C. Evaluation of Studies

One could certainly question the methodologies of all these empirical studies on the standards of proof. At the least, many questions exist as to the studies' applicability to the real world.[373] But for me, one defect dominates all others. Most of the studies to date may have simply asked the wrong questions and so yielded answers of limited usefulness.

For example, investigations showing that surveyed judges and jurors vary in translating standards of proof into specific probabilities lose much of their relevance upon realization that factfinders may not quantify or make other fine categorizations when actually applying the standards. Instead, they might proceed by making only approximate or fuzzy determinations. Indeed, they may never have to measure absolute likelihood at all. Instead, they might proceed by comparing beliefs and disbeliefs.

---

369. Schwartz & Seaman, supra note 228, at 16 (footnote omitted).

370. See supra note 358.

371. 3 Kevin F. O'Malley, Jay E. Grenig & William C. Lee, Federal Jury Practice and Instructions: Civil § 104.03 (6th ed. 2011):

> Those of you who have participated in criminal cases will have heard of "proof beyond a reasonable doubt." The standard of proof in a criminal case is a stricter standard, requiring more proof than a preponderance of evidence. The reasonable doubt standard does not apply to a civil case and you should put that standard out of your mind.

372. See supra text accompanying note 50.

373. See John Monahan & Laurens Walker, Social Science in Law 68–75 (7th ed. 2010) (discussing validity in general); DeMatteo & Anumba, supra note 333, at 15–19 (assessing optimistically the external validity of jury research).

Therefore, I doubt that one can conclude from the prior empirical work much more than the four general conclusions listed just above. For further conclusions, the research might need redoing.

A recent article takes an interesting step in the direction of a restart.[374] Cambridge psychologist Mandeep K. Dhami has conducted experiments using a new measurement of factfinders' certainty called a membership function. The idea is that a linguistic probability will have a peak meaning but also include a spread of probabilities, creating a fuzzy set. So, she had each of her subjects indicate the extent to which given probability values belong to a phrase like "beyond a reasonable doubt," measuring the extent on a 0 ("not at all") to 100 ("absolutely") scale. Creating such a membership function for self-reporting the meaning of the standard of proof, instead of using a point probability, yielded some promising results. On the one hand, the mean of the peak meanings of beyond a reasonable doubt was 96%, which was higher than the meaning given by other research methods; the membership-function method also showed less variability among individuals' meanings; and changing the content of judicial instructions had little effect on output—what all this means is that methodology might have been driving the results of the prior research. On the other hand, the new measure was no more accurate in predicting the subjects' verdicts in the experiment's manslaughter case.

She can thus conclude: "The present findings highlight the need to reevaluate the reliability and validity of past research findings on quantifying reasonable doubt and on the effects of judicial instructions on reasonable doubt, because they may been affected by the method used to measure interpretations."[375]

I concur with her, but would extend the conclusion. Future empirical study must contemplate not only that factfinders might be employing fuzzy logic but also that standards of proof might call for merely the relative comparison of beliefs and disbeliefs. To get the right answers about this decisional process, researchers must ask the right questions. Properly conducted research could turn out to reveal that factfinders are quite capable of performing their actual task.

---

374. Mandeep K. Dhami, On Measuring Quantitative Interpretations of Reasonable Doubt, 14 J. Experimental Psychol.: Applied 353 (2008).

375. Id. at 362.

Chapter IV

Competing Visions of How People Handle Different Standards of Proof

The gaps in the empirical data leave plenty of room for theories to compete. In the competition, the dominant view of how factfinders process evidence and apply the standard of proof has been probabilistic.[376] Accordingly, I have been using its idiom up to here. I indeed find probability quite expressive as an idiom in this realm. Thus, I do not stand with the courts and commentators who rail against probabilities to explain factfinding.

Anti-Probabilist Rejectionism

There has, of course, been some judicial resistance to any idea of a probabilistic standard, particularly in older cases. Courts have sometimes stated that even the preponderance standard requires convincing the jury of the truth of an allegation.[377] "In order to entitle himself to a finding in his favor his evidence must not only be of greater convincing power, but it must be such as to satisfy or convince the minds of the jury of the truth of his contention."[378] Occasional academics reject probabilism too.[379]

---

376. See generally Eggleston, supra note 25; Symposium, Decision and Inference in Litigation, 13 Cardozo L. Rev. 247 (1991); Symposium, Probability and Inference in the Law of Evidence, 66 B.U. L. Rev. 377 (1986). On subtheories, see Ball, supra note 12, at 809–12 (treating frequentist theory); Tribe, supra note 230, at 1344–50 (treating subjective theory).

377. See 2 McCormick on Evidence, supra note 10, §339, at 485 (citing and criticizing such cases).

378. Anderson v. Chi. Brass Co., 106 N.W. 1077, 1080 (Wis. 1906).

379. E.g., Vern R. Walker, Preponderance, Probability and Warranted Factfinding, 62 Brook. L. Rev. 1075 (1996).

For a specific but more defensible example, Professor Leonard Jaffee attacked the use of probability in analyzing proof. His premise was this: "The relevant legal norm or principle is that verdicts and judgments should determine absolutely and unequivocally the matters actually and properly before judicial tribunals and within their jurisdictions.... If 'probably' be sufficient, guessing may suffice."[380]

Accordingly, he would treat the preponderance standard to mean "weight greater than that of the presumption and evidence opposed to the position of the party with the burden of persuasion. It does *not* mean 'greater probability.'"[381] He elaborated:

> The preponderance-of-the-evidence standard—the standard of sufficiency as to an ordinary civil claim or affirmative defense—is intended to assure that the factfinder will not believe an assertion of fact without evidence *adequate in logic and experience* to support the belief. The term "preponderance" contemplates the problem of how to treat contradictory evidence. The standard reflects the law's presumption against the party with the burden of persuasion, e.g., the usual presumption that the defendant is not liable as the plaintiff claims. In this latter respect, the term "preponderance" contemplates the requirement that plaintiff's evidence, if true, be weightier than the presumption in favor of defendant. So, the standard is also intended to insure that the plaintiff's assertion of fact will not be believed without evidence adequate in logic and experience to support the belief vis-a-vis a contrary presumption and defendant's evidence.[382]

Similarly, as to the intermediate standard: "The stricter civil standard, like the other two, is a reflection of what society will countenance as weighty or forceful enough to justify (or make society comfortable in) imposing on the defendant the kind of loss that the applicable substantive or remedial law supplies. It is *not* a reflection of an assessment of what degree of probability is needed .... The standard in any case is normative, not statistical, and a more demanding standard creates a heavier, but not mathematically greater, burden of persuasion. The intermediate civil standard simply involves a requirement of a greater quantum or coverage of proof.... So, defendant in the intermediate-standard civil case is presumed *clearly* nonliable—until proved liable by con-

---

380. Leonard R. Jaffee, Of Probativity and Probability: Statistics, Scientific Evidence, and the Calculus of Chance at Trial, 46 U. Pitt. L. Rev. 925, 945 (1985).
381. Id. at 938.
382. Id. at 937.

vincing evidence that is both contrary to that presumption and of greater weight."[383] Finally, as to the standard of beyond a reasonable doubt: "What must be shown in a criminal cause is guilt, not probable guilt."[384]

I can understand the genesis of the *cris de coeur* from these and other theorists, who lament the costs of any intrusion of probabilistic mathematics into the very human process of proof.[385] I even share many of their concerns. I certainly believe that one has to think beyond probabilism when one tries to understand the depths of factfinding—or when one tries to reconcile the empirical findings of the preceding chapter. But I do not find anti-probabilist rejectionism a promising path toward developing that deeper understanding. So I return to the traditionally probabilistic view as a starting point.

A. Traditional View: Probability Theories

The wonderful "new evidence" scholarship has made tremendous progress toward a deeper understanding.[386] Those scholars have made strides by shifting the focus of evidence scholarship from rules of admissibility to the nature of proof, while opening the door to interdisciplinary insights including those from psychology.

---

383. Id. at 942–43.

384. Id. at 939.

385. See, e.g., Charles Nesson, The Evidence or the Event? On Judicial Proof and the Acceptability of Verdicts, 98 Harv. L. Rev. 1357, 1363–65, 1377–78 (1985) (arguing that the process of proof aims at generating acceptable statements about past events and thus at projecting behavioral norms to the public); Tribe, supra note 230 (writing the classic version of the lament, in which the author stressed not only the risk of misuse of mathematical techniques, including inaccurate meshing of numerical proof with soft or unquantifiable variables, but also the undercutting of society's values, including the dehumanization of the legal process); Adrian A.S. Zuckerman, Law, Fact or Justice?, 66 B.U. L. Rev. 487, 508 (1986) (arguing that probabilistic assessment diminishes "the hope of seeing justice supervene in individual trials," while the author portrayed factfinding as an individualized but value-laden process).

386. See generally Twining, supra note 2, at 237–48; Richard Lempert, The New Evidence Scholarship: Analyzing the Process of Proof, in Probability and Inference in the Law of Evidence: The Uses and Limits of Bayesianism 61 (Peter Tillers & Eric D. Green eds., 1988); Roger C. Park & Michael J. Saks, Evidence Scholarship Reconsidered: Results of the Interdisciplinary Turn, 47 B.C. L. Rev. 949 (2006). Although "new," this work represented the necessary return to abandoned efforts by past greats such as Wigmore. See, e.g., Anderson et al., supra note 365 (building on John Henry Wigmore, The Science of Judicial Proof As Given by Logic, Psychology, and General Experience, and Illustrated in Judicial Trials (3d ed. 1937)).

The work here has led some to make the traditional probabilism more rigorous mathematically. After considering the major forays in that direction in this Part A, I shall take a look at work that tries to integrate psychology more fully into the theory, work done both by psychologists and by legal academics, in Parts B and C.

Subjective Probability and Bayes' Theorem to Explain Processing of Evidence

What the law should or does tell the factfinder to do is a partly separate question from what factfinders can do, actually do, or think they are doing. Surprisingly, even mathematicians cannot agree on how a factfinder ideally *should* perform the task of processing evidence, and so cannot unanimously guide the law on the path to take.[387] The most popular candidate for rigorously evaluating and combining related evidence is the Bayesian approach to subjective probabilities.[388]

Subjective probability theory allows us to speak of the likelihood of a single event. A subjective probability measures an individual's personal judgment about how likely a particular event is to occur or has occurred. The theory is "based on the notion that it makes sense to ask someone what he would do if offered a reward for guessing correctly whether any proposition, designated X, is true or false. If he guesses that X is true under these circumstances, we say that *for him* the subjective probability of X, written $P(X)$, exceeds fifty percent. Symbolically, $P(X) > .5$. If he would be equally satisfied guessing either way, then we say that, for him, $P(X) = .5$."[389] Upon expanding the measure into a complete scale of probabilities from zero to one and postulating the usual logical operators, subjective probabilities follow most of the rules of frequentist probabilities.[390]

Bayes' theorem links the perceived probability before and after observing evidence. The starting point is $P(A)$, the prior probability of A. Then the posterior probability of A, after accounting for evidence B, is $P(A|B)$; this is a so-called conditional probability, which may be read as the probability that A will occur if B is known certainly to have occurred. $P(A|B)$ calculates to be $P(A)$ mul-

---

387. See generally Symposium, Artificial Intelligence and Judicial Proof, 22 Cardozo L. Rev. 1365 (2001).

388. See generally Sharon Bertsch McGrayne, The Theory That Would Not Die (2011) (recounting the centuries of controversy generated by Bayes' theorem).

389. Tribe, supra note 230, at 1347 (citing the innovative work of Leonard J. Savage, Foundations of Statistics (1954)).

390. See id. at 1347–48. Compare id. at 1348 n.63 (accepting the product rule because he is assuming bivalence), with infra text accompanying note 540 (rejecting the product rule for subjective probabilities in factfinding).

tiplied by the support B provides for A, a support that Thomas Bayes (or really Pierre Simon Laplace) equated to P(B|A) / P(B).

Despite its internal mathematical soundness, and despite the many insights it generates for law, many observers from various disciplines have voiced serious doubts about whether Bayes' theorem should be seen to play a broad role in legal factfinding.[391] First, its prior probability comes out of thin air, as some sort of subjective guess. The more objective supposition of 50%, on the thought that the fact is either true or false, comports neither with reality nor with where the law tells the factfinder to begin, and it produces inconsistencies when there are more than two hypotheses in play.[392] Second, Bayes' theorem leaves no place for indeterminacy, thus painting the world as black and white even though most of the world appears in shades of gray. It accordingly does not handle well the situation of conflicting or scarce information, using a fudge factor to account for the state of the evidence.[393] Third, its mathematical approach is not realistic, of course. It does not conform to the way humans in ordinary life arrive at prior probabilities or the way they combine them with new evidence to produce posterior probabilities.[394]

In the end, even overlooking its theoretical problems, this mathematical model is just too unrealistic a representation of human cognition. Humans instead use intuitive techniques in a nonquantitative and approximate fashion. Consequently, the law has generally left the assessment of evidence to its factfinders' instinctive treatment.

Confidence Intervals to Explain Applying of Standard

The most intriguing attempt by theoreticians to redeploy probability in order to explain standards of proof, as opposed to explanations of how to

---

391. See, e.g., Nancy Pennington & Reid Hastie, Juror Decision-Making Models: The Generalization Gap, 89 Psychol. Bull. 246, 262–68 (1981); Glenn Shafer, The Construction of Probability Arguments, 66 B.U. L. Rev. 799, 809–16 (1986). Compare Paul Bergman & Al Moore, Mistrial by Likelihood Ratio: Bayesian Analysis Meets the F-Word, 13 Cardozo L. Rev. 589, 590 (1991) (attacking), with D.H. Kaye, Commentary, Credal Probability, 13 Cardozo L. Rev. 647 (1991) (defending).

392. See State v. Spann, 617 A.2d 247, 254 (N.J. 1993) (".5 assumed prior probability clearly is neither neutral nor objective"); Jaffee, supra note 380, at 980–85.

393. See Lea Brilmayer & Lewis Kornhauser, Review: Quantitative Methods and Legal Decisions, 46 U. Chi. L. Rev. 116, 135–48 (1978).

394. Compare Samuel Kotz & Donna F. Stroup, Educated Guessing: How to Cope in an Uncertain World (1983) (discussing the sophisticated techniques of theory), with Craig R. Callen, Notes on a Grand Illusion: Some Limits on the Use of Bayesian Theory in Evidence Law, 57 Ind. L.J. 1 (1982) (discussing the simplified practices of law).

process proof, lies in the work of Professor Neil Cohen.[395] He advanced a new theory of standards of proof based on the statistical concept of confidence intervals. His theory entailed a different way of describing how sure a factfinder is, employing not only a point estimate of probability but also a level of confidence, with sureness increasing as either component rises.

The motivating idea was that a point estimate of likelihood in two cases could represent vastly different states of proof. One case might involve proof that is very precise in establishing the point estimate. The other might involve circumstantial evidence consistent with a wide range of possibilities surrounding the point estimate. These cases seem so different that anyone would assume that the latter requires a higher point estimate before the factfinder credits the plaintiff with satisfying the standard of proof.

The statistical means for capturing the spread of the evidence is the confidence interval. This second-order probability concept conveys that one is confident, to a specified level, that the true probability is within the interval. Cohen would require the whole interval to exceed the probability threshold of the standard of proof. So, to satisfy the preponderance standard, the whole interval would have to fall above 50%. Expressing the other standards presented more of a problem for his approach.

The result of his scheme would be that before finding for the plaintiff, the factfinder has to be pretty confident that the true probability exceeds the standard of proof's threshold. But the specified level of confidence, in Cohen's view, should not be the scientists' ninety-five percent, because that would overly favor defendants. Instead, the specified level of confidence would be fixed in each case at such level that the chance of an error favoring the defendant equaled the chance of an error favoring the plaintiff.

Neil Cohen's brilliant attempt ultimately failed.[396] No one any longer adheres to it.[397] The reason is not merely that the approach is extraordinarily compli-

---

395. Neil B. Cohen, Confidence in Probability: Burdens of Persuasion in a World of Imperfect Knowledge, 60 N.Y.U. L. Rev. 385 (1985) (advancing a new theory of standards of proof based on the statistical concept of confidence intervals); see Robert H.A. Ashford, Commentary, Take What You Have Gathered from Coincidence: The Importance of Uncertainty Analysis, 66 B.U. L. Rev. 943, 945–46 (1986) (generalizing Neil Cohen's argument); Richard D. Friedman, Commentary, Generalized Inferences, Individual Merits, and Jury Discretion, 66 B.U. L. Rev. 509, 512–19 (1986) (incorporating Neil Cohen's argument).

396. Compare Neil B. Cohen, Commentary, The Costs of Acceptability: Blue Buses, Agent Orange, and Aversion to Statistical Evidence, 66 B.U. L. Rev. 563, 569 (1986) (qualifying his own argument), and Neil B. Cohen, Conceptualizing Proof and Calculating Probabilities: A Response to Professor Kaye, 73 Cornell L. Rev. 78, 91–93 (1987) (conceding that confidence relates solely to the probability of avoiding false positives), with D.H. Kaye,

cated, even though it is. One cannot specify the required level of confidence simply, no less picture it; human factfinders could never apply the approach, or even use it as a helpful image. Nor is the reason a theoretical objection, although such objections exist. The confidence interval is a frequentist concept that does not easily extend to the subjective probabilities of the legal context.

The real reasons for rejecting the attempted elaboration go beyond such concerns. One problem is that the confidence interval has nothing to do with what the standard of proof is trying to do. First-order probabilities enable minimizing the expected cost of error, while second-order probabilities merely express one feature of the factfinders' state of mind—although the former may correlate with the latter, these two are separate measures that can diverge. Another problem is that using the confidence-interval approach would have substantial practical impact on outcomes without justification. It would make it considerably harder for plaintiffs to recover in all cases—and it would never allow recovery in a case with relatively thin evidence that nevertheless shows that the defendant's liability is more likely than not.

B. Psychologists' Attacks: Confidence Theories

The first step going down a more promising path to understanding requires us to build on the distinction between the factfinder's evaluating and combining evidence, on the one hand, and the factfinder's applying the standard of proof to that evidential output, on the other hand. How does the factfinder proceed through those two steps to reach a decision? No one knows exactly. Psychologists cannot tell us exactly how people assess evidence, while they can tell us almost nothing about how people measure assessments of evidence against a standard of proof. Their neglect of the latter step becomes more troublesome as psychologists push us farther away from a Bayesian approach for assessing evidence.

Commentary, Do We Need a Calculus of Weight to Understand Proof Beyond a Reasonable Doubt?, 66 B.U. L. Rev. 657, 667 n.22 (1986) (suggestively criticizing Neil Cohen's argument), and D.H. Kaye, Apples and Oranges: Confidence Coefficients and the Burden of Persuasion, 73 Cornell L. Rev. 54, 54, 56–58 (1987) (expanding his criticism).

397. But see Luke Meier, Probability, Confidence, and the "Reasonable Jury" Standard, available at http://ssrn.com/abstract=2179236 (Nov. 21, 2012) (resurrecting confidence intervals for use in the burden of production).

1. Processing the Evidence

Introspection might suggest that there is a knowledge arc, leading up by induction and abduction, and then down by deductive testing.[398] The upward arc rests on observations, which generate new hypotheses explaining the observations. The downward arc involves testing the hypotheses to reach conclusions.

Throughout the arc, there is evaluation and combination of evidence by some method. To expose that method, social scientists have tried to model the cognitive black box by experimentally comparing inputs and outputs. The models that result may be atomistic or holistic in operation.[399]

One atomistic result is the model called *information integration theory*.[400] It tries to describe how humans naturally evaluate and combine information to produce judgment. Although only one of many contesting theories, and a relatively optimist one at that, information integration theory has suggestive powers making description worthwhile. According to the theory, the human decisionmaker who has to make a finding on a fact's existence would begin with an initial impression, or predisposition, and then would process additional pieces of information. Each of these, including the initial impression, would receive a scale value, which is a measure of the likelihood of the fact's existence. Each would also receive a weighting factor, which is a measure of evidential importance that takes into account both directness and credibility. The decisionmaker would then combine these into a weighted average that determines the fact's existence.

More broadly accepted is the *story model* of evidence-processing.[401] It holds that the factfinders, over the legal process's course, construct from the evi-

---

398. See David A. Schum, A Science of Evidence: Contributions from Law and Probability, 8 Law Probability & Risk 197, 203–04 (2009) (crediting David Oldroyd, The Arch of Knowledge (1986), for this image).

399. See Mark Schweizer, Comparing Holistic and Atomistic Evaluation of Evidence, http://ssrn.com/abstract=2184242 (Nov. 1, 2012) (showing that holistic methods produce more polarized views).

400. See Kaplan, supra note 343; see also Dennis J. Devine, Jury Decision Making 21–40 (2012) (discussing a variety of juror-level and jury-level models); Jennifer Groscup & Jennifer Tallon, Theoretical Models of Jury Decision-Making, in 1 Psychology in the Courtroom, supra note 333, at 41 (sketching various models); Pennington & Hastie, supra note 391 (evaluating various models).

401. See generally Jeffrey T. Frederick, The Psychology of the American Jury 296–99 (1987) (providing a brief overview of the story model of evidence-processing); Reid Hastie, Steven Penrod & Nancy Pennington, Inside the Jury 22–23 (1983) (providing a brief summary of empirical studies supporting the story model); Paula L. Hannaford, Valerie P. Hans, Nicole L. Mott & G. Thomas Munsterman, The Timing of Opinion Formation by Jurors in Civil Cases: An Empirical Examination, 67 Tenn. L. Rev. 627, 629–32 (2000) (discussing

dence the story that makes maximal sense. The factfinders then choose, among the available decisions, the one that fits best with the constructed story:

> Several authors have recently proposed a model for juror decisionmaking based on the concept of a story as an organizing and interpreting schema. The story model attempts to explain how jurors organize and interpret the vast amount of information they encounter at trial and apply the appropriate decision criteria....
>
> ... The jurors construct a story adequately describing what happened. At the conclusion of the trial, they construct the verdict categories based on the instructions given by the judge. The individual juror arrives at his decision by determining the best match between his story and the available verdict categories. The task of the jury in deliberations then becomes one of selecting a story from among those offered by the jurors and fitting it to the available verdict options.[402]

Such psychological theories accept that humans do not naturally use perfectly "rational" techniques, but instead use less accurate "intuitive" techniques. Additionally, the employed techniques are subject to all sorts of heuristics and other biases.[403] The factfinders would take an instinctive stab at assessing all the related evidence. Moreover, the factfinders' performance of the cognitive process would usually be approximate and nonnumerical. That is, any judged likelihood would find expression in terms of a limited set of broad categories such as more likely than not, high probability, and almost certainty.

"three predominant models of jury decision making"); Jill E. Huntley & Mark Costanzo, Sexual Harassment Stories: Testing a Story-Mediated Model of Juror Decision-Making in Civil Litigation, 27 Law & Hum. Behav. 29, 29 (2003) (presenting research that "extends the story model to civil litigation and tests a story-mediated model against an unmediated model of jury decision-making"); Nancy Pennington & Reid Hastie, The Story Model for Juror Decision Making, in Inside the Juror: The Psychology of Juror Decision Making 192 (Reid Hastie ed., 1993) (detailing the story model and summarizing empirical studies testing it); Dan Simon, A Third View of the Black Box: Cognitive Coherence in Legal Decision Making, 71 U. Chi. L. Rev. 511, 559–69 (2004) (arguing that factfinders consider evidence holistically rather than atomistically).

402. Frederick, supra note 401, at 296–97 (citations omitted). Compare Reid Hastie, What's the Story? Explanations and Narratives in Civil Jury Decisions, in Civil Juries and Civil Justice 23, 31–32 (Brian H. Bornstein et al. eds., 2008) (expanding the theory to allow for a party's multiple stories), with Michael S. Pardo, The Nature and Purpose of Evidence Theory, 66 Vand. L. Rev. (forthcoming 2013), available at http://ssrn.com/abstract=2060340, at 41 (discussing the theory's difficulties in handling multiple stories).

403. See supra Chapter II-B.

2. Applying the Standard

What this book is *not* about—and this caution is critical—is how the factfinders process the evidence in the first place. Thus, I do not choose a side in the main battlefield of Bayesians versus non-Bayesians over the model for evidence-processing. Although I myself find the psychologists' theories on holistic and rather nonprobabilistic assessment of evidence very well supported, and convincing based on my experience, I realize that ascertaining the actual approach for processing evidence would be an exceedingly difficult endeavor.

In this book, to circumvent such difficult problems, I assume that the factfinders have somehow assessed a hypothesized fact. Then I focus on the step when the factfinders measure the processed proof against the standard of proof—that is, not the *evidence-processing* step but the *standard-of-proof* step.

Previous academic disputes as to standards do not overlap with the disputes over how to assess and analyze evidence.[404] Application of a standard of proof is a substantially different step from evidential inference or argument. Nevertheless, I am not saying that the two steps are entirely distinct in operation, or even in timing. I suspect that the standard of proof influences evidence processing, and also that the processing step will infect the standard's application. I further suspect that full understanding of each step must await simultaneously understanding both steps. Instead, what I am saying is that the two steps are theoretically separable—and that they are separate enough operationally to warrant my separate discussion of the standard-of-proof step, pending further research into the empirical underpinnings.

So, looking only at that standard-of-proof step, how do the factfinders supposedly decide whether the burdened party has established its version of fact strongly enough? The reader's initial reaction could very well be to ask what turns on the answer to my question. I think quite a lot. Most obviously, how the law sets and formulates its standards of proof should depend on the answer. And in practice it matters what the law says about its standards of proof. Finally, the setting and formulating of these standards are certainly not beyond debate: theorists disagree strongly over the nature of the ultimate step of applying the

---

404. See Tillers & Gottfried, supra note 238, at 142 (observing the difference between processing evidence and applying standards of proof); cf. Pardo, supra note 402, at 8 (calling these two stages the micro-level and the macro-level of proof). Two Belgian scholars helpfully distinguished the formulation of beliefs during a "credal" stage (from the Latin for believe) and decisionmaking during the "pignistic" stage (from the Latin for a bet). Philippe Smets & Robert Kennes, The Transferable Belief Model, in Classic Works of the Dempster-Shafer Theory of Belief Functions 693 (Ronald R. Yager & Liping Liu eds., 2008).

standard, as I am trying to demonstrate in this chapter on alternative visions of the standards of proof. The standards therefore seem primed for reconsideration. I therefore want to resolve, based on current knowledge, how the law should set and formulate them.

Law's Stance

The law seems to make the standard-of-proof step probabilistic, even though the law does not so treat the evidence-processing step. The ultimate requirement of applying the standard of proof looks unavoidably like a request for placement on a likelihood scale, albeit on a coarsely gradated and nonnumerical scale of likelihood. But the law's stance raises the question of whether the standard-of-proof step is probabilistic in reality.

I have just finished contending that factfinders do not apply any rigorous probabilistic technique in the processing of evidence, and that they may indeed be wholly nonprobabilistic in that processing. Still, the standard-of-proof step could be probabilistic. There is nothing inconsistent about nonprobabilistic factfinders subsequently fulfilling, at least in some intuitive way, the straightforward probabilistic task of (1) estimating subjective probability, by having looked at the evidence to measure roughly the probability of fact X's existence, and (2) comparing it to a set scale of gradations, such as asking whether the fact is more likely than not or whether it is almost certain.[405] That is to say, a nonprobabilistic model of the evidence-processing step, such as the story model, could be consistent with this more probabilistic approach to the standard-of-proof step.

Performing such a probabilistic standard-of-proof step would be feasible. People are capable of applying, if told effectively to do so, a simple standard of proof imposed by law. Finders of a fact can focus separately on the question of how probable it is that the fact is true. They are quite capable of making gross distinctions in likelihood, such as by distinguishing in application between the preponderance standard and the criminal standard upon proper instructions. No need exists for them to quantify the probability.[406]

I admit that it is easier to imagine a law-trained judge undertaking a deliberate and probabilistic approach to the standard of proof. But I can also pic-

---

405. See Richard D. Friedman, "E" Is for Eclectic: Multiple Perspectives on Evidence, 87 Va. L. Rev. 2029, 2044–46 (2001) (discussing a theory "[c]losely associated with Bayesian probability theory," called Bayesian decision theory, which posits that decisionmaking is "based on the expected value of any course of action").

406. See supra Chapter III.

ture jurors performing this task. First, the judge delivers careful instructions in vaguely probabilistic terms that require the jurors to approach the standard of proof by a separate step. Second, the assignment is really not so demanding, as it requires only an intuitive comparison of rough probability to a coarsely gradated scale. Third, jury deliberations could help immensely in performing the task. We know that jurors often do not reach a decision until the deliberations phase,[407] and that jurors can use the standard of proof as an argument during deliberations.[408] Group discussion could reinforce the duty to relate one's inner conviction to some likelihood in the outside world and could illuminate how to perform the task.[409]

After all, we perform such a task constantly in real life. We all competently apply standards of proof similar to the law's. I might decide to go see a particular movie, rather than stay home, only if going to the movie is more likely than not to deliver increased pleasure. Countless decisions rest on cost minimization, where one decides on a particular route over all available alternatives because it is likely the best way to go, or the happiest. Other decisions may entail a higher standard, because one weighs errors in one direction more heavily than in the other direction. I might decide to marry a particular person only if I am really, really sure that this is the route to go.

Psychology's Contribution

Nevertheless, I shall not simply assume that factfinders follow this probabilistic route of comparing their sensed subjective probability to the coarsely

---

407. See Shari Seidman Diamond, Beyond Fantasy and Nightmare: A Portrait of the Jury, 54 Buff. L. Rev. 717, 758–61 (2006) (discussing the effect of jury deliberations on juror decisionmaking); Hannaford et al., supra note 401, at 640 fig.3 (graphing the percentage of jurors who made up their mind at different stages of a trial and thereby showing that more jurors formed a decision in the deliberations stage than in other stages); David H. Kaye, Valerie P. Hans, B. Michael Dann, Erin Farley & Stephanie Albertson, Statistics in the Jury Box: How Jurors Respond to Mitochondrial DNA Match Probabilities, 4 J. Empirical Legal Stud. 797, 815–18 (2007) (explaining the effect of jury deliberations on a mock criminal trial for robbery in which expert testimony on mitochondrial DNA sequencing was presented).

408. See Robert J. MacCoun & Norbert L. Kerr, Asymmetric Influence in Mock Jury Deliberation: Jurors' Bias for Leniency, 54 J. Personality & Soc. Psychol. 21, 30 (1988) (suggesting that "deliberation tends to amplify the effects of these instructions"); supra text accompanying note 352.

409. On the utilization of standards by a *group* of factfinders, see Allison Orr Larsen, Bargaining Inside the Black Box, 99 Geo. L.J. 1567, 1608 (2011). On the requisite agreement among a group of decisionmakers, such as requiring unanimity on each necessary finding but not on the evidence, grounds, or theories supporting the findings, see Field et al., supra note 10, at 1424–25.

gradated and nonnumerical scale of likelihood. I first would want to hear what the experts have to say.

Yet psychologists have contributed little on the standard-of-proof step. (I am referring here to how the factfinders internally handle the standard of proof. I think that psychology has plenty to teach indirectly about how the law can optimally structure its standards,[410] but that it has less to say about the factfinders' actual application of the standards.) The psychological mechanism for implementing a standard of proof remains to be discovered. It seems safe to say that, for the time being, science has given the law no firm reason to abandon its traditional hope that its intuitive factfinders roughly estimate likelihood and measure the estimate against the standard. I shall eventually develop arguments against abiding by that traditional hope, but psychologists have not helped in building those arguments.

3. Psychological Mechanism of Confidence

As I say, psychologists have done little to extend their insights from the factfinder's processing of proof to the different question of the factfinder's handling of the standard of proof. The only serious work on the latter cognitive process comes from Germany, where an article by Professor Christoph Engel took a step forward by offering a behavioral account of how the factfinder actually implements a given standard.[411] His account is worth considering at this point.

Engel's article initially sets forth the story model of evidence-processing. As already explained, it holds that the factfinder gradually constructs from the evidence the story that makes maximal sense. The factfinder then chooses, among the available decisions, the one that fits best with the story it has constructed. Engel then posits that along the way, and by a similarly automatic or unconscious process, the factfinder generates a level of confidence in the decision by considering the degree of coverage (which means the story accounts for all the evidence), coherence (which means it is internally consistent, plausible with respect to the factfinder's world knowledge, and complete without striking gaps in expected components), and uniqueness (which means the absence of plausible alternative stories). The clearer the view of the case that the chosen story delivers to the factfinder, the more confident the factfinder will be.

---

410. See supra Chapter II-B.
411. Engel, supra note 343.

Engel next turns to the literature on "coherence-based reasoning."[412] He does so primarily to stress the dangers in this unconscious process whereby the factfinder strives to make sense of the evidence. A major danger is the so-called coherence shift: the factfinder, in constructing its narrative, will tend to overvalue consistent evidence and devalue conflicting evidence. This cognitive failing will increase the level of confidence as well as the incidence of errors.

He finally reaches the law on standards of proof. Here is his real contribution, because earlier psychological models, including the story model, failed altogether to give attention to the standard-of-proof step in decision-making. He posits that standards can act to set off a "somatic marker," an emotional trigger that gets the factfinder's juices flowing in a direction that will offset the bias of the coherence shift. In particular, if attached to one of the potential outcomes, the standard can serve as a warning of the undesirability of a false finding in that direction. A high standard of proof makes the factfinder feel more accountable, inclining it to avoid a falsely positive result. "When instructed to convict only if guilt is beyond a reasonable doubt, subjects apply a stricter standard of coverage, coherence, and uniqueness."[413] A low standard of proof such as the preponderance of the evidence leaves the factfinder freer to decide either way. "By contrast, the preponderance-of-the-evidence instructions can be interpreted as a tool for exonerating jury members from personal responsibility. Society is happy with quite a number of materially wrong judgments. Accountability is reduced to avoiding gross errors."[414]

To summarize, one new idea is that the bulk of factfinding is an unconscious process, powerful but dangerous, which generates a level of confidence in connection with which the factfinder could apply the standard of proof. The other new idea is that the only role of the law on standards of proof is to intrude beneficially on the unconscious process by using a high standard to marshal human emotions against cognitive bias. I find this brace of ideas stimulating. But I hesitate to accept either the breadth of Engel's psychological explanation or the narrowness of the role he leaves to law.

---

412. See generally Simon, supra note 401, at 511 (explaining coherence-based reasoning, whereby the factfinder looks for the account with maximal coherence, utilizing a connectionist cognitive architecture in which "the decision-making process progresses bidirectionally," that is, facts determine conclusions while conclusions affect facts in return).

413. Engel, supra note 343, at 461.

414. Id. at 464.

Confidence's Supposed Role in Standards

Recall that the question is how, psychologically speaking, does a factfinder apply a standard of proof to fact *X*, be it a simple fact or a more complexly formulated narrative. What does Engel teach? The short answer is that Engel gave little detail about how the factfinder applies the standard. Instead, he talked mainly of evidence-processing. He mentioned the well-recognized concept of confidence. He then appeared to equate the standard of proof to confidence: "The psychological correlate of the standard of proof is confidence."[415] But he failed to explain how confidence could actually work as a standard. In his attempt to establish a role for psychological confidence in explaining legal standards of proof, his lack of detail enabled him to evade three tough explanatory steps.

First, how does the factfinder generate a usable confidence level, where confidence has the psychological meaning of how sure the factfinder feels about its output? The task, according to prior research, seems to require considering the coverage, coherence, and uniqueness of the factual account. Formulating a confidence level with sufficient clarity to apply the standard of proof would be no easy mental task. Presumably, humans would be performing this complex task on the unconscious level, and so it defies precise explanation. His lack of precision here is therefore understandable.

Second, why should we rely on confidence, which is admittedly a very shaky measure? Here, I suppose, his argument is that humans can do no better with any other alternative measure. But much empirical research shows that confidence has a weak linkage to accuracy.[416] The reasons include that the evidence-providers can easily manipulate the level of confidence as by the order of presentation, that the factfinder's generation of confidence falls subject to all sorts of biases such as the coherence shift's confirmation bias, and that confidence depends on many external factors including self-image. "The confidence we experience as we make a judgment is not a reasoned evaluation of the probability that it is right. Confidence is a feeling, one determined mostly by the coherence of the story and by the ease with which it comes to mind, even when the evidence for the story is sparse and unreliable. The bias toward coherence

---

415. Id. at 458.

416. See generally David Dunning, Self-Insight: Roadblocks and Detours on the Path to Knowing Thyself 6–9, 37–61 (2005) (describing the tendency of people to be overconfident and positing a theory of how we develop self-judgment).

favors overconfidence. An individual who expresses high confidence probably has a good story, which may or may not be true."[417]

Third, and most important, how does the felt level of confidence translate into whether or not the evidence meets the standard of proof? His suggestion is that the standard of proof demands a specific level of confidence from the factfinder in its view on fact X. Thus, a high criminal standard demands great confidence, whereas a preponderance standard would settle for a shaky conclusion. The criminal factfinder and the noncriminal factfinder would both be looking at whether they somehow "believe" the fact is true, but might have to be much more confident in that belief if the case were a criminal one. This attempt at brief description shows that confidence is no self-explanatory tool for handling ambiguous evidence and also that confidence would be an especially clumsy tool for administering a preponderance standard in a legal system choosing to deploy it in pursuit of error-cost minimization.

Relation of Engel's Approach to Confidence Intervals

A surer grasp of Engel's approach comes from comparing it to the just-discussed statistical notion of the confidence interval. In fact, Engel buttresses his bridge between the standard of proof and psychological confidence by a discussion of statistical significance.[418] He claims that under the criminal standard there must be enough evidence to make the factfinder more than ninety-five percent confident that the null hypothesis (not guilty) is not true. Right off the bat, this view presents a couple of difficulties.[419]

First, Engel does not combine a point estimate with a confidence interval, as Neil Cohen did. Engel looks only at the confidence measure. But statistical

---

417. Daniel Kahneman, The Surety of Fools, N.Y. Times, Oct. 23, 2011 (Sunday Magazine), at 30, 32 ("We are prone to think that the world is more regular and predictable than it really is, because our memory automatically and continuously maintains a story about what is going on, and because the rules of memory tend to make that story as coherent as possible and to suppress alternatives. Fast thinking is not prone to doubt."); see Kagehiro, supra note 243, at 194 (observing that former jurors exhibited high confidence in their low comprehension of the standards of proof); supra note 216 and accompanying text.

418. See Engel, supra note 343, at 443–46. He equates his confidence-based standard of proof to statistical significance. "The legal order is in the same position as a statistician." Id. at 441.

419. See David H. Kaye, Statistical Significance and the Burden of Persuasion, Law & Contemp. Probs., Autumn 1983, at 13, 17, 23 & n.47 (appreciating "why one cannot identify a unique level of 'statistical significance' that would correspond to proof satisfying the burden of persuasion appropriate to a given type of case"); D.H. Kaye, Do We Need a Calculus of Weight to Understand Proof Beyond a Reasonable Doubt?, 66 B.U. L. Rev. 657 (1986) (applying his insight specifically).

significance does not necessarily imply a high probability, nor does the absence of statistical significance necessarily imply a low probability. Unacceptable results, particularly of convicting the innocent, will follow unless the criminal standard requires a high estimate of likelihood.[420]

Note that I am not contending that the criminal standard of proof could not contain a confidence measure in addition to, rather than in lieu of, a required likelihood. Maybe the presence of that extra something would explain why Engel intuits that the criminal standard has a subjective element that is lacking in the preponderance standard.[421] Further, the culturally fraught criminal standard of proof and its wordy formulation could convey, on an emotional level, the message to the factfinder's unconscious that there is this need for personal conviction based on confidence in guilt, plus a very high likelihood of guilt.[422] But Engel embraces confidence alone.

Second, it is difficult to express communicatively the preponderance standard in Engel's terms, because it would have to involve bidirectionally equalized significance levels. He does not undertake this task, but instead jumps to conclude that preponderance is very tolerant of error. Because Engel believes that the standard of proof asks only how confident the factfinder is, he naturally concludes that a lower standard, and hence lower confidence, means more errors. He therefore believes that the preponderance standard "tolerates a substantially higher error rate" than the criminal standard.[423]

That view is simply incorrect. Requiring either high confidence or high probability will greatly increase the number of false negatives, while such a strategy limits false positives. Preponderance without a confidence test, although relatively tolerant of the falsely positive type of error, will minimize the expected number of total errors. Rather than tolerating "a substantially higher error rate," it ensures a substantially lower error rate than the criminal standard. Therefore, to reformulate Engel's position into Cohen's more sensi-

---

420. See Simon Blackburn, Think: A Compelling Introduction to Philosophy 224–25 (1999) (criticizing scientific research for inferring correlation and causation from shaky results).

421. See Engel, supra note 343, at 436–37, 441–42, 461–63 (saying that the high standard looks for a personal conviction).

422. See id. at 460–62. Although a confidence-based component of the criminal standard is conceivable, I ultimately contend that the law does not impose one. See infra text accompanying note 587.

423. Engel, supra note 343, at 444 (citing as sole support James Brook, Inevitable Errors: The Preponderance of the Evidence Standard in Civil Litigation, 18 Tulsa L.J. 79, 85 (1982), a fine early article whose point was to defend the preponderance standard on the ground that it was error-minimizing).

ble terms, the signal sent to the factfinder by the preponderance standard is to be dispassionately indifferent as between false negatives and false positives.

These incorrect views lead Engel to conclude that the only proper standard is confidence and, indeed, high confidence. He therefore has to conclude that the lower standards of likelihood that the common law utilizes in noncriminal cases are completely ill-advised.[424]

Confidence's Prescriptive Problems

In any event, this confidence test—even if one could sensibly flesh it out to mean confidence in the required likelihood existing—is not how the standard of proof *should* work. The legal standard of proof wants to ask how likely the fact is, but this confidence measure answers with how sure the factfinder is in its belief. In brief, this sort of confidence is a kind of second-order probability that is supplemental to the first-order probability with which standards of proof should be concerned. Keeping the focus on likelihood is the route to minimizing the expected cost of erroneous decisions.

The first-order/second-order distinction is the key to seeing where Engel went wrong. Confidence need not be a second-order measure. The classic psychological research on confidence aimed at measuring sureness that some proposition was true.[425] Confidence there worked as a kind of first-order probability. But Engel is marrying confidence to the standards of proof, which already ask how true the proposition is. If confidence is to add any meaning, it would have to be measuring sureness in the application of a standard of proof: how sure am I that the evidence meets the standard? Confidence thus becomes a kind of second-order probability.

Any version of an Engel-type confidence measure could at most serve as an imperfect surrogate for first-order probability. It may be that as probability goes up, confidence tends to go up too.[426] But correlation does not mean that the two measures are equivalent. Confidence does not necessarily imply a high probability, nor does the absence of confidence necessarily imply a low prob-

---

424. See infra Chapter VI.

425. See, e.g., Koriat et al., supra note 216.

426. It would at least have been more sensible to assume that as the facts get farther away from the standard of proof's cutting edge, confidence will increase. "Subjects are most confident in their decision if they believe the case to be clear, i.e., if they acquit and subjective probability of guilt is low, or if they convict and subjective probability of guilt is high." Engel, supra note 343, at 461; see also id. at 453.

ability. To focus on confidence is either to focus on the wrong thing or to conflate confidence and probability.[427]

A telling counterexample to the equivalence of confidence and probability comes from a hypothetical that I posed on a recent examination. The disputed fact was which of two dead people had been driving a very negligently crashed car and which was the passenger; the evidence was that the car's owner was driving on departure for the long trip and normally did not let others drive, but the accident scene provided no proof on the driver's identity, and no other proof was available.[428] In that hypothetical, the factfinder could be highly confident that on all available evidence the owner was slightly more likely than not the driver. If the standard of proof turns on estimated likelihood, the factfinder could find liability under a preponderance standard but could not find it beyond a reasonable doubt. Given the factfinder's sky-high confidence, however, an approach that ties the standard of proof exclusively to second-order confidence in probability would, totally unacceptably, conclude the car owner was the driver under the criminal standard for confidence!

My point is that a factfinder could be *very* confident in its determination that the fact was just *slightly* more likely than not, so that confidence and probability are not equivalent. But a confidence theorist, converting the vague definition of confidence into a virtue, might respond that the factfinder in my hypothetical should not be very confident because of the paucity of evidence and the availability of a plausible alternative story: the theorist would prefer to say that we want the factfinder to be confident in the "truth" rather than confident that the evidence shows a fact to be more likely than not. I would rejoin with an altered hypothetical in which there is a mountain of evidence all pointing to the car owner being slightly more likely the driver, including some hypothetical scientific evidence establishing a point estimate of sixty percent. The theorist would presumably still decide against the plaintiff, to keep "confidence" from collapsing into first-order "probability." More generally, I would rejoin that the common-law factfinder is not supposed to hold an unavoidable paucity of evidence against the burdened party, but is instead in such a situation supposed to decide likelihood based on the evidence.

---

427. See D.H. Kaye, Apples and Oranges: Confidence Coefficients and the Burden of Persuasion, 73 Cornell L. Rev. 54, 58 (1987) (exposing neatly, by formal and general proof, the persistent misunderstanding "of the relationship between 'significance' and 'confidence,' on the one hand, and the posterior probability and the burden of persuasion, on the other").

428. For the full hypothetical, see Fredric R. Merrill & Dominick R. Vetri, Problems and Materials on Federal Courts and Civil Procedure 249–53 (1974).

Epistemology provides another route to expose the difference between confidence and probability. The epistemological aim of evidence law is that the factfinder should construct a belief that corresponds to the outside world's truth.[429] Probability is a measure of the chance of that correspondence existing between finding and reality. An alternative, but less desirable, approach would be for the factfinder to seek an evidential construct (or agree to a construct) that coheres with the rest of the world image inside the factfinder's head. Confidence is a measure of the degree of that coherence between the new belief and all the old beliefs. Psychologists might approve of this strategy of looking to confidence, so celebrating the civil law's "subjective" approach over the common law's "objectivism."[430] Such a strategy is understandable, in that people prefer looking to an inside feeling rather than to any outside measure—and so might operationalize an inquiry about probability of a fact by changing it into an inquiry about confidence that the fact obtains—because of their assumption that one has better cognitive access to the state of one's own mind. But philosophers instruct us that the inside world does not provide steadier ground than the outside world.[431] And more to my point, the law has no reason to interest itself in any such internal feeling, which would be irrelevant to societal needs. Instead, society wants the law to pursue an optimal outcome in terms of reality. Accordingly, the law by its standard of proof seeks to force the factfinder, in the final decisional step, to link its inside mental state to the outside real world.

Confidence's Descriptive Difficulties

Regardless of the desirability of looking to probability, it could be that many factfinders *do* look to confidence when called upon to apply a standard of proof in actuality. But given the overall fogginess of the supposed interaction between felt confidence and the standard of proof, it was foreordained that Engel would provide no empirical showing that factfinders interpret standards of proof so as to impose a confidence test. A very valuable series of experiments he conducted measured both subjects' confidence levels in their decision and also their subjective probabilities that the defendant committed the act, showing that the

---

429. See Ronald J. Allen & Brian Leiter, Naturalized Epistemology and the Law of Evidence, 87 Va. L. Rev. 1491, 1497–503 (2001) (explaining empirically based epistemology in the context of the law of evidence).

430. See Engel, supra note 343, at 436–37, 441–42, 461–63. But see infra text accompanying note 608.

431. See Timothy Williamson, Knowledge and Its Limits 94–98, 106–09, 190–93 (2000) (developing an anti-luminosity argument).

two are distinguishable, but it failed to show whether either drives decision.[432] Other research suggests that confidence levels are not driving decision.[433]

The psychological research on confidence may have a lot to teach us about how factfinders process evidence to generate a sense of likelihood. But confidence does not explain the subsequent application of the standard of proof, and there is no evidence that factfinders apply the standard in a way that turns on the level of confidence. It would therefore be unsound to assume that factfinders in applying the standard of proof invoke some unspecified and unproven confidence-based approach, which would be both inaccurate and undesirable to apply. It would be sounder to assume that factfinders do what the law actually and soundly tells them to do: work with their sense of likelihood, even if in some rough and intuitive manner.

Role of Law in the Psychological Process

Whether one accepts as the desirable or the actual manner of implementing the standard of proof either (1) a confidence-based process in the unconscious or (2) the traditional view of a more deliberate (even if largely intuitive) evaluation of rough likelihood, there remains the question of what the law's contribution to the mental process is or should be.

On this question, a psychologist might see the law's formulation of a high standard of proof as merely a way to pull a trigger that on an emotional level conveys to the factfinder's unconscious the message to protect the defendant. The high standard drives home the duty to take factfinding seriously and to demand a considerable feeling of conviction before finding for the burdened party.[434]

Legal academics tend to see the law as trying to do more by its standard of proof than so signal the factfinders. The law expresses a higher standard as a way to inform the factfinder that the burdened party must provide a stronger showing in terms of likelihood. The law also says it actively wants the factfinder

---

432. See supra text accompanying note 361.

433. See Schwartz & Seaman, supra note 228, at 39 (finding that the assigned standard of proof affects decision, but finding no relationship between the experimental subjects' confidence in their decisions either for or against plaintiff and the assigned standard of proof). Indeed, Engel himself seems to be abandoning confidence as an explanation. See Andreas Glöckner & Christoph Engel, Can We Trust Intuitive Jurors? Standards of Proof and the Probative Value of Evidence in Coherence-Based Reasoning, 10 J. Empirical Legal Stud. 230, 241 (2013).

434. Cf. Robert J. MacCoun, The Burden of Social Proof, 119 Psychol. Rev. 345, 347–48, 354–55, 362 (2012) (arguing that standards of proof operate more as a social influence than a decisional one).

to perform in this way. Importantly, the law's standards seem empirically to succeed in their mission of tilting the playing field in the intended direction.

Moreover, the law is obviously trying to accomplish some social aim by adjusting the standard of proof to treat criminal cases differently from civil cases. It applies a high standard to criminal cases, but a lower standard for noncriminal cases, while treating still other cases in a middle way. The law by its tripartite standards of proof consistently tries to minimize expected error costs. Because costs of error obviously differ in different settings, the law is forced to apply multiple standards of proof: preponderance of the evidence, clear and convincing proof, and proof beyond a reasonable doubt. The elevated standards help to avoid the high social costs of false positives, as in convicting the innocent, and the preponderance standard minimizes expected social costs in any setting where false positives are no more costly than false negatives. The law by its chosen standard expresses a preference among the many possible goals of procedure. Importantly, the law appears to be relatively effective in this pursuit too.

C. Legal Academics' Attacks: Other Theories

To summarize, the law's assumption that its intuitive factfinders follow its instructions—that they roughly estimate likelihood and measure the estimate against the given standard—holds up very well against the attacks to date of mathematicians and psychologists.

Accordingly, most legal academics have not embraced a confidence-based approach to standards of proof. They tend instead to split between antiprobabilists and probabilists. A few, however, search for a middle way. They do so by trying to integrate the existing sketchy interdisciplinary insights into the traditionally probabilistic approach.

1. Theoretical Potpourri

Looking for a via media, academics might try further to reconceive probability.[435] The most-cited work, even if not the most-followed, is that of the philosopher L. Jonathan Cohen.[436] He developed, as an alternative to Pascalian

---

435. Compare, e.g., Lea Brilmayer, Second-Order Evidence and Bayesian Logic, 66 B.U. L. Rev. 673 (1986), with, e.g., Craig R. Callen, Commentary, Second-Order Considerations, Weight, Sufficiency and Schema Theory: A Comment on Professor Brilmayer's Theory, 66 B.U. L. Rev. 715 (1986).

436. See Cohen, supra note 230; L. Jonathan Cohen, The Role of Evidential Weight in Criminal Proof, 66 B.U. L. Rev. 635 (1986); see also infra text accompanying note 532.

(or mathematicist) probability, a Baconian (or inductive) theory of probability. In championing inductive methods, Baconian theory looks not only at the evidence presented, but also at the evidence not available. It makes *evidential completeness* a key criterion, and thereby stresses an important concern.

Academics might instead espouse a new way to view traditional formulations of the standards of proof.[437] They try to construe preponderance, clear and convincing, and beyond a reasonable doubt without relying so heavily on probability theory. However, there is not much room here, before slipping into anti-probabilist rejectionism.

2. Relative Plausibility

The most promising of the latter efforts to reimage the factfinder's handling of the standard of proof lies in the insightful relative-plausibility theory of Professor Ron Allen.[438] It draws on the psychological literature. It also shows a nontraditional embrace of *relative judgment* by the factfinder, in preference to humans' weaker skills at absolute judgment of likelihood.[439]

Allen builds on the story model of evidence-processing to produce another theoretical brand of holism. The relative-plausibility theory posits that the factfinder constructs the story (or stories) that the plaintiff is spinning and another story (or stories) that the defendant is spinning. The factfinder then compares the two stories (or collections of stories) and gives victory to the plaintiff if the plaintiff's version is more plausible than the defendant's.[440] This

---

437. E.g., Alex Stein, Foundations of Evidence Law (2005) (arguing for viewing the standards in terms of allocation of risk), reviewed by Ronald J. Allen, 29 Law & Phil. 195 (2010); cf. Alex Stein, An Essay on Uncertainty and Fact-finding in Civil Litigation, with Special Reference to Contract Cases, 48 U. Toronto L.J. 299, 302 (1998) ("Allocation of this risk constitutes a moral rather than epistemological issue.").

438. See Ronald J. Allen & Sarah A. Jehl, Burdens of Persuasion in Civil Cases: Algorithms v. Explanations, 2003 Mich. St. L. Rev. 893, 929–43 (summarizing Allen's previous work on the theory).

439. See Edward K. Cheng, Reconceptualizing the Burden of Proof, 122 Yale L.J. 1254, 1258, 1262 (2013) (arguing that statisticians perform hypothesis testing by comparison, so that "evidence scholars need only let go of their love for $p > 0.5$"; but incorrectly assuming that theory calls for comparing the plaintiff's story to each of the defendant's stories "separately, not simultaneously," and then retreating to an assumption that juries so behave); supra note 187 and infra note 443.

440. The *weight of the evidence* methodology in science is a similar approach, as is the *differential diagnosis* approach in medicine that diagnoses by successively eliminating plausible causes of a medical condition to reveal the best explanation. See Milward v. Acuity Specialty Prods. Grp., Inc., 639 F.3d 11, 18 (1st Cir. 2011) (admitting expert evidence based

choice between alternative competing narratives is largely an ordinal process rather than a cardinal one.

Allen's ordinal comparison cannot easily explain standards of proof higher or lower than preponderance of the evidence.[441] Its more obvious, and admitted,[442] difficulty is that it does not track well what the law tells its factfinders about how to proceed, and it diverges from the law by compelling the nonburdened party to choose and formulate a competing version of the truth. Its more serious difficulty is that by the theory's own assumptions, comparing the plaintiff's story to the defendant's story, rather than to all versions of nonliability, will result in plaintiffs' recovering more often than normatively desirable.[443] Finally, Allen's theory comes with baggage, such as requiring acceptance of the story model.[444]

---

on the weight of the evidence approach: "The scientist must (1) identify an association between an exposure and a disease, (2) consider a range of plausible explanations for the association, (3) rank the rival explanations according to their plausibility, (4) seek additional evidence to separate the more plausible from the less plausible explanations, (5) consider all of the relevant available evidence, and (6) integrate the evidence using professional judgment to come to a conclusion about the best explanation."); Westberry v. Gislaved Gummi AB, 178 F.3d 257 (4th Cir. 1999) (admitting expert evidence based on differential diagnosis). These methods involve consideration and analysis of alternative explanations to get the one that best explains the evidence, a mode of reasoning called *inference to the best explanation*. Allen is drifting in his thinking in this direction. See Ronald J. Allen & Alex Stein, Evidence, Probability, and the Burden of Proof, 55 Ariz. L. Rev. (forthcoming 2013), available at http://ssrn.com/abstract= 2245304; Ronald J. Allen & Michael S. Pardo, Juridical Proof and the Best Explanation, 27 Law & Phil. 223 (2008). However, Larry Laudan, Strange Bedfellows: Inference to the Best Explanation and the Criminal Standard of Proof, 11 Int'l J. Evidence & Proof 292 (2007), powerfully demonstrates that inference to the best explanation holds little additional promise of explaining or illuminating standards of proof.

441. See Friedman, supra note 405, at 2046–47. But cf. Ronald J. Allen, The Nature of Juridical Proof, 13 Cardozo L. Rev. 373, 413 (1991) (attempting to explain the beyond-a-reasonable-doubt standard as not being satisfied if the factfinder "concludes that there is a plausible scenario consistent with innocence," while admitting that the clear-and-convincing standard is "troublesome" under his theory because it seems cardinal); Allen & Leiter, supra note 429, at 1528 (saying that the prosecution must "show that there is no plausible account of innocence").

442. See Ronald J. Allen, Standards of Proof and the Limits of Legal Analysis, http://ssrn.com/abstract=1830344, at 14 (May 3, 2011).

443. See infra note 585. Realization of this difficulty leads some theorists to argue that the aim of the system is not truth but, say, acceptability of decision. See Nesson, supra note 385.

444. See Craig R. Callen, Commentary, Kicking Rocks with Dr. Johnson: A Comment on Professor Allen's Theory, 13 Cardozo L. Rev. 423 (1991).

Important Methodological Note:
Standards of Proof As Being Unique Among Standards of Decision

As should be apparent by now, I am considering the standards of proof as a separate problem to explain. Others have sensed that the standards of proof are unique among standards of decision. That may help to explain why the empirical research concentrates so heavily on the standards of proof. It may also explain why standards of proof so often employ the unique vocabulary of preponderance of the evidence, clear and convincing evidence, and beyond a reasonable doubt, rather than choosing among the usual terms of (1) slightest possibility, (2) reasonable possibility, (3) substantial possibility, (4) equipoise, (5) probability, (6) high probability, and (7) almost certainty.

I shall develop in the next chapter that the unique feature of the standard of proof is that we expect the factfinder to ignore indeterminate, or uncommitted, belief and then compare belief in a fact's truth to belief in its falsity. The other standards of decision do not require these extra steps and so involve only a direct estimation of likelihood. Thus, the probabilist approach suggested above—roughly estimating likelihood and measuring the estimate against the given standard—works adequately for those standards of decision.

For example, we can state the standard of *review* simply in terms of the law's coarsely gradated scale of possibilities and probabilities, without the complications involved in the standard of *proof*. The reason is that we do not expect the judge to retain uncommitted belief in applying a standard of review. The "evidence" for applying the standard is complete. We want from the judge the likelihood of error in the decisionmaker's finding for the winner, with the complement being the likelihood of correctness in finding for the winner.

Similarly, trial-court review of jury decisionmaking involves a measure of the likelihood of error, rather than an attempt at stating the likelihood of truth. For example, reference to a "reasonable" jury in motions for judgment as a matter of law reflects the fact that on such a motion the judge is reviewing the jury's hypothesized application of the standard of proof. The judge's standard of decision turns on whether a jury could not reasonably, or rationally, find for the nonmovant. That is, the movant must show that a verdict for the nonmovant, given the standard of proof, is not reasonably possible.

Other standards of decision involve a measure of the likelihood of effect, as in harmless-error analysis and other trial motions. The decisionmaker can employ the coarsely gradated scale of likelihood.

Or, in the case of police actions, the standards involve a direct measure of the likelihood of truth on that scale. We want the police officer deciding whether to detain and search to measure suspicion on an absolute scale. We do not want the officer to say that he or she has almost no idea of the truth, but the scrap of suspicion outweighs any suggestion of innocence. The officer's suspicion must meet the absolute standard of decision. The law sets the standard low in recognition of the usual unavailability of evidence.

Even some matters that look a lot like the standards of proof seem to operate differently. For example, the prima-facie-showing approach used as a jurisdictional test for overlapping jurisdictional fact[445] is not really a standard of proof. The latter is a type of judicial standard that specifies the level of sureness required of a factfinder to decide that a contested fact exists but does so as part of a proof process to establish what the system will treat as truth. Instead, this prima-facie-showing standard acts as a sort of trigger to open the merits of the case. It involves only a direct estimation of likelihood. It is an ordinary standard of decision.

So, my upcoming refinement of the probabilist approach—challenging that it always entails comparing a sensed subjective probability to the coarsely gradated scale of likelihood—will extend only to the standard of proof. Having surveyed the refinement attempts of others in this chapter on the standard of proof, I shall describe my own refinement in the following chapter.

I am not, however, insisting that the standard of proof *must be* unique, or that logic rather than practice drives its special treatment. A legal system could treat some of the other standards of decision in the manner by which we treat the standard of proof. Consider for example England's treatment of overlapping jurisdictional fact. In a case where jurisdiction under the Brussels Regulation turned on the place of contractual performance, the High Court explained its standard:[446]

> The burden on the proponent of the jurisdiction under Art.5, and the proponent of exclusive jurisdiction under Art.23, is to establish a good arguable case that the requirements of those articles are satisfied. The trial of preliminary issues about matters going to jurisdiction is strongly to be discouraged, so that the necessary good arguable case must be demonstrated at an interim hearing, upon

---

445. See supra Chapter II-C-2.

446. Morley v. Reiter Eng'g GmbH, [2011] EWHC 2798, at ¶¶ 4–7 (Ch.) (declining jurisdiction).

the basis of written evidence which is neither tested by disclosure or cross-examination, to which the ordinary civil standard of proof on balance of probabilities is therefore inappropriate.

In *Konkola Copper Mines plc v Coromin Ltd* [2006] EWCA Civ.5 at para 86, Rix L.J. said that:

> "Thus it is possible that given the flexibility of the 'good arguable case' test, the answer could simply be that the applicant should make out a case which is sufficient in the circumstances to render it just to derogate from the established jurisdiction, but which still remains short of proof on the balance of probabilities. If, therefore, in terms of a provisional argument at an interim stage which properly stops short of a trial mode, the applicant fails to make out such a case, then, because he bears the burden of proof, he fails."

In *Canada Trust Co. v Stolzenberg* (No.2) [1998] 1WLR 547, at 555, Waller L.J. said:

> "It is also right to remember that the 'good arguable case' test, although obviously applicable to the ex parte stage, becomes of most significance at the inter partes stage where two arguments are being weighed in the interlocutory context, which, as I have stressed, must not become a 'trial'. 'Good arguable case' reflects in that context that one side has a much better argument on the material available. It is the concept which the phrase reflects on which it is important to concentrate, i.e. of the court being satisfied or as satisfied as it can be having regard to the limitations which an interlocutory process imposes that factors exist which allow the court to take jurisdiction."

In *Bols Distilleries BV v Superior Yacht Services Ltd* [2007] 1WLR 12, Lord Rodger, giving the judgment of the judicial committee of the Privy Council specifically approved Waller LJ's formulation and, at para 28, continued:

> "In practice, what amounts to a 'good arguable case' depends on what requires to be shown in any particular situation in order to establish jurisdiction. In the present case, as the case law of the Court of Justice emphasises, in order to establish that the usual rule in Art.2(1) is ousted by Art.23(1), the claimants must demonstrate 'clearly and precisely' that the clause conferring jurisdiction on the court was in fact the sub-

ject of consensus between the parties. So, applying the 'good arguable case' standard, the claimants must show that they have a much better argument than the defendants that, on the material available at present, the requirements of form in Art.23(1) are met and that it can be established, clearly and precisely, that the clause conferring jurisdiction on the court was the subject of consensus between the parties."

In that one passage, the High Court starts out with the accepted European law that equates to the U.S. prima-facie-showing approach[447]—but then the High Court unwittingly wanders to a requirement that the proponent have "a much better argument on the material available," which is a comparative approach much like our standard of proof applied on a truncated record. The High Court thereby shows that the prima-facie showing could be treated as a standard of proof, if the system were so minded.

---

447. See Montani v First Dirs. Ltd., [2006] IEHC 92, at ¶21 (H. Ct.) (Ir.) (upholding jurisdiction under Brussels Regulation) ("I am satisfied, equally, that there must be some evidence to ground the plaintiff's claim to jurisdiction. However, I stress that the inquiry which I must make, and I hold that I must make an inquiry, is not a determination of the issues ...."); Bundesgerichtshof [German Federal Court of Justice] Feb. 24, 2005, docket number I ZR 101/02, translated in [2006] I.L. Pr. 7, at ¶9 (upholding jurisdiction under Brussels Regulation) ("It is not relevant to an assessment of jurisdiction whether the defendant actually behaved contrary to the rules of competition. It is sufficient that such conduct has been alleged and cannot be excluded from the outset." (citation omitted)).

Chapter V

Data and Visions as to Standards of Proof Reconciled

Despite all the advances of the "new evidence" scholarship sketched in the last chapter, that new work has tended to remain either too wedded or overly hostile to subjective probabilities for evaluating evidence and Bayes' theorem for combining evidence, and so caused the debates to become "unproductive and sterile."[448] In any event, the debates have left unsolved some troubling problems and paradoxes in our law on proof.

The "New Logic"

One specific diagnosis of this shortcoming is that the new evidence tended to neglect the contemporaneous advances in logic.[449] The new, so-called non-classical logic looks and sounds much like standard logic but refuses to accept some critical assumption.[450] Most commonly, the assumption rejected is that every proposition must either be true or be false, an assumption called the principle of bivalence. But if propositions are not bivalent, so that both P and not$P$ can be true and false to a degree, then one can show that sometimes P equals not$P$—which is a rather disquieting contradiction.[451] Fashioning the new logic thus faced some challenges in its development.

---

448. Peter Tillers, Trial by Mathematics—Reconsidered, 10 Law Probability & Risk 167, 170 (2011). But see Roger C. Park et al., Bayes Wars Redivivus—An Exchange, 8 Int'l Comment. on Evidence iss. 1, art. 1 (2010), available at http://www.bepress.com/ice/vol8/iss1/art1.

449. See Brilmayer, supra note 435, at 688–91 (suggesting that diagnosis); Tillers, supra note 448, at 171 (similar). Some Bayesians, however, were sympathetic to the new logic. See, e.g., David A. Schum, Probability and the Processes of Discovery, Proof, and Choice, 66 B.U. L. Rev. 825, 847–53, 865–69 (1986).

450. See Theodore Sider, Logic for Philosophy 72–73 (2010).

451. See Peter Suber, Non-Contradiction and Excluded Middle, http://www.earlham. edu/~peters/courses/logsys/pnc-pem.htm (1997).

The first move in the new logic of special interest to lawyers relates to and builds on the branch of modern philosophy, beginning with Bertrand Russell's work, that struggled with the problem of vagueness.[452] Work on vagueness addresses matters such as the famed sorites paradox of ancient Greece ("sorites" comes from the Greek word for heap):

- Premise 1: If you start with a billion grains of sand, you have a heap of sand.
- Premise 2: If you remove a single grain, you still have a heap.
- Conclusion: If you repeat the removal again and again until you have one grain of sand left, then you will by logic still have a heap.
- Paradox: But there is no heap. Thus, heap equals non-heap. Two true premises yield an absurd conclusion. (Or—to picture the paradox in another common way—start with Tom Cruise's full head of hair, and begin plucking hairs, yet Tom will by logic never become bald.)

At some point the heap undeniably became a non-heap. Was there a fixed boundary? No, this is not a way out—at least according to most philosophers. A different path taken in the attempt to avoid the paradox leads to the embrace of *many-valued logic*.[453] This form of logic boldly declines the simplification offered by two-valued, or bivalent, logic built on a foundation of true/false with an excluded middle.[454] It instead recognizes partial truths. Both a

---

452. Bertrand Russell, Vagueness, 1 Australasian J. Psychol. & Phil. 84 (1923); see Bertrand Russell, The Philosophy of Logical Atomism, in Logic and Knowledge 175, 180 (Robert Charles Marsh ed., 1956) ("Everything is vague to a degree you do not realize till you have tried to make it precise, and everything precise is so remote from everything that we normally think, that you cannot for a moment suppose that is what we really mean when we say what we think."); see also, e.g., Timothy Williamson, Vagueness (1996); Hartry Field, No Fact of the Matter, 81 Australasian J. Phil. 457 (2003) (countering the Williamson view); Hartry Field, Vagueness, Partial Belief, and Logic, in Meanings and Other Things (G. Ostertag ed., forthcoming 2013), available at http://philosophy.fas.nyu.edu/docs/IO/1158/schiffer2004b.pdf (incorporating ideas similar to fuzzy logic); Hartry Field, Indeterminacy, Degree of Belief, and Excluded Middle, 34 Noûs 1, 20 (2000) (referencing work on belief functions).

453. See generally J.C. Beall & Bas C. van Fraassen, Possibilities and Paradox: An Introduction to Modal and Many-Valued Logic (2003).

454. Another way to see the problems that bivalence entails is to ponder the liar's paradox, represented by a sentence like "This sentence is false." Because classical logic insists that the sentence be either true or false, one inevitably ends in a loop of contradiction and hence paradox. See generally Liars and Heaps (J.C. Beall ed., 2003); Kevin M. Clermont, Foreword: Why Comparative Civil Procedure?, in Kuo-Chang Huang, Introducing Discovery into Civil Law, at xviii n.50 (2003) (mentioning self-contradictory statements).

statement and its opposite can be true to a degree. In other words, sometimes you have neither a heap nor a non-heap, but something that falls in between, with the statement "this is a heap" being both true and not true.[455]

The second interesting elaboration of the new logic involves developments in the field of *imprecise probability*.[456] This field of mathematics provides a useful extension of probability theory whenever information is conflicting or scarce. The approach can work with many-valued logic as well as with two-valued logic. The basic idea is to use interval specifications of probability, with a lower and an upper probability. Despite its name, imprecise probability is more complete and accurate than precise probability in the real world where probabilistic imprecision prevails. In fact, traditional bivalent probability (within which I include the doctrine of random chance as well as the much newer subjective probability) appears as a special case in this theory. The rules associated with traditional probability, except those based on assuming an excluded middle, carry over to imprecise probability.

All this logic may be new, but it has an extended history of forerunners. Threads of many-valued logic have troubled thinkers since before Aristotle embraced bivalence,[457] even if their thoughts found more receptive soil in the East than in the West.[458] Imprecise probability goes back to the nineteenth century.[459] Nevertheless, the new logic has enjoyed a recent flowering, inspired by the development of quantum mechanics and instructed by those just-described advances in philosophy and mathematics.

---

455. The new logic gives a pretty good answer to the sorites paradox itself, by allowing a response to "heap vel non?" in terms of a degree of heapness rather than a yes-or-no response. See Bart Kosko, Fuzzy Thinking: The New Science of Fuzzy Logic 94–97 (1993). But it is not a perfect answer, say the super-sophisticated. See R.M. Sainsbury & Timothy Williamson, Sorites, in A Companion to the Philosophy of Language 458, 475–77 (Bob Hale & Crispin Wright eds., 1997) (saying that it does not do justice to higher-order vagueness); Nicholas J.J. Smith, Fuzzy Logic and Higher-Order Vagueness, in Logical Models of Reasoning with Vague Information (Petr Cintula et al. eds., forthcoming 2013), available at http://www-personal.usyd.edu.au/~njjsmith/papers/SmithFuzLogHOVag.pdf (similar). But see Endicott, supra note 28, at 77–136.

456. See generally Peter Walley, Statistical Reasoning with Imprecise Probabilities (1991). This theory is distinct from confidence intervals.

457. See James F. Brulé, Fuzzy Systems—A Tutorial, http://www.austinlinks.com/Fuzzy/tutorial.html (1998) (recounting the history briefly).

458. See Kosko, supra note 455, at 69–78 (giving an impassioned attack on the West's hostility to many-valued logic, but also fleshing out the historical account).

459. See George Boole, An Investigation of the Laws of Thought on Which Are Founded the Mathematical Theories of Logic and Probabilities (London, Walton and Maberly 1854) (doing the early work); John Maynard Keynes, A Treatise on Probability (1921).

"Fuzzy logic." The particular bloom known as fuzzy logic finds its roots in the seminal 1965 article by Berkeley Professor Lotfi Zadeh.[460] His critical contribution was to use degrees of membership in a fuzzy set running from 1 to 0, in place of strict membership in a *crisp* set classified as yes/no or as either 1 or 0. Yet fuzzy logic is not at all a fuzzy idea.[461] It became a formal system of logic, one that is by now highly developed and hence rather complicated.[462]

I do not mean to suggest that fuzzy logic resolves all the philosophical problems of vagueness (or that it is especially popular with pure philosophers). I am suggesting that fuzzy logic is a very useful tool for some purposes. Of course, it has become so well-known and dominant because of its countless practical applications, especially in the computer business and consumer electronics.[463] But its theory is wonderfully broad, extending easily to degrees of truth. It thereby proves very adaptable in imaging truth just as the law does. Indeed, of the various models for handling uncertainty, fuzzy logic seems to capture best the kinds of uncertainty that most bedevil law.[464] Unsurprisingly, then, writers have previously voiced suspicions that it might relate to legal standards of proof.[465]

Herein, fuzzy logic will provide a handle on how to represent our understandings of likelihood for legal purposes. But it will not be an exclusive tool. "In order to treat different aspects of the same problems, we must therefore apply various theories related to the imprecision of knowledge."[466] Another, compatible theory will function herein as a description of how to make decisions based on those likelihood understandings.

---

460. L.A. Zadeh, Fuzzy Sets, 8 Info. & Control 338 (1965).

461. Zadeh substituted the term "fuzzy" for "vague" more to be provocative than to be descriptive. See Kosko, supra note 455, at 19–20, 142, 145, 148.

462. For an accessible introduction, see Timothy J. Ross & W. Jerry Parkinson, Fuzzy Set Theory, Fuzzy Logic, and Fuzzy Systems, in Fuzzy Logic and Probability Applications 29 (Timothy J. Ross et al. eds., 2002).

463. See Kosko, supra note 455, at 157–200 (describing fuzzy computer systems).

464. See Liu Sifeng, Jeffrey Forrest & Yang Yingjie, A Brief Introduction to Grey Systems Theory, in 2011 IEEE International Conference on Grey Systems and Intelligent Services 1, 6 (2011).

465. See, e.g., Clermont, supra note 225, at 1122 n.36; Schum, supra note 449, at 865–69.

466. Mircea Reghiş & Eugene Roventa, Classical and Fuzzy Concepts in Mathematical Logic and Applications 354 (1998) (referencing Glenn Shafer's work on imperfect reasoning); see David A. Schum, The Evidential Foundations of Probabilistic Reasoning 41, 200–01 (1994) (disbelieving that it is "possible to capture all of this behavioral richness within the confines of any single formal system of probabilities").

"Belief functions." Useful for that purpose is Rutgers Professor Glenn Shafer's imposing elaboration of imprecise probability from 1976.[467] His work on belief functions built a bridge between fuzzy logic and traditional probability, and in the process nicely captured our legal decisionmaking scheme.[468] He used the word "belief" to invoke neither firm knowledge nor some squishy personal feeling, but rather the factfinders' attempt to express their degree of certainty about the state of the real world as represented by the evidence put before them.[469] By allowing for representation of ignorance and indeterminacy of the evidence, he enabled beliefs to express uncertainty, again on a scale running from 1 to 0.[470] Indeed, his theory of belief functions rests on a highly rigorous mathematical base, managing to get quite close to achieving a unified theory of uncertainty.[471]

Belief function theory does not constitute a system of logic, unlike fuzzy logic. Instead, it is a branch of mathematics, like traditional probability.[472] Just as probability serves two-valued logic by handling a kind of uncertainty that the underlying logic system does not otherwise account for, belief function theory delivers mathematical notions that can extend many-valued logic. While probability treats first-order uncertainty about the existence of a fact, belief function notions supplement fuzzy logic by capturing and expressing the indeterminacy resulting from scarce information or conflictive evidence concerning the fact. Shafer's theory is thus similar to a scheme of second-order

---

467. Glenn Shafer, A Mathematical Theory of Evidence (1976) (using "evidence" in a much broader sense than legal evidence), reviewed by Lotfi A. Zadeh, AI Mag., Fall 1984, at 81, 83, available at www.aaai.org/ojs/index.php/aimagazine/article/download/452/388 (treating Shafer's theory as a version of fuzzy logic's possibility theory); Glenn Shafer, Perspectives on the Theory and Practice of Belief Functions, 4 Int'l J. Approximate Reasoning 323 (1990).

468. See Ron A. Shapira, Economic Analysis of the Law of Evidence: A Caveat, 19 Cardozo L. Rev. 1607, 1614 (1998) ("In the legally relevant literature, it was Professor Glenn Shafer who introduced fuzzy measures as appropriate formalizations of epistemic functions.").

469. See Shafer, supra note 391, at 801–04. But cf. David Christensen, Putting Logic in Its Place 12–13, 69 (2004) (saying that some use "belief" as an unqualified assertion of an all-or-nothing state of belief); L. Jonathan Cohen, Should a Jury Say What It Believes or What It Accepts?, 13 Cardozo L. Rev. 465 (1991) (using "belief," for his purposes, in the sense of a passive feeling).

470. For an accessible introduction, see Schum, supra note 466, at 222–43.

471. See Didier Dubois & Henri Prade, A Unified View of Uncertainty Theories (unpublished manuscript Mar. 7, 2012).

472. See Irving M. Copi, Carl Cohen & Kenneth McMahon, Introduction to Logic ch. 14 (14th ed. 2011).

probability,[473] which the preceding chapter showed to have hitherto failed both the statistically minded and psychologically minded as a way to explain standards of proof.

One could view belief in a fact as a black box, starting analysis at the post-belief stage and thereby avoiding my preliminary foray into fuzzy logic: an anti-probabilist might say that the factfinder somehow forms a belief and that the law's concern lies in how the factfinder should handle that belief. However, I view degrees of belief as resting on degrees of certainty, thus necessitating initial consideration of how the factfinder formulates uncertainty.

Relation to Law

My thesis is that a better explanation of what the law does with proof lies in the new logic than in two-valued logic and its probability. The explanation is indeed so good that one must entertain the notion that the law assumed and embraced the tenets of the new logic long before logicians caught up with the law.

Such an embrace by the law would not be that surprising. Law was one of the first of society's endeavors in which things appeared as neither completely true nor completely untrue. Aristotelian two-valued logic did not work for such partial truths. The common law seemed, early and intuitively, to draw many-valued logic from natural language and daily life. At about the same time, in the late eighteenth century, law and nascent probability theory began interacting. That interaction caused the law to become more open about accepting uncertainty. However, traditional probability's inherent appeal prevented observers, unknowingly indoctrinated in classical bivalent logic, from seeing the law's deep logical underpinning for what it really was.[474]

Now the time has come to excavate law's multivalent foundation. The site chosen for excavation is my subject of standards of proof. The prevailing but contested view is that factfinders should determine facts by this line of probabilistic reasoning: although given imperfect evidence, they should ask themselves what they think the chances are that the burdened party would be right if the truth were somehow to become known.[475]

---

473. Cf. Schum, supra note 449, at 868 (distinguishing belief functions from second-order probability).

474. Otherwise, probabilistic theorizing influenced the law only lightly until it began quite recently a major assault. The first effective volleys of that assault on the law arguably were John Kaplan, Decision Theory and the Factfinding Process, 20 Stan. L. Rev. 1065 (1968), and Michael O. Finkelstein & William B. Fairley, A Bayesian Approach to Identification Evidence, 83 Harv. L. Rev. 489 (1970).

475. E.g., Brown v. Bowen, 847 F.2d 342, 345 (7th Cir. 1988) ("the trier of fact rules for the plaintiff if it thinks the chance greater than 0.5 that the plaintiff is in the right").

So, how would fuzzy logic and belief functions better explain standards of proof? The initial step in tying the new logic to law is to admit that the process of proof investigates a world that is not a two-valued world where disputed facts are either true or false. Instead, a good portion of the real world is a vague, imprecise, or many-valued world, where partial truths exist. Or, at the very least, we shall never know whether a disputed fact is certainly true or false. So, the probability of truth is not the only relevant legal question. A second step is to recognize that the factfinder's complexly constructed belief is the more relevant question. We are not as concerned with how certain the factfinder is in a world of random uncertainty, as we are with the degree of truth the factfinder constructs in a world of vague imprecision. The third step builds on the idea that the factfinder will believe facts as true to a degree. We can speak of degrees of belief. Indeed, on the basis of incomplete, inconclusive, ambiguous, dissonant, and untrustworthy evidence, some of the factfinder's belief should remain indeterminate. The output is not a probability, but what a logician would call a nonadditive degree of belief in the fact's existence.[476] In the fourth step, the standard of proof will call on the factfinder to weigh those degrees of belief.

The key distinction between probabilities and degrees of belief is subtle, as attested by the confusion among people discussing proof over the long years. Both systems numerically quantify uncertainty by using numbers in the unit interval $[0,1]$. But the distinction's consequences are not subtle. Degrees of belief handle imprecision better than traditional probability theory, and they better capture the effect of imperfect evidence. Also, abandoning probabilities opens the door to the logicians' powerful tools for handling beliefs: fuzzy logic provides a way to represent imprecise views of the real world, and belief functions give the tools for translating beliefs about facts into legal decisions.

Another justification for so conceptualizing the process of proof is that several significant paradoxes of the law will melt away and die off. Most paradoxes result from the limits on existing frames of reference and tools for analysis. But one can get a handle on many seeming paradoxes of proof by utilizing newly available frameworks and tools. As I say, this chapter's view of proof works so well in this regard that it appears to have been all along the law's intuitive conceptualization of proof. Thus, after decades of reading, thinking, and writing about standards of proof, I feel as if I am finally beginning to understand them.

---

476. See Shapira, supra note 468, at 1613–16 (distinguishing additive from nonadditive). Consequently, a belief and a belief in its negation will most often not add to one. See generally Rolf Haenni, Non-Additive Degrees of Belief, in Degrees of Belief 121 (Franz Huber & Christoph Schmidt-Petri eds., 2009).

Present Project

This chapter will attempt to make good on these grand claims, which I forward tentatively despite my sometimes assertive tone. I shall sequentially discuss the four steps of factfinding: (A) assessing evidence related to a single fact, (B) conjoining separate assessments of different facts, (C) analyzing the resultant beliefs, and (D) applying the standard of proof. At each step, I shall weave in the relevant learning from the new logic and then show how it illuminates a key feature of the law of proof: (1) the gradated scale of likelihood, (2) the conjunction paradox, (3) the burden of production, and (4) the burden of persuasion.

The primary focus of the chapter is descriptive and explanatory, not prescriptive other than by implication. I seek to reveal what the law actually tells its factfinders to do. Over the centuries the law's charge to factfinders has evolved, by a process entailing considerations of both ideal factfinding and also human limitations. I am not championing new ideals or new limitations. My real interest here lies in exposing the proof process that the law has chosen. I believe and shall try to demonstrate that the law has embraced what became the new logic, likely because that version of logic captures the epistemic function of law better than classical logic and probability theory.

A deeper understanding of what the law says about its process of proof could surely lead to more knowledge and to improved law. It could stimulate new research into how factfinders actually decide. It could lead to legal reforms, such as clearer instructions on the standards of proof. But reform is not the present exploratory project. Indeed, one message of this chapter might be that the law currently does a much better job in structuring factfinding than one would guess by reading its many critical commentators.

To encapsulate, the aim of this chapter is to apply the new logic to the law. The conclusion will be that this logic snaps onto the law as a seemingly perfect fit.

A. Expressing Assessments

This part will convey the basics of fuzzy logic, when used as a way to gauge degrees of truth based on assessment of evidence related to a disputed fact. Then, this part will show how the law has seemingly employed fuzzy logic to construct, for use in its standards of decision, a gradated scale of likelihood stretching across the spectrum from the slightest possibility up to virtual certainty.

Important Methodological Note:
Overview of Fuzzy Logic

We tend to forget that our classical logic system rests on the critical assumption of bivalence: every proposition must either be true or be false, taking a value of 1 or 0. The traditional probability theory built on classical logic rests on the same assumption: probability represents the random uncertainty that the proposition is actually true or false, one or the other. The bivalent assumption pays off, in that classical logic turns out to be very useful. But like Euclidean geometry and Newtonian physics, classical logic is a very useful oversimplification that gives wrong answers around the edges of its assumptions.[477] Surprisingly, the law's task of factfinding is on the edge. Classical logic starts delivering wrong answers when the factfinder needs to conjoin elements or aggregate theories.

The cure lies in deploying a more general logic system. Many-valued logic, of which fuzzy logic is the most familiar variant, does not assume bivalence. It allows a proposition to be true to a degree, taking some value between 1 and 0. It uses a degree of membership in a *fuzzy* set running from 1 to 0, in place of *crisp*-set membership classified as yes/no or as either 1 or 0.

Take as an example the set *A* of men from five to seven feet tall. This would be a crisp set. Contrast the set *H* of men somewhere near six feet. It is a fuzzy set. So, not-so-tall-at-all Tom might be completely in set *A* but have a degree of membership in *H* of .25. If a classical probabilist says, "There is a 25% chance that Tom is tall," the speaker supposes that Tom is either tall or not tall, and given imperfect evidence he thinks that it is only 25% likely that Tom would end up in the tall category upon accurate measurement. But when a fuzzy logician says, "Tom's degree of membership within the set of tall men is .25," he means that Tom is not so tall at all. The difference is real and considerable. It derives from the fact that the classical probabilist is assuming bivalence, so that one is tall or not, while the fuzzy logician is speaking of a world where one can be more or less tall. As the evidence improves, the probabilistic chance of not-so-tall-at-all Tom's being tall will drop toward zero, but the fuzzy measure will hold steady. If

---

477. By the way, Euclidean geometry and Newtonian physics, both based on classical logic, break down in the face of general relativity and quantum mechanics, which take down classical logic's bivalence assumption. See Michael Dummett, Is Logic Empirical?, in Truth and Other Enigmas 269 (1978).

someone is interested in Tom's tallness, the fuzzy measure is both more natural to seek and more useful to know.

Fuzzy sets can treat much more than this kind of vagueness. They can handle all kinds of fact subject to proof. Fuzzy logic can treat "event imprecision": was what Tom did blameworthy or, more accurately, to what degree was it blameworthy? But it can also handle "event occurrence": how likely is it that Tom did those acts?

Indeed, it can encompass all of traditional probability, by expressing probability as membership in a set (that is, probability is the degree to which the imagined universe of all tries would belong to the set of successful tries). A resultant virtue is that fuzzy logic can combine measures of event occurrence and event imprecision.

We can thus envisage the fuzzy set of true facts and ask, for a particular proposition, what its degree of membership in that set is. Such degrees of truth turn out to be an excellent way to capture the kinds of uncertainty that most bedevil law.

In sum, degrees of truth constitute an inclusive measure of uncertainty, built right into the fuzzy logic system. This system therefore does not need to append bivalent logic's probability theory for random uncertainty, which is incidentally an add-on that can accurately handle only one of the various kinds of uncertainty that the world throws at us. Still, fuzzy logic ends up looking much like bivalence plus probability, the reason being that a multivalent logic is the more general system. It includes bivalent logic as a special case. That is, a world of black or white is a special, extreme case of the world actually shaded in grays.

Let me interject here that the choice of logic system, classical or fuzzy, does not pivot on "how one views the world." It turns on how one chooses to represent the world. You can represent the world as if it were all black and white. Or, for some purposes, you can reject bivalence in order to represent the world of grays more realistically. The advantage of using the more inclusive and less simplified logic system of multivalence is that it gives more accurate answers in many situations.

1. Zadeh's Fuzzy Logic

a. Basics of Theory

Fuzzy logic envisages degrees of membership in a so-called fuzzy set, with membership valued anywhere between 0 and 1. That is, x's membership in a fuzzy set H of the universe X may take values throughout the whole interval $[0,1]$, rather than just the two values of 0 and 1. This range allows a more complete and accurate expression of membership, when membership is imprecise.

Take as an example the set A of men from five to seven feet tall. This would be a so-called crisp set. Membership of element x in set A, represented by $\chi_A(x)$, is not vague. The values of χ_A can thus be only either 0 or 1, at least if we ignore complications at the nanoscale level.

Contrast the set H of men somewhere near six feet. It is a fuzzy set. Membership of element x in H, represented by $\mu_H(x)$, is imprecise. The values of μ_H may start at 0 for a tiny person, but they soon increase by some function to a value of 1 at precisely six feet, and then start decreasing. The membership function could be linear, but it can take on any shape as appropriate.

So Tom might be completely in set A but have a degree of membership in H of .5. The accompanying graphs represent these two sets, with the graph labeled (a) representing the crisp set of men from five to seven feet tall and with (b) being one representation of the fuzzy set of men somewhere near six feet tall.[478]

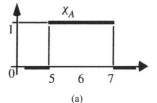

(a)

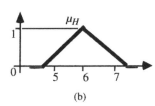

(b)

Linguistics

Important to note is the role of qualifying language in the prior example as a means of expressing membership. *Evaluative linguistic expressions* are words like small, medium, and big; another example is about, roughly, or near, when used in contrast to not-at-all or really. These words may not be a large part of our natural language. Yet, they are an important part of that language. They do a lot of work. People use them all the time to evaluate a thing or situation and to communicate their evaluation. People thereafter use them for classification, decisionmaking, and other tasks.

---

478. The figure comes from Ross & Parkinson, supra note 462, at 30.

People employ *linguistic hedges* to modify their evaluations further. Words such as very or extremely, and fairly or almost, are examples. These words allow people to create a gradated scale for their evaluations. The cross-hatched sketch represents a scale for size, ranging from v_L as the left bound of values that are very small, through medium, and on to v_R as the right bound of values that are very big.[479]

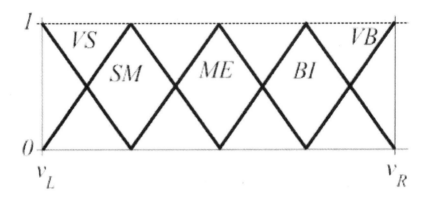

This scale actually consists of three overlapping fuzzy subsets based on the evaluative linguistic expressions of small, medium, and big. Linguistic hedges subdivide the three subsets as suggested by the four smaller triangles at the top, perhaps equating to very small, almost medium, almost big, and very big. The result is seven gradations of meaning.

These seven categories and labels are imprecise. But they are supposed to be, and they work quite well in real life. Fuzzy logic better comports to our understanding of the real world than does classical bivalent logic with its excluded middle. In the real world, boundaries of things often appear indistinct, thus making important or even essential the human ability to process fuzzy information.

Some research suggests that such verbal categories work better than numerical translations.[480] On the one hand, considerable empirical work on the legal standards of proof suggests that factfinders show considerable confusion in comprehending and translating the standards into numerical probabilities, so supporting a verbal approach to standards of proof. On the other hand, not only is such translation unnecessary, but also it might be a wrongheaded step

---

479. The figure comes from Vilém Novák, Modeling with Words, http://www.scholar-pedia.org/article/Modeling_with_words (2008).

480. See Zimmer, supra note 242, at 180.

if fuzzy logic is really in use. Other research indicates that the categories work best as a matter of natural language if they are equally sized and shaped.[481]

Evaluating and Combining Evidence

Fuzzy logic has formal rules for combining likelihoods,[482] once evaluated by one method or another.[483] Moreover, to jump ahead to belief functions, the theoretical work thereon consists mainly of developing tools for combining pieces of evidence to determine a likelihood. In particular, its very prominent Dempster-Shafer rule governs the task.[484] That rule is very complicated, because it abstractly addresses the problem in the most general terms possible (Bayes' theorem turns out to be a special case of that approach).[485] The rule is also quite contested, generating many competitors.[486]

In the end, these formal approaches are clearly not realistic representations of human cognition.[487] Humans do not naturally use rational techniques like

---

481. See id. at 166.

482. See Petr Hajek, Fuzzy Logic, in The Stanford Encyclopedia of Philosophy (Edward N. Zalta ed., 2010), available at http://plato.stanford.edu/archives/fall2010/entries/logic-fuzzy/ (discussing also the varying versions of fuzzy logic).

483. Cf. Brulé, supra note 457 ("The skeptical observer will note that the assignment of values to linguistic meanings (such as 0.90 to 'very') and vice versa, is a most imprecise operation. Fuzzy systems, it should be noted, lay no claim to establishing a formal procedure for assignments at this level; in fact, the only argument for a particular assignment is its intuitive strength. What fuzzy logic does propose is to establish a formal method of operating on these values, once the primitives have been established.").

484. See Glenn Shafer, A Mathematical Theory of Evidence 6, 57–67 (1976) (using orthogonal sums); Jeffrey A. Barnett, Computational Methods for A Mathematical Theory of Evidence, in Classic Works of the Dempster-Shafer Theory of Belief Functions, supra note 404, at 197, 198–204. By the Dempster-Shafer rule,

we construct a belief function to represent the new evidence and combine it with our "prior" belief function—i.e., with the belief function that represents our prior opinions. This method deals symmetrically with the new evidence and the old evidence on which our prior opinions are based: both bodies of evidence are represented by belief functions, and the result of the combination does not depend on which evidence is the old and which is the new.

Shafer, supra, at 25.

485. For a comparison of Bayesian probability judgments and belief functions, see Glenn Shafer & Amos Tversky, Languages and Designs for Probability Judgment, in Classic Works of the Dempster-Shafer Theory of Belief Functions, supra note 404, at 345.

486. See Kari Sentz & Scott Ferson, Combination of Evidence in Dempster-Shafer Theory 17–27 (Sandia Nat'l Labs. 2002), available at http://www.sandia.gov/epistemic/Reports/SAND2002-0835.pdf (describing thirteen alternatives).

487. See Schum, supra note 449, at 852–53 (recounting the lack of empirical support).

the Dempster-Shafer rule any more than they calculate Bayes' theorem; they instead use intuitive techniques in a nonquantitative and approximate fashion. Consequently, as already noted, the law has generally left the combination of related evidence evaluations to its factfinders' instinctive treatment.

Fortunately, fuzzy logic is not dogmatic on the method used to evaluate or combine pieces of evidence that reinforce or undermine each other. It is compatible with the factfinders' combining all the related evidence by any means. Just one possibility would be an instinctive stab at information integration's weighted average, described above.[488] In fact, a weighted-average approach commonly appears in the decisionmaking process of today's fuzzy computer programs.[489]

In any event, my interest in this chapter is not so much the initial eyeing of evidence, but rather the subsequent steps that build to a standard of proof's application. For my purposes, the new logic mainly illuminates a way for people to express their views of the evidence, prior to handling those views according to established rules of reasoning such as conjunction and aggregation. That is, fuzzy logic in this broad sense gives a new and effective way to explore humans' expression of their assessment.[490] And it then opens the door to subjecting those expressions to so-called approximate reasoning, which despite its name can be quite rigorously performed.[491]

I therefore will not pursue fuzzy logic's detailed rules, which constitute the new logic in a narrow sense, nor will I weigh the disputes over the rules' details. Naturally enough, the law built on the intuition that partial truths exist, but it never adopted all the formal complications for combining related evidence evaluations that logicians have refined since 1965. (Still, fuzzy logic could have much to offer in understanding the instinctive factfinder's eyeing of the evidence. For example, fuzzy logic in the broad sense developed below would illuminate the conjunction and aggregation of separate facts within an element of claim or defense.[492] Fuzzy logic in its narrow sense might shed indirect light on the

---

488. See supra text accompanying note 400.

489. See Kosko, supra note 455, at 176–80 (describing its use in fuzzy computer systems).

490. See Novák, supra note 479 ("Mathematical fuzzy logic has two branches: *fuzzy logic in narrow sense* (FLn) and *fuzzy logic in broader sense* (FLb). FLn is a formal fuzzy logic which is a special many-valued logic generalizing classical mathematical logic.... FLb is an extension of FLn which aims at developing a *formal theory of human reasoning*.").

491. See Ronald R. Yager, New Paradigms for Reasoning with Uncertain Information, 13 Cardozo L. Rev. 1005, 1017–24 (1991) (explaining approximate reasoning).

492. This approach would handle the uncertainty of whether an imprecise event occurred at all. See, e.g., Charles M. Yablon, On the Allocation of Burdens of Proof in Corporate Law: An Essay on Fairness and Fuzzy Sets, 13 Cardozo L. Rev. 497 (1991) (treating a transaction's fairness as a fuzzy set, while trying at the same time to account for subjec-

weighing of pieces of evidence that reinforce or undermine each other in determining a fact.[493])

b. Fuzziness Versus Probability

I propose considering the broad version of fuzzy logic as the legal model for human expression of uncertainty, in preference to assuming a probability-based bivalent view. The significance of adopting it for this purpose will become evident upon distinguishing a fuzzy statement from a traditionally probabilistic one.

A few anticipatory words of qualification are in order. I am not an anti-probabilist. I am not arguing against a probabilistic approach if "probabilistic" carries its capacious sense of accepting uncertainty and mathematically accounting for it. I am arguing against traditional probability theory when appended to a bivalent view of the world. What I am proposing is a nontraditional means for expressing uncertainty.

Describing Different Uncertainties

Both a traditionally probabilistic description and a fuzzy one can be accurate statements, but they describe different states. The key distinction is that probability here depends on the existence of a crisply bivalent world. Fuzzy logic accepts an imprecisely multivalent world.

On the one hand, fuzziness is a way, for example, to describe event imprecision. It measures what has occurred—actually, the degree to which the event occurred—which can be vague. On the other hand, probability is a way to describe event occurrence. It can measure the chance that the event will occur or not.

The probability of whether an event occurs in a bivalent world is normally random, as contrasted with the nonrandom uncertainty of vagueness that fuzziness additionally measures. Probability expresses the chance of whether something will occur, all the while knowing it will occur or not on an all-or-

---

tive probability of occurrence); cf. supra note 11 and accompanying text.

493. See John MacFarlane, Fuzzy Epistemicism, in Cuts and Clouds: Vagueness, Its Nature, and Its Logic 438 (Richard Dietz & Sebastiano Moruzzi eds., 2010), available at http://johnmacfarlane.net/fuzzy-epistemicism.pdf, at 22–29. For a specific example, when an inference rests on an inference, their combined likelihood does drop. But their combined likelihood can still nudge up or down the likelihood established by the other evidence, making the inference upon inference relevant to processing all the evidence into an assessment. See Cohen, supra note 230, at 68–73, 267–69 (discussing the difficulty of assessing "inference upon inference").

nothing basis. It is a mathematical supplement to bivalent logic, used to account for that one kind of uncertainty. Fuzziness expresses vagueness as a degree of membership. It builds its inclusive measure of uncertainty right into the basics of the multivalent logic system.

Probability conveys what we know, when in possession of only partial knowledge, about whether an event will occur. With more information, the uncertainty in the probability will dissipate, and if the event's occurrence becomes known the probability itself will morph into a value of 1 or 0. By contrast, fuzziness conveys all the information we have about an event, which most often ends up expressed as a partial truth. More information will increase the fuzziness of set membership, because any crisp lines become harder to maintain. That is, as one acquires more information about the world, one sees a greater need for measuring fuzziness in lieu of bivalent categorization.

Probabilism and fuzziness can describe much more than events. Maybe another example would help. If a probabilist says, "There is a 30% chance that Tom is tall," the speaker supposes that Tom is either tall or not tall, and given imperfect evidence he thinks that it is only 30% likely that Tom would end up in the tall category upon accurate measurement. But when a fuzzy logician says, "Tom's degree of membership within the set of tall men is .30," he means that Tom is not very tall at all. The difference is real and considerable. It derives from the fact that the probabilist is assuming bivalence with an excluded middle, so that one is tall or not, while the fuzzy logician is speaking of a world where one can be more or less tall.

Choosing Between Models

Which model to use, probability or fuzzy logic, depends on what one is trying to describe. If the fact in question is or is assumed to be nonvague, and thus readily distinguishable from its opposite, and its occurrence is subject only to random uncertainty, then probability is appropriate. For a probability example: will I pick a black ball from the urn? However, if the fact is vague, and most facts in the world are vague, fuzzy logic is the way to go. For a fuzzy example: how black is this grayish ball?

The choice between probabilism and fuzziness is important. The kind of statement one can make will depend on the choice made. "You paint one picture of the world if you say there is a 50% chance that an apple sits in the refrigerator. You paint a different picture if you say half an apple sits in the refrigerator."[494] The two models are not fully interchangeable, even though

---

494. Kosko, supra note 455, at 15.

people tend to treat them so. People use probability loosely for any sort of uncertainty. They use it to express fuzziness. But it is inappropriate for that purpose.

I am coming to the choice that the law has made. But at this point, it is natural for the reader to jump to the conclusion that the law in its factfinding usually wants to know if an apple is in the refrigerator, not whether it is half eaten. The court wants to know if Tom was or was not the alleged perpetrator. Just to slow you up, however, I point out that in legal factfinding no one is ever going to be able to look inside the refrigerator. Also, much more significantly, I can pose another example that makes it much less clear which sort of statement the law seeks. Think of a somewhat sloppily drawn circle: is it more appropriate to say (1) there is a 90% probability that it is a perfect circle or (2) it has a .90 membership in the set of circles?[495] An analogy to the circle would be the law's trying to determine fault, when degrees of fault are the reality. But also analogous would be causation, consent, coercion, good faith, intent, and a host of other legal issues. After all, remember that Bertrand Russell saw all of natural language as vague.[496] Many, many legal issues are fuzzy concepts, in that they draw indistinct lines, most often unavoidably—and many of these fuzzy concepts are subjects of proof through litigation.[497]

So, the important choice between probabilism and fuzziness is not an easy one. Bearing on that choice, however, consider three advantages of fuzzy logic.

First, it is more accurate than probability whenever one encounters non-random uncertainty, such as vagueness. It picks up the extra information about vagueness, extra information expressed in natural language but lost upon classification into a crisp set. Recall that fuzziness includes the imprecision of an event, while probability describes only the chance of the event. The precision of probability thus turns out to be a vice rather than a virtue. Probability has

---

495. See id. at 44–46 (using this image).

496. See supra note 452. Others go beyond Russell to contemplate the existence of vague objects. See Michael Morreau, What Vague Objects Are Like, 99 J. Phil. 333 (2002).

497. See Endicott, supra note 28 (arguing that vagueness plays a significant role in law, a role not owing solely to the vagueness of language); Katz, supra note 28, at 139–56 (cataloging examples of vague concepts); Andrei Marmor, Varieties of Vagueness in the Law, http://ssrn.com/abstract=2039076 (Apr. 12, 2012) (articulating the different types of vagueness in law, beyond those entailing only a simple sorites sequence); Scott Soames, Vagueness in the Law, in The Routledge Companion to Philosophy of Law 95 (Andrei Marmor ed., 2012) (bridging between philosophical logic and legal philosophy). Consequently, legal scholars are increasingly using fuzzy logic. See Michael T. Nguyen, Note, The Myth of "Lucky" Patent Verdicts: Improving the Quality of Appellate Review by Incorporating Fuzzy Logic in Jury Verdicts, 59 Hastings L.J. 1257, 1261 (2008) (listing examples).

the advantage of bivalent simplicity, but it will often be misleading in the real world of fuzziness:

> The question is not whether the glass is half empty or half full. If we had to say all or none, the question is, is the glass full or empty. [Either answer is a half-truth.] That is the real state of the world. We don't mean that there is a 50% probability that the glass is full. We mean half a glass. If for some cultural reason we limit what we say to the two bivalent options of all or none, true or false, yes or no, then we pay the price ....[498]

Second, the precision of probability becomes particularly troublesome when trying to gauge a probability resting on imperfect evidence that leaves a lot indeterminate. Fuzzy expression can better handle incomplete, inconclusive, ambiguous, dissonant, and untrustworthy evidence.[499] The degree of membership in a fuzzy set can itself be imprecise or otherwise uncertain, making what is called an *ultrafuzzy* set (or a type-2 fuzzy set, which operates as an initial step toward type-*n* fuzzy sets and operates in contrast to the type-1 fuzzy sets discussed up to here).[500] Basically, representation of the uncertainty in the degree of membership comes out in a third dimension from each degree of membership represented in two dimensions.[501] The third dimension can be projected back into the two dimensions to create the footprint of uncertainty (or FOU, which I mention just to suggest how cool the terminology in this field gets). Of course, the logical operators become much more complicated to account for this third dimension.[502] However, here there is no reason to explore the sophistication of logical operators for ultrafuzzy sets, because the law seems to treat all meas-

---

498. Kosko, supra note 455, at 25–26; see id. at 33 ("At the midpoint you cannot tell a thing from its opposite, just as you cannot tell a half-empty glass from a half-full glass.").

499. See generally Maciej Wygralak, Vaguely Defined Objects (1996).

500. See, e.g., Mark Jablonowski, An Ultra-fuzzy Model of Aggregate Growth in Catastrophic Risk Potentials, 2008 Annual Meeting of the North American Fuzzy Information Processing Society, available at http://ieeexplore.ieee.org/xpl/freeabs_all.jsp?arnumber= 4531214.

501. See Jerry M. Mendel, Type-2 Fuzzy Sets and Systems: An Overview, IEEE Computational Intelligence Mag., Feb. 2007, at 20, available at http://sipi.usc.edu/~mendel/ publications/MENDEL%20CI%20Magazine%202007.pdf.

502. See Nilesh N. Karnik & Jerry M. Mendel, Operations on Type-2 Fuzzy Sets, 122 Fuzzy Sets & Sys. 327 (2001); see also Jerry M. Mendel, Type-2 Fuzzy Sets and Systems: How to Learn About Them, IEEE SMC eNewsl., http://www.my-smc.org/news/back/2009_ 06/SMC-Mendel.html (June 2009); MacFarlane, supra note 493, at 28 n.13.

ures of truth simply as type-1 fuzzy sets and instead roughly accounts for other second-order-like uncertainty through belief functions.

Third, another advantage of fuzzy logic is that it is the more inclusive system. Many-valued logic includes two-valued logic. Being a form of many-valued logic, fuzzy logic neither requires nor forbids that anything be of an on-or-off nature, true or false, completely inside a set or outside that set. The two-valued logic of probability demands the existence of sets with strict membership classifications exclusively, an in-or-out characteristic symbolized respectively by values of either 1 or 0. But those crisp sets are a kind among fuzzy sets. Bivalence is a special case of multivalent logic. The world of black or white is a special, extreme case of the world shaded in grays.

In many situations, a single fact is subject both to vagueness and to occurrence uncertainty. Although probability theory can say little on how to reason about things that are not completely true or false, fuzzy logic can handle the more mixed and complex situations. For an example back on earth of what might be called "normative" uncertainty,[503] it might be that there was a .70 blameworthy act. Or while the act was completely blameworthy, there was a 70% chance that it occurred, creating "factual" uncertainty. But what about a 70% chance of a .70 degree of fault? Then, the two kinds of uncertainty need to be integrated.[504]

Moreover, a decision may rest on a number of facts, some of which demonstrate only occurrence uncertainty, while others show some vagueness as well. The need in decisionmaking to combine these factfindings counsels the use of one logic system, because "we cannot coherently countenance two different kinds of degree of belief."[505] To combine the facts, a common currency is necessary.

The inclusiveness of fuzzy logic suggests its use for each fact and for combining evaluations of different facts. Indeed, it can effortlessly express even a traditional probability as membership in a set, that is, probability is the de-

---

503. See Ariel Porat & Eric A. Posner, Aggregation and Law, 122 Yale L.J. 2 (2012) (coining the terms "normative aggregation" and "factual aggregation"). Philosophers had already plowed this ground, distinguishing a "vagueness-related partial belief" from a "standard uncertainty-related partial belief" or, better, taking-to-be-partially-true from partially-taking-to-be-true. See MacFarlane, supra note 493, at 15–18.

504. See supra note 493 and accompanying text.

505. Nicholas J.J. Smith, Degree of Belief Is Expected Truth Value, in Cuts and Clouds, supra note 493, at 491, 491, available at http://www-personal.usyd.edu.au/~njjsmith/papers/smith-degrees-belief-truth.pdf (cataloging the difficulties that would come from entertaining both probabilities and degrees of belief, when the two underlying logic systems employ different operators).

gree to which the imagined universe of all tests would belong to the set of positive results.[506] This compatibility is essential. It allows easy combination of a randomly uncertain set with an imprecise set, in accordance with fuzzy logical operators.

In sum, fuzzy logic provides the needed common currency. It can handle all kinds of facts, and can do so much better than probability. The legal reader cannot dodge my argument by concluding that fuzziness reaches, if any, only some kinds of facts. Instead, fuzziness handles facts exhibiting random uncertainty as well as those showing vagueness, facts embodying both factual uncertainty and normative uncertainty, and factual events and legal constructs.[507] Law could choose fuzziness as its sole mode of measurement.

c. The Law's Choice

My concern in this chapter is primarily to unearth what the law actually tells its factfinders to do. Even if in the end it remains up in the air as to which model, fuzzy logic or probability, would be the superior vehicle for the legal proof process, my real interest here is in which model the law actually chose. This is a descriptive rather than prescriptive question: which model better expresses the law's scale of likelihood of truth, which better explains the legal treatment of the well-known conjunction paradox, and which better effectuates the burdens of production and persuasion? On the descriptive question, I believe and shall try to demonstrate that the law embraces fuzzy logic.

In its instructions to factfinders, the law does not explicitly distinguish between probabilism and fuzziness. It instead speaks in terms of a common currency, mixing the questions of whether and how much an event occurred. Whether the issue is occurrence or blameworthiness of an act, the law deals only in degrees of truth. Asking for a single measure of uncertainty makes sense only in fuzzy logic, because it accounts for the various kinds of uncertainty. Relying instead on the mathematical supplement of the probability calculus would be so awkward and incomplete as to be nonsensible. I therefore submit that the law treats all measures of truth simply as fuzzy sets.

I would further submit, if pressed, that the reason for the law's choosing to speak in terms of degrees of membership is that they behave more appropriately than probabilities in a world filled with various kinds of uncer-

---

506. See Kosko, supra note 455, at 55–64 (calling this set "the whole in the part").

507. See Mark Colyvan, Is Probability the Only Coherent Approach to Uncertainty?, 28 Risk Analysis 645 (2008); Bart Kosko, Fuzziness vs. Probability, 17 Int'l J. Gen. Sys. 211 (1990).

tainty.[508] Imagine that the law is trying to determine if Tom was at fault. A number of features of this issue of fault indicate that the actual and better approach for law is fuzzy logic. First, we shall never know the answer as a 1 or a 0. Therefore, we should not be worrying too much about specifying the chance of a 1 turning up. Second, ours is not a crisp world, so the law is often not interested in establishing that the truth value of an element is a 1 or a 0. Instead, it wants to ascertain whether the element has a sufficient truth value for the purpose at hand. Third, any conclusion based on evidence is necessarily uncertain for five reasons: "Our evidence is 'never complete', is usually 'inconclusive', is frequently 'ambiguous', is commonly 'dissonant' to some degree and comes to us from 'sources having imperfect credibility.'"[509] Fourth, the factfinder might entertain thoughts of both randomness and vagueness, that is, both a sense that Tom was .70 likely to have been completely at fault and also that Tom was at fault to a .70 degree. Fifth, given that some issues in a case might demand the more inclusive measure of imprecision, logical coherency requires that the same type of measure apply to every issue.

I am not calling for a major shift in conceiving the standards of proof. After all, fuzzy logic is not antithetical to classical logic. All I am saying is that the law appreciates that more kinds of uncertainty than that of event occurrence are at play. The law therefore uses a logic appropriate to the task. Fuzzy logic moves its measure of uncertainties into the basics of the system, rather than leaving their treatment to some sort of afterthought. That nonradical move does not call for an overhaul of legal language or imagery, and it even makes many legal consequences easier to comprehend.

Indeed, I am not even saying that if we recognize the role of multivalence, we need to abandon the probability idiom. It can be quite expressive in the realm of standards of proof. Nonetheless, when plunging to the depths, we need always to remember that the legal foundation is ultimately fuzzy in nature. Here is a last clever image to make the point as to what the law deals in:

> Suppose you had been in the desert for a week without drink and you came upon two bottles marked K and M [and marked, respectively, with a .91 membership in the fuzzy set of potable liquids and a .91 probability of being a potable liquid]. Confronted with this pair of

---

508. See Shapira, supra note 468, at 1614–15 (arguing for the superiority of degrees of belief).

509. Schum, supra note 398, at 216 (quoting Rudolf Carnap, An Introduction to the Philosophy of Science 51 (Martin Gardner ed., 1966)).

bottles, and given that you must drink from the one that you chose, which would you choose to drink from? Most people, when presented with this experiment, immediately see that while K could contain, say, swamp water, it would not (discounting the possibility of a Machiavellian fuzzy modeler) contain liquids such as hydrochloric acid. That is, membership of 0.91 means that the contents of K are fairly similar to perfectly potable liquids, e.g. pure water. On the other hand, the probability that M is potable "equals 0.91" means that over a long run of experiments, the contents of M are expected to be potable in about 91% of the trials. In the other 9% the contents will be deadly— about 1 chance in 10. Thus, most subjects will opt for a chance to drink swamp water.[510]

2. Legal Application: Gradated Likelihood

The way to apply fuzzy logic to factfinding in the legal system is to envisage the fuzzy set of true facts and ask for x, as a particular element of a claim or defense, what is its degree of membership in that set. Recall that membership represents how much a variable is in the set. The membership here will be partial. It will tell how true the factfinder finds the element to be. One could express $\mu(x)$ as truth(x). Membership thereby creates degrees of truth.[511]

While this membership will turn on likelihood of truth in a sense, it is in a sense different from the classical understanding of the factfinder's subjective probability that the element is true. Such subjective probability crisply deals with the probability of x being in actuality 1, while fuzzy logic vaguely deals with a degree of truth. The degrees of truth range from 0 to 1 in fuzzy theory, but in practice they find expression most often as words, or evaluative linguistic variables that use linguistic hedges to cover all the intervals of partial truth between completely false and completely true.

---

510. Bogdan R. Kosanovic, Fuzziness and Probability, http://www.neuronet.pitt.edu/ ~bogdan/research/fuzzy/fvsp/fvsp.html (Feb. 8, 1995) (emphasis omitted). In early 2012 some congressional offices received threatening letters containing a suspicious powder. The letter promised additional mailings and said there was a "10 percent chance that you have just been exposed to a lethal pathogen." Andrew Taylor, Congressional Offices Receive Mailed Threats, http://news.yahoo.com/congressional-offices-receive-mailed-threats-220538717.html (Feb. 23, 2012).

511. See Richard Bellman & Magnus Giertz, On the Analytic Formalism of the Theory of Fuzzy Sets, 5 Info. Sci. 149, 151–52 (1973) (showing the equivalence between fuzzy sets and fuzzy statements).

Fuzzy logic's schema well describes the law's scale of likelihood that I have previously documented.[512] For a significant example, the law today limits its choice to no more than three standards of proof—preponderance, clearly convincing, and beyond a reasonable doubt—from among the infinite range of probabilities stretching from slightly probable to virtual certainty; the law did not always recognize this limitation, but with time the law has acknowledged that the conceivable spectrum of standards coalesced irresistibly into three. For another example, the harmless-error doctrine frequently invokes one of three low possibilities of an error's effect on outcome. More generally, the law's standards of decision invoke a coarsely gradated scale of likelihood stretching across the broader spectrum from the slightest possibility up to virtual certainty.

The reason for this coarse gradation partly lies in the cognitive psychology literature. Cognitive limitations leave humans able only weakly to judge likelihood on any sort of scale. Studies of humans' weak absolute judgment, restricted short-term memory, and use of biased heuristics all support the limited capability of humankind. Those studies suggest that a step-like scale of intervals accords with how humans naturally process such information: judged likelihood customarily finds expression in terms of a very small set of broad verbal categories. Today, in all the probability and logic theories, there seems to be an emerging sense of the need to confront the limited precision of humans in gradating their beliefs.[513] It might therefore be more psychologically feasible to ask legal factfinders for an approximate degree of truth than for their precise view of probability.

Perhaps the law, by an intuitive but wise reconciliation with cognitive limitations, has already optimized by conforming to the coarsely gradated scale of likelihood already in people's customary use. The law usually does, realistically can, and optimally should recognize only seven categories of uncertainty and imprecision in its standards of decision: (1) slightest possibility, (2) reasonable possibility, (3) substantial possibility, (4) equipoise, (5) probability, (6) high probability, and (7) almost certainty. First, this book's description of seemingly diverse legal doctrines demonstrated that standards of decision tend to fall, often in groups of three, into the seven customary categories. Second, a review of cognitive psychology revealed humans to be "boundedly rational." Third, combining the observation with the science suggested that the system-

---

512. See supra Chapter II.

513. See Terrence L. Fine, [The Axioms of Subjective Probability]: Comment, 1 Stat. Sci. 352, 353 (1986).

atic structure of the standards reflects the law's reconciliation with those cognitive limitations. For those reasons, I espouse viewing the seven gradations as degrees of truth in the broad sense of fuzzy logic (although I would redraw the separate gradations to be equally sized and shaped).

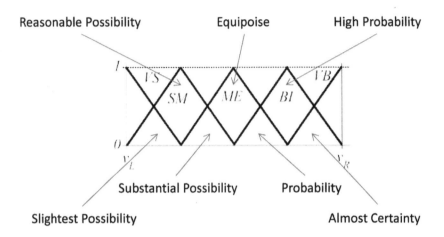

Thus, fuzzy logic accommodates the cognitive limitations of humans. Fuzzy logic offers a rich approach to elaborating the law's gradated scale of likelihood. Its real value, however, is that it captures the epistemic function in law better than probability. We want to know the belief in truth of a factual element, not the chance that the element will turn out to be 100% true.

B. Conjoining Assessments

This part will explain that probability's product rule for conjoined events does not apply in fuzzy logic. Then, this part will show how the law relies on fuzzy logic when it applies the standard of proof to each element of claims or defenses, without worrying about applying the standard to conjoined elements.

To follow this part, it is first necessary to step back and consider the nature of logic systems. Unbeknownst to us lay people, the way logic works is to start by assuming a basic representation of the world, then specify a small group of operators that suffices to generate a complete and internally sound system, and finally test the system to see if it makes sense in our world and hence can be useful. Logic is therefore more of an art, around the edges, than the laity would guess.

First, as to assumptions: One must begin with "genuine logical truths," or basic assumptions about the world.[514] For my purposes, the key assumption of classical logic is that every proposition must either be true or be false. This key assumption of bivalence, rather hidden from view, has a huge impact on a very practical problem that the law must confront: conjoining the effect of evidence. Because the impact derives from the effect of an underlying assumption, exposure of that impact will not involve merely pointing out some obviously mistaken logical step. Exposure will necessarily be the more subtle endeavor of tracing assumptions.

Second, as to operators: One constructs any system of logic by stipulating a small but adequate number of logical operators, or connectives, such as set theory's intersection (or propositional logic's conjunction or ∧ or AND), union (or disjunction or ∨ or OR), and negation (or ~ or ¬ or NOT). They are the premises that generate an internally sound and complete system.[515]

Third, as to testing: One can generate a logic system from any adequate group of operators. It will be internally sound on a formal level, but it will not be useful unless the operators make sense in our world as we understand it. What makes sense is the philosophical question of what things constitute "genuine logical consequences."[516] But philosophers have to punt on this question, saying that operators make sense if their consequences seem to make sense to us.

1. Fuzzy Operators

a. Minimum and Maximum

The power of the fuzzy conceptualization becomes more obvious when one considers the combination rules of fuzzy logic. These can become quite complicated, but for our purposes those of special interest are the most basic fuzzy operators, which we need to compare to the classical versions.

Classical Logic's Operators

This bivalent system, which recognizes only the two values of true and false, stipulates the following functions for conjunction and disjunction:

truth(x AND y) = 1 if both x and y are true, but 0 otherwise
truth(x OR y) = 1 if either x or y is true, but 0 otherwise

---

514. See Sider, supra note 450, at 1–2, 6–11.
515. See id. at 25, 35–37, 67–80 (showing also that in going beyond two-valued logic, one needs to stipulate the implication operator as well).
516. See id. at 1–2, 6–11.

Another way to state these two functions is this:

$$truth(x \text{ AND } y) = minimum(truth(x), truth(y))$$
$$truth(x \text{ OR } y) = maximum(truth(x), truth(y))$$

A different format in which to stipulate an operator is by truth table. The one for negation indicates that the negative of 1 is 0, and vice versa:

~	
1	0
0	1

All things bivalently logical flow from these three stipulations.

Fuzzy Logic's Operators

Those three operators for fuzzy logic are just the same, except that they must extend to give results for values between 0 and 1.[517] Thus, the AND and OR functions work this way for sets in fuzzy logic when x and y can take any value from 0 to 1:[518]

$$truth(x \text{ AND } y) = minimum(truth(x), truth(y))$$
$$truth(x \text{ OR } y) = maximum(truth(x), truth(y))$$

So, let X be the universe, and let A be one fuzzy set and B be another fuzzy set in the universe. The two sets might be independent, in the sense that the degree of membership in one set has no effect on the degree of membership in the other set, but they need not be. Designate the membership of element x in A as $truth(x)$, and the membership of element y in B as $truth(y)$. Then, the truth of the conjunction of x and y equals the smaller of the truth of x and the truth of y.

For an example involving a common element, let X be the universe of men, and let A be the set of tall men and B be the assumedly independent set of smart

---

517. See Brian R. Gaines, Fuzzy and Probability Uncertainty Logics, 38 Info. & Control 154 (1978) (showing that the operators for fuzzy logic and probability theory are the same until one adds the assumption of the excluded middle).

518. For elaborations of fuzzy intersection and union, see Radim Bělohlávek, George J. Klir, Harold W. Lewis III & Eileen Way, On the Capability of Fuzzy Set Theory to Represent Concepts, 31 Int'l J. Gen. Sys. 569, 575 (2002); Ronald R. Yager, Connectives and Quantifiers in Fuzzy Sets, 40 Fuzzy Sets & Sys. 39 (1991).

men. So, if Tom is a .30 member of *A* and a .40 member of *B*, then Tom is a .30 member of the set of tall and smart men. The intersecting set becomes smaller, but Tom's degree of membership in it does not decrease below the lower of his tallness and smartness levels. In other words, the truth value for the intersection would be the minimum value of the two memberships in *A* and *B*.

Fuzzy logic injects set theory's mathematical techniques into propositional logic. The accompanying figure may help to visualize the intersection or conjunction function, the so-called MIN operator, by indicating the shaded intersection of the two sets, where μ gives the degree of membership of an element in the fuzzy set.[519] Along the *x*-axis, for any *z* that falls in the intersection, the degree of membership therein will be the degree of membership in *A* or *B*, whichever has the lower membership line at that point *z*.

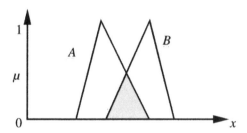

Justifying Fuzzy Operators

There are several signs that fuzzy logic makes sense. To begin, fuzzy logic does not produce nonsensical results. For example:

> The simplest and most fundamental qualitative law of probability is the *extension rule*: If the extension of *A* includes the extension of *B* (i.e., $A \supset B$), then $P(A) \geq P(B)$. Because the set of possibilities associated with a conjunction *A*&*B* is included in the set of possibilities associated with *B*, the same principle can also be expressed by the conjunction rule $P(A\&B) \leq P(B)$: A conjunction cannot be more prob-

---

519. The figure comes from Ross & Parkinson, supra note 462, at 33; see also id. at 34–36 (extending the MIN operator from a common element's membership in multiple fuzzy sets to the relationship of *x*'s and *y*'s memberships in different fuzzy sets, which would change the image into a mapping by Cartesian product of the multiple memberships onto the same interval of [0,1]).

able than one of its constituents. This rule holds regardless of whether
A and *B* are independent .... Furthermore, it applies not only to the
standard probability calculus, but also to nonstandard models ....[520]

The MIN rule in fuzzy logic conforms to the extension rule by setting the conjoined probability of elements, whether or not independent, as equal to the
least likely element.

More than that, the MIN rule affirmatively makes sense as the way for conjoining
multivalent values. Tom really appears to be a .30 member of the set of tall and
smart men. It is therefore the way to combine truth degrees more generally.[521]

Furthermore, fuzzy logic is not wildly different from classical logic. It does
not require a radical overhaul of worldview. The choice posed is between (1)
fuzzy logic and (2) bivalent logic with its probability overlay. In essence, fuzzy

---

520. Tversky & Kahneman, supra note 213, at 19, 20 (emphasis omitted).

521. The proof would go as follows. Reasoning backward from what is necessary for a
system to make sense,

$$x \wedge x = x \quad (1)$$
$$x \vee x = x \quad (2)$$
$$x \wedge y \leq x \quad (3)$$
$$x \vee y \geq x \quad (4)$$

while associativity and distributivity need to prevail as well,

$$(x \wedge y) \wedge z = x \wedge (y \wedge z) \quad (5)$$
$$x \vee (y \wedge z) = (x \vee y) \wedge (y \vee z) \quad (6).$$

Then, using (2) and (3),

$$x \wedge (x \vee y) = (x \vee x) \wedge (x \vee y) \leq x$$

and, using (4) and (6),

$$x \vee (x \wedge y) = (x \vee x) \wedge (x \vee y) \geq x$$

and their having been shown to be equal, and both $\leq$ and $\geq x$,

$$x \wedge (x \vee y) = x \vee (x \wedge y) = x \quad (7).$$

Now, designate *y* as the lesser or equal of the two truth values *x* and *y*. There should be a *z*
such that $x \wedge z = y$, which allows the final conversions with the use of (7) and of (5) and
(1), respectively:

$$x \vee y = x \vee (x \wedge z) = x = \text{MAX}(x, y)$$
$$x \wedge y = x \wedge (x \wedge z) = (x \wedge x) \wedge z = x \wedge z = y = \text{MIN}(x, y).$$

See Bellman & Giertz, supra note 511, at 152–55 (proving that the MIN and MAX operators "are not only natural, but under quite reasonable assumptions the only ones possible"
for fuzzy sets); D. Dubois & H. Prade, A Review of Fuzzy Set Aggregation Connectives, 36
Info. Sci. 85, 89–92 (1985) (showing that conjoined membership must of course be less
than or equal to the minimum membership, but that accepting a value less than that minimum would produce nonsensical results). Thus, although a multivalent system could theoretically adopt a different operator for conjunction, the MIN rule is the one that best fits
with other reasonable assumptions to make maximal sense.

logic says only that we should account for the undeniable imprecision of the world by altering the system's operators, rather than by some awkward after-thought squeezed into the probability calculus.

At bottom, though, fuzzy logicians are arguing that their logic is different because it makes more sense than classical logic. "There are many reasons to get interested in nonclassical logic, but one exciting one is the belief that classical logic is *wrong*—that it provides an inadequate model of (genuine) logical truth and logical consequence."[522] The argument is that classical logic, by assuming the principle of bivalence, assumes one too many logical truths. It assumes a world where everything appears as on the left in the accompanying figure.[523]

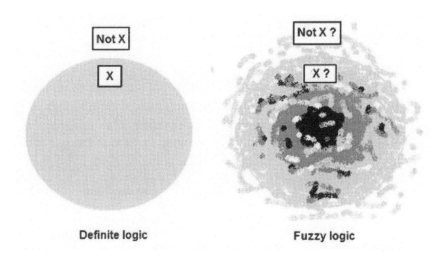

Definite logic   Fuzzy logic

b. Product Rule Contrasted

The reader should nevertheless be sensing that something odd is afoot. Indeed, this is where most readers will abandon ship. After all, the probability operation for AND is multiplication of the probabilities of independent events.[524] But fuzzy logic tells us to apply the MIN operator even for independent events.

---

522. Sider, supra note 450, at 72.

523. The figure comes from 3 Avi Sion, Logical and Spiritual Reflections ch. 4, http://www.thelogician.net/6_reflect/6_Book_3/6c_chapter_04.htm (2008).

524. For interdependent events, the probability operation for conjunction is P(A) multiplied by P(B|A). Meanwhile, fuzzy logic tells us still to apply the MIN operator, which is so much easier to comprehend and apply.

Applying Different Rules

Think of a room with ten men each 5'6" tall. We might think of each as .30 tall. What would we term the tallness of the ten men as a group? It would still be .30 by the MIN operator. It would not be .30^{10}, a very tiny number yielded by the product rule to reflect the remote chance of them all turning out to be truly tall.

Now if the room has ten men, with three "short" men 5'6" or below and three "dumb" men, then one man picked at random has a .09 chance of being both short and dumb, assuming independence. So, here the product rule applies.

That is, the probability operator is not inconsistent with the fuzzy operator. The two just contemplate different contexts. Indeed, the two are fundamentally consistent, because traditional probability is a special case of fuzzy logic's more general theory of uncertainty. So, it is not that one of these theories of uncertainty is correct and the other is wrong. It is that one theory can include the other.

For random uncertainty in an ascertainably bivalent world, the probability operator will give the right answer, but so would the MIN rule. First, if the world were crisp, and x and y were known to be either true = 1 or false = 0, then their conjunction would be either 1 if both were true or 0 if not. In this narrow setting, the probability and fuzzy operators are equivalent. That is, the product rule would be no different from the MIN operator: truth(x)·truth(y) = minimum(truth(x), truth(y)). Second, in either logic system, the chance of complete conjunction of currently unknown variables—that x and y will both turn out independently to be 1, or completely true—will be the product of their individual probabilities.[525] Say the respective probabilities are 50% and 40%. But under the rigorous assumption of an ascertainably bivalent world, the degrees of membership are different. The membership of x is not .5. It is 1 in half the cases and 0 in the other half, while y so splits in two-fifths and three-fifths of the cases. Then, $x = 1$ in half of the two-fifths in which $y = 1$, and only in that 20% of the cases will the MIN rule yield truth(x AND y) = 1.

Remember that there are multiple kinds of uncertainty, including the indeterminacy resulting from scarce information or conflicting evidence and also the uncertainty characterized as either vagueness or randomness. If one tries to deal with the variedly uncertain real world, the more inclusive approach to conjunction becomes appropriate. In a fuzzy world, the product rule retreats to a specialized role, applying only when the independent values of x and y happen to be randomly uncertain without being vague. The product of prob-

---

525. The product will make most sense in connection with frequentist probabilities. Still, the uncertainty could concern unique events, because one can speak of the subjective probability of x and y turning out to be either true = 1 or false = 0.

abilities gives the chance of things, which can take only a value of 1 or 0, coming up as 1 in two independent trials under conditions of random uncertainty. The conjunction of degrees of truth is telling you how much you believe two statements put together. The latter is more general.

In sum, the product rule is not a feature only of classical logic. Both under classical logic with a probability overlay and under fuzzy logic, the MIN rule will reduce to the product rule—if one assumes bivalence and then adds an assumption of random independence. But the product rule will prevail under either system only if the elements under consideration are always ascertainable to be completely true or completely false. Thus, the question becomes whether one should so assume bivalence.

Choosing Between Rules

Because both the product rule and the MIN operator can give correct, but sometimes different, answers, they must be giving answers to different questions or, rather, questions resting on different assumptions. The product of probabilities is answering a question different from what the conjunction of degrees of truth is answering. The nature of the desired answer will determine the correct question to ask and, hence, whether the product rule or the MIN operator is appropriate to apply.

First, as a thought exercise, ponder which is the correct question to ask when one wants to know if Tom is tall and smart. Begin with the two membership statements given above—Tom is a .30 member of A and a .40 member of B. Those numbers mean something like "Tom is not so tall" and "Tom is not so smart."

The fuzzy combination would yield: "Because Tom is not so tall and Tom is not so smart, Tom is not such a tall, smart man." The MIN operator yields a .30 belief in that intersection. The traditionally probabilistic calculation, however, would yield: "Because Tom is not so tall and Tom is not so smart, Tom is likely a short, dumb man." The chance of a tall and smart Tom according to the product rule is .12, not .30, so that the product is lower than either truth(x) or truth(y).

This calculation by the product rule would be appropriate for certain kinds of decisions (and bets), but seems inappropriate for determining one's belief in Tom's membership in the set of tall and smart men. Multiplication of probabilities gives the chance that Tom is both completely tall and completely smart, while what we want to know is the degree to which he is both tall and smart. The inappropriateness becomes much more obvious as one combines more and more elements in the calculation, such as tall, smart, rich, and bald men. The product calculation will approach .00, even if some of the values are very high. The fuzzy combination, however, will go no lower than the minimum truth value. In other words, a fuzzy conjunction of very true statements is very true, not almost completely untrue.

Second, one might try to classify a thing as a chair and as a red object. If the thing has some of the characteristics of a chair[526] and some pinkish hue, one would give it, perhaps, a .60 membership in the set of chairs and a .51 membership in the red set. Now, if one had to give it a membership in the class of red chairs, one would say .51 for this reddish chair-like thing. One would not apply the product rule to say .31.

The same analysis would apply even if all furniture were definitely a chair or not, and an observer who glimpsed a piece of furniture under certain conditions was 60% sure it was a chair, as long as no way exists now to determine with certainty whether it was a chair. When would one apply the product rule for probabilities? One would do so when things are completely chairs or not and red or not, and you cannot see the thing, but you have an idea of the likelihood of chairishness and redness. To compute the chances of what bivalent values one will see when the thing is uncovered, and the thing becomes clearly a chair or not and red or not, one would use the product rule.

Many sorts of legal situations call for the product rule. In manipulating and evaluating statistical evidence, the factfinder would often use it.[527] In calculat-

---

526. See H.G. Wells, A Modern Utopia 381 (1905) ("I would undertake to defeat any definition of chair or chairishness that you gave me").

527. A colleague gave this illustration:

Suppose that the Black Death strikes some town in England in 1349. Let's suppose that by the end of the year it kills 500 of the 1000 people then living in the town. A historian today is interested in figuring out whether ten particular people who lived in the town at the beginning of 1349 were killed by the Black Death later that year. The historian searches through the cemeteries, through church records and through other materials but comes up empty. There is simply no specific credible evidence about how any of these ten died. The historian can't even figure out how old each of them was at the time and thus adjust the odds based on different survival rates for different ages. Accordingly, his best guess is that for each of the townspeople, there is 50% probability that he or she died from the Black Death. Now the historian wants to know what are the odds that all ten died from the Black Death. The product rule says it's 1/1024 (unless there's some reason to think these are connected events, like they shared a household, so let's assume no info is known about such things). Fuzzy logic says it's one in two, which seems very obviously wrong. Indeed, assuming again that we know nothing further about any of the inhabitants of the town, fuzzy logic would tell us that the odds that *everyone* in the town died from the Black Death are one in two, but we know—because we assumed it to begin the inquiry—that the odds that everyone in the town died of the Black Death are zero. Only half of the inhabitants died of the Black Death. This seems to me a proof by contradiction of the applicability of the product rule to this sort of case.

E-mail from Michael Dorf to author (June 3, 2012, 22:04 EST).

ing the odds of future events, as in computing expected costs on a motion for a preliminary injunction, the product rule would be appropriate.[528] There is a proper realm for the product rule, just as there is one for the straightforward application of the MIN rule. The question before us is whether a significant share of legal applications of the standard of proof falls into the latter realm.

Third, picture a column of 100 coins, 30 of them heads randomly placed, and another column of 100 coins, 40 of them heads randomly placed. Then only about 12 paired rows will have two heads. Or picture a column of 100 people, 30 of them tall people randomly placed, selected from a universe where people are either completely tall or completely short; and picture another column of 100 more people, 40 of them smart people randomly placed, selected from a universe where people are either completely smart or completely dumb. Then only about 12 paired rows will be persons tall and smart, respectively. Now, picture instead a column of varying beliefs in the tallness of 100 people selected from a universe where people have the tallness trait distributed naturally, aligned from tall down to short, and another column of 100 beliefs about persons, aligned from smart down to dumb. The beliefs concerning the thirtieth pair from the bottom will be not so tall and not so smart, respectively, while the twelfth pair from the bottom will be a diminutive dim couple.

The Law's Choice

Traditional probability and degrees of truth do therefore differ. They behave differently in the conjunction setting. Put simply, the product rule gives the random chance of the simultaneous and independent occurrence of multiple crisp elements, while the MIN operator measures the intersection of sets. Once lawmakers have in mind the difference between the product rule and the MIN operator, they have to decide which the law should apply.

Imagine the law is trying to determine if Tom himself was at fault, that is, whether the perpetrator was Tom and whether the perpetrator was at fault. A number of features of this compound question indicate that the better approach for law is fuzzy logic. First, the two parts of the question are epistemically very different, one being a factual event and the other a legal construct; the law needs

---

528. See John Leubsdorf, The Standard for Preliminary Injunctions, 91 Harv. L. Rev. 525, 542 (1978) ("The court, in theory, should assess the probable irreparable loss of rights an injunction would cause by multiplying the probability that the defendant will prevail by the amount of the irreparable loss that the defendant would suffer if enjoined from exercising what turns out to be his legal right. It should then make a similar calculation of the probable irreparable loss of rights to the plaintiff from denying the injunction. Whichever course promises the smaller probable loss should be adopted." (footnote omitted)).

commensurable measures to combine them. Second, as already argued, the law should not be worrying too much about the chance of a truth value of 1 turning up; instead it should ascertain whether the element has a sufficient truth value. Third, in establishing past truths, the law should be even less concerned with the chance of a 1 repetitively turning up; applying the product rule to subjective probabilities for legal factfinding actually seems illogical.[529]

That third point is indeed determinative. One can similarly make the point by distinguishing between ex ante probabilities, used to make predictions of what you will eventually know, and ex post probabilities, used to decide what actually happened even though you will never know for sure. If you are placing a bet predicting whether two randomly uncertain events will independently happen together, then multiply their probabilities. But if you are looking back to the past, then you need a different operator. You are no longer trying to figure the odds of two things being sure, but rather how sure you are that one thing happened while you remain somewhat sure that the other happened. "The ex post probability for complete instantiation of the causal law is equal to the lowest ex post probability for instantiation of any constituent element."[530]

In other words, we want to know if it is a reddish chair, not what the chances are that it is 100% a chair and also 100% red. We want to know if Tom's fault is sufficiently true, not the chances of somehow discovering both the perpetrator certainly to be Tom and the perpetrator to be completely at fault. Here is another way to see this. If Tom is 60% likely the perpetrator, and the perpetrator is 70% at fault, the 60% figure means that it is 60% likely that Tom is surely the person who was 70% at fault. We thus have a 60% chance of Tom's being legally at fault, just as the MIN rule would say.

While the MIN rule seems the obvious choice if identity is a matter of occurrence uncertainty and fault is a matter of imprecise vagueness, I think it still should apply even if both factfinding percentages measure only random uncertainty. Having different operators for different kinds of elements, leading to some weird hybrid calculation unknown to current law, would be more than awkward. But I am arguing that the MIN rule is the right approach, not just a convenient one. A 60% chance of the weakest link represents the chance that

---

529. See Didier Dubois & Henri Prade, A Set-Theoretic View of Belief Functions: Logical Operations and Approximations by Fuzzy Sets, in Classic Works of the Dempster-Shafer Theory of Belief Functions, supra note 404, at 375, 403 (rejecting the application of "arguments deriving from the study of statistical experiments"); MacFarlane, supra note 493, at 13 (saying that the product rule here "just seems wrong").

530. Richard W. Wright, Proving Facts: Belief Versus Probability, in European Tort Law 2008, at 79, ¶45 (Helmut Koziol & Barbara C. Steininger eds., 2009).

all the other elements are more likely than not to exist. Because a 70% chance of fault is good enough for liability, we should not further account for that chance of finding complete fault. To multiply the chances, getting 42%, would be double counting, as it represents the chances of *fully* establishing both identity and fault. The chances of proving completely each of multiple elements simultaneously would be an odd inquiry when the law does not demand complete proof of any. Because establishing every element to 100% is not what the law calls for, the chances of doing so are irrelevant. The relevant inquiry comprises how likely the weakest element is, given that all the other elements would simultaneously be stronger.

Provability Versus Probability

Reactions of colleagues have convinced me that elaboration of this assertion, even in multiple ways, is necessary. So, up to this point, I have established that the MIN and product rules are both valid operators, but they govern in different realms. Which, then, should govern in applying the standard of proof?

In explaining the law's choice, let me begin with the contrary intuitive yearning to apply the product rule. If element A is 60% likely and element B is 70% likely, if both A and B either occurred or did not, and if the law wants to allow recovery only if A and B both occurred, then it does seem that the plaintiff should lose on this 42% showing.

My initial counterargument is that this result is tough on plaintiffs. Multiple elements would stack the deck against real-world plaintiffs, who must live with the imperfections of available evidence. Imagine some other plaintiff having proven four elements each to 70%. That plaintiff has done a really good job in presenting a strong case. The plaintiff has well established each element before passing to the next one. The plaintiff has done exactly what we should demand. Yet this plaintiff would lose with a miserable 24% showing under the product rule. What happened? How did a strong case become a sure loser? Regardless of how, plaintiffs apparently would lose strong cases they really should win. Moreover, defendants at fault would not be receiving a corrective message. These errors would detrimentally affect economic efficiency.

Perhaps the law should not interest itself in the probability of the elements all turning out to equal 1, if only the veil on perfect knowledge were lifted. If every event and thought were somehow videotaped, then we would be partially living in an ascertainably bivalent world, and the law's approach to standards of proof might have to change. But I think the law should not imagine the real world to be a videotaped one. Adopting a false assumption simply in order to make a familiar math tool available is usually indefensible. The law should not ask the odds of the elements bivalently and conjoinedly existing on the video-tape. The law instead should ask how well the burdened party has proven its case. The factfinder needs to operate on the basis of its resulting internal beliefs about the world, rather than pretending that external knowledge is attainable.

Provability, not probability, is the law's concern. Forming a belief as to what happened, rather than a prediction about a veil-lifting that will never happen, is the aim. The law wants to know whether the state of our knowledge based on proof justifies recovery. Fuzzy logic vaguely deals with the "probably provable," while traditional probability crisply deals with the "provably probable."[531]

Expression of this provability comes in terms of membership, to a degree, in the set of true statements, with the degree measured as a truth value. Provability of one element does not detract from the provability of another. An easily provable A and an easily provable B mean that it will be easy to prove A and B. The intersection of sets represents the interaction of elements, and the MIN rule governs the intersection of sets. Consequently, if the plaintiff proves element A to 60% and B to 70%, then the provability of the case being in the set of (A AND B) is 60%.

The plaintiff has shown that the conjoined claim is 60% provable and the defense 40% provable. That is, the belief in the claim is stronger than its negation (the belief that one or the other element or both elements failed). To minimize errors, the law should decide in conformity with the stronger belief. If the law were to deny liability in these circumstances because of some attraction to bivalent probability theory, more often than not the law would be wrong. Giving the plaintiff a recovery and the defendant a loss thus is economically efficient. Accordingly, the law should and does instruct the use of the mathematically sound way to combine beliefs, here the MIN rule.

This key distinction between probability and provability was at the heart of Oxford philosopher L. Jonathan Cohen's almost impenetrably brilliant book entitled *The Probable and the Provable*.[532] He argued that the task of the law

---

531. Cf. Schum, supra note 466, at 243 (discussing belief functions, and crediting Judea Pearl, Bayesian and Belief-Functions Formalisms for Evidential Reasoning: A Conceptual Analysis, in Readings in Uncertain Reasoning 540, 571 (Glenn Shafer & Judea Pearl eds., 1990), for this phrasing).

532. Cohen, supra note 230, reviewed by David A. Schum, 77 Mich. L. Rev. 446 (1979), and Carl G. Wagner, 1979 Duke L.J. 1071; see also Bertrand Russell, Human Knowledge: Its Scope and Limits 359–61 (1948) (arguing comparably that his "degrees of credibility" do not follow the product rules of traditional probability); Haack, supra note 11, at 217–18 (arguing comparably that her "degrees of warrant" do not follow the product rules of traditional probability); MacFarlane, supra note 493, at 12–22 (arguing against the product rule and in favor of the MIN rule). The line of argument of the latter, id. at 13–14 (footnote omit-

court is to decide, by use of inductive reasoning, what is provable. Importing traditional probability into the project, such as the product rule, produces a whole series of anomalies. Instead, the conjunction rule for inductive reasoning is this: "The conjunction of two or more propositions ... has the same inductive probability ... as the least" likely conjunct.[533]

Thus, the respective realms of the MIN and product rules do not turn on the nature of the fact issue, but on the question the system wishes to pose. Which image fits the factfinding endeavor: the betting table or set theory? I think that standards of proof are looking for provability based on set theory. They therefore take the same approach to facts involving occurrence uncertainty as they do to facts involving vagueness.

Monty Hall's Contribution

Why do smart people so resist accepting that provability differs from probability? "When the plaintiff proves one element to 60% and another to 70%, their conjunction is 42%—and I am sticking to it!" Well, for every complex problem there is an answer that is clear, simple, and wrong.[534]

---

ted), is worth quoting:

1. If classical semantics is correct for vague discourse, then borderline propositions are either true or false; no finer distinctions are made.

2. If borderline propositions are either true or false, then (since we don't know which truth value they have) our attitudes toward them must be attitudes of uncertainty-related partial belief.

3. If our attitudes towards borderline propositions are attitudes of uncertainty-related partial belief, they ought to obey norms of probabilistic coherence.

4. We regard the propositions *Jim is tall*, *Jim is bald*, and *Jim is smart* as independent. That is, we don't think Jim's being bald (or smart, or bald and smart) would make it any more likely that he is tall, and so on.

5. Probabilistic coherence demands that our credence in the conjunction of several propositions we take to be independent be the product of our credences in the conjuncts.

6. But it is not the case that we ought to have much less credence that Jim is bald and tall and smart than we have that he is bald.

7. Therefore, classical semantics is not correct for vague discourse.

533. Cohen, supra note 230, at 266; see id. at 89–91, 265–67 (arguing that the law's interest in provability, given the "inapplicability of betting odds" to "unsettlable issues," means that probability's product rules should not apply).

534. That thought always gets credited to Mencken. See, e.g., BrainyQuote, http://www.brainyquote.com/quotes/quotes/h/hlmencke129796.html. But it represents quite a journey from his actual words. H.L. Mencken, Prejudices: Second Series 158 (1920) ("there is always a well-known solution to every human problem—neat, plausible, and wrong"). A related thought is Einstein's, "Everything should be made as simple as possible, but not

Their reaction irresistibly brings to mind the usual reaction to the celebrated Monty Hall problem. "It is customary for books about probability to try to persuade otherwise intelligent people that they are lousy when it comes to reasoning about uncertainty…. In presenting the Monty Hall problem to students I have found the common reactions to follow the well-known five stages of grief."[535] There is denial, anger, bargaining, depression, and then acceptance.

Consider the related "sibling gender problem."[536] A few years back you saw Tom walking down the street with his son. Your companion said that she remembers he has two children. What are the chances that the other child is a boy? The answer is ⅓, because the equally probable possibilities are BB, BG, and GB. But if your companion had said that the elder child was a boy, the answer would be ½! The additional information, seemingly irrelevant, provides ordering that affects the odds.

If you resist the result, and persist with ⅔ odds that the younger child is a girl, I propose the following gamble to you. You will bet on whether a hidden flipped coin is heads. But before placing the bets, I flip another coin, and it comes up tails. You then should believe there is a ⅔ chance that the hidden coin is heads, and so should offer me better than even money.

The effect of additional information emerges from this sequence: Flip two coins. What are the odds that they will both be heads? ¼. If you know one of them was heads, what are the odds they both were heads? ⅓, because knowing the result of one flip tells us something about the other. If instead you know the first flip was heads, what are the odds they both were heads? ½.

After you have progressed through a couple of the stages of grief toward acceptance of these results, consider that traditional probability is generating all

---

simpler." See, e.g., "Quotable Quotes," Reader's Dig., July 1977, at 42; Collected Quotes from Albert Einstein, http://rescomp.stanford.edu/~cheshire/EinsteinQuotes.html (1995). Although many sources repeat this quote or a variant, neither I nor others have been able to locate it in Einstein's writings or speeches. See The New Quotable Einstein 290 (Alice Calaprice ed., 2005) ("Everyone seems to know it, yet no one can find its original source.").

535. Jason Rosenhouse, The Monty Hall Problem: The Remarkable Story of Math's Most Contentious Brainteaser 5 (2009). The literature here is immense. One nifty entry was a report on how overlooking the additional-information effect on probabilities had invalidated decades of research on cognitive dissonance. John Tierney, And Behind Door No. 1, a Fatal Flaw, http://www.nytimes.com/2008/04/08/science/08tier.html (Apr. 8, 2008) ("Even some of the smartest mathematicians initially come up with the wrong answer to the Monty Hall Problem. Perhaps the best way to understand it is to play the game yourself."). The article links to a site, http://www.nytimes.com/2008/04/08/science/08monty.html#, that allows you to play the game repetitively and so build to the right strategy.

536. See Rosenhouse, supra note 535, at 26, 138–41, 147–48.

those emotions. When a problem calls for rejecting bivalence, you should expect that sometimes the answer will be similarly nonobvious. For example, reconsider a plaintiff trying to prove the identity of the perpetrator being Tom and also to prove the perpetrator being at fault. True, if the randomized odds are 60% and 70%, the odds of Tom being at fault are 42%. The product rule gives that result. But if the plaintiff has proved fault to 70%, the odds on the remaining question of Tom being the perpetrator are 60%. The MIN rule sets the likelihood of the conjunction at 60%.

Using the setting of the more familiar "Bertrand box paradox"[537] for elaboration of the shift to multivalence, imagine that there is an identity box and a fault box, each containing a ball that is either black for liability or white for nonliability. The two balls came, respectively, from an urn with 600 of 1000 balls being black and from another urn with 700 of 1000 being black. The odds of the two balls both being black are 42%. But if you uncover or otherwise decide that the fault box has a black ball, the odds of the identity ball being black are 60%.

What is going on? The adherents of 42% are assuming that the pairings are randomized. But in inductively and abductively proving a case—by establishing two truth values or fuzzy provabilities—the plaintiff was ordering the information.[538] The plaintiff thereby removed the randomization feedback loop between the boxes, a randomization of information essential to the 42% calculation.

Under its standard of proof, the law has decided to act on the basis of a partially proved case, not on the basis of the probability of a fully proved case. Fault proven to 70% will never convert to 1 or 0. That means that 30% of the results are not findings of nonfault, but erroneous failures to find fault. Fault having satisfied the standard of proof, the 30% of pairings of nonfault with disputed identity then become errors. To minimize errors, the factfinder should consider only the 70% of pairings that match established fault with disputed identity. Because 60% of those pairings will result in liability and 40% not, deciding in line with the 60% showing will minimize errors and optimize efficiency.[539]

---

537. See id. at 14–16. It runs: Three boxes respectively contain two black balls, two white balls, and one black ball and one white ball. You pick a ball from one box, and it is black. What are the odds that it came from the mixed box? The answer: ⅓.

538. Recall my illustration of the two ordered columns of tall and smart people, supra text accompanying note 528.

539. Another colleague challenges me, after putting aside problems of market share and statistical evidence, to "assume the plaintiff's decedent took a drug either from manufacturer D1 or from manufacturer D2 (the drugs are identical). Assume 60% probability of D1 and 40% of D2. Assume further that it is 60% likely that the drug (from whichever manufacturer) actually caused the death. So 4 possibilities: D1's drug caused the death (36%); D2's drug caused the death (24%); neither D1 nor D2 caused the death (40%). Why

Perhaps, however, that explanation retains too much of the frequentist imagery. The sounder approach would recognize that the law deals not with the odds of magically revealing that the contention is fully true, it deals with partial truths. Not caring about the odds of unattainable truth, the law wants to know what to do with the partial truths it unearths: how can we use those partial truths to decide in a way that minimizes expected error costs? Proof of an element to .50 produces a half-truth, which will never convert by revelation into something other than a half-truth. A half-truth conjoining with a near certainty yields, by the MIN rule, a half-truth in the universe of overall stories covering the two elements. More tellingly, that half-truth conjoining with a separate half-truth yields an overall story that is halfway convincing, rather than merely a quarter-truth.

Now imagine in place of the two elements a long string of elements each shown to be half proven. In combining these partial truths, the boundaries of elements do not matter, because the storyteller is simply connecting pieces to establish an overall partial truth. The chain of the pieces is as strong as the weakest link. Thus, the result is a halfway-convincing overall story, not the infinitesimally likely story suggested by the product rule's measure of the odds of every element being revealed as 1. The law must act optimally in light of the facts that it has, rather on the basis of the odds of getting facts it will never have.

Even if you thereby accept that you should think in terms of partial truths rather than odds, you have to make an affirmative effort to avoid bivalent notions sneaking back into your analysis. Return to the thought experiments. If

---

should P collect against D1?" E-mail from George Alan Hay to author (June 7, 2012, 11:15 EST) (names of parties altered). I respond in this way:

- You are proposing a thought experiment, in which we pull off the veil to reveal a bivalent scheme and then randomly distribute the cause over the identity results. The drug as cause of death sometimes becomes a 1, but in 40 out of 100 cases it will become 0. The zeros fall randomly, instead of dropping out.
- However, that thought experiment has no relevance to what the law or economic theory should do based on the actual proof. It changes the problem, and does so in ways that affect what law and economics would do with respect to D1's liability. In the case against D1, liability when the cause will randomly be either 1 or 0 is a different question from liability when the plaintiff has proved cause to 60%.
- So, I am indeed saying that P has a 60% provable case against D1, and should win just as the law says. P enjoys a truth value of 60% on the proposition that D1 made the drug, and another of 60% that the drug caused the death. This means that the proposition that D1's drug caused the death is 60% a member of the set of true statements. In other words, given the current state of our knowledge, P has 60% of full proof against D1. To decide against P would be to favor a defendant with 40% of a defense.

you view 60% as the odds of that vanished thing you glimpsed having been a chair, while you judge the hue to have been .51 red, but you know there is no way to see that thing again, the partial truth on which to proceed is that it was .51 a reddish chair. Refusing to accept the MIN rule's version of the truth will always involve choosing a lesser truth at some step in telling the overall story of a series of two, or more, elements. The best you could do would be to choose the opposite of the least-proven element; but then the partial truth of all other stories combined would amount to the partial truth of that opposite, the partial truth of the combination of all other stories being the opposite's truth conjoined with the certainty of all alternatives as to other elements. Combining all stories alternative to the .51 partial truth of a reddish chair amounts to only a .49 partial truth. Therefore, acting on the basis of odds to conclude it was not a reddish chair (that is, accepting the product rule's mistaken suggestion that it was 69% established to be not a reddish chair) would increase your error rate.

In sum, fuzzy logic is the correct tool for handling things that will always remain neither wholly true nor wholly false. Classical logic can handle only things that eventually reveal themselves to be true or false. Therefore, fuzzy logic is the tool that will minimize errors in legal factfinding.

Role of Assumptions

Here lies the key to the paradox. If one assumes bivalence, then one must convert fault to 1 or 0 before proceeding. The mathematically sound way to conjoin absolute truths is the product rule. As a means of simplification traditional probability handles only absolute truths, but the law needs to deal with partial truths. If one instead acknowledges multivalence through one's assumptions, one should proceed with fault standing as a partial truth. The mathematically sound way to conjoin partial truths is the MIN rule. Therefore, recognition that the plaintiff can prove any element only to a degree produces an element-by-element approach.

Instinctive resistance to the MIN rule derives from residual yearning to apply a multiplicative rule of traditional probability to a problem it cannot handle, the problem of fuzzy provability. It can handle only randomly uncertain estimates of independent events in a binary world, because it is built on the logical assumption of bivalence. When an assumption no longer prevails, one cannot apply the rules built on the assumption. We tend to forget that mathematical constructs operate only within their assumed system, and that the probability calculus assumes all events will take a value of either one or zero. Multivalence calls for new math. We must move up to MIN.

There is more at work obscuring the picture. Even if one acknowledges that the multiplicative rule should apply only in an abstract world of bivalence, one

will not intuitively sense the subtle shift in a problem's setting from a bivalent assumption to a multivalent reality in which the middle is no longer excluded. The shift can be almost imperceptible. But when the problem is
finding facts of which one will never be sure, the picture must be painted in
multivalent grays.

The bottom line is this: *as an artifact of bivalence, the product rule does not apply
to subjective probabilities for factfinding.* This position is not anti-probabilist. To
the contrary, my position is that we should conceive probability correctly. The
law is not asking for a measure of the probability that each of the elements will
reveal itself to be completely true rather than completely false, but instead the
law asks whether each is sufficiently true to impose liability accurately. *Multivalent logic answers the probability question that bivalent logic cannot, namely, how to
proceed most accurately to the next step when a fact must remain partially proven
rather than magically revealed as true or false.*

I therefore submit that degrees of truth behave more appropriately here
than bivalent probabilities, as the law has long recognized. That recognition constitutes a powerful piece of evidence—adding to many other pieces that I have
already marshaled—that the law's standard of proof employs fuzzy logic in
preference to classical logic.

Fuzzy logic is the proper way to combine partially proved facts. Note that
I am resting on positive arguments for the appropriateness of fuzzy logic. Additionally, there are practical arguments against the product rule. It might be
cognitively challenging to apply.[540] Or the effect of an element-by-element approach might offset the inefficiencies of other legal rules.[541] But I do not need
to rely on these practical arguments.[542]

---

540. See Robert Cooter, Adapt or Optimize? The Psychology and Economics of Rules
of Evidence, in Heuristics and the Law 379 (G. Gigerenzer & C. Engel eds., 2006); Porat &
Posner, supra note 503, at 47–48.

541. See Alex Stein, Of Two Wrongs That Make a Right: Two Paradoxes of the Evidence
Law and Their Combined Economic Justification, 79 Tex. L. Rev. 1199 (2001).

542. Some such arguments, however, are just wrong. For example, some argue that for
jury decisionmaking the necessity of convincing multiple factfinders means, by virtue of
the Condorcet theorem and the supermajority requirement, that the plaintiff's task is way
too demanding; accordingly, to ameliorate the difficulty of proof, the system does not impose the additional demand of a product rule and instead proceeds element-by-element.
See Saul Levmore, Conjunction and Aggregation, 99 Mich. L. Rev. 723, 734–45 (2001).
This position rests on several errors. See Allen & Jehl, supra note 438, at 904–19; Paul H.
Edelman, On Legal Interpretations of the Condorcet Jury Theorem, 31 J. Legal Stud. 327,
343–48 (2002). To me, the most obvious error lies in ignoring that a decision for the defendant also requires the agreement of the multiple factfinders.

In any event, my central question, again, is which representation the law actually employs for its standard of proof. Here, as I have already said, and as I shall show in the upcoming resolution of the conjunction paradox, I am confident that it is degrees of truth across the board.

c. Negation Operator

Accepting the usefulness of fuzzy logic prompts interest in other fuzzy operators. Another basic one is negation. Here $\text{truth}(\text{not}x) = (1 - \text{truth}(x))$, just as in classical logic. The negation is the complement.[543]

However, the whole fuzzy set and its complement do not necessarily add to unity, because fuzzy logic does not obey the law of the excluded middle. The accompanying graphs demonstrate this fact, with the graph labeled (a) representing the fuzzy set A by the solid line and its complement by the dotted line and with (b) representing by its dark upper line the union of A and its complement by operation of the MAX function.[544]

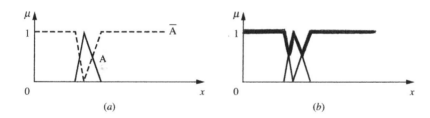

(a)   (b)

The serrations in the upper line in the right-hand graph show that A and its complement do not add to equal the universe X, reflecting that the law of the excluded middle does not hold. There will be an area where beliefs are neither in the set of belief nor in the set of disbelief, but instead are indeterminate.

---

543. But cf. Bellman & Giertz, supra note 511, at 155–56 (showing that other negation operators are theoretically possible).

544. The figure comes from Timothy J. Ross, Fuzzy Logic with Engineering Applications 37 (3d ed. 2010).

2. Legal Application: Conjunction and Aggregation Paradoxes

The payoff of the fuzzy logic approach emerges as one realizes how it affects the view of the proof process.

Conjunction Paradox

Consider the best-known statement of the infamous conjunction paradox:

> We purport to decide civil cases according to a more-probable-than-not standard of proof. We would expect this standard to take into account the rule of conjunction, which states that the probability of two independent events occurring together is the product of the probability of each event occurring separately. The rule of conjunction dictates that in a case comprised of two independent elements the plaintiff must prove each element to a much greater degree than 50%: only then will the plaintiff have shown that the probability that the two elements occurred together exceeds 50%. Suppose, for example, that a plaintiff must prove both causation and fault and that these two elements are independent. If the plaintiff shows that causation is 60% probable and fault is 60% probable, then he apparently would have failed to satisfy the civil standard of proof because the probability that the defendant *both* acted negligently and caused injury is only 36%.
>
> In our legal system, however, jurors do not consider whether it is more probable than not that all elements occurred in conjunction. Judges instruct jurors to decide civil cases element by element, with each element decided on a more-probable-than-not basis. Once jurors have decided that an element is probable, they are to consider the element established, repress any remaining doubts about it, and proceed to consider the next element. If the plaintiff proves each element by a preponderance of the evidence, the jury will find in his favor.... Thus, jurors may find a defendant liable even if it is highly unlikely that he acted negligently, that is, the conjoined probability of the elements is much less than 50%. In such cases, the verdict fails to reflect a probable account of what happened and thus fails to minimize the cost of judicial errors....
> ....
>
> ... Although courts direct juries to consider and decide each element seriatim, juries do not consider each item of evidence seriatim when deciding whether a given element is proved. The jury must decide each element by looking at all of the evidence bearing on proof of that

element. Thus, although the jury does not assess the conjunction of the elements of a case, it does decide each element by assessing the conjunction of the evidence for it.[545]

The implications are profound but boggling. Allowing recovery on a 36% showing of causation *and* fault is not only unfair but inefficient. How embarrassing for the law!

For another boggle, ponder the apparent criticality of how exactly the ancients (and moderns) divided our causes of action and defenses into elements: the more subdivisions, the lower the conjunctive probability that would produce victory.[546] And yet: "Anyone who has ever litigated a real case knows the exact opposite of the conjunction paradox is true: the more disputed elements the plaintiff has to prove, the *less* likely the plaintiff is to prevail.... [A]lthough it is possible that a particular plaintiff could obtain an unjust verdict in a case with several disputed elements, [there is an increased] probability that the jury will find at least one element to be less likely than not."[547]

Admittedly, the conjunction paradox turns out to be not such a serious problem in practice. Only one element might be in dispute, or the disputed elements might not be really independent. The judge might not clearly state, or

---

545. Nesson, supra note 385, at 1385–88 (footnotes omitted); see A.P. Dawid, The Difficulty About Conjuction, 36 Statistician 91 (1987). Professor Nesson saw the paradox as illustrating his broad thesis that the law's process of proof aims at generating acceptable statements about past events and thus at projecting behavioral norms to the public, rather than at reaching probable conclusions in a search for truth:

> Application of the more-probable-than-not test to each element produces the most acceptable conclusion as to that element. The conjunction of these conclusions constitutes a story that is more probable than any other story about the same elements. Suppose, for example, that the elements of a story are A and B, and A (70%) is more probable than not-A (30%), and B (60%) is more probable than not-B (40%). The conjunction (A & B) (42%) may not be more probable than its negation (not-(A & B)) (58%). But the conjunction (A & B) (42%) is more probable than any other version: (A & (not-B)) (28%), ((not-A) & B) (18%), or ((not-A) & (not-B)) (12%). The application of the more-probable-than-not standard of proof on an element-by-element basis will produce the single most probable story.

Nesson, supra note 385, at 1389–90 (footnotes omitted). See generally J.S. Covington, Jr., The Structure of Legal Argument and Proof 347–57 (2d ed. 2006).

546. See James A. Henderson, Jr., Fred Bertram & Michael J. Tōke, Optimal Issue Separation in Modern Products Liability Litigation, 73 Tex. L. Rev. 1653, 1655–59, 1667–75 (1995).

547. David A. Moran, Jury Uncertainty, Elemental Independence and the Conjunction Paradox: A Response to Allen and Jehl, 2003 Mich. St. L. Rev. 945, 946–47, 950.

the jury might not fully understand, the proper element-by-element approach to the standard of proof.

Or, because humans might tend to construct a story for the whole case rather than proceeding element-by-element, the factfinder might end up applying the standard of proof to the conjoined elements. In fact, many psychologists agree that the factfinder naturally constructs such stories, although perhaps not in a very systematic manner.[548] The broadly accepted story model of evidence processing holds that the factfinder, over the trial process's course, constructs from the evidence the story that makes maximal sense; and the factfinder then chooses, among the available decisions, the one that fits best with the constructed story.

If the jurors construct a story for the whole case, or otherwise cognitively process the entirety while the trial progresses, and then the judge instructs on standard of proof, it might be that the jurors actually apply the standard to the whole claim or defense. It might also be that, being human, a judge when acting as factfinder proceeds in essentially the same manner, testing whether the already conjoined elements are more likely than not.

Indeed, by providing obscure instructions only at the end of oral trials, the law seems determined to encourage overall consideration and to discourage applying the standard of proof element-by-element. Although the judge does instruct literally in element-by-element terms,[549] this may work only to encourage the jurors' detailed evaluation of the evidence and to stress the requirement that any story must contain all of a series of elements—just as many evidence rules may work to brake any undesirable tendency of the factfinder to rush toward creating a story.[550]

So, the conjunction paradox may not inflict great practical effects. Nonetheless, the big theoretical problem of the conjunction paradox will unavoidably pose at least some practical difficulties. The law sometimes enforces its element-

---

548. See supra text accompanying note 401.

549. 3 O'Malley et al., supra note 371, § 104.01:

> Plaintiff has the burden in a civil action, such as this, to prove every essential element of plaintiff's claim by a preponderance of the evidence. If plaintiff should fail to establish any essential element of plaintiff's claim by a preponderance of the evidence, you should find for defendant as to that claim.

See Allen & Jehl, supra note 438, at 897–904 (criticizing Dale A. Nance, Commentary, A Comment on the Supposed Paradoxes of a Mathematical Interpretation of the Logic of Trials, 66 B.U. L. Rev. 947, 949–51 (1986) (finding this instruction ambiguous)).

550. See Bruce Ching, Narrative Implications of Evidentiary Rules, 29 Quinnipiac L. Rev. 971 (2011); Lisa Kern Griffin, Narrative, Truth, and Trial, 101 Geo. L.J. 281 (2013); Doron Menashe & Mutal E. Shamash, The Narrative Fallacy, 3 Int'l Comment. on Evidence iss. 1, art. 3 (2006), available at http://www.bepress.com/ice/vol1/iss1/art3.

by-element theory and thereby impedes the holistic practice. An obvious example would be when the judge requires a special verdict that asks the jury to find each element by a preponderance.[551] The conjunction paradox therefore remains troubling, and theorists twist themselves into pretzels trying to explain it away.

It would be troubling, however, only if theory really calls for the product rule. But theory does not. Instead, it invokes the MIN rule. The truth of the conjunction equals the minimum of the truths of the elements. If each element is more likely than not, then the truth of the conjunction is more likely than not. To use the above example, if the plaintiff shows that fault is .60 true and that causation is .60 true, then he has shown to .60 that the defendant *both* acted negligently and caused the injury.

Thus, there is no conjunction paradox. It implodes under the force of fuzzy logic. The MIN operator provides that belief in the conjunction will match the least likely element, which has already passed the standard of proof. The MAX operator meanwhile indicates that belief in the negative of the conjunction, that is, in the disjunction of each element's negation, will never reach equipoise. The story of liability will not only be the most believable story, but will be more believable than all the stories of nonliability combined.

Comfortingly, under the MIN rule, *applying the standard of proof element-by-element works out to be equivalent to applying it to the whole conjoined story.* So, if the factfinder actually does follow the story model, that practice would not directly endanger the standard of proof. The apparent criticality of the number of elements melts away too. Because the MIN rule applies to each set of evidence to be conjoined, it does not matter logically where the law draws formal lines between elements, or whether the elements are independent or interdependent. Nor does it matter if I sloppily labeled identity as an element in my examples above.[552] "Element" would best serve merely as a synonym for a finding necessary to a cause of action.

Moreover, the proof process within elements is not dissimilar to the proof process between elements. Within elements, the factfinder uses intuitive techniques in a nonquantitative and approximate fashion to find facts. For separate facts within elements, the factfinder uses the fuzzy operator for conjunction,

---

551. See Elizabeth G. Thornburg, The Power and the Process: Instructions and the Civil Jury, 66 Fordham L. Rev. 1837, 1857–63 (1998).

552. See Cohen, supra note 230, at 267 ("So on the inductivist analysis, if the plaintiff gains each of his points on the balance of probability, he can be regarded as gaining his case as a whole on that balance…, without any constraint's being thereby imposed on the number of independent points in his case or on the level of probability at which each must be won.").

which works in a style similar to that between elements. For alternative facts, the factfinder uses the fuzzy operator for disjunction, making the finding if any of the alternatives meets the standard of proof. The resulting noncriticality of how we break up a cause of action means, for example, that the variable granularity of special verdicts presents no theoretical problem.

The law does seem to know what it is doing, then. Whenever it phrases its instruction to require applying the standard of proof element-by-element, it is instructing to apply the MIN operator. But do actual factfinders apply the MIN operator as they should and as the law tells them to do? We do not know. Some experimental evidence arguably suggests that the lay person tends to apply the product rule rather than the MIN operator.[553] Nevertheless, no sign exists that factfinders in the legal system are using the product rule. After all, a concern that they were ignoring the product rule generated the unfounded fear of the conjunction paradox in the first place.

Aggregation Paradox

Scholars also invoke a converse paradox, involving multiple independent theories that are alternative routes to the same conclusion, whether that conclusion is a judgment in a case with multiple counts or a decision on a particular claim or an element of a claim. These observers lament that the law denies relief to a supposedly deserving plaintiff (or to a defendant with multiple defenses almost proved):

> Consider a case involving three different legal theories and three different factual foundations. Plaintiffs deserve to win if one of the sto-

---

553. See Gregg C. Oden, Integration of Fuzzy Logical Information, 3 J. Experimental Psychol.: Hum. Perception & Performance 565 (1977). His experiment involved having students judge the degree of truthfulness of statements like "a chair is furniture" and "a pelican is a bird," and asking them for the degree to which both statements together were true. The students seemed to use the product rule rather than the MIN rule. But it seems to me that the students could have interpreted these statements as verifiably being either completely true or completely false, thus making the product rule appropriate. Moreover, other experiments indicate that people do use fuzzy operators. See Rami Zwick, David V. Budescu & Thomas S. Wallsten, An Empirical Study of the Interpretation of Linguistic Probabilities, in Fuzzy Sets in Psychology 91, 114–16 (Tamás Zétényi ed., 1988) (indicating that people do not use the product rule naturally). In any event, in the legal system any human failing to conjoin properly would be offset by the human tendency to construct a story for the whole case instead of proceeding element-by-element. Cf. Tversky & Kahneman, supra note 213, at 19 (discussing biases that tend to ignore conjunction); Amos Tversky & Derek J. Koehler, Support Theory: A Nonextensional Representation of Subjective Probability, in Heuristics and Biases, supra note 208, at 441 (same).

ries embodying one legal theory is true; defendants deserve to win only if all of their competing stories are true (for if this is false, one of the plaintiff's stories is true). For example, assume the plaintiff has alleged defective design, defective manufacture, and failure to warn theories. If the probability of each is .25, the "probability" of each not being true is .75, but, the probability of at least one being true is $1 - .75^3 = .58$, and perhaps plaintiff should win, even though the individual probabilities of each being false is .75.[554]

The lamenters are quite serious, sometimes abandoning the restriction that theories be alternative routes to the same conclusion and even extending their point to parallel conclusions in the criminal law. Thus, some startlingly argue for *conviction* on the basis of a number of offenses *almost* proved:

> Should a court convict a defendant for an unspecified offense if there is no reasonable doubt that he committed an offense, even though the prosecution cannot prove his guilt as to a particular offense beyond a reasonable doubt? Stated otherwise, is committing an offense sufficient for a conviction or must a prosecutor establish what this offense is to justify a conviction? This Article contends that, under certain conditions, a prosecutor should not have to establish the particular offense committed by a defendant—proof that the defendant committed an offense should be sufficient.[555]

Others have tried to explain, and thereby to justify as a practical or prudential matter, why the law illogically ignores the paradox.[556] In a new arti-

---

554. Allen & Jehl, supra note 438, at 939 (citing Levmore, supra note 542, at 745–56); see Massachusetts v. U.S. Dep't of Health & Human Servs., 682 F.3d 1 (1st Cir. 2012) (striking down DOMA on both equal protection and federalism grounds), noted in Mike Dorf, Is the First Circuit's Opinion in the DOMA Case Insufficiently "Fuzzy"?, http://www.dorfonlaw.org/2012/06/is-first-circuits-opinion-in-doma-case.html (June 4, 2012).

555. Alon Harel & Ariel Porat, Aggregating Probabilities Across Cases: Criminal Responsibility for Unspecified Offenses, 94 Minn. L. Rev. 261, 261–62 (2009). On aggregation in criminal sentencing, see Kevin Bennardo, A Quantity-Driven Solution to Aggregate Grouping Under the U.S. Sentencing Guidelines Manual, available at http://ssrn.com/abstract=2148133 (Sept. 20, 2012).

556. E.g., Frederick Schauer & Richard Zeckhauser, On the Degree of Confidence for Adverse Decisions, 25 J. Legal Stud. 27, 41–47 (1996) (conceding the probability argument regarding multiple crimes almost proved, but arguing that the criminal law still should not convict for reasons of abundant caution).

cle, Ariel Porat and Eric A. Posner go on the offense.[557] They attack the law's general refusal to multiply the probabilities of claims and defenses, and then argue for overhauling the law to cure this logical mistake. Their *Aggregation and Law* is an article beautifully developed by admirable scholars. But it rests squarely on the premise that refusal to multiply probabilities in legal factfinding is illogical.

Is it? Few indeed have questioned whether ignoring the paradox is illogical. I do. My position is that the paradox that motivated Porat & Posner's whole article simply does not exist. Instead, modern logic demonstrates that the tort plaintiff who supported three theories each to .25 has proved his case to only .25 and so should lose, just as the plaintiff does lose under current law. Therefore, the law should not, and does not, aggregate by multiplying probabilities.

To begin, both under classical logic with a probability overlay and under fuzzy logic, the MAX rule will reduce to the familiar De Morgan's rule for aggregation—*if* one assumes bivalence and then adds an assumption of independent statements. De Morgan's rule provides that the aggregation of two independent statements (say, each .25 likely) equals the negation of the product of the negations of those statements ($1 - .75^2 = .44$).

The explanation of De Morgan's rule is that if values can be only 1 or 0, then the probability measures of, say, 50% and 40% for two propositions mean no more than an expectation that in five out of ten and four out of ten times the value will turn up as 1. Thus, given the assumption of independence, only in half of the four times when the second proposition is 1 will the first be 1, that is, 20% of the time. As to aggregation, $1 - (1 - .50)(1 - .40) = 70\%$ of the time one or the other proposition or both will be 1. The MAX rule then tells us that in those 70% of the cases, truth(x OR y) = 1.

De Morgan's rule applies in many situations, namely, those dealing with randomly uncertain estimates of independent events' likelihoods in binary circumstances. Think of drawing black or white balls from urns. Or think of manipulating statistical evidence to prove a claim. But are Professors Porat and Posner correct in thinking that it should apply across-the-board to legal factfinding, even between theories?

---

557. Porat & Posner, supra note 503. Astoundingly, Professors Porat and Posner double down on the criminal law example. Not only would they convict for one crime out of two separate crimes *almost* proved, but they would acquit for one crime out of two even when each is proved beyond a reasonable doubt but the odds of the defendant's having committed *both* crimes is mathematically less certain (after all, they argue, 96% x 96% = 92%). Id. at 35–36. They thereby fall out of the aggregation fallacy and into the conjunction fallacy.

The alternative approach would not assume bivalence. Let H be one fuzzy set and B be another fuzzy set in the universe. The two sets might be independent, in the sense that the degree of membership in one set has no effect on the degree of membership in the other set, but they need not be. Designate the membership of element x in H as truth(x), and the membership of element y in B as truth(y). Now, fuzzy logic says to stick with the more general MAX rule. Under it, the truth of the aggregation equals the larger of truth(x) and truth(y).

For a more specified example, let H be the set of tall men and B be the assumedly independent set of smart men. So, if Tom is a .25 member of H and a .40 member of B, then Tom is a .40 member of the set of either tall or smart men. The aggregated set becomes larger, so Tom's degree of membership in it does not increase above the greater of his tallness and smartness levels. Significantly, we are not interested in the odds of Tom being completely tall or completely smart, which is the odd question that De Morgan's rule would answer.

Turning to legal applications, fuzzy logic would apply the same MAX rule if one were trying to determine if Tom either committed a tort or breached a contract. The MAX rule would displace De Morgan's rule.

Ay, there's the rub: the MAX rule gives a different answer than De Morgan's rule gives for aggregating theories. Which does the law apply? The law applies the MAX rule. Why? Because De Morgan's rule applies only if classical logic's assumption of bivalence holds for factfinding, and it does not.

Let me use this aggregation, or multiple theory, paradox to explain further that nonintuitive point about bivalence. Imagine a claim A that is 25% likely to be valid and an independent claim B that is 40% likely to be valid.

Some scholars, but not the law, say that the likelihood of (A OR B) is equal to $1 - (.75 \cdot .60) = 55\%$, and therefore the plaintiff should win. I am saying, however, that the likelihood of (A OR B) is equal to that of the likelier of A and B, that is, 40%, and therefore the plaintiff should lose.

It is easy to say that I am being obtuse, because anyone can intuit that the probability of A and B's aggregation must be higher than either. But the fact that the law says otherwise, that a widely accepted logic system built on multivalence says otherwise, and that some pretty bright lights shining in philosophy's vast literature on vagueness say otherwise should give pause to intuition. Let me present three hypotheticals to suggest my counterargument.

First, for modeling **event imprecision**, imagine a claim A for tort, where the defendant did acts that were 25% bad, and an independent claim B for contract, where the defendant did acts that constituted 40% of what would be an unquestionable breach. These are members of fuzzy sets. The breaching quality of the acts has no bearing on the tortiousness of the acts, that is, the 40% showing has no effect on the 25% showing. The likelihood of their aggregation is 40%, so that we can say only that the plaintiff went 40% of the way toward proving liability. One way to understand aggregation is to realize that this hypothetical is just like not-so-tall-at-all and not-so-smart Tom. A factfinder would have no interest in the chance that Tom is either completely tall or completely smart; in any event, De Morgan's rule would yield an aggregation of about 0% likelihood, because the chance of Tom's being completely tall and the chance of his being completely smart are about 0% and 0%. Instead, the factfinder would have interest in Tom's degrees of membership in the set of tall men (25%) and in the set of smart men (40%); he is therefore a .40 member of the set of tall or smart men. Another way to visualize the aggregation of two fuzzy sets, A (acts constituting a tort) and B (acts constituting a breach), comes in the accompanying figure.[558] The degree (μ) to which a set of facts (z), located on the x-axis, constitutes either a tort or a breach is indicated by the membership line for A or B, whichever is higher at point z.

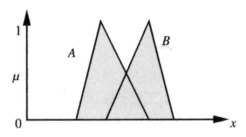

Second, for modeling **bivalent chance**, imagine a ball A drawn from an urn with only 25% black balls among white balls, and a ball B drawn from another urn with 40% black balls. The chance that at least one of them will be black (and let us say that black represents liability), when the drawn balls are both revealed, is 55% by De Morgan's rule. In a sense, the act of revealing the balls to be white or black affects the odds, because the balls must be either white or black and only one has to be black. If one turns up black, this takes the pressure off the other's being black.

Third, for modeling **event occurrence**, imagine a claim A for tort, where the defendant was actually 25% likely to have done the bad tortious acts alleged, and an independent claim B for contract, where the defendant was ac-

---

558. The figure comes from Ross & Parkinson, supra note 462, at 33.

tually 40% likely to have done the bad breaching acts alleged. Assume that all available evidence would not change those numbers, which is what I mean by the word "actually." Is this third situation more like the first or the second situation? All our intuitions, honed by life-long exposure to traditional probability theory, point us to the second. But the real world of imprecision and other uncertainty makes the appropriate analogy the first situation.

Now let me flesh out my counterargument. I start by noting that the law always asks in the same way whether the plaintiff has proven a fact by satisfying the standard of proof—regardless of the *nature* of the factual finding, be it a finding on an imprecise matter or a finding regarding random uncertainty. To aggregate the findings, the law applies the MAX rule—it is thereby saying that a number of theories *almost* proved do not combine to produce liability.

There are many reasons for the law so to use fuzzy logic in thinking about the real world. In the course of legal factfinding, fuzzy logic alone can handle the frequent situations where the issues involve event imprecision. It alone can handle the situation where the law must combine a finding of event imprecision as in the first hypothetical case with a finding of event occurrence as in the third case. It alone can smoothly handle the situation where the two claims are not independent. And of course we would never want to ask real factfinders to make the probability determinations that De Morgan's rule necessitates for calculation.

Yet I am not merely contending that fuzzy logic is convenient, but rather that it is the right vehicle for accurate factfinding. As I have implied, the easy case for my position is the first of the three: traditional probability cannot handle event imprecision any better than it can handle Tom's tallness or smartness. But I am not conceding the harder third case of event occurrence. Thus, I contend the MAX rule is the way to go even when combining two independent and alternative findings on the likelihood that liability occurred in fact.

An initial step here is to observe that the law's embrace of the MAX rule seems commonsensical. A number of failures do not create a success. A plaintiff should not be able to raise likelihood by framing alternative independent arguments.

Only by drawing inspiration from the betting table can scholars construct an argument to the contrary. Yet drawing balls from an urn is a bad analogy to factfinding, because in the proof process we shall never be able to lift the veil in order to see the color of the "balls" that represent facts found. In establishing facts in the courtroom we shall never know the full truth, because all we can ever find is a degree of truth. Thus, we are not concerned with whether something is fully true—whether a truth value of 1 will turn up—but whether it seems to have a sufficient truth value to support liability. We are concerned not with whether we picked from the urn a black ball that we shall never see, but rather with how black is this grayish ball that we can see. De Morgan's rule thus answers a question that the law is not asking.

In the urn case, 25% for the first urn's ball represents the chance of black turning up. That 25% carries over to the second ball in the sense of increasing the odds to 55% that at least one of the balls will be black. Note, however, that if the ball from urn A reveals to be white, the chance of the ball from urn B being black is 40%, not 55%.

When the law finds claim A to be 25% likely, it is not saying that in twenty-five of a hundred cases liability will come up as 1. It is saying that a valid tort claim does not exist. In those twenty-five cases, a finding of liability would be an error. Those twenty-five hypothetical decisions on claim A are not 1s to be distributed randomly among a hundred hypothetical decisions on claim B, but instead are errors to be discarded before going forward. When the law proceeds to claim B, no trace of the 25% liability on claim A carries over to affect the B inquiry. Claim B remains 40% likely. (Indeed, if claim A's result bore on independent claim B, the result would be relevant evidence to prove claim B; it is not, because logically it has nothing to say about how to decide claim B.)

There lies the key to this paradox. The law has made a finding of partial truth on claim A, not a prediction on how things would turn out in a bivalent world. There is no sense in having factfinders fix the odds of 1 turning up if only knowledge were perfect. The aim instead is their measuring belief in the facts based on imperfect evidence. Thus, even for a *single* fact subject only to random uncertainty of occurrence, their measure of likelihood is a belief rather than a traditional probability. Confusion arises because expression of a partial truth sounds so much like a traditional probability. But provability (the formation amidst uncertainty of a belief as to what happened that is sufficient to justify liability), not probability (the odds that 1 will turn up), is the law's concern.

When factfinders have to combine *multiple* facts' measures of likelihood, they should employ the operator for combining beliefs, not calculate the odds of 1s turning up. Belief that claim A failed and belief that claim B failed will together produce a belief that both claim A and claim B failed. That belief will be stronger than its negation, that is, the belief that one or the other claim or both claims succeeded. To minimize errors, the law should decide in accordance with that stronger belief. If the law were to impose liability in these circumstances because of some attraction to bivalent probability theory, more often than not the law would be wrong in finding liability, and that is not economically efficient. Consequently, the law should and does instruct the use of the mathematically sound way to combine beliefs, here the MAX rule.

We are ready to reconsider the third case of a 25% probable tort claim and a 40% probable contract claim. More complete evidence will not arrive to change the likelihoods—and we cannot pull off the veil to show what really happened, we shall not get to see if the "ball" is truly black, we shall never get to reduce the world to bivalence. It was the reduction to bivalence that affected the joint odds in the urn case. Unlike the drawn balls whose probabilities will change upon unveiling, the likelihoods in the third case will never be anything but 25% and 40%. If we can never convert the likelihood of a claim to one or zero, then all we can say is that the defendant is liable to a certain degree. That is, when we can never know with certainty what happened, a likelihood of occurrence is not different from a degree of misfeasance: a likelihood of occurrence is not a traditional probability, it is a fuzzy set.

Now consider the strongest argument in rebuttal. It would concede that fuzzy logic might apply in most cases, but maintain that traditional probability should apply in a very pure hypothetical of event occurrence. So, the rebutter would have us imagine a factfinder being 40% sure that a driver caused each of ten different car accidents, where "cause" is unrealistically assumed to have an accepted meaning and to be an on/off matter (note that the issue is causation rather than fault, and note that the fact of multiple independent accidents is not relevant to causation of any particular accident, which stays at 40% likely):

- Does the factfinder think, if he or she could only lift the veil, that causation of at least one of the accidents would have a truth value of 1? Yes, of course. In this betting situation, the residual chance of causation carries over, as risk, from one accident to the next. De Morgan's rule gives the risk that at least one accident will occur, but does not tell which one.
- Does the factfinder believe that the driver caused any specific accident? No, as long as the issue is causation of an accident, not free-floating risk of a nonspecified accident. If the factfinder believes, based on the evidence, that the driver did not cause the first accident or the second one or the other ones, then the factfinder will believe that the driver did not cause any particular accident. That is, the driver having caused any one of the ten accidents is a .40 member of the set of true statements.
- Should we change tort law to impose proportional liability on proof of negligent behavior that imposed a significant risk but without proof of its causing any particular accident in suit? Maybe, although that question is a complicated one of substantive law. There hides the trick played by the rebutter. The rebuttal starts to answer how probability works in determining cause, but switches the question to whether law should impose liability for risk without causation. That latter question is a matter of substantive policy, not a puzzle of probability. We cer-

tainly should not adopt any such substantive reform on the basis of faulty arguments that probability theory dictates the reform.[559]

In conclusion, the aggregation paradox would arise only if theory really calls for application of De Morgan's rule. But theory does not. Instead, sound theory invokes the MAX rule. The truth of the aggregation equals the maximum of the findings' truths. Likewise, *the law is not asking for a measure of the probability that one of the claims will reveal itself to be completely true rather than completely false, but instead the law seeks the likelihood of one of the claims*

---

559. Professors Porat and Posner's cited exceptions, where the law arguably seems or ought to aggregate by multiplying probabilities, actually constitute changes to the substantive law rather than exceptional applications of traditional probability to factfinding:

- Their prime example of market-share liability changes the elements of the cause of action (substituting risk of harm for cause in fact) and does so not at all for probability reasons but solely for substantive reasons. Cf. Mark A. Geistfeld, The Doctrinal Unity of Alternative Liability and Market-Share Liability, 155 U. Pa. L. Rev. 447 (2006) (attempting to make market-share liability look less radical). Market-share liability thus nvolves a move comparable to the imposition of strict liability.
- The authors also draw illustrations from the realm of proportional liability. See Porat & Posner, supra note 503, at 6–7, 26. But whether a polluter caused a particular cancer is a factual question (on which one would not multiply probabilities) different from the legal question of whether tort law should impose liability for the pollution's increased risk of cancer (on which one could multiply probabilities). See David A. Fischer, Proportional Liability: Statistical Evidence and the Probability Paradox, 46 Vand. L. Rev. 1201, 1201 (1993) (criticizing, on substantive grounds, proposals that called for "modifying traditional tort rules to permit plaintiffs to recover from a defendant who contributed to the risk of causing the plaintiff's harm without proving that the defendant actually caused the harm").
- For a completely different example of theirs, constitutional law's choice to apply strict scrutiny to hybrid free-exercise claims does not even involve factfinding. See Porat & Posner, supra note 503, at 48–49.

That there is no connection between their examples is unsurprising, as there is no stopping point to their theory of probabilistic aggregation, and so it straddles many settings. Yet they do take some reforms off the table. For example, unlike aggregation as to causation, they would not aggregate "almost negligent" behaviors, given that "two or more instances of 'almost negligent' behavior are even more socially desirable than one." Id. at 67. Why this limit to their aggregation? The reason is that in their view, the rejected reforms are undesirable as a matter of substantive law. See id. (referencing "cases where normative aggregation makes little sense because of the nature of the substantive law in question"). The rejected reforms are, however, just as much of an offense to their understanding of probability theory. Thus, the authors' arguments about probability theory are irrelevant to the line they draw between desirable and undesirable reforms.

being sufficiently true to impose liability. Thus, there is no aggregation para-dox. It implodes under the force of fuzzy logic.

Again, the law seems to know what it is doing.

C. Analyzing Beliefs

My ultimate focus on fuzzy provability pushed traditional probability far-ther into the background, so setting the stage for a shift of focus onto beliefs as being at the core of the standards of proof. This part will introduce belief func-tions into the mix, in order better to represent how imperfect evidence keeps factfinders from committing all of their belief. Then, this part will use this the-ory to explain why the law's initial burden of production starts the factfinders at point zero. While the energizing idea introduced heretofore has been mul-tivalence, the unlocking idea henceforth will be the nonadditivity of beliefs.

1. Shafer's Belief Functions

a. Basics of Theory

I have already implicitly advocated that we treat the degree of S's truth, which is a degree of membership in the set of true facts, as a degree of belief in S as a true proposition. The broad version of the theory of belief functions will now give us a handle on how to manipulate such beliefs.[560] It will also pro-vide us with a better mental image for representing indeterminacy.[561] I there-fore continue with a minor normative undercurrent.

In factfinding, I contend, we should not ask how likely S is but rather how much we believe S to be a real-world truth based on the evidence, as well as how much we believe notS—while remaining conscious of indeterminacy and so recog-nizing that part of our belief will remain uncommitted. Beliefs can range any-where between 0 and 1. If the belief in S is called Bel(S), then $0 \leq \text{Bel}(S) \leq 1$.

Consider belief function theory's treatment of a single factual hypothesis. Take as an example the issue of whether Katie is dead or alive, with S representing death. Although you have no tangible evidence, three witnesses said she is dead. One seems somewhat credible. But you think that another saw a differ-

---

560. See Shafer, supra note 484, at 35–37.

561. See Liping Liu & Ronald R. Yager, Classic Works of the Dempster-Shafer Theory of Belief Functions: An Introduction, in Classic Works of the Dempster-Shafer Theory of Belief Functions, supra note 404, at 1, 2–19 (recounting also the history of belief function theory).

ent woman's body, which discounts the evidence of death but gives no support to her being alive. And you think that the third was lying as part of a cover-up of her escape from captivity, which is compatible with both S and notS and so gives some thin support to her being alive. In sum, this evidence supports your .5 belief that she is dead, or Bel(S). That evidence also supports your weaker belief that she is alive, with Bel(notS) coming in at .2. That is, Bel(notS) is not determined by the value of Bel(S). The remaining .3 is indeterminate, meaning she could be either alive or dead because the evidence is imperfect. The defects in evidence might be probative, affecting Bel(S) and Bel(notS); but the defects might be nonprobative, so that they just leave some belief uncommitted. (This example actually involves a so-called power set of four beliefs: S, notS, neither S nor notS, and either S or notS. The belief in the "null" of neither alive nor dead is set by definition to be 0. The belief in the "catchall" of either alive or dead is 1.0.)

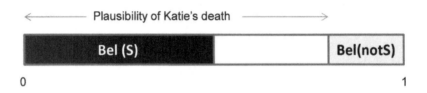

Belief is sometimes called the lower probability. Bel(S) is the extent to which you believe Katie to be dead. The upper probability bound represents "possibility" in Zadeh's terminology or "plausibility" in Shafer's.[562] It is the extent to which you think her being dead is plausible, that is, the sum of the affirmative belief plus the indeterminate belief. The plausibility that she is dead is .8, being .5 + .3. (A traditionally expressed probability of her being dead would fall somewhere within the range from the lower to the upper probability.) The plausibility that she is alive totals .5, being .2 + .3. Plausibility equals one minus the belief in the opposite.

Belief functions thus harness the idea of imprecise probability to capture indeterminacy. Although they can be used with ordinary expressions of probability, combining belief functions with fuzzy logic's degrees of truth and its

---

562. See Barnett, supra note 484, at 200–01 (providing a neat mental image for these bounds); A.P. Dempster, Upper and Lower Probabilities Induced by a Multivalued Mapping, 38 Annals Mathematical Stat. 325 (1967); L.A. Zadeh, Fuzzy Sets as a Basis for a Theory of Possibility, 1 Fuzzy Sets & Sys. 3 (1978).

operators makes an even bigger step toward understanding.[563] The resultant beliefs can be expressed, if expression is ever necessary, as coarsely gradated beliefs. In addition to the benefits of utilizing natural language, these terms capture the uncertainty and imprecision in determining the belief. Thus, in lieu of expressing beliefs in terms of decimals, one should use the coarse gradations of (1) slightest possibility, (2) reasonable possibility, (3) substantial possibility, (4) equipoise, (5) probability, (6) high probability, and (7) almost certainty.

In the end, the representation of findings in the form of beliefs captures the effect of imperfect evidence, which was a rallying cry of Baconian theorists. The move from probability to belief is also a slight nod to the civil-law emphasis on inner belief as captured by its *intime conviction* standard,[564] and to the frequent *cris de coeur* of theorists who lament any intrusion of probabilistic mathematics into the very human process of proof. Finally, belief functions can make a contribution to understanding law independently of fuzzy theory, as I shall try to show.

b. Negation Operator

By traditional probability theory, the probability of a hypothesis's negation equals 1 minus the probability of the hypothesis. If Katie is 60% likely dead, she is 40% likely alive.

Under the scheme of belief functions, Bel(S) and Bel(notS) do not necessarily add to 1, because normally some belief remains uncommitted. Thus, for Katie, Bel(S) = .5 and Bel(notS) = .2, so the sum of determinate beliefs adds to .7. We are now squarely in the realm of nonadditive beliefs.

The *complement of Bel(S)* equals (1 – Bel(S)), but this gives the plausibility of notS, not the belief in notS. Indeed, the plausibility of notS equals (Bel(notS) + uncommitted belief). Hence, there is a big difference between the complement and the *belief in the negation*: the difference is the uncommitted belief. Belief function theory thus utilizes the very useful distinction between a lack of belief and a disbelief. After all, disbelief and lack of belief are entirely different states of mind.[565]

---

563. See Dubois & Prade, supra note 529, at 375 (arguing for the basic compatibility of the two approaches); John Yen, Generalizing the Dempster-Shafer Theory to Fuzzy Sets, in Classic Works of the Dempster-Shafer Theory of Belief Functions, supra note 404, at 529 (showing how to form beliefs about membership in a fuzzy set); cf. Schum, supra note 466, at 266–69 (observing that one can fuzzify belief functions).

564. See infra Chapter VI.

565. See Bellman & Giertz, supra note 511, at 155–56 (showing that negation can have multiple meanings).

c. Lack of Proof

Traditional probability encounters legendary difficulties with a state of ignorance.[566] The reason is that it cannot distinguish between lack of belief and disbelief. In classical terms, S = 0 means that S is impossible. And it means that notS is certain. No amount of evidence could alter an impossibility or a certainty into a possibility under Bayes' theorem.[567] As a way out, probabilists sometimes assert that the ignorant inquirer should start in the middle where the probabilities of S and notS are both 50%. But this trick does not accord with the actual probabilities or with the law's instructions.[568]

Meanwhile, one of the great strengths of belief function theory is that it well represents a state of ignorance.[569] An inquirer, if ignorant and well-behaved, starts at zero, not at a 50% belief. When Bel(S) = 0, it does not mean that S is so highly unlikely as to be impossible. It means there is no evidence in support. Accordingly, the inquirer starts out with everything indeterminate, because the lack of evidence makes one withhold all of one's belief. Although Bel(S) = 0, Bel(notS) equals zero too. The uncommitted belief is the entirety or 1, meaning that S is completely plausible, as is notS. In other words, the inquirer does not believe or disbelieve S. Belief function theory thus utilizes the very useful distinction between disproof and lack of proof.

2. Legal Application: Burden of Production

Let me start with some background on how the law has traditionally viewed the burden of proof, say, in a jury trial. The burden of proof dictates who must produce evidence and ultimately persuade the factfinder on which elements of the case. Burden of proof thus encompasses two concepts: burden of production and burden of persuasion. The burden of production might require either party at a given time during trial to produce evidence on an element or suffer the judge's adverse determination on that element; one party has the initial burden of production on any particular element, but that burden may shift during the trial if that party produces certain kinds or strengths of evidence. The burden of persuasion requires a certain party ultimately to

566. See, e.g., Richard Lempert, The New Evidence Scholarship: Analyzing the Process of Proof, 66 B.U. L. Rev. 439, 462–67 (1986).
567. See Brilmayer, supra note 435, at 686–88.
568. See supra note 392 and accompanying text.
569. See Shafer, supra note 484, at 22–24 ("representation of ignorance").

persuade the factfinder of the truth of an element or suffer adverse determination on that element.

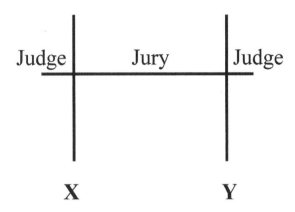

Imagine a single disputed issue of typical fact on which the plaintiff bears the initial burden of production and the burden of persuasion. Then imagine a grid representing the judge's disagreement with a potential verdict for the plaintiff, or equivalently the judge's view of likelihood of error in such a verdict, with disagreement or likelihood decreasing from one on the left to zero on the right.[570] It is important to realize that this diagram represents the likelihood of jury error in finding that the disputed fact exists, not the judge's view of the evidential likelihood that the disputed fact exists. In other words, this diagram represents the judge's thought process in externally overseeing the jury that acts as factfinder, not the judge's thought process as if the judge were finding facts. Alternatively stated, this diagram represents the burden of production, not the burden of persuasion.

The plaintiff in the imagined case starts at the left of the diagram. If he presents no evidence, the judge would ordinarily grant a motion for judgment as a matter of law against him. He is consequently bound to go forward with his evidence until he satisfies the judge that a reasonable jury would be warranted in finding for him. That is, he must get to line X in order to make a jury question of the imagined single issue of fact, doing so by presenting evidence. The plaintiff's getting to or beyond line X means that although the

---

570. See 9 Wigmore, supra note 10, § 2487; cf. McNaughton, supra note 86 (offering alternative diagrams).

judge might still disagree with a verdict for the plaintiff, the judge thinks a reasonable jury could find that the plaintiff sustained his persuasion-burden, and therefore the judge will hold that the plaintiff sustained his production-burden. If the plaintiff does not get to line X, that means that the judge would so vehemently disagree with a verdict for the plaintiff as to consider the jury irrational, and so the judge can grant the motion for judgment as a matter of law. Line X, again, represents the judge's view on the limit of rationality in the jury's finding for the plaintiff, rather than the judge's view of the evidential likelihood that the disputed fact exists. For example, if the judge disbelieved all of the plaintiff's abundant evidence, but still acknowledged that a reasonable jury could believe it, then the judge should rule that the plaintiff has carried his production-burden, because a reasonable jury could conclude that the plaintiff sustained his persuasion-burden.

This diagrammatic scheme works pretty well to represent the law's approach. Moreover, the diagram helps in understanding other concepts and special rules. A *permissive inference* (and res ipsa loquitur is one in the view of most courts[571]) describes an inference that a jury is authorized but not required to draw from certain evidence; in other words, the inference satisfies the plaintiff's production-burden by getting the case to line X, although not beyond line Y. A true *presumption* (such as the presumption against suicide as the cause of death) shifts the burden of production to the opponent after the introduction of the evidential premise; in other words, the presumption puts the case to the right of line Y and so requires the jury to find the presumed fact, unless the opponent introduces enough evidence to carry her production-burden and push the case at least back into the jury zone between Y and X.[572]

Among special rules, certain kinds of evidence will not satisfy an initial burden of production. To satisfy that burden, the burdened party cannot rely on the opponent's failure to testify,[573] on mere disbelief of the opposing testimony,[574] or on demeanor evidence drawn from the opponent's testimony.[575] Similarly, naked statistical evidence normally will not satisfy the initial burden of production.[576] However, any of these kinds of evidence is perfectly proper to

---

571. See John Farley Thorne III, Comment, Mathematics, Fuzzy Negligence, and the Logic of Res Ipsa Loquitur, 75 Nw. U. L. Rev. 147 (1980) (justifying the doctrine by use of fuzzy logic).

572. See Fed. R. Evid. 301.

573. See Stimpson v. Hunter, 125 N.E. 155 (Mass. 1919).

574. See Cruzan v. N.Y. Cent. & Hudson River R.R. Co., 116 N.E. 879 (Mass. 1917).

575. See Dyer v. MacDougall, 201 F.2d 265 (2d Cir. 1952).

576. See Guenther v. Armstrong Rubber Co., 406 F.2d 1315, 1318 (3d Cir. 1969) (dictum) (saying, in a case where the plaintiff had been injured by an exploding tire, that a 75-

introduce as a supplement to positive evidence that satisfies the initial burden of production.[577] The idea behind these special rules is that they are necessary to protect the notion of an initial burden of production, which serves to facilitate early termination of weak claims or defenses, to safeguard against irrational error, and to effectuate other process and outcome values.[578] In the absence of these special rules, any burdened party could produce enough evidence to reach the jury, this evidence possibly being merely in the form of silence, disbelief, demeanor, or general statistics (such as that the defendant manufactured 60% of the supply of the injury-causing device of unknown provenance). Perhaps we harbor a special fear of the jury's mishandling of such evidence when undiluted by other admitted evidence and consequently rendering an unreasoned verdict for the proponent based either on prejudice without regard to the evidence or on undue deference to such bewildering evidence. To avoid such an outcome, and to ensure that the burden of production means something, the judge should require sufficient evidence of other kinds. Once the proponent clears that hurdle, the tribunal should allow the feared evidence its probative effect.

At first glance, this whole accepted scheme seems fairly compatible with traditional probability. One diagrammatic qualification coming from the new logic would be that representing the judge's view of jury error as a fuzzy interval rather than a point would better capture reality.

But the biggest difficulty for traditional probability is fixing the starting point. The probabilist might assume that when you know nothing, the rational starting point is 50% (thus, many a Bayesian would make 50% the initial prior probability). Indeed, some experimental evidence indicates that lay people do tend to start at 50%.[579] Then, if the plaintiff offers a feather's weight of evidence, he would thereby carry not only his burden of production but also his burden of persuasion.

The real-life judge, however, hands only defeat to the plaintiff with nothing more than a feather's weight of evidence, and does so by summary means.

---

to-80% chance it came from the defendant manufacturer was not enough for the case to go to the jury). For a more complete consideration of statistical evidence and its ultimately nonparadoxical nature, see Field et al., supra note 10, at 1352–56 (explaining how a factfinder converts statistical evidence into a belief).

577. See, e.g., Baxter v. Palmigiano, 425 U.S. 308, 316–20 (1976) (treating failure to testify).

578. See Summers, supra note 5.

579. See Martin & Schum, supra note 345, at 390–93 (surveying a small sample of students for their odds of guilt used as the prior probability, which turned out to be 1:1 or 50%).

Why is that? The law says that we should start not at 50% but at the far left, and to get to X requires more than a feather's weight. The proper representation of lack of proof is zero belief in the plaintiff's position, but also zero belief in the defendant's position. The full range of belief is properly uncommitted. That insight makes sense of the notion of the burden of production. It also suggests that, in starting at zero belief, the law is proceeding by belief function theory.

D. Applying Standards

This part will introduce the idea of comparing belief and disbelief of a fact, which the factfinder would do after putting any indeterminate belief aside. Then, this part will demonstrate how the law already conceives of its three standards of proof as different ways of so comparing belief and disbelief.

1. Comparison of Beliefs

My conceptualization has thus far led me to think that the law should not and does not employ the traditional academic view of the proof process resting on a two-valued logical approach. Factfinders instead determine their beliefs as fuzzy degrees of real-world truth based on the evidence, just as the law expects of them. Eventually they end up with Bel(S) and Bel(notS), falling between 0 and 1, but not necessarily adding to 1. What then do they do?

So, finally, I come to the matter of applying a standard of decision. The law dictates that factfinders decide by subjecting their fuzzy beliefs to a standard of proof in order to come to an unambiguous output. That is, at this point the law forces factfinders back into what looks like a two-valued logic, by forcing them to decide for one party or the other. Such disambiguation is not a practice unique to law. All fuzzy computer programs end with a step that produces an unambiguous output, a step called *defuzzification*.[580]

As already observed, application of a standard of proof is a step separable from evidential argument. Psychologists have contributed almost nothing here, leaving the dispute to logicians so far. On the logic front, I contend that speaking in terms of two-valued logic tends to mislead on standards, just as it does elsewhere. Admittedly, the determined theorist could pursue the two-valued image of traditional probability. Then the ultimate task of

---

580. See Kosko, supra note 455, at 172 (describing the step in fuzzy computer systems).

applying a standard of proof would unavoidably involve placement on a scale of likelihood.

A better understanding of standards of proof would result from thinking in terms of many-valued logic and belief functions, however. Even though decisionmaking requires converting from a many-valued logic to an output that sounds two-valued, the law does not need to require enough evidence to make the fact more likely than 50% or whatever. The path to decision might involve only comparing Bel(S) and Bel(notS) while ignoring the indeterminate belief. All the factfinder need do is compare the strengths of belief and disbelief. By requiring only a comparison, belief functions would never require placement on a scale of likelihood.[581]

2. Legal Application: Burden of Persuasion

a. Traditional View

In going from discussing the burden of production to explaining the academic view of the burden of persuasion, I need to use a different diagram, one that represents the internal thought process of the factfinder in ultimately weighing the evidence. The grid now measures the factfinder's view of the evidential likelihood that the disputed fact exists, with likelihood increasing from 0% on the left to 100% on the right.

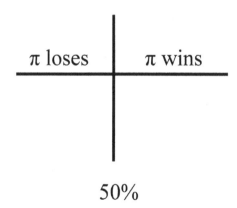

π loses   π wins

50%

---

581. See Smith, supra note 505, at 503 (describing a betting scheme based on such comparison). For the mathematics involved, see Smets & Kennes, supra note 404, at 703–11.

The plaintiff in an imagined civil trial again starts at the left. By presenting evidence on the issue, he must get beyond the midpoint to win. That is, he must show that it is more likely than not that the disputed fact exists. If after the plaintiff has given his best shot the factfinder thinks that he has not passed the 50%-line, then the factfinder should decide for the defendant.

A necessary qualification is that even under this traditional view, this diagram serves mainly as an impetus to thinking about these matters, rather than as a source of definitive statements thereon. For example, the diagram does not mean that a 50%-line exists in reality. The psychological truth is that equipoise is more of a zone, or range of probabilities, than a line. A range of evidential states may strike the factfinder as evenly balanced.

Again, this diagrammatic representation of the traditionally viewed burden of persuasion appears fairly compatible with traditional probability. But having to draw a fat 50%-line encourages a reconsideration of the proof standards. And that reconsideration leads to reformulating those standards to reflect the role of the new logic. The conclusion will be that this diagram for the burden of persuasion is fundamentally misleading. The diagrammed view thus needs redrawing rather than mere refinement. The law does not and should not conform to the traditional academic view.

b. Reformulated View

Recall that the law has settled on three standards of proof that apply in different circumstances: (1) The standard of preponderance of the evidence translates into more-likely-than-not. It is the usual standard in civil litigation, but it appears throughout law. (2) Next comes the intermediate standard or standards, often grouped under the banner of clear and convincing evidence and roughly translated as much-more-likely-than-not. These variously phrased but equivalently applied standards govern on certain issues in special situations, such as when terminating parental rights. (3) The standard of proof beyond a reasonable doubt means proof to a virtual-certainty. It very rarely prevails outside criminal law.

Now, consider using the considerable powers of relative judgment by the factfinder rather than absolute judgment of likelihoods. What could preponderance of the evidence, or its translation of more-likely-than-not, mean in a comparative sense?

One could compare the proof to some threshold. Although one could say that the proof must exceed 50%, this formulation does not accord with the import of real cases. The law does not require the completeness of proof that would be necessary to get a belief above 50%. The law is willing to rest decisions on the evidence presented.[582]

The law does not inquire which side has the stronger evidence, however. It looks instead to belief in the burdened party's position.[583] Although one still could measure the belief against some absolute measure, say, requiring that Bel(S) exceed 50%, the better approach is to invoke the more powerful human ability of relative judgment by comparing beliefs. One could compare Bel(S) relative to Bel(notS).[584]

In comparing them, Bel(notS) is the belief in the negation of S, not the complement of Bel(S). It represents how much the factfinder actively disbelieves S, the fact in dispute. The comparison thus should look at actual belief in S and actual disbelief of S.

If you were to work with only those two beliefs, and discard the indeterminate belief, the most obvious course in civil cases would be to say that the burdened party should win if and only if Bel(S) > Bel(notS). You would decide for the plaintiff if Bel(S) exceeds Bel(notS), but decide for the defendant if Bel(S) does not exceed Bel(notS). This standard not only is readily comprehensible but also avoids any need to quantify beliefs.

The comparative approach to the civil standard of proof does not mean that the nonburdened party needs to formulate a competing version of the truth, other than negation. A belief in the falsity of the burdened party's version of the truth may develop naturally in the course of trial. It could arise even upon hearing only the burdened party's evidence. The nonburdened party's evidence, if any, should contribute to raising Bel(notS).

Relatedly, the nonburdened party need not fight imaginary fights. Some scholars worry that looking at negation puts the burdened party in the impossible situation of disproving every alternative possibility.[585] But that worry

---

582. See Laudan, supra note 440, at 304–05 ("The trier of fact cannot say, 'Although plaintiff's case is stronger than defendant's, I will reach no verdict since neither party has a frightfully good story to tell'. Under current rules, if the plaintiff has a better story than the defendant, he must win the suit, even when his theory of the case fails to satisfy the strictures required to qualify his theory as the best explanation.").

583. See McBaine, supra note 14, at 248–49.

584. See Cohen, supra note 230, at 255 ("The cardinal question to be settled by the trier of fact may always be construed as this: on the facts before the court, is the conclusion to be proved by the plaintiff more inductively probable than its negation?"); supra note 187.

585. See, e.g., Michael S. Pardo, Second-Order Proof Rules, 61 Fla. L. Rev. 1083, 1093–94 (2009) (footnotes omitted) (speaking of the comparison imposed by more-likely-than-not, but using "negation" in the sense of the complement of Bel(S)):

[The comparison] might mean the likelihood of the plaintiff's factual allegations

comes from confusing lack of belief with disbelief. Disbelieving S entails the degree to which the factfinder thinks S is false. The mere possibility of other states of the world in which S is not true go into the uncommitted belief, not into Bel(notS); recall that the "plausibility" of notS equals Bel(notS) plus the uncommitted belief; again, the degree of believing that Katie is not dead, or actually alive, is quite different from envisaging the chance that she is possibly alive. The proposed comparison involves the belief in notS, and does not involve the plausibility of notS.

Now, as to the other two standards of proof, clear and convincing evidence should mean Bel(S) >> Bel(notS).[586] This standard would not be that difficult to apply. We are quite used to such a standard of being clearly convinced, in life and in law. Judges apply it on a motion for a new trial based on the verdict's being against the weight of the evidence. Appellate courts use it in reviewing judge-found facts. Those standards of decision mean that it is not enough to disagree with the jury or the judge; the reviewer must think there was a serious error.

However, the cases do not make very evident what clear and convincing means. Alternatively, or perhaps additionally, it imposes a requirement about the completeness of evidence. It may require admission of enough evidence to reduce uncommitted belief to the point that Bel(S) exceeds the plausibility of notS. I am open to those viewpoints, but unconvinced so far. In the mean-

---

versus the negation of those allegations, or it might mean the likelihood of the plaintiff's allegations versus the likelihood of the defendant's alternative allegations. The first interpretation appears to better fit the instructions, but it fails .... If the plaintiff must prove that some fact, X, is more probable than its negation, *not-X*, then the plaintiff should have to show not only the probability that the state of the world is such that X is true, but also the probability of every other possible state of the world in which X is not true. This would mean that in order to prevail, plaintiffs would have to disprove (or demonstrate the low likelihood of) each of the virtually limitless number of ways the world could have been at the relevant time. This would be a virtually impossible task, and thus, absent conclusive proof, plaintiffs would lose. This would plainly be inconsistent with the goals of the preponderance rule, and thus some comparison with the defendant's case is necessary.

In order to facilitate the goals of the preponderance rule, the plaintiff ought to prevail whenever the likelihood of his allegations exceeds that of the defendant's.

586. See McBaine, supra note 14, at 263 (proposing an instruction to the effect that "the probability that they are true or exist is substantially greater than the probability that they are false or do not exist"); Edmund M. Morgan, Instructing the Jury upon Presumptions and Burden of Proof, 47 Harv. L. Rev. 59, 67 (1933) ("its truth is much more probable than its falsity"); cf. Laudan, supra note 440, at 299–300 (discussing attempts to append such notions to the approach of inference to the best explanation).

time, one could partially capture this requirement by explicating clear and convincing to the factfinder as the standard that lies between preponderance and reasonable doubt.

As to proof beyond a reasonable doubt, it is different in kind. It must mean more than Bel(S) >> Bel(notS). Placing separate demands on Bel(notS) and Bel(S), it should mean that no reasonable doubt persists and that no great uncommitted belief remains.[587]

No reasonable doubt means that no reasonable person could hold Bel(notS) > 0. On the view that anything is possible, zero as a coarsely gradated degree of belief equates to a "slightest possibility." Therefore, Bel(notS) > 0 refers to a step up from the slightest possibility of innocence. No reasonable factfinder should see a "reasonable possibility" of innocence. In other words, for a conviction the prosecutor must show that no reasonable possibility of innocence exists.

No great uncommitted belief reflects the idea that Bel(S) cannot be weak, measured in an absolute sense. We do not want to convict when, although there is some evidence of guilt, we really do not know what happened. The belief in guilt must outweigh all alternative possibilities, including fanciful ones. The *belief* in guilt must at least exceed the *plausibility* of innocence, so that Bel(S) > .50. Given the usual limits on available evidence, achieving such a high degree of absolute belief represents a demanding standard.[588]

That proof beyond a reasonable doubt differs in kind—it seems not to be simply Bel(S) >>> Bel(notS)—implies that the law could create significantly more than three standards of proof. Not being restricted to the three categories of likelihood above equipoise, the law could play in various other ways with the comparison of Bel(S) and Bel(notS). But it does not. The law sticks with three standards of proof. Perhaps it does so in deference to the pattern of other standards of decision, which look directly at the decisionmaker's perceived category of likelihood and which can therefore not realistically and feasibly multiply the standards available. Or perhaps the law simply recognizes that decisionmakers already have enough trouble distinguishing among three standards of proof.

---

587. See Allen & Leiter, supra note 429, at 1528 (saying that the prosecution must "show that there is no plausible account of innocence"); McBaine, supra note 14, at 266 (proposing an instruction to the effect that a reasonable doubt exists when "you cannot honestly say that it is almost certain that the defendant did the acts which he is charged to have done"); cf. Laudan, supra note 440, at 300–02 (discussing attempts to append such a notion to the approach of inference to the best explanation).

588. On justifying what still may seem to be a low threshold, Bel(S) > .50, see supra text accompanying note 68.

Compatibility of Reformulated and Current Standards

A reader always entertains the temptation, upon seeing what looks like a plea for reconceptualization, to dismiss it as a pie-in-the-sky academic musing. When the reconceptualization involves the standards of proof, the specialists have the added temptation of dismissing it as another of the common anti-probabilist rants or pro-probabilist paeans. After all, if my view were a sound one, someone would have come up with it before. So I hasten to undercut my contribution by stressing that my ideas are not that new. I am trying little more than to explain what the law has been doing all along.

The easiest way to grasp the lack of newness is to picture an alternative fashion of converting from fuzzy beliefs back into a two-valued output. Picture a normalization process of disregarding the indeterminate beliefs and scaling Bel(S) and Bel(notS) up proportionately so that they add to one. Call the recalculations b(S) and b(notS). If Bel(S) = .50 and Bel(notS) = .20, then b(S) = .71 and b(notS) = .29. These new numbers represent much less mental distance from the traditional view of standards of proof, because b(S) > b(notS) if and only if b(S) > .50. Thus, preponderance could retain a meaning of likelihood exceeding 50%, while clear and convincing means much more likely than 50% and beyond a reasonable doubt means almost certainty. This alternative renders my conceptualization much less jarring, and it also demonstrates that I did not pull my formulations out of thin air.

Yet, I resist taking that normalization route. First, converting to additive beliefs would reintroduce the probabilistic imaging that originally led us astray into all the problems and paradoxes of the traditional view. Second, I contend that directly comparing Bel(S) and Bel(notS) actually conforms better to the actual law than the probabilistic view does. Third, normalization requires measurement of b(S) and b(notS), a complicated step otherwise unnecessary, and a step that is much more difficult for humans than relative judgment.

The evidence at trial will support S to an extent while supporting notS to another extent, and the reformulated standards say that the factfinder need only compare these two fuzzy beliefs. How does the current law actually state, say, preponderance of the evidence? Consider a couple of classic cases.

In *Livanovitch v. Livanovitch*,[589] the trial court gave the following charge: "If ... you are more inclined to believe from the evidence that he did so deliver the bonds to the defendant, even though your belief is only *the slightest degree*

---

589. 131 A. 799 (Vt. 1926).

greater than that he did not, your verdict should be for the plaintiff."[590] The appellate court said:

> The instruction was not erroneous. It was but another way of saying that the slightest preponderance of the evidence in his favor entitled the plaintiff to a verdict.… All that is required in a civil case of one who has the burden of proof is that he establish his claim by a preponderance of the evidence.… When the equilibrium of proof is destroyed, and the beam inclines toward him who has the burden, however slightly, he has satisfied the requirement of the law, and is entitled to the verdict. "A bare preponderance is sufficient, though the scales drop but a feather's weight." This rule accords with the practice in this state as remembered by the justices of this court, and is well supported by the authorities.[591]

In *Lampe v. Franklin American Trust Co.*,[592] one of the defendant's contentions was that the note in suit had been altered after it had been signed by the defendant's decedent. The trial court refused the defendant's request for an instruction that the jury should find that the instrument was not the decedent's note "if you find and believe that it is *more probable* that such changes or alterations have been made in the instrument after it was signed by the deceased and without his knowledge and consent, than it is that such alterations and changes were made at or about the time that the deceased signed the instrument and under his direction and with his knowledge and consent."[593] Holding the refusal to have been proper, the appellate court said:

> The trouble with this statement is that a verdict must be based upon what the jury finds to be facts rather than what they find to be "more probable." … This means merely that the party, who has the burden of proof, must produce evidence, tending to show the truth of those facts, "which is more convincing to them as worthy of belief than that which is offered in opposition thereto."[594]

These two cases' formulations sound contradictory. But if one interprets the quotations as speaking in terms of the coarsely gradated belief in the fact compared with the coarsely gradated belief in the fact's negation, based on the evidence presented, the apparent contradiction evaporates. They both seem

---

590. Id. at 800.
591. Id.
592. 96 S.W.2d 710 (Mo. 1936).
593. Id. at 723.
594. Id. (quoting Rouchene v. Gamble Constr. Co., 89 S.W.2d 58, 63 (Mo. 1935)).

to be saying that the burdened party should win if and only if Bel(S) > Bel(notS).

Other courts sometimes express more divergent views of the standard of proof. Some writers conclude that courts interpret the probabilistic approach to preponderance in one of three ways: (1) "more convincing," which requires the burdened party to tell a better tale than the opponent tells; (2) "more likely than not," which requires a showing of the fact's existence stronger than the showing of its nonexistence; or (3) "really happened," which requires a showing by evidence of what probably transpired outside in the real world.[595] My approach would conform to the middle option of (2), rather than either (1) relative plausibility or (3) absolute measure.

In the end, I submit that comparison of coarsely gradated beliefs is an accurate representation of what the law tells a factfinder to do with a standard of proof. In civil cases, the factfinder has to find that Bel(S) is more likely than *not*, which means Bel(S) > Bel(notS). Or as the judge tells the jurors, preponderance means that the evidence "produces in your minds belief that what is sought to be proved is more likely true than not true"[596] or "more probably true than false."[597] By literally instructing factfinders to decide between S and notS, the law effectively urges them to focus on those two fuzzy beliefs and compare them.

c. Implications of Reformulation

My views, then, are not seditious. Overall I merely contend, in accordance with the new logic's teaching, that the law charges factfinders to form a set of fuzzy factual degrees of belief that would conform to a coarsely gradated scale, while leaving some belief uncommitted in the face of imperfect evidence, and then to apply the standard of proof by comparing their resultant belief in the burdened party's version to their belief in its negation. Many observers of the legal system would find that contention, putting its slightly new vocabulary to the side, unobjectionable.

Tracing the implications of my contention reveals its hidden powers, however. It implies that the factfinders at the end of a case would properly apply the standard to each separate element. It also implies that the factfinders should

---

595. See, e.g., Covington, supra note 545, at 99–100; cf. supra note 27 (locating these three views on a broader spectrum of disagreement).

596. 3 O'Malley et al., supra note 371, § 104.01.

597. Nissho-Iwai Co. v. M/T Stolt Lion, 719 F.2d 34, 38 (2d Cir. 1983) ("The term 'preponderance' means that 'upon all the evidence ... the facts asserted by the plaintiff are more probably true than false.'" (quoting Porter v. Am. Exp. Lines, Inc., 387 F.2d 409, 411 (3d Cir. 1968))).

start the case, being in a state of ignorance with lack of proof, at a zero belief. Thus, two paradoxes in the nature of legal proof simply vaporize. The four parts of this chapter generate related insights.

First, the linguistic evaluations that humans tend to use in their fuzzy logic, as opposed to quantifications, nicely express the law's development of a coarsely gradated scale of possibilities and probabilities: (1) slightest possibility, (2) reasonable possibility, (3) substantial possibility, (4) equipoise, (5) probability, (6) high probability, and (7) almost certainty. And the coarseness of the scale of likelihood means that the factfinder in comparing beliefs will not have to draw paper-thin distinctions.

Second, when the factfinders face multiple elements, it has long appeared that they seek the most believable story by applying the standard of proof to each element. But theorists worry that this conjoined story itself may not meet the standard of proof. Rest assured, because the law knows what it is doing. The MIN operator demonstrates that belief in the conjunction will match the belief in the least likely element, which has already passed the standard of proof.

Third, the notion of burden of proof becomes much clearer. The paradoxical difficulties in applying the burden to weak proof dissipate. For an example, a directed verdict motion by a civil defendant meshes the burden of production with the new view of the preponderance standard. The motion requires the judge to ask if no reasonable jury could view $Bel(S) > Bel(notS)$.[598] At the end of the plaintiff's case, if a reasonable $Bel(notS)$ could equal 0 (effectively a "slightest possibility"), then the inequality requires a compatibly reasonable $Bel(S)$ to exceed 0 (effectively a "reasonable possibility"). That the plaintiff must have established a reasonable possibility is the embodiment of the burden of production, and it is what keeps the plaintiff from surviving with a mere feather's weight of evidence. An illustrative situation would be where the plaintiff has produced a little evidence, but it is "pure" evidence that gives the defendant no support.[599] If a reasonable jury could find for the plaintiff on such proof, the judge should deny the directed verdict motion. If the defendant then produces no effective evidence during the rest of the trial, but moves again for a directed verdict at the end of all the evidence, the judge should deny the motion and the case should

---

598. The reference to a "reasonable" jury reflects the fact that on such a motion the judge is reviewing the jury's hypothesized application of the standard of proof. The judge's standard of decision turns on whether a jury could not reasonably, or rationally, find for the nonmovant. That is, the defendant must show that a verdict for the plaintiff, given the standard of proof, is not reasonably possible.

599. See Liu & Yager, supra note 561, at 18–19 (discussing Liebniz's notions of pure and mixed evidence).

go to the jury. The jury, if it were to take the same view of the evidence as the judge hypothesized, could find for the plaintiff—even on such thin evidence.

Fourth, a new understanding of how to apply the standard of proof to the party with the burden of persuasion follows naturally, even if not inevitably, from the foregoing logical conceptualization of the nature of proof. The standard should concede that upon incomplete, inconclusive, ambiguous, dissonant, and untrustworthy proof, some of our belief will remain indeterminate. The standard should look only to committed belief, comparing belief in the burdened party's version versus disbelief.

Not only does this comparative approach comport with the natural cognitive method that follows from telling the factfinders they must decide for one side or the other, but also it does nothing to interfere with the current procedural and substantive functioning of the standard of proof. For example, the traditional view of the preponderance standard as a showing of a probability greater than 50% appeared appropriate for civil cases: among competing fixed standards, it minimizes the expected number of erroneous decisions and also the expected sum of wrongful amounts of damages, which is the goal that the law apparently has chosen to pursue. My reformulated standard has the same error-minimizing properties, but achieves them in the real world where the principle of bivalence does not hold and where some indeterminacy prevails. For an idea of a proof adapted from a probabilist's proof, let $b(S) = p$ be the apparent probability that the defendant is liable (for D dollars) under a two-valued view. If $\text{Bel}(S) > \text{Bel}(\text{notS})$, then $p > \frac{1}{2}$; call p by the name p_1 in that case. If $\text{Bel}(S) \leq \text{Bel}(\text{notS})$, call it p_2. On the one hand, under the preponderance standard, the expected sum of false positives and false negatives over the run of cases is $\sum[(1 - p_1)D + p_2 D]$. On the other hand, under a very high standard that eliminates false positives, the analogous sum is $\sum[p_1 D + p_2 D]$. Therefore, given that $(1 - p_1)$ is less than p_1, the reformulated preponderance standard lowers the system's expected error costs.

To close, a comprehensive example would perhaps be beneficial. Suppose that someone has seriously injured Suzie, in circumstances suggesting fault. She sues Tom, which means that she must prove his identity as the tortfeasor—as well as fault, causation, and injury. She introduces a fair amount of evidence.

- First, the factfinder would assess that evidence and might conclude as follows: (1) The evidence points to Tom being the perpetrator. If the factfinder were a bettor, he would put the odds at 3:2, or 60%. Using words, he would say that Tom was probably the perpetrator. (2) The question of fault was a tough one. There are uncertainties as to what was done, but there is also a vagueness concerning how blameworthy the supposed acts really were. The factfinder needs commensurable measures, so that he can evaluate a mix of random and nonrandom uncertainty. If forced to assess all the evidence on this issue and put it on a scale of truth running from zero to one, he would say .7. He might feel more comfortable saying fault was probable or more. (3) The acts, whatever they were, apparently caused the injury. Proximate cause is about as vague and multivalent as a legal concept can get. The factfinder is pretty convinced nevertheless. He would put causation at .8, or highly probable. (4) Suzie's injuries are not really very vague or uncertain. He would put this element of the tort at .95, or beyond a reasonable doubt. Note that the new conceptualization changes nothing, to this point, regarding the factfinder's task as traditionally envisaged.

- Second, the factfinder may want to combine these findings. They are a mixture of probabilities and degrees of truth. But viewing them all as degrees of truth invokes the MIN operator, so that he can say that Suzie's story comes in at .6, or probable. Suzie should win, by use of fuzzy logic.

- Third, this approach does not do a terribly good job of accounting for the state of the evidence. It still poses an odd question to the factfinder: given imperfect evidence, what is the degree to which the plaintiff is right? Belief functions work better here to reflect the factfinder's actual knowledge: belief starts at zero, and some belief will remain uncommitted in the absence of perfect evidence. That is, on a fact to which the standard of proof applies, the belief function route is the one to take, rather than invoking the simplistic scale of likelihood just described. Instead of saying that Tom's fault is probable, the factfinder should speak and think in terms of degrees of belief.

- Fourth, although belief functions do not require placement on a scale, the factfinder in effect might end in believing Suzie's position on Tom's fault to be only substantially possible. That situation does not mean that Suzie should lose, however. The factfinder might, if forced to express likelihood, believe the falsity of Tom's fault merely to a reasonable possibility. All the factfinder must do is to compare belief and disbelief: all that preponderance of the evidence requires is that the strength of the factfinder's belief that Tom was at fault must exceed his belief that Tom was not at fault. Belief functions thus add the idea that the factfinder in such a case must have a belief in the case's truth stronger than his belief in its falsity. While some of the factfinder's belief remains uncommitted, he did find Suzie's position to be a good one: more likely true than false. So, Suzie should still win, by use of belief functions.

In conclusion, this chapter deployed the new logic—in particular, fuzzy logic and belief functions in their broad senses—to conceptualize the standards of proof. This was not a heavily prescriptive endeavor, which would have tried to argue normatively for the best way to apply standards. Instead, it was mainly a descriptive and explanatory endeavor, trying to unearth how standards of proof actually work in the law world. Compared to the traditionally probabilistic account, this conceptualization conforms more closely to what we know of people's cognition, captures better what the law says its standards are and how it manipulates them, and improves our mental image of the factfinders' task. One virtue of the conceptualization is that it is not radically new, as it principally acts to confirm the law's ancient message that factfinders should simply compare their nonquantified views of the fact's truth and falsity. The conceptualization leaves the law's standards essentially intact to accomplish their current purposes. Another virtue is that it nevertheless manages to resolve some stubborn problems of proof, including the fabled conjunction paradox. Thus, for understanding the standards of proof, degrees of fuzzy belief work better than traditional probabilities.

Chapter VI

Comparative (and Historical) Puzzle as to Standards of Proof

The subject of this chapter is a striking divergence between common-law and civil-law countries' standards of proof in noncriminal, or civil, cases. In England and the United States, the standard of proof sounds "probabilistic" in the capacious sense of accepting uncertainty: civil claims ordinarily must be proved by a preponderance of the evidence, that is, the party with the burden of persuasion must prove the fact to be more likely than not. In civilian countries, the standard seems strange to us: it says that a civil claimant must in effect convince the trier of fact that the claimant's assertions are true.

The common law treats the standard of proof as centrally important. Strangely enough, the civilian world rather casually requires the civil litigant with the burden to prove the fact to a much higher probability, identical or similar to the criminal law's virtual-certainty requirement.

Thus, for example, the classic study of German civil procedure makes this passing observation on standards of proof:

> What is the degree of conviction to which the civil court must be brought in ordinary situations before it is justified in holding that the burden of establishing a proposition has been met? [A German treatise says]: "The judge may and must always content himself with a degree of certainty that is appropriate for practical life, one which silences doubts without entirely excluding them." Evidently a rather high degree of probability is called for, and there is a tendency toward at least verbal equation of the civil with the criminal standard.[600]

---

600. Benjamin Kaplan, Arthur T. von Mehren & Rudolf Schaefer, Phases of German Civil Procedure (pt. 1), 71 Harv. L. Rev. 1193, 1245 (1958) (footnotes omitted); see also Arthur T. von Mehren, Some Comparative Reflections on First Instance Civil Procedure: Recent Reforms in German Civil Procedure and in the Federal Rules, 63 Notre Dame L. Rev. 609 (1988).

According to a more recent sketch, the situation is this:

> The law ... in Germany, as contrasted with United States law, es-
> chews different standards of proof. Under the German system, the
> judge must be convinced beyond a reasonable doubt, whether the suit
> involves private, criminal, or public law (administrative and consti-
> tutional) issues. The reasonable doubt standard is inapplicable only in
> the exceptional circumstance in which a statute specifically mentions
> some other standard to be applied.[601]

So, Germany applies, with some exceptions,[602] a reasonable-doubt standard
in civil cases. The very existence of legislative or judge-made exceptions, as in
Germany, confirms the existence of a normally high civil standard. Thus, German law today does differ from U.S. law on the standard in civil cases.[603]

Beyond Germany, other civil-law countries follow suit, with the result that
the civil-law and common-law formulations of the civil standard of proof in
general differ starkly. This difference qualifies now as obvious truth, justifying
an encyclopedia's summary:

> In continental European law, no distinction is made between civil and
> criminal cases with regard to the standard of proof. In both, such a
> high degree of probability is required that, to the degree that this is pos-
> sible in the ordinary experience of life itself, doubts are excluded and
> probability approaches certitude. In the common-law countries the
> degree of probability required in civil cases is lower than that called for
> in criminal matters.[604]

---

601. Juliane Kokott, The Burden of Proof in Comparative and International Human
Rights Law 18 (1998) (footnotes omitted).

602. See Peter Gottwald, Fact Finding: A German Perspective, in The Option of Litigating
in Europe 67, 77 (D.L. Carey Miller & Paul R. Beaumont eds., 1993) (stressing the importance of exceptions that apply a preponderance standard "with regard to prima facie cases,
to causation, to negligence and to assessment of damages"); cf. Per Olof Ekelöf, Be-
weiswürdigung, Beweislast und Beweis des ersten Anscheins [Evaluation of Proof, Burden
of Proof, and Prima Facie Proof], 75 Zeitschrift für Zivilprozess 289 (1962) (criticizing the
logic of such exceptions).

603. See Patrick Kinsch, Entre certitude et vraisemblance, le critère de la preuve en
matière civile, in De code en code 455, 459 (2009). But cf. Peter L. Murray & Rolf Stürner,
German Civil Justice 310–13 (2004) (stressing lack of clarity in German law on the civil
standard).

604. Heinrich Nagel, Evidence, in 7 Encyclopædia Britannica: Macropædia 1, 2 (1974),
available at http://www.britannica.com/EBchecked/topic/197308/evidence/28368/The-bur-
den-of-proof.

For the standard of proof on the criminal side, the civilians set a high standard, requiring what some call *une intime conviction*, or an inner, deep-seated, personal conviction of the judge. This high criminal standard, whatever one chooses to call it, has its champions, who claim its superiority over the common-law standard of beyond a reasonable doubt, seeing it as clearer, as more expressly focused on a subjective belief or moral certainty as an absolute threshold, or as more squarely a burden imposed on the prosecution.[605] In actual practice, however, the civil-law and common-law standards for criminal cases are likely equivalent.[606]

The significant and surprising departure from the common law, then, is that civilians say they apply the same or a very similar standard in noncriminal cases as they do in criminal cases. The party who bears the burden in a civil case must satisfy the judges, to the point of *intime conviction*, of the existence of the pertinent fact. The civil law "demands the same high degree of the judge's conviction in civil matters as in criminal matters: only facts established with certainty, or with that high degree of probability that one until recently called moral certainty, can be accepted by the judge in civil cases."[607] My concern in this chapter lies with this marked difference from the common-law standard of preponderance of the evidence.

In theory, instead of asking whether some fact X (say, that the defendant executed the promissory note disputed in a noncriminal lawsuit) is more likely true than not, the civil law asks whether the fact is so probable as to create an inner and deep-seated conviction of its truth. Civilians d so in all courts, including their administrative courts. That is, instead of a standard requiring merely a preponderance of the evidence, they apply their *intime conviction* standard. What exactly does *intime conviction* mean? Civilians are usually vague on this point, only occasionally muttering something definitive. Then it might

---

605. E.g., Solan, supra note 60, at 106, 118, 145.

606. See Michael Bohlander, Principles of German Criminal Procedure 8 (2012); Mireille Delmas-Marty, La preuve pénale, 23 Droits 53, 59–60 (1996) (observing, however, initially: "*Le degré de certitude qui conditionne la décision de culpabilité est une des questions les plus obscures du droit pénal.*"); Kinsch, supra note 603, at 458. Indeed, some civil-law countries are expressly adopting the phrase of beyond a reasonable doubt. For one example, in 2009 Belgium enacted a statute that substituted a beyond-a-reasonable-doubt standard in criminal cases for *intime conviction*, with Article 327 of the Belgian Code of Criminal Procedure saying: "The law provides that the accused may be convicted only if it is apparent from the evidence admitted that he is guilty beyond reasonable doubt of the offence with which he is charged." See Stephen C. Thaman, Should Criminal Juries Give Reasons for Their Verdicts: The Spanish Experience and the Implications of the European Court of Human Rights Decision in Taxquet v. Belgium, 86 Chi.-Kent L. Rev. 613, 624 (2011).

607. Kinsch, supra note 603, at 459 (translated).

even sound like proof beyond a shadow of a doubt. The essence, though, is that they want to be very sure before upholding the burdened party's proof. Alternatively stated, they are much more willing to accept a false negative than a false positive.

The difference is not that the civil-law standard is subjective while the common-law standard is in some sense objective. That distinction is illusory.[608] Civilians do look for an inner conviction, but they expect the judge to base that conviction on the evidence.[609] Common-law formulations do speak more directly of the evidence, but they actually look to the factfinders' belief based on that evidence.

The critical difference between the two systems, therefore, is that the civil law demands a stronger belief before their factfinders decide for the burdened party in a civil case. If civilians are not actually practicing what they are preaching, then unearthing their law in action would be an important thing to do. Assuming instead, as it might be fair to do, that the standards of proof operate in practice as they are stated in texts, then this striking difference between common-law and civil-law rules not only has great practical importance, but also suggests a basic difference in attitudes toward the process of trial and subtle differences between the two systems' procedural objectives.

I am focusing on the civil-law systems, but their approach to standards of proof appears to prevail in other legal traditions.[610] Thus, the common-law approach could fairly be termed the common-law exception. U.S. lawyers accept their own lower standard of proof as a significant policy choice and an

---

608. See Moritz Brinkmann, The Synthesis of Common and Civil Law Standard of Proof Formulae in the ALI/UNIDROIT Principles of Transnational Civil Procedure, 9 Unif. L. Rev. (n.s.) 875, 881–82 (2004). This point is driven home by the fact that some civilians invoke their standard's subjectivity not as a mark of distinction but as proof of similarity to common-law standards. "It is this subjective element that allows German courts to operate in much the same way as their American counterparts ...." Gerhard Wagner, Heuristics in Procedural Law, in Heuristics and the Law, supra note 540, at 281, 283.

609. Civil-law countries differ on whether the judges must merely arrive at an *intime conviction* or must go on to state the reasons on which they based judgment, specifying in writing why they were convinced and thus meeting a standard of explicable conviction or *conviction raisonnée*.

610. See, e.g., Mary Ann Glendon, Michael Wallace Gordon & Christopher Osakwe, Comparative Legal Traditions 903 (1985) (explaining that Soviet law did not distinguish between degrees of proof, but instead required "inner conviction of the judge" in all civil as well as criminal cases); I.V. Reshetnikova & V.V. Iarkov, Grazhdanskoe pravo i grazhdanskii protsess v sovremennoi Rossii [Civil Law and Civil Procedure in Contemporary Russia] 168–71 (1999) (saying that the same standard still applies under art. 56 of the new Russian Civil Procedure Code).

unquestionably proper one. Most of them are ignorant of the rest of the world's law to the contrary; they react with disbelief upon having it explained; but upon being convinced of reality, they quickly conclude that foreigners have been misguided to reject something so obviously valid.

Yet, the comparative literature has largely overlooked the subject of standards of proof. Indeed, the lack of attention is even stranger than the fact itself of the common law's adherence to its lonely position. The silence is downright bizarre. Standards of proof are not an obscure point. The disagreement between the civil and common law here is deep and evident enough that even an encyclopedia notes it, as above quoted. But strangely, for the longest time almost no one seemed to make much of the difference, in the United States or elsewhere.[611] Recently, though, the articles of a few commentators and the increasing prominence of international courts seem to have generated at least some interest in the comparative puzzle, so discussion has commenced in both the civil-law and common-law camps. This is good. This subject needs attention. Insights abound.

---

611. E.g., Ugo A. Mattei, Teemu Ruskola & Antonio Gidi, Schlesinger's Comparative Law (7th ed. 2009) (giving no discussion); Konrad Zweigert & Hein Kötz, Introduction to Comparative Law (Tony Weir trans., 3d rev. ed. 1998) (same). Some comparativists alluded to the puzzle. Professor Mirjan R. Damaška's book, Evidence Law Adrift (1997), compared the law of proof in the civil and common law. American-published but European-informed, the book briefly observes the oddity of civil-law standards of proof: "Surprisingly, the [criminal] standard of [*intime*] conviction is often said to be applicable in civil cases as well." Id. at 40 n.29 (citations omitted). But cf. id. at 114 n.78 (stressing that exceptions exist to the high civil standard). Neither his book's general theme on evidence law nor his specific preference for civil-law methods of proof sheds light that would lessen the surprise. See id. at 114 (observing that a high civil standard is unexpected, given the dispute-resolution purpose of civil proceedings on the Continent), 121 (observing that the lesser devotion to truth on the noncriminal side would warrant a less demanding standard of proof than on the criminal side). For instance, he says that civilians view themselves as less technically legalistic, more real-world and scientific, than common lawyers in their approach to truth-finding. See id. at 11–12. But he realizes that any such superiority fails to explain the civil-law standards of proof. See id. at 89 ("At the outset, it should be made clear that these [shortcomings of common-law factfinding] are not to be found in the sphere of reasoning about the validity of proof," but in the passivity of Anglo-American factfinders and in the methods for putting evidence before them.).

A. Variations

1. English Approach

Take England as another common-law example on the standards of proof. England recognizes two standards: balance of probabilities for civil cases and beyond a reasonable doubt for criminal cases.[612] Previously, courts waffled on this purity a good deal, expressing the allure of intermediate standards.[613] Lord Denning put the argument for multiple standards thus:

> It is of course true that by our law a higher standard of proof is required in criminal cases than in civil cases. But this is subject to the qualification that there is no absolute standard in either case. In criminal cases the charge must be proved beyond reasonable doubt, but there may be degrees of proof within that standard.
>
> ... So also in civil cases, the case may be proved by a preponderance of probability, but there may be degrees of probability within that standard. The degree depends on the subject-matter. A civil court, when considering a charge of fraud, will naturally require for itself a higher degree of probability than that which it would require when asking if negligence is established. It does not adopt so high a degree as a criminal court, even when it is considering a charge of a criminal nature; but still it does require a degree of probability which is commensurate with the occasion.[614]

As in the United States, the English law treats the standard of proof as centrally important. Different civil and criminal standards clearly exist, with lots of attention expended over the years on what those different standards should be. Although this long, candid debate continues as to details, certain basic propositions enjoy wide acceptance.

Everyone agrees, as a rational matter, on this: "The establishment of the truth of alleged facts in adjudication is typically a matter of probabilities, falling

---

612. See Sec'y of State for Home Dep't v. Rehman, [2003] 1 A.C. 153 (H.L. 2001); Rosemary Pattenden, The Risk of Non-Persuasion in Civil Trials: The Case Against a Floating Standard of Proof, 7 Civ. Just. Q. 220 (1988).

613. See Adrian Keane, The Modern Law of Evidence 91, 95–101 (5th ed. 2000) (observing some intermediate standards in practice); Ennis McBride, Is the Civil "Higher Standard of Proof" a Coherent Concept?, 8 Law Probability & Risk 323 (2009) (arguing that recent House of Lords' decisions failed to settle the debate).

614. Bater v. Bater, [1951] P. 35, 36–37, [1951] 2 All E.R. 458, 459 (C.A. 1950).

short of absolute certainty."[615] Furthermore, as an instrumental matter, the law should try to set the required probability at levels that serve the system's aims. In short, it is candid, rational, and desirable to recognize that factfinding is a matter of probability and that the system should seek to optimize its probabilistic standards of proof.[616]

In setting its standard of proof for civil cases, England like the United States has overcome the appealing but unsound lay intuition that outcome should not swing from no recovery to full recovery on the basis of a slight shift in the weight of evidence. Instead, the common law pursues an error-cost minimizing strategy, by routinely applying the balance of probabilities or the preponderance of the evidence as the civil standard and not some higher standard. Also worth noting is that the aim in imposing one of the higher standards of proof often is heavily substantive in nature. The lower standard has the procedural aim of providing the parties with a level playing field. But a higher standard usually aims to influence the outcome of the case. Therefore, the common law demands a special reason before it will impose one of the higher standards on certain kinds of cases. The civil law does not, and that is the critical difference.

Room for debate still exists as to what the standard of balance of probabilities or preponderance of the evidence practically means.[617] Moreover, lots of room exists to elaborate the finer theoretical points of probabilistic proof and consequent liability, such as the recent elaboration of the proper role for statistical evidence. The point here is simply that such debate occurs in a lively and open fashion in England and the United States, against the background of acceptance of some sort of more-likely-than-not standard for civil cases.

The contrast is to civilian lawmakers and commentators, who have done some such work on the implications of proof standards,[618] but not very

615. Twining, supra note 2, at 76.

616. See Richard D. Friedman, Anchors and Flotsam: Is Evidence Law "Adrift"?, 107 Yale L.J. 1921, 1946 (1998).

617. For an intriguing exploration, see Rhesa Shipping Co. v. Edmunds, [1985] 1 W.L.R. 948, 955 (H.L.) (rejecting the Sherlock Holmes dictum that "when you have eliminated the impossible, whatever remains, however improbable, must be the truth").

618. E.g., Pierre Widmer & Pierre Wessner, Révision et unification du droit de la responsabilité civile: rapport explicatif 241–46 (c. 2000) (explaining Swiss law-reform proposals on liability); Fabienne Hohl, Le degré de la preuve dans les procès au fond, in Der Beweis im Zivilprozess 127, 137 (Christoph Leuenberger ed., 2000) (describing the current Swiss approach and calling for reform, but concluding: "Par conséquent, une vraisemblance simple, chiffrée pour les besoins de la démonstration à 51%, ne devrait jamais suffire."); see Per Olof Bolding, Aspects of the Burden of Proof, 4 Scandinavian Stud. L. 9, 18 (1960) (arguing for a probabilistic approach and the preponderance standard—against "the classical view of the

much,[619] so judges there have to muddle through the cutting-edge problems without guidance. The common law too can hide some aspects of proof from view, as it has done with the conjunction problem of element-by-element application of the standard of proof—here common lawyers have proceeded with their heads in the sand, albeit with acceptable results, as I explained in the preceding chapter. But civilian lawyers bury their heads farther, never even perceiving a conjunction problem: "In this respect there is a notion of 'fact' which has received little or no attention from either the courts or doctrinal writers. 'Fact' as used in the statute and by the courts probably comes close to that of 'ultimate fact' in common law parlance: that which, once established, causes the court to apply legal rule X rather than legal rule Y. Virtually no attention is given to intermediate facts ...."[620]

2. French Approach

Let us then take France as the civil-law example.[621] France, of course, is a prototypical civil-law country in most respects, including its civil proce-

---

burden of proof, which is that the judge may find himself, after having made the evaluation of evidence, in one of three different situations. About the fact X he may have arrived at the conviction (1) that it does not exist, or (2) that it does exist, or (3) that there is uncertainty about its existence," and thus decide against the burdened party in cases (1) and (3).); F. Taroni, C. Champod & P. Margot, Forerunners of Bayesianism in Early Forensic Science, 38 Jurimetrics J. 183 (1998) (discussing, inter alia, studies of proof in the Dreyfus case).

619. See Barbara J. Shapiro, "Beyond Reasonable Doubt" and "Probable Cause": Historical Perspectives on the Anglo-American Law of Evidence 253–55 (1991).

620. James Beardsley, Proof of Fact in French Civil Procedure, 34 Am. J. Comp. L. 459, 466–67 (1986) (discussing French law of proof). But cf. François Terré, Introduction générale au droit 413–15 (1991) (discussing elements of fact in French law of proof).

621. See generally John Bell, French Legal Cultures (2001); John Bell, Sophie Boyron & Simon Whittaker, Principles of French Law (2d ed. 2008); Walter Cairns & Robert McKeon, Introduction to French Law (1995); Christian Dadomo & Susan Farran, The French Legal System (2d ed. 1996); Christel de Noblet, French Legal Methodology (2004); Brice Dickson, Introduction to French Law (1994); Catherine Elliott, Carole Geirnaert & Florence Houssais, French Legal System and Legal Language (1998); Catherine Elliott, Catherine Vernon & Eric Jeanpierre, French Legal System (2d ed. 2006); Introduction to French Law (George A. Bermann & Etienne Picard eds., 2008); Eva Steiner, French Law (2010); Eva Steiner, French Legal Method (2002); Terré, supra note 620; Andrew West, Yvon Desdevises, Alain Fenet, Dominique Gaurier & Marie-Clet Heussaff, The French Legal System (2d ed. 1998); Martin Weston, An English Reader's Guide to the French Legal System (1991); Zweigert & Kötz, supra note 611, at 74–131; Claire M. Germain, French Law Guide (July 2004), http://www.lawschool.cornell.edu/library/whatwedo/researchguides/french.cfm. A good source for actual French law, in French and English, appears at http://www.legifrance.gouv.fr/.

dure.[622] I admit that while French law overall might be prototypical, it is no longer strongly typical of civil law: French civil procedure law surely differs in important ways from that of other civil-law countries.[623] All I am contending is that France is not an atypical representative.[624]

Moreover, our precise concern in this chapter is why the civil-law standard of proof in civil cases is so much higher than the common-law standard. France serves well for this more detailed inspection of the standards of proof. I am not contending that all civil-law systems employ exactly the same civil standard in the same manner. But the differences are smaller here than in the rest of law. "With respect to the standard of proof, however, the differences within the family of civil law systems appear to be negligible."[625]

So, let us begin with a survey of French procedure for civil cases. That procedure is partly inquisitorial, to use the terminology of legal mythology. But that description holds true only as long as one concentrates on the statutory powers of investigation bestowed on the French judge.[626] If one looks beyond the statute books, the French procedure for civil cases appears to be a mixed system, as are most civilian systems.[627] Indeed, according to the best descrip-

---

622. See generally Loïc Cadiet & Emmanuel Jeuland, Droit judiciaire privé (7th ed. 2011); Gérard Couchez, Procédure civile (12th ed. 2002); 2 European Civil Practice 139–77 (Alexander Layton & Hugh Mercer gen. eds., 2d ed. 2004); European Traditions in Civil Procedure 25–68 (C.H. van Rhee ed., 2005); Serge Guinchard & Frédérique Ferrand, Procédure civile: droit interne et droit communautaire (28th ed. 2006); Peter Herzog & Martha Weser, Civil Procedure in France (1967); Thierry Bernard & Hedwige Vlasto, France, in 2 Transnational Litigation: A Practitioner's Guide (John Fellas gen. ed., 2004); Robert W. Byrd & Christian Bouckaert, Trial and Court Procedures in France, in Trial and Court Procedures Worldwide 138 (Charles Platto ed., 1990); J.A. Jolowicz, Civil Procedure in the Common and Civil Law, in Law and Legal Culture in Comparative Perspective 26 (Guenther Doeker-Mach & Klaus A. Ziegert eds., 2004); Christine Lécuyer-Thieffry, France, in International Civil Procedures 241 (Christian T. Campbell ed., 1995); Raymond Martin & Jacques Martin, France, in 1 International Encyclopaedia of Laws: Civil Procedure (Piet Taelman ed., 2005); Renée Y. Nauta & Gerard J. Meijer, French Civil Procedure, in Access to Civil Procedure Abroad 131 (Henk J. Snijders ed. & Benjamin Ruijsenaars trans., 1996); Xavier Vahramian & Eric Wallenbrock, France, in International Civil Procedure 213 (Shelby R. Grubbs ed., 2003).

623. For a broader survey of procedure, see European Civil Practice, supra note 622.

624. See generally O.F. Robinson, T.D. Fergus & W.M. Gordon, European Legal History (3d ed. 2000).

625. Brinkmann, supra note 608, at 879.

626. See West et al., supra note 621, at 286–88, 291–98.

627. See J.A. Jolowicz, On Civil Procedure 175–76, 218–21 (2000).

tion in English of modern French factfinding in actual practice, the French system is largely adversarial.[628]

In French litigation, the parties fix the issues, and ultimately they must prove their cases. The preparatory judge, called *le juge de la mise en état*, in practice seldom uses the statutory powers to investigate, and so controls more than directs factual investigation in the pretrial phase.[629] Although the French system is thus quite adversarial, the parties lack any substantial methods of discovery, a U.S. innovation that the French disdain. "Since the lawyers are not only disinclined but powerless to engage in real factual investigation and since the court is reluctant to use the powers which it enjoys, the perception of fact by the court tends to be based entirely on an evaluation of documents submitted by the parties and exchanged between them .... While the exchange of documents may sometimes serve to uncover useful evidence, it is not seen as a device whose principal aim is the discovery of evidence ...."[630] As a result, a party's case usually consists of documents already in the party's possession.

Any high standard of proof makes burdens of proof critical to outcome. The French system has no need to make fine distinctions among burdens of production and persuasion,[631] so we can, as the French do, speak just of burden of proof, or *la charge de la preuve*.[632] The party with the burden loses if a key fact is unproven or remains uncertain. The French plaintiff must prove all elements of the claim, while the defendant must prove affirmative defenses. As to allocating elements between claim and defense, the theory is to impose the burden on the party who seeks to upset an existing situation. That party "must establish every fact which conditions the existence of the right he invokes. He need not prove the absence of a fact which could have obstructed the birth of this right. Nor is he bound to show the absence of defects which might destroy his right."[633] The implications of this theory prove rather obscure in application, allowing the actual allocation of the burden between the parties to

---

628. See Beardsley, supra note 620.

629. See Joëlle Godard, Fact Finding: A French Perspective, in The Option of Litigating in Europe, supra note 602, at 57, 57–61.

630. Beardsley, supra note 620, at 467, 474.

631. But cf. Xavier Lagarde, D'une vérité l'autre: Brèves réflexions sur les différentes cultures de la preuve, 130 Gazette du Palais 2020, 2023 (2010) (distinguishing along these lines *la charge de l'administration de la preuve* from *le risque de la preuve*).

632. See Herzog & Weser, supra note 622, at 310. One also encounters the expression *le fardeau de la preuve*.

633. Claude Giverdon, The Problem of Proof in French Civil Law, 31 Tul. L. Rev. 29, 41 (1956) (footnote omitted).

follow familiar considerations of fairness and policy, such as access to proof, unlikeliness of contention, and substantive disfavor.[634] Further, legal presumptions play a large role in shifting the burden. Thus, for illustration, the plaintiff must prove fault, causation, and harm in tort cases, but the burden on causation shifts when the defendant was responsible for the equipment involved in the tort.[635] The burden of proof therefore does a lot of the work in arriving at a just decision, such as worrying about when the little guy goes up against the big guy.[636]

At the end of the civil process, there is a public hearing, or *audience*, before a three-judge panel, which prominently includes the preparatory judge. The *avocats* debate the import of previously investigated facts that appear in the dossier. The judges in principle engage in free evaluation of the evidence, although a number of legal hierarchies of proof do persist. For instance, even beyond an extensive statute of frauds, documentary proof definitely tends to outweigh oral accounts, which must have been reduced to writing anyway.[637] That is, the French do not have a pure version of "free evaluation," but rather a mixed system that retains some of the old spirit of "legal proof."[638]

On the evidence before them, the judges must decide.[639] They decide by majority vote in secret, with no publicly expressed dissent.[640] In announcing their decision in writing, the judges must explain their factfindings.[641] The judgment must show that their inner conviction comports with logic and ex-

---

634. See Frédérique Ferrand, Preuve ¶¶ 112–172, in 4 Encyclopédie Dalloz: Répertoire de procédure civile (2006).

635. See Herzog & Weser, supra note 622, at 310–16; West et al., supra note 621, at 286; C.N. Ngwasiri, The Role of the Judge in French Civil Proceedings, 9 Civ. Just. Q. 167, 167–68 (1990).

636. See Kinsch, supra note 603, at 461; cf. Field et al., supra note 10, at 1047–49 (explaining how judges, in the old days of trial by ordeal, oath, and battle, manipulated the mode and burden of proof to produce the just outcome); F.W. Maitland, The Forms of Action at Common Law 15–19 (1936) (same); Peter T. Leeson, Ordeals, 55 J.L. & Econ. 691 (2012) (same).

637. See Godard, supra note 629, at 61–65; Lagarde, supra note 631, at 2022–23.

638. See Jolowicz, supra note 627, at 213–15; infra text accompanying note 688.

639. See Jolowicz, supra note 627, at 211–13.

640. See Bell et al., supra note 621, at 110; Herbert J. Liebesny, Foreign Legal Systems: A Comparative Analysis 320 (1981).

641. See Code de procédure civile [C.P.C.] art. 455 (Fr.) ("*Le jugement doit être motivé.*"); Jean-Marc Baïssus, Common v. Continental: A Reaction to Mr. Evan Whitton's 1998 Murdoch Law School Address, 5 Murdoch U. Elec. J.L. No. 4, at ¶ 68 (Dec. 1998), http://www.murdoch.edu.au/elaw/issues/v5n4/baissus54.html.

perience,[642] albeit in a brief and uninformative manner that cannot express doubt.[643]

Clearly, the French system, like every legal system, is not ideally suited to the search of truth. As a perceptive French commentator put it: "In the first place, he who undertakes the search must have full liberty of investigation on the question to be resolved. Secondly, if he considers that the results of his search are not satisfactory, he must have the power of not concluding or of concluding only provisionally. Very clearly, these two possibilities must be refused to the civil judge."[644] The prevailing situation, in which the decisionmakers must render an umpireal decision on limited party-produced evidence, makes the burden and standard of proof critical.

So, at last, what is the French standard of proof? The French do not really have a word for this concept, although recently one does see the phrase *le degré de la preuve*.[645] Typically civilian, the standard is the same for civil and criminal cases:

> [T]he standard of proof required in civil and penal law in France is the same: the judge has to be convinced, without a shadow of a doubt, of a person's fault, be it penal or civil. In other words, there is in French law a direct relationship between the civil tort and the penal fault. The outcome is that where a civil and a penal action are concurrently pending, the civil case is stayed until the penal decision is taken. To avoid any delay for victims, they are given the possibility of joining their civil action to the criminal proceedings, which they do in the immense majority of cases. They enjoy the added advantage of seeing the prosecution doing the hard work of establishing proof of guilt—and footing the costs.[646]

Although the French criminal standard[647] has received some thought and discussion, it is quite hard to find even an explicit statement as to what is the French civil standard. There is a paucity of code, case, and commentary on the latter subject. First, no general statutory provision sets the civil stan-

---

642. See Mirjan Damaška, Free Proof and Its Detractors, 43 Am. J. Comp. L. 343, 345–46 (1995).

643. See Jean-Denis Bredin, Le doute et l'intime conviction, 23 Droits 21, 25 (1996) ("*La décision ne peut pas être douteuse.*").

644. Giverdon, supra note 633, at 30 (footnote omitted).

645. See Kinsch, supra note 603, at 456–57. One also encounters the expressions *le degré de certitude* or, rarely, *le quantum de la preuve* or *le critère de la preuve*.

646. Baïssus, supra note 641, ¶ 77.

647. See Code de procédure pénale art. 427 (Fr.) ("*le juge décide d'après son intime conviction*").

dard of proof.[648] The older Code Civil and the new Code of Civil Procedure do not treat the standard.[649] Second, the courts' uninformative judgments do not elaborate the civil standard of proof that they apply. There being no effective review of fact (the first level of appeal is a rehearing, the second level extends only to law[650]), appellate cases have little occasion to spell out the standard.[651] But the Cour de cassation has made clear that the party bearing the burden of proof must lose if the proof leaves any uncertainty or doubt.[652] Third, the training of judges in France covers the burden of proof in detail. But it proceeds without any mention of the standard of proof for civil cases.[653] Fourth, the long-reigning major text on civil procedure does not even mention the standard of proof.[654] Few discussions have appeared in commentary until quite recently. One of the rare articles somewhat on point sums up the doctrinal situation: "In Civil Matters.—*Intime conviction* appears in no statute. It is not defined. But one can see many similarities between the civil judge and the criminal judge."[655] A very recent, authoritative article concludes that "the civil standard is not fundamentally distinguishable, in French law, from the criminal standard: both require certainty or at least the absence of reasonable doubt."[656]

How can this obscurity prevail as to the civil standard of proof? Professor René David theorized that the *intime conviction* idea itself allowed French law simply to ignore such matters: "The indifference of French lawyers to evidentiary questions is explained basically, without doubt, by the importance in French law of the principle of the judge's intuitive conviction ...."[657] Of course, the French today realize that *intime conviction* requires only very high probability, not absolute certitude,[658] and yet a reasonable doubt will defeat the nec-

---

648. See Herzog & Weser, *supra* note 622, at 309.

649. See Code civil [C. civ.] (Fr.); C.P.C., supra note 641.

650. See West et al., supra note 621, at 300–05.

651. See Herzog & Weser, supra note 622, at 310 n.361.

652. See Kinsch, supra note 603, at 461.

653. See E-mail from Nicolas Michon, Auditeur de Justice, Orléans, to author (May 1, 2012, 12:41 EST).

654. See Guinchard & Ferrand, supra note 622.

655. Bredin, supra note 643, at 23 ("*En matière civile.—L'intime conviction n'est évoquée par aucun texte. Elle n'est pas définie. Mais on peut observer bien des ressemblances entre le juge civil et le juge pénal.*"); see also Baïssus, supra note 641, ¶ 77.

656. Kinsch, supra note 603, at 462 (translated).

657. René David, French Law 147 (1972).

658. See Bredin, supra note 643, at 23. But cf. id. at 26 (seeming confusedly to equate *intime conviction* in criminal cases with mere likelihood).

essary intuitive conviction.[659] Still, beyond these obvious insights, French legal theoreticians have not pursued probabilistic notions in any coherent or accepted way.

Nevertheless, the French have introduced exceptions for certain kinds of civil cases or issues, for which a lower standard of proof will apply.[660] An emergent example in the caselaw is that a claimant in cases on theft insurance need prove the fact of the theft and the value of the loss only to a *"vraisemblance prépondérante,"* which is less than an *intime conviction* but more than a preponderance of the evidence in the American sense; the difficulty of proof and the desire to preserve the protection of insurance have produced this exception.[661] Another example is the growing use of presumptions on the issue of causation in civil cases, not merely to shift the burden of proof, but tacitly to lower the standard of proof.[662]

Now, obviously, I am here dealing with the law on the books, not the law in action. I am not suggesting that French judges operate without a more general awareness that criminal cases are "different" from civil cases. But in the main French judges accommodate the difference of civil cases through manipulation of the burden of proof rather than the standard of proof.

An Illustration

Our concern rests on the general level. But for some purposes, a specific example might be useful. I can use the example employed in one of the earliest modern analyses of standard of proof: "A sues B on a note, whose execution B denies."[663] Given indeterminate handwriting samples, one can imagine various bodies of evidence by which A tries to prove execution of the promissory note and by which B rebuts, with conflicting witnesses to the surrounding circumstances: "Two apparently credible persons testify affirmatively. One, somewhat more credible, testifies negatively. The testimony of the two, or of the one, would have been believed, had it not been contradicted by that of the one or of the two."[664] Assume there is no other evidence.

---

659. See id. at 27 (*"Seul le doute sérieux s'impose à l'intime conviction. Ce doute doit être argumenté, cohérent, raissonnable. Ce doit être un vrai doute."*). But cf. id. at 25 (seeming confusedly to equate serious doubt in criminal cases with probability of innocence).

660. See Kinsch, supra note 603, at 464–70.

661. See id. at 466.

662. See id. at 467–70.

663. William Trickett, Preponderance of Evidence, and Reasonable Doubt, 10 Forum (Dick. L. Rev.) 75, 77 (1906).

664. Id. at 76.

With this closely balanced body of evidence, and even without party or expert testimony, the common-law factfinder could find for A, given a corresponding reaction to the three witnesses' credibility. Contrariwise, the civil-law factfinder could not faithfully apply its standard of proof and still find for A. After all, no one would be ready to convict B of a crime based on this body of evidence.

In particular, consider this case arising in France. Let us assume that it was a nonnotarized note of a nonmercantile nature. French pretrial proceedings would consist of an exchange of pleadings and of documents. Thus, the body of evidence would consist of documents, including writing samples as well as party-obtained and exchanged written witness statements, or *attestations*.

The preparatory judge could, but usually would not, order other measures taken: first, the preparatory judge could order an *enquête*, for orally questioning witnesses in chambers and then summarizing their responses in a written report to the dossier;[665] second, the preparatory judge could hear the parties' unsworn versions in chambers, *la comparution personnelle*, which the judge would summarize for the dossier;[666] and third, the preparatory judge could seek written expert opinion from a *technicien*, or might even send the whole fact dispute to a judge-chosen expert for a common-law-like mini-trial pursuant to the so-called *expertise* device.[667] The judges avoids the first two devices, because there is no reward for getting more involved in the facts, and using the devices will instead sacrifice "the gain in legitimacy that application of the usual rules of proof bestows on his decisions."[668] The third route is more palatable because delegating the task avoids the blow to the judge's legitimacy.[669]

In any event, eventually the judge would have to decide the fact dispute. On any such closely balanced body of evidence, the burden of proof, after applying any presumptions, would be critical. The civil law's high civil standard of proof, imposed on the ultimately burdened party, should be determinative. Here the burden to prove execution falls on A.[670] Thus, the high civil standard of proof likely preordains poor A's doom.

---

665. See C.P.C., supra note 641, arts. 288, 290, 293; West et al., supra note 621, at 288, 295–96; Beardsley, supra note 620, at 476–77, 478–80.

666. See C.P.C., supra note 641, art. 291; West et al., supra note 621, at 288, 295; Beardsley, supra note 620, at 464, 469.

667. See C.P.C., supra note 641, art. 292; West et al., supra note 621, at 296–97; Beardsley, supra note 620, at 469, 480–85.

668. Lagarde, supra note 631, at 2023.

669. See id. ("*S'il ne peut éviter la question de preuve, il peut en partie la déléguer en ordonnant une expertise.*").

670. See C. civ., supra note 649, arts. 1323–1324; cf. U.C.C. §3-308(a) (imposing the burden of persuasion on the same party under U.S. law).

Partie Civile

One French procedure deserves renewed discussion, because it reveals what the French are really doing with their standard of proof. Demonstration that outcomes in like civil cases differ under the civil-law and common-law standards of proof exists in the peculiarly French practice of joining civil claims to parallel criminal cases.[671]

The high criminal standard directly and unavoidably affects outcome in those French civil cases that the plaintiff chooses to join with the criminal proceedings, acting as a so-called *partie civile*. In contrast even to most of its neighbors, French law recognizes criminal-to-civil preclusion, so that the outcome of a civil case cannot contradict a prior criminal conviction or indeed an acquittal.[672] This French rule follows from the French courts' belief that they are applying the same standard of proof in criminal and civil cases. Therefore, a loss on the criminal case generally will dictate a loss on the joined civil case. If the defendant gets off on some criminal technicality or some peculiar element of or defense to the crime, then the *partie civile* can still recover if it proves civil liability. But the *partie civile* cannot argue guilt if the court found guilt not to exist, nor can the *partie civile* argue that it bears a lighter standard of proof.[673]

Even more interestingly for my purpose, French plaintiffs prefer to join their civil cases to parallel criminal proceedings whenever possible, in order to save time, effort, and money and to gain leverage. They do not seem to think that they are losing an advantage in bringing a separate civil case. In other words, potential civil plaintiffs seem to realize that even in a purely civil case there is

---

671. See Patrick Campbell, A Comparative Study of Victim Compensation Procedures in France and the United States: A Modest Proposal, 3 Hastings Int'l & Comp. L. Rev. 321 (1980); Jean Larguier, The Civil Action for Damages in French Criminal Procedure, 39 Tul. L. Rev. 687 (1965); Edward A. Tomlinson, Nonadversarial Justice: The French Experience, 42 Md. L. Rev. 131, 148 n.52 (1983); supra text accompanying note 646. On related practices in other civil-law countries, see Mattei et al., supra note 611, at 855–62.

672. See West et al., supra note 621, at 229–31 (explaining the principle of *la chose jugée au criminel a autorité sur le civil*). Many civil-law countries do not go this far with preclusion. After all, civil-law countries do not grant much collateral estoppel, especially as to nonparties. They nonetheless achieve an outcome similar to France's by allowing the introduction of the criminal dossier as evidence in the civil action. See Mattei et al., supra note 611, at 861.

673. See Michel Redon, Cour d'assises ¶¶ 494–495, in 3 Encyclopédie Dalloz: Répertoire de droit pénal et de procédure pénale (2010). The exception for civil plaintiffs who can prove their case without the issue that led to acquittal appears to have misled Professor Richard Wright into thinking that France has abandoned its general rule of the criminal result controlling the civil result. See Wright, supra note 530, ¶ 24.

a presumption of the defendant's innocence. This practice tends to establish that French courts actually do apply the criminal law's high standard of *intime conviction* in purely civil cases.[674]

3. Japanese Approach

Other civil-law countries certainly do differ in important ways in their civil procedure law. So we should take a look across the globe. The major reference work available in English on Japanese civil procedure has this to say on the standard of proof in Japan's civil cases:

> Since the Code makes no mention of degree in the required conviction of the judge, opinions on the point are not wholly in agreement. Some authorities contend that conviction based on "a preponderance of evidence" is sufficient, while others appear to insist that a conviction "beyond a reasonable doubt" is necessary even in a civil trial. The latter seems to be the prevailing view, which is best represented in the following statement: "The free conviction principle requires the judge to find facts according to his conviction. Although he need not be convinced so firmly that there is no room for finding otherwise, he is required to be convinced at least to such an extent that people in general might behave in daily life, relying on his finding with full satisfaction. The judge can find a certain fact true only when he has been convinced that it is ninety-nine per cent true; he may not, when he has been convinced it is seventy per cent true, but thirty per cent untrue."[675]

---

674. Incidentally, as a result of the civil law's distaste for collateral estoppel based on mere civil proceedings, rather than as a result of acknowledging different standards of proof, there is no civil-to-criminal preclusion, even in France. See Robert C. Casad, Issue Preclusion and Foreign Country Judgments: Whose Law?, 70 Iowa L. Rev. 53, 63–65 (1984). There is one arena in which the difference in standards might expose itself: international civil-to-civil preclusion. Within France's narrow realm of issue preclusion, an interesting question would be whether a French civil court should refuse to credit an American civil finding because it rested on a mere preponderance of the evidence. But the French seem not to have focused on this possible impediment to recognition, consistently with their lack of interest in standards of proof. See Bernard Audit, Droit international privé 395–407 (3d ed. 2000).

675. Takaaki Hattori & Dan Fenno Henderson, Civil Procedure in Japan § 7.05[13][b] (Yasuhei Taniguchi, Pauline C. Reich & Hiroto Miyake eds., 2d ed. 2000) (footnotes omitted) (quoting H. Kaneko, Risshō sekinin [Responsibility for Adducing Proof], in 2 Minji soshō -hō kōza [Lectures on the Law of Civil Procedure] 568 (1954)); see also Minsohō [Japanese Code of Civil Procedure] art. 247 ("In rendering a judgment, the court shall, considering

The same book immediately proceeds to quote a leading Supreme Court medical malpractice case: "Proving of a causal relationship in litigation, unlike in natural science, which permits no doubt, requires a high degree of probability [kōdo no gaizensei] that a certain fact (or facts) induced the occurrence of a specific result. This means putting all of the evidence together and examining it according to logical and experiential rules. It is necessary and sufficient that the judge has acquired, through the proof, a conviction [kakushin] of the existence of such a relationship to the degree that an average person will not entertain any doubt."[676]

We can set in Japan the case of A v. B, the ordinary action on a note that the defendant denies executing.[677] This particular example of the specialized issue and its related evidence may be more typical of U.S. cases than Japanese cases. Japan's legal system might often be able to avoid a case that in the end looks like this one. Whether or not such avoidance is commendable, such avoidance may allow the Japanese more easily to live with their high standard of proof. But sometimes cases similar to the example will reach trial in Japan. The standard of proof then applied is our concern. The outcome would be that the Japanese factfinder could not faithfully apply its elevated standard of proof and still find for A.

Of course, Japan inherited its high standard of proof from, and still shares it with, the civil-law countries. Most of those countries apply their high standard with a bit of obliviousness. Japan demonstrates a greater awareness of what it is doing,[678] however, as well as entertaining more debate about the ac-

---

the entire import of the oral argument and the result of the examination of evidence, and based upon its freely determined conviction, decide whether or not the allegations of fact are true."); Joseph W.S. Davis, Dispute Resolution in Japan 314 (1996); Carl F. Goodman, The Rule of Law in Japan 358–59 (2d rev. ed. 2008); Hiroshi Oda, Japanese Law 422 (3d ed. 2009); Takeshi Kojima, Japanese Civil Procedure in Comparative Law Perspective, 46 U. Kan. L. Rev. 687, 708–09 (1998); Supreme Court of Japan, Outline of Civil Litigation in Japan, http://www.courts.go.jp/english/proceedings/civil_suit_index/ (2006) ("When the court, considering all the allegations and evidence, has been convinced of whether the claim sought by the plaintiff should be granted or not, the court concludes oral argument and fixes a date for the rendition of judgment."); Craig P. Wagnild, Civil Law Discovery in Japan: A Comparison of Japanese and U.S. Methods of Evidence Collection in Civil Litigation, 3 Asian-Pac. L. & Pol'y J. 1, 7–8 (2002).

676. Miura v. Japan, 29 Minshū 1417, 1419–20 (Sup. Ct., Oct. 24, 1975); cf. Oda, supra note 675, at 187 (seeming to treat this case as governing only the issue of causation).

677. Cf. Hattori & Henderson, supra note 675, § 9.04 (describing the optional special action on a bill or check).

678. See, e.g., Shōzō Ōta, Saiban ni okeru shōmeiron no kiso [The Basis of Proof Theory in Adjudication] (1982) (examining the theories and cases on standard of proof under Japanese and German law).

tual standard prescribed and applied.[679] The result is that Japan now seems to have nudged its civil standard down from the level of beyond a reasonable doubt, although it remains well above preponderance of evidence and still at least resembles the very high standard supposedly applied in criminal cases.[680] So, we can call the Japanese civil standard a high-probability standard.[681] Moreover, for the proof of damages, the Japanese Code of Civil Procedure now allows the court to reduce the standard of proof.[682] "This device is intended to

---

679. See, e.g., Shigeo Itō, Jijitsu nintei no kiso [The Basis of Finding Facts] 158, 162–63, 171 (1996) (arguing that the civil standard is high, but no longer as high as the criminal standard).

680. The law calls for a beyond-a-reasonable-doubt standard of proof in Japan's criminal cases. See Hattori & Henderson, supra note 675, §7.05[13][b], at 7–77 n.468; J. Mark Ramseyer & Minoru Nakazato, Japanese Law: An Economic Approach 172 (1999).

Incidentally, in the Japanese district courts, the defendants contest guilt in only about 7% of the criminal cases, and convictions follow in 99% of those contested cases. See id. at 178–82 (the authors' U.S. data are unreliable because of the authors' treatment of dismissed cases). The comparable U.S. figures were 9% and 77%, respectively. See Annual Report of the Director of the Administrative Office of the United States Courts 225 tbl.D-4 (1995).

The comparatively high conviction rate in Japan is noteworthy. As an explanation, the overworked Japanese prosecutors perhaps pursue only their strongest cases, see Ramseyer & Nakazato, supra, at 181–82, or bureaucratic pressures perhaps psychologically induce Japanese judges to avoid acquittals, see id. at 179.

Yet high conviction rates prevail generally in civil-law countries, see Markus Dirk Dubber, American Plea Bargains, German Lay Judges, and the Crisis of Criminal Procedure, 49 Stan. L. Rev. 547, 585 (1997) (citing a trial conviction rate over 96% in Germany), where explanations tailored to Japan do not work so well. Some attribute the high conviction rate to the European inquisitorial system of criminal procedure, see Grant H. Carlton, Equalized Tragedy: Prosecuting Rape in the Bosnian Conflict Under the International Tribunal to Adjudicate War Crimes Committed in the Former Yugoslavia, 6 J. Int'l L. & Prac. 93, 100 n.59 (1997), an explanation that in turn does not work so well in the more adversarial Japan. See Oda, supra note 675, at 436–42.

One could cite other factors, such as the wider right to jury and the unavailability of appeal from acquittal in the United States. But it is possible that civilian judges are generally biased toward conviction. See Frank K. Upham, Review Essay, Political Lackeys or Faithful Public Servants: Two Views of the Japanese Judiciary, 30 Law & Soc. Inquiry 421, 431–39 (2005). In trying to explain completely Japan's and other civilian countries' sky-high conviction rates, one has to wonder whether judges' having to live with a nominally high standard of proof in civil cases has caused them by habit to dilute the similar standard of proof in criminal cases, applying it less rigorously than they would if civil and criminal standards were clearly distinguished as in the United States.

681. See Huang, supra note 454, at 140 (concluding that the Japanese standard of proof in civil cases is similar to the U.S. intermediate standard of clear and convincing evidence).

682. Japanese Code of Civil Procedure, supra note 675, art. 248 ("In cases where it is determinable that damages have arisen, if it is extremely difficult to prove the amount

enable the court to render a judgment in accordance with common sense by adjusting the standard of proof to reflect reality."[683]

In sum, in Japan the prevailing standard ordinarily requires the party who bears the burden in a civil case to satisfy the judge, to the point of a high probability, of the existence of the pertinent fact.[684] Although Japanese law is thus unique, this comparative foray reveals anew the striking divergence between civil-law and common-law standards of proof in civil cases: Japan requires proof to at least a high probability, while England and the United States require only that the burdened party prove the fact to be more likely than not.

B. Histories

How did the doctrines get to where they are today?

1. Civil Law

Early on, the civil-law systems employed the medieval method of legal proof, or *la preuve légale*. It assigned weights to specified classes of evidence, such as admissions and oaths, and prescribed exactly when a set of evidence amounted to so-called full proof. Legal proof's requirement of full proof, acting similarly to other ancient manners of "proof," avoided the necessity of formulating or even contemplating expressly different standards of proof for criminal and civil cases.[685]

Probability theory began to interplay with both the civil law and the common law in the eighteenth century. Legal theorists and the examples they forwarded made early contributions to the rapid advances in the mathematics

---

thereof from the nature of the damage, the court may determine a proper amount of damages on the basis of the entire import of the oral argument and the result of the examination of evidence.").

683. Kojima, supra note 675, at 709; see Yasuhei Taniguchi, The 1996 Code of Civil Procedure of Japan—A Procedure for the Coming Century?, 45 Am. J. Comp. L. 767, 785 (1997) ("This change can be said to be more substantive than merely procedural.").

684. On Japanese rules for shifting the burden, see Goodman, supra note 675, at 358–59; Hattori & Henderson, supra note 675, §7.05[13][a], [14]; Huang, supra note 454, at 143–53; Oda, supra note 675, at 422.

685. See Randall Lesaffer, European Legal History 274 (2009) ("This rigorous system [of legal proof] bears witness to a lack of confidence in the powers of judgment of the judges. The step from a blind faith in divine judgment to faith in human judgment proved too great [without a jury to hide behind]."); Leubsdorf, supra note 27, at 8–9.

and philosophy of probability, and then the interaction flowed back the other way.[686] This intellectual ferment resulted from a recent revolution in the way people looked at the world: " 'Probability' from the ancient world to the late seventeenth century traditionally had lumped together the noncertain, the seemingly true, and the merely likely. When evidence was unclear…, the result was probability or mere opinion, not knowledge. A late seventeenth-century development, however, suggested that probability consisted of a graduated scale that extended from the unlikely through the probable to a still higher category called 'rational belief' or 'moral certainty.' "[687] Given the legal proof regime, however, probability theory could manifest itself only through readjustment of the weight appropriate to each class of evidence.

Then the French Revolution imposed its intellectual effects broadly on the civil law. It largely overthrew legal proof in favor of the old Roman principle of free evaluation of the evidence, or *la liberté de la preuve*. Modern civilians take pride in their free evaluation principle, contrasting it with the common law's exclusionary rules of evidence that are partly attributable to the jury.[688] Putting aside the merits of that debate, the focus of this chapter remains the much starker disagreement between civil law and common law on the standards of proof, the degree of necessary persuasion.

Not being accustomed to requiring anything but full proof, civilians naturally came to apply a standard of *intime conviction* to all freely evaluated cases, criminal and civil alike, rather than probabilistic standards of proof.[689] "Imposing strict guidelines and rules on the judge as to how strong the evidence has to be, maybe even expressing them by a numerical probability, would have undermined the tendency to do away with legal proof."[690] Indeed, with the exuberance of root-and-branch abolition of the old method of legal proof, probability theory fell out of civilian favor. "Although Voltaire's criticisms and the Revolutionary reforms were aimed at the legal system of [*preuve légale*], the mathematical applications to jurisprudence may have been tainted by association."[691]

Thus, the Continentals stopped thinking and talking about the matter of standards of proof, throughout subsequent periods of history in which prob-

686. See Shapiro, supra note 619, at 1–41, 123–24, 220–23, 253–55; Barbara J. Shapiro, A Culture of Fact: England, 1550–1720, at 8–33 (2000); Éric Desmons, La preuve des faits dans la philosophie moderne, 23 Droits 13 (1996); Leubsdorf, supra note 27, at 28–31.
687. Shapiro, supra note 619, at 8.
688. See Damaška, supra note 642, at 343–48.
689. See Damaška, supra note 611, at 114 n.78.
690. Brinkmann, supra note 608, at 888.
691. Lorraine Daston, Classical Probability in the Enlightenment 354 (1988).

abilistic thinking waned and waxed in other disciplines.[692] The very obscurity of the *intime conviction* standard allowed the Continentals to avoid the whole subject.[693]

2. Common Law

Early moves in the direction of expressing common-law standards of proof simply gave the matter, in Bacon's terms, to the "juries' consciences and understanding."[694] From there, the common law evolved toward an expressed standard of inner conviction. "Seventeenth- and early eighteenth-century trials abound in references to 'conscience,' and writers on conscience often used the trope of 'an inner tribunal.' "[695]

By the turn into the eighteenth century, the common law's criminal and civil juries were basing decisions on a relatively free evaluation of the evidence presented in court, and the authorities had come to understand the task of evaluating conflicting sets of evidence to reach a rational conclusion.[696] Probability theory arrived on the scene, and the law did not sense pressures to back away. The common law was ready to take a major leap forward, hand in hand with probability theory. The common-law systems would continue their reciprocal interactions with those insights over the ensuing centuries.

As an additional background matter, it could be argued that the common law, in that same time period, was intuitively drawing many-valued logic from natural language and daily life.[697] Doing so would have caused the common law to become even more open toward accepting uncertainty.

In any event, by the late eighteenth century, the common law evolved to have the judges begin instructing juries in Lockean[698] terms of degrees of cer-

---

692. See Shapiro, supra note 619, at 253; Friedman, supra note 616, at 1944–46.

693. See supra text accompanying note 657.

694. 1 William Holdsworth, A History of English Law 333 n.6 (7th ed. 1956) (quoting a 1607 proclamation for jurors by Francis Bacon); see Shapiro, supra note 619, at 11.

695. Shapiro, supra note 619, at 14; see Leubsdorf, supra note 27, at 18–23.

696. See Shapiro, supra note 619, at 3–12.

697. See supra text accompanying note 474.

698. See John Locke, An Essay Concerning Human Understanding bk. IV, ch. XV, §2 (Roger Woolhouse ed., Penguin Classics 1998) (1690) ("there being degrees [of probability], from the very neighbourhood of certainty and demonstration, quite down to improbability and unlikeness, even to the confines of impossibility; and also degrees of assent from full assurance and confidence, quite down to conjecture, doubt, and distrust"); id. ch. XVI (saying that the highest degree of probability occurs when our own and all others' experience confirms the testimony of fair witnesses to create near certainty, such as that fire warms; the next degree is when "I find by my own experience, and the agreement of all

tainty.[699] Criminal cases became subject to the probabilistic standard of "beyond a reasonable doubt."[700]

Although the evolution of the lower civil standard is murkier, it began to diverge from the criminal standard in dictum and in commentary shortly thereafter,[701] as Professor John Leubsdorf's research is beginning to illuminate.[702] But only over the nineteenth century, with the criminal standard acting as a catalyst, the express specification of "preponderance of the evidence" or "balance of probabilities" slowly emerged in jury instructions.[703] And the low standard for civil cases has since undergone a lengthy process of refinement, as attested by the high number of cases struggling with the concept until relatively recently.[704]

3. Historical Causation of Divergence

Why precisely did the common-law standards change?

The modern institution of the jury appears to have been especially effective in facilitating this progress toward gradated standards of proof. At the least, the correlation between the existence of the civil jury[705] and the development of the preponderance standard seems perfect. Countries that used the civil jury came to apply the preponderance standard.[706] Quebec nicely demonstrates the influence of Anglo-American procedure on the civil standard of proof.

---

others that mention it, a thing to be for the most part so, and that the particular instance of it is attested by many and undoubted witnesses"; the third degree rests on "fair testimony" creating belief; but conflicting evidence can lead to belief or to wavering, doubt, distrust, or disbelief).

699. See Damaška, supra note 611, at 51–54.

700. See Shapiro, supra note 619, at 21–25; Sheppard, supra note 53.

701. See Harold J. Berman & Charles J. Reid, Jr., The Transformation of English Legal Science: From Hale to Blackstone, 45 Emory L.J. 437, 482 & n.87 (1996).

702. See Leubsdorf, supra note 27, at 15–18, 31–33.

703. See id. at 33–37, 39–50.

704. See supra text accompanying note 14.

705. See World Jury Systems (Neil Vidmar ed., 2000).

706. See La. Code Evid. Ann. art. 302(1) (exhibiting a similar result in Louisiana, another somewhat mixed system that has the civil jury); L.H. Hoffman, The South African Law of Evidence 365–67 (2d ed. 1970) (same for South Africa, which formerly had the civil jury in some provinces according to H.R. Hahlo & Ellison Kahn, The Union of South Africa 214–15, 221, 235, 237, 257 (1960)); W.A. Wilson, Introductory Essays on Scots Law 57, 67 (1978) (same for Scotland, which has the civil jury). Moreover, courts of equity followed the old civilian approach of legal proof until they later absorbed the common law's standards of proof. See Michael R.T. Macnair, The Law of Proof in Early Modern Equity 263–66, 288–89 (1999); cf. 2 McCormick on Evidence, supra note 10, §340, at 488 n.15 (illustrating an opposite spillover, from equity to law, as to standards of proof).

There, the common-law approach heavily infiltrated the prevailing French procedural system from 1785 onward, creating an adversarial procedure that included until recently the civil jury. Consequently, a preponderance of the evidence, or balance of probabilities, standard now governs in Quebec, as it does in the rest of Canada.[707]

Beyond correlation, the relation might be causal. Because of the criminal jury's need for judicially verbalized instructions, the common law had to acknowledge openly the role of random uncertainty and vague imprecision in decisionmaking and thus confront probability and logic—while the civil law could sweep such matters under the rug and so freeze in time its underdeveloped notions of proof. Perhaps in anticipation of the civil jury's like need for instruction, theoreticians then started molding the lower civil standard. To the extent the civil jury did act as proximate cause of the differentiated common-law standards, the civil jury has worked yet another of its benefits, helping not only to induce fair, efficient, and effective standards but also to force more broadly an honesty about the nature of decisionmaking.[708]

Determining the cause of a legal rule can be tricky, however. Common-law adversariness could instead be the root cause of the prevailing law, as it thrusts the imperfection of evidence, and hence the need for a standard of proof, out into the open. Alternatively, the common law's judges, who faced the need for an articulated standard of proof and had the lawmaking power to formulate even such a fundamental feature of their legal system, could constitute the root cause of its articulation of standards. Or, finally, the common law has shown a broad tendency to be explanatory, as in its judicial opinions and its legal writings, so this general openness could instead be the root cause of the divergence from civilian law. Most likely, the structure and function of the common-law court—bifurcated with a lawmaking *judge* controlling a lay *jury*, and operating with *openness* in an *adversary* setting—played in combination a contributory causal role in developing standards that acknowledged gradated uncertainty.

Nonetheless, the desire or need to articulate a standard does not necessarily dictate what the standard will be. The common law has indeed thought

---

707. See John E.C. Brierley & Roderick A. Macdonald, Quebec Civil Law 52 & n.96, 689 n.11, 690–91, 696 (1993); Kinsch, supra note 603, at 459–60.

708. See Damaška, supra note 611, at 54 ("In short, problems pertaining to factfinding that are expressly regulated and highly visible in the fish-bowl world of jury trials remain veiled from view in Continental procedure, shrouded by the secrecy of the deliberation room."). The jury's role affected the specific content of the common-law standards too, as group deliberation and the unanimity requirement produced more intersubjective standards of proof. See id. at 36 n.23, 38–40.

much more about its standards of proof than has the civil law. The common law consciously chose its low standard for civil cases to pursue error-cost minimization. In that sense, then, sound policy was the specific cause of the preponderance standard itself.

C. Explanations of Difference's Persistence

In the previous section, I described how civil-law and common-law systems came to adopt different approaches to proof in the late eighteenth century. The Revolution in France brought a radical simplification of evidence law; this reform in turn led civilian lawyers to disapprove, or at least to ignore, refined standards of proof. In England and the United States, there was no similar disruption in legal procedure, so the law of evidence continued to evolve in a way that increasingly incorporated probabilistic concepts; consistently, at an early stage common-law judges and lawyers thought through the problem of standards of proof in order to craft appropriate instructions for juries and otherwise to adapt to common-law procedure.

Yet, historical causation of divergence does not explain why the two systems have continued to adhere to their different standards over the centuries. Studying the past may reveal the answer why the common law lowered its standard of proof in civil cases, but it fails to illuminate why the civil law persists in declining to follow suit down to today. If the policies behind the common-law developments are so sound, why has the civil law, even in the absence of the jury, not yet evolved in a similar direction? Mere inertia of the post-Revolution tradition could not be that powerful. History alone cannot explain why standards of proof remain strikingly different.

For a first stab, one could build historical causation into a current explanation. It might run along the line that the code-heavy civil-law system exhibits a particular mental outlook, an outlook based on an Enlightenment belief in consistent and complete absolutes that make accessible a single correct answer—in contrast to the procedure-dominated common-law system that displays a Romantic allegiance to relativism and pluralism, which increases comfort with uncertainty.[709] Such an insight might, at the least, be quite useful in understanding some of our differences in methodologies for making and

---

709. See Vivian Grosswald Curran, Romantic Common Law, Enlightened Civil Law: Legal Uniformity and the Homogenization of the European Union, 7 Colum. J. Eur. L. 63, 64, 70–71 (2001).

applying law. Further, with their emphasis on "conviction" in the *intime conviction* standard, the civil-law countries were perhaps signaling their devotion to belief in truth, a belief thoroughly compatible with a Cartesian worldview. Such an approach fit better with an inquisitorial ideal than it did with an adversarial model, allowing it to persist for centuries. One could then argue, and French theorists have very recently done so upon awakening to the importance of this issue, that here lies the explanation of the current split between civil law and common law on standards of proof.

A leading commentator in France maintains that the key is this cultural difference flowing from our different traditions.[710] Thus, he says, the French believe in truth but do not take proof seriously, while common lawyers do not believe in truth but take the proof process seriously:

> In this sense, one can say the French jurist believes in truth while the common-law jurist does not. The former thinks that truth has an absolute value and consequently is pessimistic on the chances of reaching it by trial. The latter does not give such value to truth but thinks that a well-organized trial will be able to reach it.[711]

Other French commentators make the same observation, but do so more approvingly of their homegrown approach. They say that in the United States people are content to let the adjudicator choose the winner of two contesting accounts of the truth, while the Romanists look to the "minister of truth" for a pronouncement. In France "*la vérité est une et indivisible*," and so for a French jurist conceiving of gradations of the truth is "*une hérésie intellectuelle*."[712] A specific example that these French like to invoke for demonstrating that Americans are not concerned with *la vérité* is our acquittal of O.J. Simpson and subsequent assessment of his civil liability on the same facts. A criminal jury applying the standard of beyond a reasonable doubt acquitted Simpson of killing two persons, while a civil jury applying the standard of preponderance was later free to find him liable for the same act. Acceptance of those two results supposedly demonstrates that we do not care about truth.[713]

---

710. See Lagarde, supra note 631, at 2020.

711. Id. at 2021 (translated, and footnote omitted).

712. Antoine Garapon & Ioannis Papadopoulos, Juger en Amérique et en France: Culture juridique française et *common law* 129–30, 133–34 (2003) (attributing this difference largely to the split between Catholicism and Protestantism).

713. See id. at 131; Myron Moskovitz, The O.J. Inquisition: A United States Encounter with Continental Criminal Justice, 28 Vand. J. Transnat'l L. 1121 (1995).

I like this cultural explanation. Despite superficial convergences, our deeper cultures arguably remain quite different. This explanation's implicit emphasis centers on a split between bivalence and multivalence as worldview. It thus fits my theories wonderfully. At the least, the cultural difference might contribute in part to a full explanation of the standards of proof. But I must admit that I find the explanation too neat to be the full explanation.

Is culture that constant across the broad civil-law world? France and Japan are more different than alike. Because of important differences among civil-law countries' laws and cultures, any narrow explanation like this is likely to fail.

Anyway, do the civil law and the common law really still view contested truth in such different ways? Any such cultural difference in outlook seems unable to illuminate the very concrete and practical problem of why the two systems' judges would differ on how to decide, on the same conflicting evidence, whether B executed a note. No civilian, whatever the details of his or her cultural outlook, would contend that whether B executed the note has an answer that is certain.[714] The supposedly bivalent outlook of civilians might make their high standard of proof on civil cases less jarring to them, but a bivalent inclination is too abstract to explain their high standard's continued existence.

Finally, how does culture explain that most civil-law countries, including Germany, France, and Japan as already noted, have deemed it appropriate to adjust their standard downward in some or all cases? They recognize that sometimes a high standard, resting on a bivalent comprehension of absolute truth, is a suboptimal social policy.

So, then, why do the two systems broadly continue to treat standards of proof so differently? More pointedly, common lawyers cannot stop wondering— in light of their conviction that the preponderance of the evidence standard is a better way to allocate legal responsibility in civil cases—why civilian legal systems continue to adhere to what seems to them to be the unrealistic and potentially unfair and inefficient standard of *intime conviction* in civil cases.

A fuller explanation than history or culture is necessary. Something *within* standards of proof must be playing a role. In the following subsections, I offer a series of possible endogenous explanations of the persistent divergence.

I shall begin with commonly voiced explanations that, in my view, contribute only minimally to an understanding of the problem. Although some of these explanations suggest how the unitary standard for criminal and civil cases

---

714. See Valérie Lasserre-Kiesow, La vérité en droit civil, 186 Recueil Dalloz 907 (2010) (establishing the relativity of legal truth, while observing that evidence law highlights that relativity).

has managed to escape remark in civilian systems, they do not provide a *motivation* for its persistence. Then, I shall turn to more purposive explanations, including what I believe is the best explanation: suppression of the probabilistic nature of factfinding gives judgments an appearance of legitimacy, which all courts, including civilian courts, closely guard.

1. Inattention to the Problem

One quick explanation for why civilian legal systems have retained the standard of *intime conviction* in civil cases is that the scholars who shape the civil law have failed to advert sufficiently to the problem of proof. It is undeniable that the civilians have exhibited a much lower level of interest in the subject of standards of proof. While the United States and England buzz with interest, France has shown remarkably little interest in its standards of proof. Even if France is less self-aware as to its standard of proof than some of its neighbors, the continental situation nevertheless appears basically consistent: "There is elaborate caselaw on [standard of proof] in the United States, but the concept is less known to continental lawyers who generally assume that the judge needs to be 'fully persuaded' in all types of cases. Only a few modern [continental] scholars have demonstrated interest in alternative standards of proof ...."[715]

Scholarly inattention may be due to the civilians' disdain for the study of proof, or it may be due to a lack of understanding of uncertainty. The first does not universally apply, and the second is simply implausible.

a. Disdain

Civilian legal systems may have retained their high standard of proof in civil cases because their influential scholars view the problems of proof as below them. If we look to France, there does indeed appear to be a general lack of interest in, or disdain for, civil procedure and especially evidence law within the French academy.[716] These have not been serious subjects in the university curriculum until recently.[717] The little study that is done in these fields has tended to be aridly formal: "Despite statutory, and a great deal of doctrinal, concern

---

715. Kokott, supra note 601, at xvii–xviii, 18 (citing German scholarship that expresses interest in the preponderance standard, including Gerhard Kegel, Der Individualanscheinsbeweis und die Verteilung der Beweislast nach überwiegender Wahrscheinlichkeit, in Das Unternehmen in der Rechtsordnung 321, 335–39 (Kurt H. Biedenkopf, Helmut Coing & Ernst-Joachim Mestmäcker eds., 1967)).

716. See David, supra note 657, at 144–49.

717. See Guinchard & Ferrand, supra note 622, at 13.

with the 'truth,' there doesn't seem to have been much serious reflection on what the courts really do."[718] In fact, according to Professor David himself: "The expression *law of evidence* does not even exist in France …."[719] Only in more recent years has a slight upswing in interest found expression in *le droit de la preuve.*[720]

French inattention to matters of procedure and evidence likely does help to explain why the civil law and the common law continue to differ, both as to their level of interest in standards and also as to their prevailing standards of proof. French inattention further helps to explain how the civil law can live with an apparently suboptimal civil standard of proof. But, of course, inadvertence has no justificatory force.

Important Methodological Note:
Maintaining a Cross-Cultural Vision Without Stereotyping

Bear in mind that the civilian standards of proof persist in other countries beyond France. That fact makes any "inattention" explanation unsatisfactory. Consider again Japan—which is not at all indifferent to or disdainful of these fields of study,[721] and which has a long history of openness to foreign ideas while adapting them to native needs.[722] Other civil-law countries, like Germany, similarly treat civil procedure as a serious subject. Therefore, something more than inattention is needed to resolve the mystery.

One needs to search for an explanation that applies across many borders. One also needs to avoid jumping to a generalization about a culture that amounts to no more than an intuitive stereotype.

---

718. Beardsley, supra note 620, at 460; see Giverdon, supra note 633, at 48 ("the French law of proof is a perfectly logical construction, quite in harmony with our cartesian character").

719. David, supra note 657, at 146; see Dickson, supra note 621, at 129; Haack, supra note 11, at 208 ("The English word 'evidence' may be qualified by 'sketchy' as well as 'complete,' by 'flimsy' as well as 'overwhelming,' by 'strong' as well as 'weak'; but the French word 'évidence' (like the English word 'evident') conveys certitude, and 'preuve'—though a somewhat less misleading translation of 'evidence' than 'évidence'—also means 'proof, demonstration.'").

720. E.g., Philippe Théry, Les finalités du droit de la preuve en droit privé, 23 Droits 41, 41 (1996) ("*Les études consacrées à la preuve en font ressortir la complexité.*").

721. See Huang, supra note 454, at 109–10.

722. See Oda, supra note 675, at 5–7.

A typical national-peculiarity approach is to postulate that Japan shares an Asian aversion to probabilistic inference.[723] There are a number of problems with proposing such a cultural rejection of the rationalist approach. First, rationalism seems fairly robust in applying consistently across scholarly disciplines and national borders, at least throughout the West.[724] Second, the research relied on by these cultural generalizers indicates that the Japanese in particular are Western, not Asian, in their approach to probabilities.[725] Third, any cultural generalization about an anti-probabilist Japan has the air of the traditionalist theories of law premised on Japanese uniqueness, theories previously discredited as explanations for such general subjects as litigation-aversion.[726]

Even if Japan were anti-probabilist, a cultural conjecture runs into three more problems in specifically explaining standards of proof. First, the Japanese took their standards as transplants from continental Europe, so that supposed Asian attitudes would not help to explain the development of Japan's standards of proof. Second, although supposed Asian attitudes might suggest that the Japanese should be more at home with continuing the civilian nonprobabilistic approach than continental Europeans, I have already documented that Japan today shows more sensitivity to the probabilistic nature of proof than most of the European countries. Third, Japan in particular and the East in general have proved much more comfortable than the West with multivalent logic over many centuries.

I am not denying that culture plays a role. My own tentative view of the effect of culture on rationalism is that, as one of many factors, culture can affect the general task of evidential reasoning—especially in the step of collecting evidence and even in the step of analyzing evidence, but less so in measuring evidence against a standard of proof. At least some aspects of

---

723. See Richard D. Friedman & J. Frank Yates, The Triangle of Culture, Inference, and Litigation System, 2 Law Probability & Risk 137, 146–48 (2003); cf. Richard E. Nisbett, The Geography of Thought: How Asians and Westerners Think Differently ... and Why (2003) (generalizing Asian differences), critically reviewed by Sherry Ortner, East Brain, West Brain, N.Y. Times, Apr. 20, 2003, § 7 (Book Review), at 17.

724. See William Twining & Iain Hampsher-Monk, Introduction, in Evidence and Inference in History and Law: Interdisciplinary Dialogues 4 (William Twining & Iain Hampsher-Monk eds., 2003).

725. See J. Frank Yates, Ju-Whei Lee, Winston R. Sieck, Incheol Choi & Paul C. Price, Probability Judgment Across Cultures, in Heuristics and Biases, supra note 208, at 271, 276, 286, 290.

726. See Kenneth L. Port & Gerald Paul McAlinn, Comparative Law: Law and the Legal Process in Japan 16–19 (2d ed. 2003).

our handling of probabilities do seem culturally based.[727] I admit that application of the standard of proof is a complicated and ultimately behavioral task.[728] Nonetheless, there is as yet no showing that advanced cultures differ in how their people compare processed proof of a fact to the standard of required likelihood.[729] At any rate, there is no basis for postulating a cultural difference between the United States and Japan as to handling standards of proof.

b. Misunderstanding

The second possibility—that civilian scholars have failed to study and reform their standards of proof because they misunderstand the character of decisionmaking under uncertainty—rests on a weak basis. Its primary support is the fact that probability did not work itself into the civil law in a nuanced form before or after the French Revolution. Thus, civilian lawyers may be a little out of practice in thinking about their law in terms of uncertainty.

The stronger form of this argument—a claim of actual misunderstanding of probability theory—is implausible, however. Surely the home of Blaise Pascal and Pierre de Fermat, just like that of G.W. Leibniz and C.F. Gauss, is at least as comfortable with probability as the colonies of the country that produced Thomas Bayes and Francis Galton.[730]

2. Avoidance of the Problem

A second type of explanation for the persistence of different standards of proof in civil-law and common-law countries is that the difference never man-

---

727. See Edwards & von Winterfeldt, supra note 208, at 250–51; George N. Wright & Lawrence D. Phillips, Cultural Variation in Probabilistic Thinking: Alternative Ways of Dealing with Uncertainty, 15 Int'l J. Psychol. 239 (1980); George N. Wright, Lawrence D. Phillips, Peter C. Whalley, Gerry T. Choo, Kee-ong Ng, Irene Tan & Aylene Wisudha, Cultural Differences in Probabilistic Thinking, 9 J. Cross-Cultural Psychol. 285 (1978). For example, culture might influence our usual response scale. Cf. Gardner, supra note 181, at 342–50, 358 (discussing terminology for colors).

728. See Schum, supra note 466, at 41.

729. See, e.g., Mo Zhang & Paul J. Zwier, Burden of Proof: Developments in Modern Chinese Evidence Rules, 10 Tulsa J. Comp. & Int'l L. 419, 453–54 (2003) (observing movement toward similar approach).

730. See generally Peter L. Bernstein, Against the Gods: The Remarkable Story of Risk (1996).

ifests itself. As this argument goes, the civil law just avoids the situations where the difference would have an impact.

This argument might rest on either of two peculiarities of civilian procedure, namely, the tight control that some civilian courts maintain over factual disputes and the vestigial notion that civilian procedure is primarily inquisitorial rather than adversarial. Neither of these two possibilities can explain why civil-law courts would deliberately retain a nonprobabilistic standard of proof, although each may help to show how the courts can usually avoid addressing the standard.

a. Nonfacts

According to some, French courts do not care much about facts: they seek quick access to an idea or concept from which to deduce, and they will not wallow in the facts as common-law judges often do.[731] For that or some other reason, French courts do exercise tight control by a variety of techniques to avoid or minimize the role of factfinding in trials. For example, the courts prevent access to evidence by denying discovery and cross-examination; they strongly value documentary evidence over oral accounts; and they employ tricks such as automatically accepting as true any proof that is uncontradicted.[732] The result, in the words of one commentator, is "an approach to factfinding which appears to have the main aim of resolving factual issues by means other than the arduous sifting of evidence."[733] In other words, despite the French ideal of free evaluation, these constraints on the availability and evaluation of evidence effectively limit factfinding, which in turn may reduce the impact of an unsatisfactory civil standard of proof.[734]

For several reasons, however, the explanation that French courts can avoid the problem of their standard of proof by avoiding factfinding is seriously in-

---

731. E.g., Pierre Legrand, European Legal Systems Are Not Converging, 45 Int'l & Comp. L.Q. 52, 69 (1996).

732. See Lagarde, supra note 631, at 2022–25.

733. Beardsley, supra note 620, at 473; see Giverdon, supra note 633; Xavier Lagarde, Vérité et légitimité dans le droit de la preuve, 23 Droits 31, 32 (1996).

734. Some scholars have argued a civilian advantage in factfinding. E.g., John H. Langbein, The German Advantage in Civil Procedure, 52 U. Chi. L. Rev. 823 (1985). But see Ronald J. Allen, Stefan Köck, Kurt Riechenberg & D. Toby Rosen, The German Advantage in Civil Procedure: A Plea for More Details and Fewer Generalities in Comparative Scholarship, 82 Nw. U. L. Rev. 705 (1988) (powerfully questioning the existence of a German advantage). See generally R.R. Verkerk, Fact-Finding in Civil Litigation: A Comparative Perspective (2010). This lends a special irony to an explanation of the civil-law standard of proof that rests on the observation that civilian judges actually resolve few disputes of fact. See Beardsley, supra note 620, at 459.

complete. First, French fact-avoidance techniques do not likely explain the difference between French and U.S. standards of proof because the United States itself has a fair number of both exclusionary evidence rules and jury control mechanisms that limit factfinding in comparable ways.[735] Second, French courts cannot avoid all factual questions: the case of A v. B, for example, calls for some decision, which will have to turn on conflicting evidence about the authenticity and circumstances of B's execution. Third, although fact-avoidance techniques are a prominent feature of French procedure, they are not characteristic of all civil-law countries. Thus, while fact-avoidance techniques may help some civil-law courts to live with their high standard of proof in civil cases, it is more than difficult to construct a general explanation on this ground.

b. Inquisition

The other version of how civil-law courts may avoid coming to grips with the problem of their standard of proof rests on the vestigial character of the civil law as an inquisitorial rather than an adversarial system. The perception that civil-law judges retain investigatory responsibility in some or even all civil cases may lead them to seek "truth" and also permit them to believe that they have found it. Being the single person or group charged with seeking information scientifically to uncover the truth may generate a different sense of what truth is, making it something not only objective but available. If judges have sole or primary responsibility for assembling and evaluating evidence, they may be able to convince themselves that the evidence is complete enough and that no real doubts remain about its meaning.[736] In contrast, the avowedly adversarial orientation of common-law procedure, with each party presenting its account of the truth (often by oral testimony), may sensitize common-law judges to the uncertainty of evidence, making truth appear elusive if not obscure. Moreover, their detached and umpireal role, combined with long experience in applying the preponderance standard of proof, may make it easier for common-law judges to accept uncertainty. Their setting generates a greater humility in the pursuit of truth.[737] Thus, it is not surprising that civil-law judges are more comfortable with the standard of *intime conviction* in civil cases than common-law judges would be.

---

735. See Jolowicz, supra note 627, at 213–15.
736. See Damaška, supra note 611, at 83.
737. See Mirjan R. Damaška, The Faces of Justice and State Authority 122 (1986) ("Troubling questions of proper standards for sufficiency of proof can be more easily resolved; where facts remain uncertain, judgment can be awarded in favor of the party who has made a better evidentiary case."); Reshetnikova & Iarkov, supra note 610, at 168–71 (predicting that increased adversariness in Russian procedure will lead to the preponderance standard).

The difficulty with this version of the "avoidance" explanation—one that uses the inquisitorial method not as a historical explanation but as a current influence—is that the association of civil law with inquisitorial procedure and of common law with adversarial procedure is largely mythical. The different images must flow from memory or theory, or from attitudes and experience on the criminal side, because on the civil side the civilian judges today are in reality much less independent than they once were. Typically, a civilian judge's independent powers extend only to calling experts and interrogating witnesses; even French judges, who possess substantial powers on paper, independently do little more than this and have ceded responsibility to adverse lawyers for gathering and presenting facts.[738] Meanwhile, common-law systems have become less adversary on the civil side.[739] In brief, civil-law and common-law proceedings today are not much different in fundamental character, as even those who champion the civil law concede.[740] So, although the civil law's conceptualization of judges as investigators may further contribute to making its standard of proof less jarring, any ongoing inquisitorial function does not survive a reality-check and so fails to explain or justify the high standard of proof in civil cases.

3. Insignificance of the Problem

A third explanation is that the difference in articulated standards of proof has negligible practical effect when the courts apply their standards. That is, whatever civil-law and common-law courts say about the level of proof required, they may find facts and decide civil cases similarly in actual practice.

Again, this explanation comes in two possible versions: perhaps the civilians do not adhere to their articulated standard in civil cases or, alternatively, perhaps both systems settle intuitively on the same standard somewhere along the spectrum between a preponderance of the evidence and an *intime conviction*. This is a potentially powerful explanation, and so requires a more careful counterargument.

a. Lip-Service

Several American scholars have suggested that the difference between civil-law and common-law articulations of the standard of proof are insignificant in practice. They have tended to doubt that the Continentals really follow their

---

738. See Damaška, supra note 611, at 106–08, 113–15.
739. See id. at 135–41.
740. See Jolowicz, supra note 627, at 175–76, 218–21.

civil standard, thinking that the Continentals simply cannot be doing what they say. Professor Peter Herzog, for example, assumed that French courts must be applying probabilities in practice.[741] Recall that Kaplan, von Mehren & Shaefer seemed to hypothesize that the civil standard in Germany is only verbally equivalent to the criminal standard.[742] Even some Continentals share this belief.[743] The best argument in support would be the amazing silence on the standard of proof both in the older comparative law studies and in current international arbitration practices.[744] If a real difference existed, it would manifest itself in observably obvious ways.

If these scholars were completely right, the whole mystery would vaporize. Concededly, it may very well be in some civil cases, such as our A v. B example where A sues on a note that B denies executing, that common sense would prevail over doctrine, and continental judges would allow judgment to rest on a balance of probabilities. But I believe their conjecture cannot reach all cases, as I shall explain after stating the other version of this "insignificance" explanation.

b. Convergence

Alternatively, it may be that neither civil-law courts nor common-law courts are faithful to their own standard, but both instead apply an intermediate standard. In one line of support for this explanation, a theoretician could argue that some more-or-less universal patterns of human perception and cognition are resistant to probabilistic analysis. When humans perceive sounds, colors, and the like, they tend to sort them into discrete categories that suppress shadings and ambiguities. Moreover, this way of sorting data can be useful, because it

---

741. See Herzog & Weser, supra note 622, at 310. For this proposition, their book cites, somewhat out of context, 7 Marcel Planiol & Georges Ripert, Traité pratique de droit civil français 851 (2d ed. 1954) ("*Puisque la règle de la neutralité enlève au juge toute initiative de la preuve, et que les éléments de sa conviction dépendent des parties, il n'est pas possible de parler de certitude judiciaire, mais seulement de probabilité.*"); see Lagarde, supra note 733, at 32. The better citation might have been to Giverdon, supra note 633, at 38 ("And this conviction will be established by the party who has furnished the more likely explanation of his position. Thus judicial proof comes down to a simple probability; it is the party who gains the better position in the argument who wins the process.").

742. See supra text accompanying note 600.

743. E.g., Bolding, supra note 618, at 19–22 (arguing that Swedish courts may in fact sometimes be applying unknowingly a preponderance standard). On the Swedish standard, see also Ruth B. Ginsburg & Anders Bruzelius, Civil Procedure in Sweden 297–98 (1965); Kinsch, supra note 603, at 462 n.31; and especially Bengt Lindell, Sweden, in 2 International Encyclopaedia of Laws: Civil Procedure ¶¶611–616 (Paul Lemmens ed., 1996).

744. See Brinkmann, supra note 608, at 875, 886–87.

allows humans to reach definite conclusions and act on them. Extending the argument, the theoretician would say that decisionmakers confronted with some strength of probabilistic data—convincing but well short of certainty—will tend to form convictions about the data's meaning, whatever the articulated standard of decision. Thus, the standard of *intime conviction*, while somewhat misleading because it suggests a very high level of certainty, and the standard of preponderance while somewhat misleading because it suggests a low level of certainty, are both beside the point as to how all factfinders naturally weigh evidence to reach categorical judgment.

A more legal line of support would look to the increasingly frequent lowering of the civil-law standard in certain places or situations, as exemplified by the aforementioned slippage in Japan's articulated standard. Other civil-law countries have very recently begun paying attention to the matter of standards of proof. Scholars are writing more. Lawmakers are beginning to make laws thereon. For another example, Austria may be readying to nudge its civil standard down to high probability, a standard lower than its criminal standard but higher than the U.S. preponderance standard.[745] China is considering adopting Uniform Provisions of Evidence that would continue the beyond-a-reasonable-doubt standard in criminal cases[746] but impose a "high probability" standard for civil cases;[747] the law would define the latter term thus: "High probability means that the probability of the existence or nonexistence of the facts proved by evidence produced by one party is clearly higher than the probability of the existence or nonexistence of facts proved by evidence produced by the other party." More startlingly, starting after the turn of the millennium, the Italian courts, while moving expressly toward a beyond-a-reasonable-doubt standard for criminal cases, have appeared to adopt more

---

745. See Walter Rechberger & Daphne-Ariane Simotta, Grundriß des österreichischen Zivilprozeßrechts [Basics of Austrian Civil Procedure Law] ¶ 580 (5th ed. 2000).

746. See John J. Capowski, China's Evidentiary and Procedural Reforms, the Federal Rules of Evidence, and the Harmonization of Civil and Common Law, 47 Tex. Int'l L.J. 455, 486 (2012) (citing art. 130). Terming of the standard in criminal cases as beyond-a-reasonable-doubt came into effect in 2013 with the new Criminal Procedure Law art. 53. See Library of Congress, China: Amendment of Criminal Procedure Law, http://www.loc.gov/lawweb/servlet/lloc_news?disp3_l205403080_text (Apr. 9, 2012).

747. See Capowski, supra note 746, at 486–87 (citing art. 141). Judicial practice, codified in 2000, had already approved a similarly lowered standard. See Zhang & Zwier, supra note 729, at 453–54 (discussing the undefined standard of "clearly higher" proof in the earlier Chinese Civil Evidence Rules art. 73); cf. Ronald J. Allen, Burdens of Proof, http://ssrn.com/abstract=2146184, at 21–22 (July 30, 2012) (questioning whether an even lower standard actually applies).

or less expressly a preponderance-of-evidence standard for civil cases.[748] Arguably, this slippage in certain countries, along with the increase in exceptions to the high civil standard even in Germany and France, represents the wave of the future for the civil law.

There is some derrière-garde skirmishing. In response to growing talk in terms of standards of proof in EU competition cases, a member of the European Commission's Legal Service has criticized such talk as a common-law intrusion.[749] "For lawyers outside common law countries, the absence of specifically defined thresholds of persuasion is natural and does not give rise to particular difficulties." He adds:

> It is submitted that the approach of the EU Courts to the assessment of evidence is better understood from the perspective of continental law systems. In civil law jurisdictions the question "how much evidence is required before a judge can conclude that a party has met its burden of proof?" does not typically receive an ex ante abstract answer in terms of probability. Or, rather, the answer tends to be "as much evidence as necessary." Necessary for what? Necessary to convince the judge. The key notion is that the evidence should be enough to persuade the judge of the facts, who will adjudicate the case on the basis of his/her personal persuasion at the end of the proceedings. It is the standard of the *intime conviction*, which applies equally in civil and criminal cases. The law does not stipulate how strong this "personal conviction" of the judge should be.

But he then goes to discuss at length the various factors that will require more or less convincing evidence, factors as variable as background probabilities and

---

748. See Wright, supra note 530, ¶¶ 21, 25, 52. In 2006, Italy amended its Criminal Procedure Code to impose a beyond-a-reasonable-doubt standard, with Article 533(1) providing: "*Il giudice pronuncia sentenza di condanna se l'imputato risulta colpevole del reato contestatogli al di là di ogni ragionevole dubbio.*" See Luca Marafioti, Italian Criminal Procedure: A System Caught Between Two Traditions, in Crime, Procedure and Evidence in a Comparative and International Context 81, 87–88 (John Jackson et al. eds., 2008); Picinali, supra note 53, at 9–10, 22–23.

749. Eric Gippini-Fournier, The Elusive Standard of Proof in EU Competition Cases, 33 World Competition 187, 189–90, 195, 202 (2010). For a similar argument concerning another international court, see Jo M. Pasqualucci, The Practice and Procedure of the Inter-American Court of Human Rights 173–74 (2d ed. 2013); Álvaro Paúl, In Search of the Standards of Proof Applied by the Inter-American Court of Human Rights, 55 Revista Instituto Interamericano de Derechos Humanos 57 (2012), available at http://ssrn.com/abstract= 1923908.

the costs of false positives and negatives. "Judging ostensibly under the same standard, courts require different degrees of persuasiveness from the evidence, depending on the interests at stake." He thus describes a "continuous sliding scale, which is the *intime conviction*." His conclusion is that the European courts can operate effectively in this way without actually speaking in terms of standards of proof.

Relatedly, a disgruntled article on this subject by an Italian author[750]— after surprisingly conceding that the common law's preponderance standard of proof is superior—argues that some civil-law countries, such as Italy and Spain[751] but not the more rigorous Germany,[752] are adamantly nonexpress about their high civil standard of proof and thereby free up their judges to apply whatever standard the judges think appropriate in the search for "truth" or "moral certainty." (His argument that civil-law countries do not really live up to their profession of a high standard supports my position that they have an ulterior purpose in professing their standard. Unfortunately, he rests his argument on pure assertion. I myself would not be comfortable in attesting that such a practice prevails in Europe. But for the purposes of argument, I am willing to take this commentator's assertion at face value.) He seems to approve of this ad hoc practice.[753] Yet I disagree with its wisdom. Such judicial discretion is obviously dangerous. Having standards of proof handled behind the scenes leads to lack of control over decisionmakers and to sloppy thinking by lawmakers. Would the typical judge be capable of the demanding task of setting a standard appropriate to the particular case or issue? Indeed, why should a lowly judge get to decide the standard of proof? As a Luxembourgeois commentator put it:

---

750. Michele Taruffo, Rethinking the Standards of Proof, 51 Am. J. Comp. L. 659, 666–69 (2003) (characterizing *intime conviction* as "a sort of black box"). I address here the one relevant, coherent, and possibly accurate criticism contained in this article by Taruffo, a former visiting professor at Cornell Law School.

751. In fact, Italy has openly reconsidered its standard, see supra note 748 and accompanying text, while Spain on most issues still requires the judge "to be fully convinced of the truthfulness of the facts." Civil Justice in Spain 139 (Carlos Esplugues-Mota & Silvia Barona-Vilar eds., 2009).

752. However, Brinkmann, supra note 608, at 882–86, extends Taruffo's argument to include Germany. Indeed, Professor Brinkmann, id. at 889–91, sees ALI/UNIDROIT Principles of Transnational Civil Procedure princ. 21.2, rule 28.2 (2006) as following this ad hoc approach in its attempted compromise through adoption of a "reasonable conviction" standard of proof.

753. Cf. Taruffo, supra note 750, at 670–71 (maintaining fashionably that truth is what judges say it is).

> This is a system, a normative system, at stake: in any event, to say that "it's all a question of the *intime conviction* of the judge, which is not susceptible to a normative control" will never be satisfying. It is not for individual judges or courts to resolve intimately and secretly this question, a question of the judicial order that must be resolved by preexisting and known rules.[754]

The lawlessness of applying an ad hoc standard of proof only increases on a collegiate court, as each judge applies his or her own chosen standard.

The leading voice on this side of the ocean to argue convergence is Professor Richard Wright[755]—but his departure point is the inferiority rather than the superiority of the common law's preponderance standard. He begins with the usual anti-probabilist distaste for deciding in terms of mere likelihood, but combines it with admiration for the civil-law's standard of proof. He contends that only by requiring the plaintiff to produce in the adjudicator an inner conviction can we achieve truth, even though he believes that inner conviction requires much less than virtual certainty in noncriminal cases. He views this superiority as so undeniable that he deduces that common-law judges are actually applying the civil-law standard. However, he is not really contending that the common-law standard is moving up. A closer reading reveals that he is mainly wary of nonparticularistic statistical evidence and admires the civil law's emphasis on belief as a prophylactic. After simply accepting the aforementioned Italian commentator's assertion that civilians have watered down their standard for noncriminal cases, he ends up urging that both systems are applying a more-likely-true-than-not test for the required belief. I agree that both the civil law and the common law look for some specified unquantifiable belief to decide civil cases. Yet I maintain that the civil law calls for a stronger belief. His vision of convergence appears to rest on wishful thinking. I see little sign that common lawyers are abandoning their allegiance to a more-likely-true-than-not showing. I see little sign that civilians are abandoning wholesale their traditional demand for a stronger conviction.

Overall on these variations of the "insignificance" explanation, I accept the possibility that either or both sides' imperfect compliance with the articulated standards of proof lessens the practical importance of differences between standards. I am willing to concede that most factual disputes would come out the same in both systems. But I suspect that such convergence must be incom-

---

754. Kinsch, supra note 603, at 456 (translated); see supra text accompanying note 25.

755. Wright, supra note 530; Richard W. Wright, Proving Causation: Probability Versus Belief, in Perspectives on Causation 195 (Richard Goldberg ed., 2011).

plete, meaning that the differently phrased standards of proof have a practical impact, both directly and indirectly. In other words, convergence is at best an incomplete explanation. And I can offer a number of reasons to doubt its force as an explanation.

First, the civil-law and common-law standards are dramatically different on their face, and when articulated standards are so different, they likely produce a real difference at least in some cases. The standard that prevails in theory should in practice affect decisionmakers, jury and nonjury. Consider again the case of A v. B, which turns on credible but conflicting testimony about the authenticity and circumstances of B's execution of a note. It seems obvious that the different standards, applied with any degree of seriousness, would produce different outcomes in this case. Under the preponderance of the evidence standard, the case is a close one; under the standard of beyond a reasonable doubt, B surely wins. Therefore, unless a lot of decisionmakers are flagrantly ignoring the formal rules with great consistency, the difference in articulated standards of proof should have some real effect on the run of legal outcomes.

Second, existing empirical data indicate that standards of proof can make a practical difference, as I detailed in Chapter III. Admittedly, existing empirical research focuses only on Anglo-American factfinding and is quite imperfect. To my knowledge, there are no studies examining the standard actually applied by civilian factfinders in civil cases, because civilian scholars have long been largely oblivious to the whole subject. Nor are there direct comparative studies, and designing a sound study would be a daunting task. Nonetheless, the existing research does suggest that factfinders, charged on the issue of a fact, can focus separately on the question of how probable it is that the fact is true. Despite some confusion, factfinders can and usually do make the gross distinction between the civil and criminal standards of proof.

Third, researchers in fact will never be able to show that outcomes in like cases are always alike under the civil-law and common-law standards of proof, because contrary proof of actual differences in application already exists. Recall the French practice of joining civil claims to parallel criminal cases. A willing plaintiff becomes *partie civile*, apparently accepting that even a purely civil case calls for the criminal standard of proof. This practice seems to establish that French courts actually do apply the criminal law's high standard of *intime conviction* in purely civil cases.

Fourth, even if researchers could show that outcomes in like cases are alike under the civil-law and common-law standards of proof, the formal difference between the standards is significant in itself, because it affects how people feel and think about adjudication. Law on the books has an effect, whatever the law in action might be. Civilians believe they are applying a unitary standard of "truth." This belief, even if illusory, deflects their attention from the questions of proof and prevents them from developing strategies for management of uncertainty. Their belief in a unitary standard also has procedural consequences, such as their criminal-to-civil preclusion rules. In the United States, the differing criminal and civil standards of proof mean that acquittal of a defendant in a criminal case does not preclude a later civil claim against the defendant based on the same factual allegation.[756] The U.S. courts think they are applying a criminal standard that is higher than their civil standard. But French law recognizes criminal-to-civil preclusion, so that the outcome of a civil case cannot contradict a prior criminal conviction or acquittal.[757] The French rule follows from the French courts' belief that they are applying the same standard of proof in criminal and civil cases.[758]

In sum, real-world fudging of the civilian standard would make it easier to live with. But whatever the factfinders are really doing in ordinary cases, the articulated difference between the civil-law and common-law standards of proof has significant practical consequences in at least some cases. The difference has a real impact. One would be making a sizable mistake to dismiss the two systems' different standards as harmless verbal formulas.[759]

4. Purposiveness Behind Standards

Thus far I have reviewed three sets of explanations for the civil-law's high civil standard of proof that succeeded in showing only why civil-law courts have not been under serious pressure to adopt a lower standard for civil cases. Perhaps, in combination with historical and cultural explanations, these suffice to explain the civil law's willingness to tolerate the effects of that standard. Still, the civil-law standard is fundamentally at odds with the state of evidence in a typical civil dispute. Certainty in knowledge is not attainable with respect to a disputed past event briefly represented through conflicting evidence. Like many judgments one makes and acts on in ordinary life, most legal disputes remain forever in a state of considerable doubt. For example, the decision-

---

756. See Restatement (Second) of Judgments § 85 (1982); cf. Fenton Bresler, O.J. Is Over There, Nat'l L.J., Nov. 5, 2001, at A21 (observing that the same is now true in England).

757. See supra note 672 and accompanying text.

758. See Kinsch, supra note 603, at 462–63.

759. See Addington v. Texas, 441 U.S. 418, 425 (1979) ("Nonetheless, even if the particular standard-of-proof catchwords do not always make a great difference in a particular case, adopting a 'standard of proof is more than an empty semantic exercise.'" (quoting Tippett v. Maryland, 436 F.2d 1153, 1166 (4th Cir. 1971) (Sobeloff, J., concurring in part and dissenting in part))).

maker's conclusion in our A v. B case simply must be a conclusion based on likelihood. In this light, the civil law's demand for "truth" in civil cases has the appearance of wilful mischaracterization, suggesting that some unstated purpose must lie behind it. I therefore remain convinced that all those explanations are incomplete, and so I should continue the search for an explanation that includes a motivation for the civil-law standard.

Accordingly, I turn now to the set of explanations that confess the civil-law's high civil standard of proof represents a significant difference from the common law, but that go on to say a policy reason underlies the civil law's choice of standard. I first divide the types of possible reasons why the civil law might affirmatively wish to retain its high standard in civil cases into two, substantive and procedural.

a. Substantive Purposes

One reason for retaining a high standard of proof might be a desire to influence the substantive outcome of litigation.[760] A high civil standard, combined with a burden of proof that already disadvantages plaintiffs by usually designating them to prove affirmatively the elements of their claims, quite obviously makes it more difficult for plaintiffs to succeed. The same high standard, coupled with rules and presumptions that sometimes shift the burden of proof, permits the law to choose between favoring plaintiffs and favoring defendants. The civil law's (1) use of its high standard of proof to influence the outcome of litigation might reflect a general hostility toward plaintiffs, who usually seem intent on disrupting the status quo, while its (2) special rules and presumptions might reflect a specific substantive policy of imposing liability on certain defendants, who in the circumstances could better shoulder the expense.[761] Alternatively, on whomever the law imposes the burden, the high standard (3) might reflect both the civil law's historical desire to constrain the judiciary, as the legislature can play a somewhat bigger role by allocating the high burden on the various elements of claim and defense, and also its historical distrust of judges, so that the law would want to limit judicial discretion or even avoid looking as if it has left any real "decision" to a judge, or (4) might perhaps reflect a desire not to trigger the state's power without strong justification.[762]

I doubt the force of this sort of explanation for the civil law's standard of proof. I can offer several arguments supporting the doubt.

---

760. Cf. Lindell, supra note 743, ¶ 614 (explaining Sweden's possibly variable standard of proof in civil cases on substantive grounds).

761. See supra text accompanying note 40.

762. See John Henry Merryman, The French Deviation, 44 Am. J. Comp. L. 109 (1996).

First, there is no general reason to prefer one side of civil litigation to the other. In criminal cases, a high standard of proof reflects the view that punishment of innocent defendants is a heavy cost, one that outweighs the cost of letting some guilty defendants go free. But in civil cases, harm to one party is as weighty as harm to the other, whether the harm takes the form of liability inflicted or injury unredressed.[763] Disruption of the status quo provides at best a weak justification for prejudicing plaintiffs. Indeed, because identifying the status quo is notoriously difficult,[764] that justification is almost weightless. Taking the A v. B case as an example, it is not clear whether A in seeking to enforce the note or B in contesting its validity is challenging the status quo, and society in fact has no reason to prefer this defendant to this plaintiff. In other examples, moreover, the parties' status as plaintiff or defendant may be interchangeable, depending on who first institutes suit. In brief, it appears that any society should be generally indifferent in civil cases between plaintiffs and defendants. It is thus hard to believe that civil-law societies, in many ways similar to common-law societies, would reach a different consensus about the relative merits of plaintiffs and defendants.

Note that I am not saying that the strong anti-plaintiff effect of the *intime conviction* standard would show up as more victories for defendants in litigated cases. Cases that fall close to whatever standard of proof applies will more heavily proceed to trial, because parties can select cases for trial. Other cases will tend to settle, creating the so-called selection effect. Under simplifying assumptions, and as a limiting implication, the result of adjudicating all those close cases would be about a 50/50 ratio of plaintiff victories to defendant victories in litigated cases, under any standard of proof. Under the preponderance standard, trials are most likely to occur when the evidence is roughly in balance; but under the standard of *intime conviction*, trials are most likely to occur when the evidence is strongly in the plaintiff's favor. The different standards will not, however, translate into different win rates observable in outcome data. Therefore, although different standards would affect the kind of cases that proceed to trial rather than settle, the standards would not necessarily affect the percentage of plaintiff wins.[765]

---

763. See supra text accompanying note 29.

764. See, e.g., Cooling v. Security Trust Co., 49 A.2d 121, 123–24 (Del. Ch. 1946) (attempting to determine the "status quo" for purposes of a preliminary injunction that had required a trustee to file exceptions in a probate proceeding in order to preserve the rights of beneficiaries).

765. See Kevin M. Clermont & Theodore Eisenberg, Do Case Outcomes Really Reveal Anything About the Legal System? Win Rates and Removal Jurisdiction, 83 Cornell L. Rev. 581, 588–89 (1998); J. Mark Ramseyer & Minoru Nakazato, The Rational Litigant: Settlement Amounts and Verdict Rates in Japan, 18 J. Legal Stud. 263, 284–85 (1989).

Second, it is easier to believe that civil-law societies, although similar to common-law societies, have reached different conclusions about the bases for imposing substantive liability in specific kinds of cases. Nevertheless, because any substantive tilt is more difficult to conceal than sometimes obscure procedural bias, one would expect the pursuit of substantive policy by disadvantaging one of the parties to prompt considerable debate. Instead, as we have noted, the whole question of standard of proof has gone largely unnoticed. It is thus hard to believe that the civil law is utilizing its high standard to achieve specific substantive ends.

Third, a high standard of proof would be a clumsy way to restrain judges or the state. All it would ensure is that judges will act, or refrain from acting, on a set of facts that might not comport with the most probable view of reality. Moreover, any judicial decision, for plaintiff or defendant, constitutes judicial activity, there being no neutral outcome. The high standard yields biased outcomes, but certainly not restraint in any desirable sense.

b. Procedural Purposes

This analysis brings us to the more promising type of reason, one that focuses on procedural rather than substantive purposes that legal systems might be pursuing through their standard of proof. To explain what I have in mind, I begin with brief background on the possible goals of civil procedure.

Scholars of procedure have attributed multiple and sometimes conflicting purposes to the civil process.[766] (1) In any legal system, dispute resolution must be a primary objective of the civil process—especially in run-of-the-mill cases—so that law can stand as a ready alternative to private revenge and self-help.[767] (2) Yet, if the legal system also aims to be fair and individualized or, for that matter, to regulate conduct and modify behavior in beneficial ways, its proce-

---

766. See, e.g., Jolowicz, supra note 627, at 71–77 (stressing aims to demonstrate the effectiveness of law, to develop the substantive law, and most importantly to effectuate the substantive ends of law); Martin P. Golding, On the Adversary System and Justice, in Philosophical Law 98, 106–19 (Richard Bronaugh ed., 1978) (discussing truth-finding, satisfaction, and protection functions of adversary procedure); Kenneth E. Scott, Two Models of the Civil Process, 27 Stan. L. Rev. 937, 937–39 (1975) (describing conflict-resolution and behavior-modification models); Sidney Post Simpson, The Problem of Trial, in David Dudley Field Centenary Essays 141, 141–42 (Alison Reppy ed., 1949) (observing that trials now aim not only to settle disputes but also to adjudicate them correctly, in accordance with "the reality of the controversies presented"); cf. Robert A. Baruch Bush, Dispute Resolution Alternatives and the Goals of Civil Justice: Jurisdictional Principles for Process Choice, 1984 Wis. L. Rev. 893, 908–21 (breaking general values down into ultimate goals).

767. See Jolowicz, supra note 627, at 69–70; Simpson, supra note 766, at 141.

dure must pursue truth, in the sense of making an accurate determination of the facts before it applies the law—because procedure that yields a reasonably accurate picture of the facts will contribute to equal treatment of litigants and to better realization of the substantive ends of law, such as protection of rights and efficient allocation of resources.[768] It might be argued that objective accuracy in factfinding is not very important in creating incentives for desirable future conduct. For this purpose, the argument might go, it is enough that actors *believe* that judicial outcomes rest on accurate factfinding. Yet, although the perception of accuracy does not equate with objective accuracy, the latter is instrumental in creating such a perception. (3) Another intertwined objective is to foster popular belief in the legitimacy of judgments.[769]

Of course, dispute resolution, accuracy-dependent, and legitimacy aims will often be at odds, because time and resources are scarce. So which predominates here?

Some accept the proposition that civil procedure in civil-law countries today concerns itself more with dispute resolution than with other aims, favoring procedures that resolve essentially private disputes while preserving public order or enhancing social harmony.[770] As one writer has observed about France, "the aim of civil litigation is to end the dispute between the parties and not necessarily to do so on the basis of historical truth.... From these traditional ideas, the Frenchman—judge, lawyer or party—has acquired a concept of

---

768. See Jolowicz, supra note 627, at 70–71; Golding, supra note 766, at 107. Of course, there will always be the additional question of how much of any goal a society wants to buy, given that time and resources are scarce. See C.H. van Rhee & A. Uzelac, The Pursuit of Truth in Contemporary Civil Procedure: Revival of Accuracy or a New Balance in Favour of Effectiveness?, in Truth and Efficiency in Civil Litigation 3 (C.H. van Rhee & A. Uzelac eds., 2012).

769. See Bryant G. Garth, Observations on an Uncomfortable Relationship: Civil Procedure and Empirical Research, 49 Ala. L. Rev. 103, 113–14 (1997) (discussing the yearning of the system's participants to augment its legitimacy); Nesson, supra note 385 (stressing the acceptability of judgments); Simpson, supra note 766, at 141–42 (discussing the value of public satisfaction). Compare Charles P. Curtis, It's Your Law 3–4 (1954) (discussing the value of party satisfaction in the United States), with Shōzō Ōta, Reform of Civil Procedure in Japan, 49 Am. J. Comp. L. 561, 575 (2001) (arguing that user satisfaction is not an aim in Japan).

770. See, e.g., Damaška, supra note 611, at 110–13, 120; cf. Anthony D'Amato, Self-Regulation of Judicial Misconduct Could Be Mis-Regulation, 89 Mich. L. Rev. 609, 623 n.52 (1990) ("Compare Plato's view of 'justice' in The Laws: institutions of justice exist to stabilize a society rather than do justice; what is impermissible is the appearance of injustice rather than injustice itself."); Friedman & Yates, supra note 723, at 143–45 (arguing that Asian adjudicatory systems aim at social harmony as a means to preserving proper social order).

civil procedure which is primarily focused on putting an end to the dispute on the basis of what, in common law perspective, may seem like a mere approximation of the truth."[771] Meanwhile, the common law does pursue truth. One piece of evidence to this effect is that the United States has overlaid its adversary procedure with an extensive nonadversarial disclosure and discovery scheme, which signals a special allegiance to truth.[772]

This proposition of differing roles for truth is not one essential to my analysis. I mention it only as a possibility. I myself doubt it.[773] Parenthetically, I do not, in so recounting the view of others that civil-law systems prefer dispute resolution over truth, mean to suggest either (1) that truth is the exclusive value of the common-law systems or (2) that common-law procedure is a better way to arrive at truth. First, like the civil law, the common law certainly pursues dispute resolution, along with other nontruth values, and perhaps does so increasingly. Second, some features of common-law adversarial procedure admittedly can thwart accurate factfinding.[774] But I have no need to enter the fray on the relative desirability of adversarial versus inquisitorial methods.[775] Although genuinely inquisitorial methods could conceivably signal a greater attachment to truth,[776] they cannot do so if they are nonexistent in practice. In actuality, both common-law and civil-law procedures are now functionally adversarial on the civil side to a large degree, thus largely mooting the debate.

Returning to the particular feature under consideration, does an assumption of the civil law's higher devotion to dispute resolution than to truth explain the high civil-law standard of proof for civil cases? At first glance, the civil law's high civil standard indeed might seem to facilitate dispute resolution, by the crude method of deterring litigation overall and thereby minimizing its associated public and private costs. Litigation costs are a real worry,

---

771. Beardsley, supra note 620, at 464, 486.

772. See generally Huang, supra note 454.

773. See Brinkmann, supra note 608, at 881 ("The starting point for all civil and common law systems is the truth as the intrinsic goal of fact-finding.").

774. See Keith A. Findley, Adversarial Inquisitions: Rethinking the Search for the Truth, 56 N.Y.L. Sch. L. Rev. 911 (2012) (lambasting the American criminal system); Golding, supra note 766, at 109–12 (discussing some flaws, as well as some benefits, of the truth-finding function of the adversary system).

775. Compare Joint Conference on Professional Responsibility, Report, 44 A.B.A. J. 1159 (1958), with Jolowicz, supra note 627, at 86, 175–82.

776. See Twining, supra note 2, at 76–77 ("For it is generally recognized that inquisitorial systems are more directly and consistently concerned with the pursuit of truth and the implementation of law than adversarial proceedings, the primary purpose of which is legitimated conflict-resolution.").

of course. However, they hardly justify skewing outcomes without regard to the merits. Moreover, once a country has established a court system, skewing outcomes by imposing a high standard of proof likely will not alleviate concerns about costs or lower the amount of litigation. Disputes will still arise, despite the high standard. Cases that fall close to the standard of proof, whatever it is, will exist in good number and will tend to go to trial. After all, a substantial number of criminal trials occur despite the criminal law's high standard of proof. Nor will different standards lead to wildly different caseloads, because the same forces that minimize the effect of a high standard of proof on the number of actual trials will also reduce its effect on the number of case filings. In short, the amount of contested litigation tends to expand to fill the system's existing capacity.[777]

Flipping assumptions, so that truth rather than dispute resolution is the civil law's greatest concern, it might seem that a standard of virtual certainty is better designed to produce true answers to disputed questions of fact than the preponderance standard. Under the civil-law view, no fact is "true" unless the judge reaches an inner conviction of its truth, because truth should not rest on chance; nor should truth be viewed as arguable when it could be found out more definitely. If civil-law procedure were genuinely inquisitorial, and if civil-law courts had unlimited time and resources, a requirement of virtual certainty could conceivably advance truth. But no court has unlimited time and resources, and civil-law procedure has become functionally adversarial. In these circumstances, the practical effect of the civil law's high civil standard of proof is not that truth will prevail, but that the party favored by the burden of proof will enjoy a huge advantage. The result in an uncertain case will be a decision for the party favored by burden-of-proof rules, rather than a decision for the party whose claim is most probably true. Wrongly rejecting claims is just as much an error as wrongly sustaining them. The error-cost minimizing preponderance standard better serves truth. Thus, the civil law's high civil standard represents a sacrifice of truth, without facilitating dispute resolution.[778]

After this look behind assumptions, neither a preference for dispute resolution nor a devotion to truth in civil cases does anything to diminish the appearance of the civil law's wilful mischaracterization—thus suggesting that another unstated and less obvious purpose must lie behind its high standard

---

777. See Clermont, supra note 329, at 1946–51, 1956–61; George L. Priest, Private Litigants and the Court Congestion Problem, 69 B.U. L. Rev. 527 (1989).

778. See Huang, supra note 454, at 141–42 (cataloguing and refuting Japanese objections to the preponderance standard).

of proof, some purpose that has nothing to do with the procedural aim of dispute resolution or truth determination. I accordingly turn to a final possible benefit that would explain why the civil law might affirmatively wish to retain its high standard in civil cases: the civil law may retain its high standard with the procedural aim of augmenting apparent legitimacy.

5. Legitimacy

a. Elaboration

The high civil-law standard of proof perhaps exists in hope of enhancing the perceived legitimacy of judicial decisions. Legitimacy in the sense used here refers to popular acceptance, which grows whenever judges act within the seemly role allocated to them.[779] Professor Takeshi Kojima, in justifying procedural reform, has described the systemic yearning for legitimacy thus: "The integrity of the judges and the correctness of fact determinations have been traditionally established features of Japanese civil justice. However, a judgment rendered by the court may not be strong enough to satisfy the sense of justice or common sense that the general public embraces."[780]

Even if the probabilistic nature of fact-finding is inevitable in our uncertain world, probabilism does produce discomfort. It also requires sophistication and imposes some destructive side-effects, at least if acknowledged by the legal system. The civil-law systems could be choosing to avoid all those ills, by refusing openly to acknowledge it. If so, they would be relying on the widespread efficacy of the people's unexamined intuition, which would yield the legitimating misimpression that requiring virtual certainty comports with finding real truth. That is, the high standard would insinuate to the parties and the public that judges will not treat facts as true on less-than-certain evidence. Moreover, civil-law judges should not appear to have free rein to call close cases or to exercise discretion. That is to say, the high standard helps them to

---

779. See Alain A. Levasseur, Legitimacy of Judges, 50 Am. J. Comp. L. 43, 45–46 (Supp. 2002).

780. Kojima, supra note 675, at 691; cf. John O. Haley, The Japanese Judiciary: Maintaining Integrity, Autonomy, and the Public Trust, in Law in Japan: A Turning Point 99, 127 (Daniel H. Foote ed., 2007), available at http://law.wustl.edu/harris/documents/2003-3HaleyJapaneseJudiciary.pdf ("Trust is the judiciary's most significant attribute."); John O. Haley, Litigation in Japan: A New Look at Old Problems, 10 Willamette J. Int'l L. & Disp. Resol. 121, 139 (2002) ("Japan by all reliable accounts has the most autonomous, corruption-free and trusted judiciary in the world.").

appear to act only when more-or-less forced to act. This rhetoric and form thus sound and appear good, and imply a seriousness of purpose and a caution in action. Finally, when the court does render judgment, the standard retrospectively implies that the evidence must have been certain and the result necessary. All these implications are admittedly appealing (but nonetheless false or misleading).[781]

Important scholarship in France has argued that French evidence law on the civil side, under the guise of truth-directed rules, aims at legitimating judicial decisions rather than finding truth.[782] Of special interest is the recent work of Professor Xavier Lagarde, the leading insider to take a critical look at French evidence law and, in particular, at burdens of proof.[783] He suggests that when the various rules of evidence that work to minimize factfinding (deference to experts, preference for signed documents, reliance on admissions, and a strictly interpreted statute of frauds) fail to yield a mechanical judgment, then the burden of proof, with its air of slight fault on the part of the unsuccessful burdened party, gives the system and its judges a last rock to hide behind.[784] A judge pronouncing the existing truth renders a more *"acceptable"* judgment than a judge who has decided what the truth is.[785]

---

781. The high standard in civil cases could also convey an appealing impression of compassion and individualized justice, because no one's legal fate turns on the basis of statistical probability. But this subtle and nonintuitive message would need to be explained to the people. Therefore, the civil law likely does not intend to send this message, given that the civil law does not enunciate its civil standard of proof too expressly, loudly, or frequently— sensing perhaps that this message could not stand up to scrutiny.

782. See Xavier Lagarde, Réflexion critique sur le droit de la preuve (1994); Henri Lévy-Bruhl, La preuve judiciaire 29 (1964) (*"[L]a preuve judiciaire a pour objet de faire obtenir par l'intéressé la ratification, l'homologation de la collectivité. Si telle est bien la fonction de la preuve judiciaire, on comprendra que la recherche de la vérité passe au second plan, ne joue qu'un rôle secondaire."*).

783. Lagarde, supra note 782, at 203–72, 355–65; Lagarde, supra note 733; Lagarde, supra note 631; see Ferrand, supra note 634, ¶ 3 (situating Lagarde's work in the evolution of French evidence law); Guinchard & Ferrand, supra note 622, at 909 (observing that the recent scholarship has *"l'immense mérite de démystifier, de faire tomber le tabou de la recherche de la vérité, quête d'un Graal, d'un absolu"*).

784. See Lagarde, supra note 733, at 38 (*"Ainsi, les règles d'attribution de la charge de la preuve évitent aux juges d'avoir à rendre des jugements de preuve dont la réalité serait trop facilement contestable."*); Lagarde, supra note 631, at 2023 (arguing that the French system blames the person who has failed to carry the burden: *"Là comme ailleurs, nul ne sait où se trouve la vérité. Mais la décision rendue est acceptable."*).

785. See Lagarde, supra note 631, at 2023 (*"D'une certaine manière, mieux vaut une justice dogmatique qu'une justice arbitraire."*).

Although Professor Lagarde's initial scholarship did not address the standard of proof, his same idea applies readily to suggest that the high standard makes that last burden-of-proof rock much bigger. By 2010, indeed, he was expanding his focus to include the standard of proof in his theory.[786]

Is there support for that theory? Circumstantial evidence exists that the high civil-law standard of proof has the important objective of legitimating judicial decisions. Taking France once more for specific example, the brief French decisions cannot express doubt, but instead must exhibit certainty.[787] In the words of one French scholar, "[t]he judge, the good judge, lives without doubt in an ocean of doubt ...."[788] The task of the judge is to convert that doubt into a judicial certainty. "The judge must pronounce the judicial truth, which will become social truth."[789]

Some empirical evidence exists that the French legal system has succeeded in its quest for legitimacy. According to one American practitioner in Paris, the French system of factfinding "appears to satisfy those who operate it and those whose claims are decided by it. It is worth noting that nothing in a sociological survey conducted in 1973 at the behest of the Ministry of Justice suggests that the French consider that the treatment of fact is a serious problem in civil procedure."[790]

Relatedly, the high standard of proof gives comfort to judges too. For example, the Japanese judge fears errors of fact more than errors of law, because factual errors will be more obvious to the parties.[791] A high standard of proof gives the judge that large rock to hide behind. The judge will not have to call evenly balanced cases. The party with the burden of proof will win only when clearly entitled to win; if that party loses, the standard of proof, not the judge,

---

786. See id. at 2024–25.

787. See Bredin, supra note 643, at 25 ("*La décision ne peut pas être douteuse.*").

788. Id. at 29 ("*Le juge, le bon juge, vit sans doute dans un océan de doute ....*").

789. Id. at 24 ("*Le juge doit dire la vérité judiciaire, qui sera vérité sociale.*").

790. Beardsley, supra note 620, at 486 & n.114.

791. Accordingly, Japanese judges receive special training in factfinding. Interview with Tadashige Ōnishi, District Judge, Fukuoka District Court, in Ithaca, N.Y. (Apr. 11, 2003). The relative fears are the reverse for U.S. judges, as shown not only by their lack of special training in factfinding, but also by the trial attorneys' duty to disclose adverse law and not adverse fact, see Field et al., supra note 10, at 287–91, and by the appellate courts' less deferential standard of review for law than for fact, see supra text accompanying note 116. The greater U.S. fear of an error of law could lie in the realization that under stare decisis a legal error will affect all of society rather than just the parties; contrariwise, the judge can still blame an error of fact on the parties' faulty adversarial presentation or on the jury.

is to blame. Likewise, the judge might duck a difficult decision, or otherwise seek to self-protect, by relying on the unrealistically high standard of proof.

b. Evaluation

Again, I do not mean to suggest inferiority by observing the civil-law systems' quest for legitimacy. Public perceptions of what courts do may be just as important as what they do in actuality.[792] Judicial myths can sometimes have great utility. Thus, civilian courts with magisterial judges, sensitive to the special need for legitimacy in a social structure historically wary of the judiciary, may have willingly continued to accept the duty to deal only in "truth." Theirs is a defensible position.

Moreover, civil-law systems of course are not alone in seeking legitimacy for their decisions. Common-law courts have had their own means of maintaining an appearance of accuracy and fairness, such as delegating factfinding to an impartial jury of citizens that supposedly embodied common sense and community values.[793] Similarly, common-law judges seek psychic comfort. The jury bestows this benefit by shouldering responsibility for decision, with the result that judges like juries.

Although legitimacy is an important objective, and its pursuit yields real benefits sought by all legal systems, I still think the civil law suffers some costs as a result of its high standard of proof in civil cases. Meanwhile, the common law enjoys some offsetting benefits from its embrace of an error-cost minimizing policy, its neutral treatment of plaintiffs and defendants, and even its frank acknowledgment of the probabilistic character of evidence.

First, the common law obtains more accurate results, by determining the most likely state of affairs in each case. In contrast, the civil law's outcomes flow from rules allocating the burden of proof, which do not always capture the realities of particular cases.

---

792. See Jolowicz, supra note 627, at 72–73.

793. An intriguing article makes an argument comparable to mine, but with respect to constitutional interpretation in the United States. Mark D. Rosen, Defrocking the Courts: Resolving "Cases and Controversies," Not Announcing Transcendental Truths, 17 Harv. J.L. & Pub. Pol'y 715 (1994). His article argues that the Supreme Court has used burden-shifting presumptions in order to reach what appear to be confident resolutions of controversial moral issues when actually the choices made are close and difficult. The Court's method lends its decisions an air of certainty and legitimacy, which in turn increases popular respect for and acceptance of its rulings. Mr. Rosen, however, suggests that this decisional method is ultimately an unstable one. He believes the Court would fare better if it candidly admitted that, as a matter of necessity, it was shaping practical solutions to difficult problems.

Second, the common-law standard of proof permits courts to maintain a more impartial stance toward litigants, because it equalizes the litigants' positions. By explicitly adopting and patrolling the preponderance standard, the common law better controls decisional bias. Contrariwise, civil-law judges might apply a haphazardly variable civil standard of proof, but the system cannot regulate the judges' modifications or even modulate them because the question of standard remains hidden. The civil law's formalistic approach thus opens the door to unthinking, or thinking, bias in decisionmaking.

Third, the common law's approach is more conducive to introspective and open development of an efficient evidence law. For example, the common law is in a better position to handle statistical evidence in this era of increasing scientization of evidence. Meanwhile, the civil law has only just begun to grapple with some fundamental liability questions, such as probabilistic problems of causation and apportioned liability.[794]

---

794. See Damaška, supra note 611, at 143–52.

Chapter VII

Normative Conclusions

A. Drawing Comparative Lessons on the Standard of Proof

I do not offer a definitive answer to the comparative puzzle as to standards of proof framed in **Chapter VI**. Sound comparative scholarship, in my view, is a delicate enterprise that demands great learning and skill.[795] A comparativist should be sufficiently immersed in the different legal cultures to understand the context in which legal rules operate and the attitudes an insider might bring to the rules. If the comparativist is not so immersed, he or she should approach the rules of a different system with modesty and respect, with the sole aim of drawing lessons about the home system. "The purpose of comparative study is to help understand what is distinctive (and problematic) about domestic law."[796] In drawing lessons for the home system, the comparativist should remain cautious. He or she should be suspicious of drawing easy generalities[797] or making confident calls for legal transplants.[798] This caution is especially appropriate for comparisons in procedure, a field marked by the interrelatedness of its parts, the latency of its values, and its inseparability from local institutional structure and even from substance. A grasp of the tiny mat-

---

795. See generally Methods of Comparative Law (Pier Giuseppe Monateri ed., 2012).

796. John H. Langbein, The Influence of Comparative Procedure in the United States, 43 Am. J. Comp. L. 545, 545 (1995); see also George A. Bermann, The Discipline of Comparative Law in the United States, in L'avenir du droit comparé 305, 306–08 (Société de Législation Comparée 2000) (discussing various aims of comparative law).

797. See Allen et al., supra note 734; Basil Markesinis, Comparative Law—A Subject in Search of an Audience, 53 Mod. L. Rev. 1, 7–10 (1990).

798. See Benjamin Kaplan, Civil Procedure—Reflections on the Comparison of Systems, 9 Buff. L. Rev. 409, 422 (1960); Konstanze Plett, Civil Justice and Its Reform in West Germany and the United States, 13 Just. Sys. J. 186 (1989); John C. Reitz, Why We Probably Cannot Adopt the German Advantage in Civil Procedure, 75 Iowa L. Rev. 987 (1990).

ter of standard of proof turns out to require a profound understanding of the legal and nonlegal context in which it functions.[799]

In the preceding chapter, the principal difficulty lay in explaining how the civil-law and common-law systems could today share general aims and yet preserve their historical difference on such a fundamental aspect as the civil standard of proof. After all, this difference of *intime conviction* versus preponderance of the evidence not only entails all sorts of practical consequences, but also implies some basic divisions on attitudes toward the nature of truth. My suspicion as to the persistent difference between the two standards, among all the possibilities explored, is that the chosen standard of proof serves a very different procedural goal in each of the legal systems. In other words, the current motivation for the difference on standards of proof, in my view, lies in subtle differences between the two systems' procedural objectives to which their standard of proof conforms.

The common law in its standards of proof consistently tries to minimize expected error costs. Because costs of error obviously differ in different settings, the common law is forced to apply multiple standards of proof: preponderance of the evidence, clear and convincing proof, and proof beyond a reasonable doubt. The elevated standards help to avoid the high social costs of false positives, as in convicting the innocent, and the preponderance standard minimizes expected social costs in the setting where false positives are no more costly than false negatives. Thus, after deeming the error-cost minimizing approach to be procedurally proper and recognizing that civil cases pose no substantive reason to weight the balance against one side of the dispute, the common law enshrined the preponderance-of-the-evidence standard.

The civil law, by contrast, applies basically the same standard of proof in all settings. In all cases, even in the face of differing costs, the civil law sends to its factfinder the strong signal to protect the nonburdened party. It follows that the civil law is not trying to seek accuracy by minimizing expected error costs. The civil law's standard must have another purpose. My best surmise remains that it is seeking the perceived legitimacy of its higher standard. The civil law seeks the legitimating benefits of the myth that its courts act only on truly true facts and not on mere probabilities. This is not entirely a forthright position.

The civil law's quest for legitimacy is by no means silly, however, even if it pursues that goal at the expense of the burdened party, whoever that party is after the law's burdens and presumptions play out in a particular case. Common-

---

799. See William Ewald, Comparative Jurisprudence (I): What Was It Like to Try a Rat?, 143 U. Pa. L. Rev. 1889 (1995).

law courts seek legitimacy elsewhere, perhaps in other myths, and thus are free to adopt preponderance of the evidence as the standard of proof that more efficiently and fairly captures the real truth of the civil case.

What is important to stress is that my explanatory difficulty did not regard which system is right or wrong, but instead lay in figuring out why the two legal systems remain apart. Therefore, I am not arguing that the civil law's approach to the standard of proof is worse or better than the common law's, but rather that it reflects a different cost-benefit analysis. The civilians have concluded that the overall cost-benefit balance favors a high standard for their noncriminal cases, reflecting a weighing of costs and benefits in their own legal context. Determining whether either legal system is wrong would not only require a surer determination of the goals underlying the system's standard of proof, but also turn on a very subtle balance of benefits and costs. The chosen standard expresses a choice among the many possible goals of procedure. Given their different purposes, the common law and the civil law differ on the appropriate standard of proof. I believe that a sophisticated analysis might reveal these different standards of proof are each right for the respective legal system.

I have thus used comparative methods mainly to illuminate the common law's standards of proof. The yield is a better understanding of the standards' origins, as well as a realization that what the common law now takes to be obvious the world's other legal systems have long rejected. This yield more than justifies my efforts at comparative study, even if the study revealed no immediate lessons for reform.

B. Conveying the Standard of Proof

Chapter V conceptualized standards of proof in a way that reconciled the competing visions mapped in Chapter IV. For applying the common-law standard of proof, that conceptualization makes one major point that is relevant to reform. The theory of belief functions reveals that the likelihood of a fact should be compared to the likelihood of its falsity, not to the possibility it is not true. One should compare Bel(S) and Bel(notS). In doing so, Bel(notS) is the belief in the negation of S, not the complement of Bel(S). It represents how much the factfinder actively disbelieves S, the fact in dispute. The comparison thus should look at actual belief in S and actual disbelief of S.

I made suggestions regarding the higher standards of proof. Here I shall expand only on preponderance of the evidence. In civil cases, if you were to work with only those two beliefs, and discard the indeterminate belief, the appro-

priate course would be to say that the burdened party should win if and only
if Bel(S) > Bel(notS). You would decide for the plaintiff if Bel(S) exceeds
Bel(notS), but decide for the defendant if Bel(S) does not exceed Bel(notS).

How should we convey this standard to the jurors? A current federal pattern
jury instruction says this:

> Plaintiff has the burden in a civil action, such as this, to prove every
> essential element of plaintiff's claim by a preponderance of the evi-
> dence. If plaintiff should fail to establish any essential element of plain-
> tiff's claim by a preponderance of the evidence, you should find for
> defendant as to that claim.
>
> "Establish by a preponderance of the evidence" means evidence,
> which as a whole, shows that the fact sought to be proved is more
> probable than not. In other words, a preponderance of the evidence
> means such evidence as, when considered and compared with the ev-
> idence opposed to it, has more convincing force, and produces in your
> minds belief that what is sought to be proved is more likely true than
> not true.[800]

I propose that it express even more clearly what is being compared. Its second
paragraph should say: "'Establish by a preponderance of the evidence' means
evidence that, as a whole, shows the fact sought to be proved is more likely
true than false. You should determine the level of your belief that the fact actually exists and also determine the level of your belief that the fact actually
does not exist. If the former belief is stronger than the latter belief, then the
plaintiff has established the fact."

Of course, thoughtful commentators have for decades proposed much the
same thing. Adjudicators should stay away from just weighing the quantity of
evidence. They should avoid thinking in terms of numerical probabilities. Professor Morgan had this suggestion:

> If the trial judge tells the jury that the burden is upon a party to
> prove a specified fact by a preponderance of the evidence, he should
> explain that this means only that they must find that the fact does not
> exist unless the evidence convinces them that its existence is more
> probable than its non-existence. Indeed, there is no need for him to
> talk of burden of proof or of preponderance of evidence. He may well
> confine his instruction on this matter to a specification of the dis-
> puted propositions of fact and a direction as to which party must fail

800. 3 O'Malley et al., supra note 371, § 104.01.

on each proposition unless the jury is convinced by the evidence that the truth of that proposition is more probable than its falsity.[801]

Professor McBaine actually composed an instruction:

The court instructs you that by the law of this state burdens of proving facts are imposed upon parties to lawsuits, and other types of legal proceedings, for the purpose of reaching wise and just decisions.

The court instructs the jury, wherever you have been instructed in other instructions in this case, that a party to this action has the burden of proving a fact or facts by the preponderance or greater weight of the evidence, that the burden of proof imposed upon that party is the following:

The burden is not a burden of merely producing a greater number of witnesses or a greater quantity of evidence. The burden therefore is not necessarily carried by the introduction of the greater number of witnesses or the greater quantity of evidence. A greater number of witnesses or a greater quantity of evidence are factors which you may take into account in determining whether the burden of proof has been carried. Neither the greater nor the lesser number of witnesses or quantity of the evidence is the sole test to be applied in determining whether the burden of proof, imposed by law, has been carried because the burden so imposed is one of convincing your minds. Belief in the truth of assertions, therefore, is not to be reached by merely calculating the numbers of witnesses or by estimating the quantities of evidence.

The burden is not a burden of convincing you that the facts which are asserted are certainly true or that they are true to a high degree of probability.

The burden imposed is to convince you upon all the evidence before you that the facts asserted are more probably true than false.

If then upon consideration and comparison of all the evidence in the case you believe that it is more probable that the facts are true than it is that they are false you must find that the facts have been proved.

If, on the other hand, you believe that it is more probable that the facts asserted are false than it is that they are true, you will find that the party upon whom this burden of proof has been placed has not proved the facts.

---

801. Morgan, supra note 586, at 66–67.

Also, if you find that the probabilities of truth and falsity are evenly balanced; that it is just as probable that the facts are true as it is that they are not true, you will find that the burden of proof imposed upon him has not been carried, because he has not proved that the facts are more probably true than not true.[802]

Much more extensive reforms would be necessary to communicate the standard of proof in a way that effectively invokes the proper standard in the factfinder's mind. Nevertheless, beyond my modest suggestion to rewrite the pattern instruction I am not prepared to go without more empirical support. **Chapter III** argued that prior empirical research asked the wrong questions and so did not produce useful answers. We need a fresh wave of research in order to see what adjudicators understand and do in handling standards of proof.

C. Stating the Standard of Decision

The conceptualization's concomitant exploration of fuzzy logic reinforced the psychological explanation of the pattern observed in **Chapter II**. The law usually does, realistically can, and optimally should recognize only seven categories of uncertainty and imprecision in its standards of decision: (1) slightest possibility, (2) reasonable possibility, (3) substantial possibility, (4) equipoise, (5) probability, (6) high probability, and (7) almost certainty. The law has indeed crystallized around these seven customary and nonquantified categories of likelihood. And the law has acted wisely in so doing, as it accommodates our psychological capabilities while still conforming to a sound logical system.

Of course, further improvement is possible. I have already suggested small reforms, such as refining appellate review of new-trial motions. The big lesson that I have preached is that lawmaking and analysis should stick ever more closely to the use of the customary and nonquantified standards of decision, in explicit recognition of a quantum-step approach to the standards of decision. The law should not be too demanding of human probability skills and accordingly should, even more consistently than it does, recognize only the seven categories of likelihood. Just as the standards of proof have coalesced toward three of the seven categories, so should lawmakers steadfastly cast other standards of decision in terms of some of the seven categories.

The *motivation* for reform lies in realizing that although the law has usually acted wisely as to standards of decision, it has sometimes faltered by depart-

---

802. McBaine, supra note 14, at 261–62.

ing from the normal pattern. The *means* consists of using the new psychological understanding to shape a better procedure. The *end* is to make sound procedure that better fits humans.

Specifically, when lawmakers confront the task of fixing a particular standard of decision, they should choose a standard based on a customary category, thereby acknowledging the quantum steps between standards. On the one hand, a coarsely gradated scale can make some such choices seem heartrending, but lawmakers should choose rather than take the fainthearted way out by leaving the standard vague. On the other hand, the limited set of standards available will define the policy choice clearly and often make it easier. Once lawmakers choose, they should express the standard in familiar language, not novel verbiage or quantification. Such lawmaking should improve comprehension and application by decisionmakers, as well as enable better control of those decisionmakers.

This proposal implies that some current standards of decision—those difficult to pigeonhole—ironically reveal not sophistication but rather either a lack of courage to make the tough choice or a lack of thought and effort in making and expressing the choice. So, for example, courts should clear up their domains where the decisionmakers cannot tell which standard prevails[803] or what the prevailing standard means.[804] Thus, for example, most appellate standards now grouped under "abuse of discretion" would convert readily to a standard of highly probable error.

---

803. E.g., Morris v. Mathews, 475 U.S. 237, 246–47 (1986):

> Accordingly, we hold that when a jeopardy-barred conviction is reduced to a conviction for a lesser included offense which is not jeopardy barred, the burden shifts to the defendant to demonstrate a reasonable probability that he would not have been convicted of the non-jeopardy-barred offense absent the presence of the jeopardy-barred offense. In this situation, we believe that a "reasonable probability" is a probability sufficient to undermine confidence in the outcome. Cf. Strickland v. Washington, 466 U.S. 668, 695 (1984)....

> The Court of Appeals thus was ... too ready to find that [the defendant] had made the necessary showing of prejudice.... [Its] "reasonable possibility" standard, which could be satisfied by "an exceedingly small showing," was not sufficiently demanding. To prevail in a case like this, the defendant must show that, but for the improper inclusion of the jeopardy-barred charge, the result of the proceeding probably would have been different.

See id. at 255 & n.3 (Blackmun, J., concurring in judgment) (calling the conflict in the new standard "particularly puzzling").

804. E.g., INS v. Stevic, 467 U.S. 407, 424 & n.19 (1984) (using "clear probability" to mean more likely than not); United Steelworkers v. Warrior & Gulf Navigation Co., 363 U.S. 574, 582 (1960) (using "positive assurance" as a standard without explanation).

Similarly, my proposal implies that lawmakers should avoid, or consider abolishing, any sliding-scale standards of decision. A sliding scale in this context means that the applicable standard of decision varies by infinite or very fine gradations of likelihood according to the circumstances. Such an approach springs from the understandable urge to be precise in dealing with situations involving many factors, but such precision is an illusion. The applicable standard properly may vary according to the circumstances, but only by quantum leaps from one customary category of probabilities to another. So, coalescence of standards into the customary categories, in reaction to the unacceptable complexity of a sliding scale, is a sign of maturity of legal doctrine.

My position is susceptible to radical misunderstanding. Several caveats should offer some immunization.

To locate anew the area in dispute, I stress my concern lies only in the form of decisionmaking that involves placement on a scale and, more particularly, testing for a required degree of certainty. I am arguing that lawmakers normally should not ask decisionmakers to make unrealistic distinctions of likelihood, say, by requiring them to find a fact only if it is more than much-more-likely-than-not but not necessarily beyond-a-reasonable-doubt. I thus do not attack all amorphous or multifactored forms of decisionmaking, which often pass under the banner of balancing and which can be wholly appropriate in many settings.

Moreover, within that specific area of dispute, I am not arguing for more sophistication or complexity. Despite superficial appearances, I am arguing for less complication, in recognition of cognitive limitations. Although decisionmaking requires a standard of decision, which in turn necessitates line drawing, I champion simpler line drawing. This book thus conveys selective sympathy—in a specific area for special reasons—with those who argue that the law has become just too complicated.[805]

D. Summary of Standards of Decision in Law

This book began its study of standards of decision by creating a taxonomy of standards. The various standards differed in terms of how certain the decisionmaker must be to decide in a particular way. Speaking in terms of degrees of certainty proved useful at the outset. After considerable consideration of cognitive psychology and fuzzy logic, that framework proved largely accurate as well as useful.

---

805. E.g., Robert F. Nagel, The Formulaic Constitution, 84 Mich. L. Rev. 165 (1985); Irving Younger, In Praise of Simplicity, 62 A.B.A. J. 632 (1976).

The major lesson to emerge as to standards of decision in general was the one just summarized: the degrees of certainty should remain nonnumerical and approximate. The law indeed conforms, stating its standards in customary terms of coarse categories of likelihood. For example, it states the *standard of review* simply in terms of its scale of possibilities and probabilities: nondeferential review, clear-error review, and almost-certain-error review. Moreover, the law does not expect the judge to leave belief uncommitted in applying a standard of review. The system wants the judge to determine, say, the likelihood of jury error in finding for the plaintiff, with the complement being the likelihood of jury correctness in finding for the plaintiff. The "evidence" for applying the standard is complete.

That major lesson implies all sorts of lower-level doctrinal lessons. For example, appellate review of new-trial motions should employ only three review standards: all issues of law should prompt the appellate court to ask simply whether it disagrees with the trial judge's decision; on factual reconsideration the appellate court should reverse a denial of a motion on the ground that the verdict was against the weight of the evidence only if it is almost certain that the trial judge erred; and all other reviewable new-trial issues should receive customary middle-level scrutiny. I will not repeat all the other doctrinal lessons drawn in this book.

The principal exception to this general scheme turned out to concern the very important standard called the *standard of proof.* This is the type of standard that specifies the level of sureness required of a factfinder to decide that a contested fact exists, when acting as part of a judicial proof process to establish what the system will treat as truth. Here a more sophisticated conceptualization that accounts for imperfections of the evidence is mandatory.

The new work on the mathematical theory of belief functions illuminates. It reveals that the unique feature of the standard of proof is that we expect the factfinder to ignore indeterminate, or uncommitted, belief and then compare belief in a fact's truth to belief in its falsity. Only then can one understand the real meaning of preponderance of the evidence, clear and convincing evidence, and beyond a reasonable doubt.

The other standards of decision, such as the standard of review, do not require that extra step of ignoring uncommitted belief and so involve only a direct estimation of likelihood. Thus, the simpler and more directly probabilistic approach of comparing that likelihood to a simple threshold works adequately for those standards of decision.

This book set out to get at the answer to the question of what are proper standards of decision—how American law should adjust in order to accommodate human, theoretical, logical, and comparative insights. The journey has been long, but has deepened understanding. The conclusion is that room for re-form exists, but that the law has done surprisingly well so far. To summarize the summary, the proper and largely prevailing approach is this:

- Because we and our law operate in an uncertain world, we employ standards of decision that are probabilistic. But our fuzzy cognition applies those standards in a nonnumerical and approximate way. We measure on a customary and coarse scale the chances of the proposition's being correct, and then compare the likelihood to the applicable standard's action threshold.

- Because we tell factfinders to decide on the basis of beliefs resting on admittedly imperfect evidence, the standards of proof turn out to be a special kind of standard of decision. The common law has frankly accepted the realities of a probabilistic environment and imperfect evidence: it tells its factfinders to set aside their uncommitted belief, and then compare their belief in the proposition's truth to their belief in its falsity. The applicable standard of proof specifies the required comparison, the law having used a cost-benefit analysis to choose among a starkly limited set of standards differing in degree and manner as to how the belief in the proposition's truth must exceed the belief in its falsity.

Index